Political Catsup

with

Economy Fries

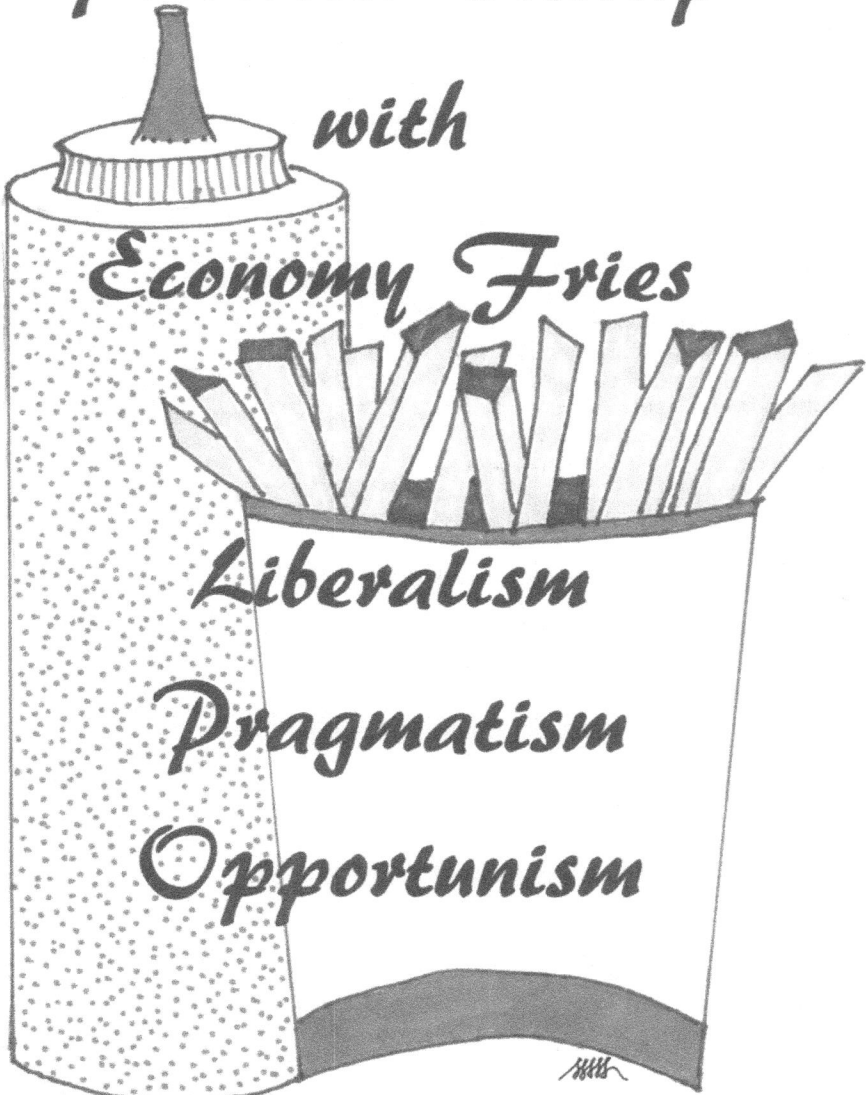

Liberalism

Pragmatism

Opportunism

Mel Scanlan Stahl

Published by Fast Car Publishing, Spokane, WA

ISBN: 978-0-9965417-1-8

Printed in the United States of America

Cover design and interior artwork by: Mel Scanlan Stahl

Table of Contents:

Why I wrote this book
and how you can use it to your advantage

When I sat in my house thinking about topics I might write about in 2011, my neighbor's house sat empty. Her house was just behind mine. She'd abandoned it after her business failed and her other job at the U.S. Postal Service became less secure. She didn't say anything to me before she left but I've heard that she went to Costa Rica. Since the U.S. economy looked beleaguered, since my neighbor had abandoned her property, since there were numerous foreclosures, record numbers of people on food stamps and unemployed, I decided to write about politics, economics and history.

I felt sorry that most Americans, including myself, didn't really know how to discuss these topics anymore. Especially since Alexis De Tocqueville, in *Democracy in America (1835)*, had once claimed that any American would discuss politics with him at the slightest opportunity. Americans had once been political participants. I wanted to find out why we changed and how to tune back into American politics. But it has seemed that we don't know how to have a conversation with anyone about politics without getting into an argument. Except for creating controversy, we mostly have forgotten what politics can do. In my determined way, I began to explore how this state of affairs came to be. I wrote a whole book about it. And by the end, I answered other questions as well.

Politics affects everything, and when I discovered what had happened to political practice in America, I found some surprises. I asked questions until I could visualize the connections between politics and everything else. First, I identified three political ideologies over American history. How could I tell the difference between them? I looked at economic policies. I looked at the kind of relationship between politics and economics. I started to define politics differently. I abandoned the term "politics," which describes what politicians do, and adopted a new term that describes the action arena of political decision making that decides "who gets what": the politic. And instead of describing economics according to economic theories, I decided to call the economy the aggregate of markets where people meet to exchange goods and services based upon a negotiated price in a mutually beneficial exchange. So the politic and economy were defined in this way and then I described them as the two powerful arms of society. How they work together is set out in policies and those policies create distinctions between political ideologies. Just doing that gave me a lot to write about.

But I wanted to capture the experience of being alive in America during each ideological period. Ideologies are never naked. They are clothed with the intentions and ideas of creative people who try to make the ideology work to achieve their goals. And political ideologies can organize benefits to some and harms to others. Or a spectrum of unequal benefits to different groups in society. So it's helpful to seek out the winners and losers under each ideology. Quotes that capture ideas and intentions for ideologies make describing politics a practical affair rooted in the lives of people. Why should I use my words to describe a political ideology when influential people have already done that? I'd rather use quotes that relate ideas and influence in the politic and then I can summarize and compare each ideology. In the U.S., there have been three different political ideologies. It's enjoyable to learn about them and see how the ideas rooted in each ideology can still affect us today.

I also paid special attention to finance, war and the law as spheres of influence that affect both the politic and economy and therefore are especially important in policy formation. If you don't balance disparate interests, then the politic and economy can become unstable. If fiscal policy and monetary policy are set up primarily to help the government to carry enormous debt and bankers to get more financial deals but not to protect solvency, for example, you can damage the economy and the politic. Likewise, constant war will drain resources out of the economy and politic. Similarly an unjust legal system that favors the powerful harms the grassroots and can create political strife that might destroy a nation. These imbalances have been seen off and on throughout human history. We are seeing them now.

I know that I said that I started this investigation and wrote a book because of economic troubles. And because Americans had lost their appetite for meaningful political discussions even though previously they'd had an avid interest in politics. And that's true, but there's a more personal reason. Changes that I saw in the job market and real estate market affected me personally after the Great Recession. I don't really believe that the U.S. recovered from the financial problems that surfaced in 2007 and those problems were rooted in bad economic policies. It was by writing my book that I came to appreciate the legal structures that failed to prevent problems in finance and real estate. And I needed to understand why our politic isn't serving the grassroots right now. Because that's where I live.

So one of the personal reasons that I wrote my book was because my boss had required me to double my productivity at work. My work had been exemplary over a long career in a technical field and I couldn't double my workload without some sort of improved technology or strategy. The company I worked for had bought a machine which failed to increase productivity and they pressured me to make it happen anyway. But neither the machine nor I could make double the work production in the same amount of time. Hired consultants agreed that my work was above the industry's standard. But the company I worked for had stopped valuing my real work and they ignored their consultants. They demanded more. In expecting a doubled production, my work was suddenly worth half as much. How could skills worth doing for eighteen years that had been in demand for decades, be worth half as much all of a sudden?

The other big personal reason was the decline of real estate prices and the decrease of market demand in real estate that happened in 2008. My property lost about 30% of its estimated value. You could argue that it may have been overvalued in a bubble-subprime-blowout, but I still couldn't really get value out of my property improvements. And when could my husband and I sell our house? With jobs hard-to-come-by after 2008, there weren't many buyers. With greater job insecurity, if my husband lost his job, after I quit mine to write this book, who would pay property taxes and living expenses? We and many other Americans felt caught in a financial trap that was set up by our Congress when it deregulated the financial industry. This was a clear incentive to me to research and write my book.

Political Catsup with Economy Fries: Liberalism, Pragmatism, Opportunism, discusses three American political ideologies and it can adapt to the needs of different kinds of readers. If you feel impatient and you want to discover the main ideas that undergird each discussion, go to Fast-Car-Analysis. If you want to reflect on higher level systems that nurture political ideologies go to the appendix to read about topics like the nation state system or the rule of law. If you want to get a person-to-person introduction to an ideology, the main body of the narrative provides quotes from ideological founders who lived then. They're found at the beginning of each ideology's discussion. If you feel lost among contingent historical events, the appendix will have a timeline to help you get oriented. And if you are the kind of person who likes the rubber-meets-the-road approach look for policy analysis in the main narrative. Sticklers will be happy to discover source references in the endnotes. If you want a quick tour, read all the Prelude, the Fast-Car-Analysis sections and the long bit about Neoliberalism. Or if you like to savor books, of course, you can just read it all.

Prelude

Here's a short-cut you can use to examine our politic and economy.

Asking about any political ideology from the perspective of political dogma wastes effort and yields little practical understanding. Consider instead the policy relationship between the politic and the economy. The politic is the action arena where people decide who gets what. The economy is the set of markets where people negotiate to decide the value and price of traded services or commodities in a mutually beneficial exchange system. The relationship between the politic and economy can be understood through policies. How does the government regulate the economy? What taxes are collected? Who are the stakeholders that influence policies? Notice that the Constitution affects political factions differently than congressional legislation affects them. How active are political factions and economic factions? What organizations concentrate and focus factional interests to motivate political change? How does money incentivize the politic? This simpler approach reveals three separate American political ideologies over the span of U.S. history: classical liberalism, modern liberalism and neoliberalism. They each have operated under the U.S. Constitution, although classical liberalism was initiated under the Articles of Confederation. Some Americans have imagined that the abandoned Articles of Confederation has been of little importance, but that's not true.

The Articles of Confederation still matters to Americans because it showed us that a weaker federal government couldn't regulate interstate trade successfully. Economic squabbling among states and a failure of leadership in managing federal and state debt were flaws in the Articles of Confederation which were repaired by drafting the U.S. Constitution differently. That's why the Articles of Confederation had a short lifespan. The document was crafted in 1777, ratified in 1781, and inspired the Constitutional rewrite by 1787. Americans wanted to improve the Articles of Confederation after trading between states became problematic because states were charging other states a tariff when commodities crossed their borders. The new Constitution organized a more powerful federal government and forbade states to charge a tariff for interstate trading. In 1789, the Articles of Confederation was replaced by the current U.S. Constitution plus the protective Bill of Rights ratified in 1791, and other amendments over time[1].

After ratification, the U.S. Constitution served as the sentinel document, according to the Supreme Court's interpretation of it, which laid out the laws of the land and the operation of the U.S. nation state, maneuvering within the nation state system (see the prelude's appendix for information on the nation state system). Always under a representative government shaped by the 1789 U.S. Constitution, different social participants have gained or lost advantages under each ideological system. Political theorists can argue at length about what ideology is better for whatever reasons, and they do. But to paraphrase Saul Alinsky, when he said something practical: "**the price of victory in politics is a viable solution**". Understanding political victory and its price is easier than examining political dogma which is mostly made to influence rather than to explain. Each ideology has faced a different set of urgent problems and American political ideologies have changed as needed to adapt to the demands of evolving circumstances within the nation state system. A consistent theme under each ideology has been the promotion of a healthy commonwealth where most capital generating property is owned by private individuals or by corporations.

Although each of the three U.S. political ideologies, classical liberalism, modern liberalism and neoliberalism have contained the word "liberalism," only classical liberalism was true liberalism. This becomes obvious by looking at the history of the nation's political and economic policies under each ideology. Classical liberalism had the greatest economic independence from government regulation and modeled itself on the idea that political freedom required economic freedom. The economy was diverse and regional. It lacked regional integration because of limited transportation and communication. The other ideologies developed later under a market economy and they diverted money out of the U.S. economy and redirected it into the politic. The economy was regulated under modern liberalism in order to increase political power for war and social welfare. Under neoliberalism economic policy has been reformatted through deregulation and regulatory reform to provide better opportunities for transnational and multinational corporations under a system of global capital circulation.

Money siphoned out of the economy to fund war and social programs during modern liberalism eventually led to government deficit and debt. Keynesias justified this debt as an acceptable policy because they believed that government spending would enhance economic activity. But Keynesianism created economic inefficiencies by withdrawing money out of the economy and applying it to political goals. Positive legal regulation of the economy was another hallmark of modern liberalism. In the case of neoliberalism, corporations have purchased political influence in Washington, money from taxes or corporate tax reprieve has been shuttled to transnational business at the expense of other economic contributors. And under neoliberalism, deregulation of financial businesses has led to financialization. Financialization's easy credit has increased the indebtedness of most businesses and most private citizens. The financialized economy is all about debt and the opportunity to borrow even more.

Based on the economy's relationship with the politic, each political ideology can be classified differently in terms of kind. Classical liberalism was true liberalism, modern liberalism was mild socialism[2] and neoliberalism has been state sponsored corporatism[3]. Classical liberalism was founded by liberals with classical and neoclassical political philosophical principles. Modern liberalism was sponsored by philosophical pragmatists who expanded the federal government's regulatory role. Neoliberalism was pushed onto the world scene by political opportunists in the UK, Europe and the U.S who took advantage of federal governments' increased power after WWII which they redirected in order to further corporate interests. Eventually transnational corporations were allowed to regulate their own industries and they gained access to mobile capital through deregulated finance.

Classical liberalism, the political ideology of the American Revolution, continued until the Civil War when the politic changed its relationship with the economy from economic liberalism to mixed economy under an income tax regime. Modern liberalism continued until the end of WWII when the Bretton Woods Conference among Allies reorganized trade agreements to promote a global economy and a global monetary system with the U.S. dollar as the international currency. Bretton Woods reduced economic nationalism by getting rid of many tariffs and opening trade. And Bretton Woods was the eventual gateway to fiat monetary systems after the managed gold system under the dollar ended during the Nixon Shock in 1971. Neoliberalism began its incarnation after WWII, and has continued into the present. Each political ideology was assembled by an organized political faction with specific ways of seeing the relationship between the politic and economy. They each wanted to succeed in a specific political and economic context, in a different context of historical challenge and under different factions of political support and opposition.

Here's how political ideologies changed in the U.S. without public recognition.

There's almost no discussion in the U.S. about changing political ideologies in American history. However strange that may seem, there are cultural reasons why it's been difficult for politicians to admit rhetorically that political change has occurred. One reason has been the "Founding Fathers". The "Founding Fathers", have been an iconic part of early American political idealism. The idea of having "Founding Fathers" originated in classical formulas for politics taken from Roman texts[4]. Greek and Roman classical studies contributed to the development of neoclassicism during the time of the early American republic's founding. Having "Founding Fathers" served the purpose of founding the nation inside a set of unchanging traditions. Classical era Greek and Roman books outlined classical "first principles" for good government. Classic ideals included the hero in warfare mentality and approved of warfare as a political prerogative. Classic ideals also included concepts about law. Law was conceived to facilitate justice for insider citizens during sequential wars of the conquering civilization where conquered people had fewer legal protections. And law would act as an impartial social technology to maintain state civility among citizens.

Classical liberal principles based on rhetorically outlined "first principles" from Classic Greek and Roman writings for good government inspired Enlightenment political writers to elaborate neoclassical "second principles" for better Enlightenment Period government. But the American Founding Father traditions approved of only the first American political ideology, classical liberalism. That historical fact has led people in American politics to resist talking about the other two ideologies. People across society have paid lip service to classical liberalism as they have proceeded to implement two later ideologies mostly while in rhetorical denial about what they were really doing. That rhetorical denial has spread political ignorance among most Americans as later ideologies took form after classical liberalism. This has caused an unfortunate lapse in America's political understanding of itself.

The political cost of refuting the Founding Father philosophies was too high to encourage political honesty when American politics changed. And change was spurred on by urgencies of changing circumstances in an internationally competitive political system. Wars in Europe, like the Napoleonic Wars (Napoleonic Era: 1789-1815), caused European nation state governments to implement income tax programs to pay for the expense of war and larger government tax levies allowed governments to grow in size and complexity. Change toward modern liberalism, allowed the U.S. to be competitive with European nations that had adopted income taxes to pay for war. If European states had income taxes then the U.S. needed them in order to compete on an equal footing. The innovation of income taxes was adopted by the Union in order to win the Civil War. A more regulated economy came along soon after as modern liberalism proceeded to meet new challenges in the context of nation states and market economies.

After WWII, the political implementation of neoliberalism happened in America under the deceitful guise of a return to classical liberal principles. The Cold War, the nation state contest between modern liberalism and communism included rhetorical opposition to communism and socialism despite the political reality of soft socialism in modern liberal America. The U.S. had already adopted a regulated American economy, income taxes and broad government oversight of business practices, even though business enterprises remained mostly privately owned. Later, the UN meeting at Bretton Woods in 1944, created a neoliberal network of "open market" trading treaties and international lending organizations. The Allied nations from WWII signed GATT treaties which removed tariffs and promoted global trade. Globalization, which had been interrupted by WWII, was renewed with help from loans by the IMF and World Bank. American politics continued to evolve under regulatory reform. The nation state system began to link diverse global economies through treaties, transnational companies and international banking. Since then, financial deregulation and mobile capital have continued to change global politics and economics.

Rather than a return to liberal principles, neoliberals have deregulated and reregulated to the advantage of global corporations. Neoliberal deconstructions have altered the role of nations in the nation state system, increased the importance of organizations in the politic and also have caused Americans to reconsider what oaths to the U.S. Constitution really mean to public servants during a global restructuring. What should politicians, public servants and other Americans think now of patriotism or treason under the globalist neoliberal restructuring program? Controversy arising from government data leaked by people like Edward Snowden in 2013, showed that many Americans have become confused about how to better protect the nation's interests—by revealing secrets or by withholding them.

These controversies have arisen for three reasons. One reason is political conflicts where corporate welfare clashes with public welfare. The second reason for controversy comes out of the mostly unexamined conflict between past American political ideologies and later ones. A third reason for controversy arises out of loyalty to the U.S. Constitution in the face of federal government objectives that reach beyond the intentions and outline of America's most sacred political document. Observations can be made about historical circumstances, political pragmatism and the dynamic interaction of the politic and the economy under each ideology and those observations help to clarify what kinds of changes have occurred in American society and why those changes have happened.

Colonial politics in small communities gave classical liberals a ferocious political ambition to establish a new nation and fix its problems.

Here's a reminder of basic history which will help lay a foundation for more in-depth analysis in upcoming chapters. The first U.S. ideological system was classical liberalism. Political problems of urgency faced by classical liberals included the generation of a new nation, addressing and repairing the shortcomings of the Articles of Confederation by constitutional convention that created a new U.S. Constitution, paying debt obligations from the American Revolution and fighting battles among competitors for American lands including Native Americans and European nations.

The American Revolution was costly not just in terms of money to pay for war itself but also because the British set up a coastal blockade and counterfeited

American Continentals[5]. According to one source, just the cost of the war in terms of money borrowed from other nations amounted to thirty million dollars of specie[6]. And that amount didn't include trade losses or destroyed property. Classical liberalism happened in a mostly agrarian population and it was politically idealistic in two ways. The first was because of classical liberal leaders' attention to Greek and Roman classical political ways of thinking. The second reason was the conscientious way that colonial leaders wanted to make their communities prosper by trying town-hall political approaches. After colonists became established they created their own community government. And some community governments had more than a hundred years to politically experiment and to mature. They were a valuable incubator of the new American political system.

The relative political independence that colonists enjoyed gave them an opportunity to provide justice and liberty to many citizens according to a regional standard. Under this system, politicians were willing to advance a new relationship of noninterference between the politic and the economy. Such a relationship had never been seen during European history. It was unique to Americans. The American system of classical liberalism provided political opportunity where voting was based on property ownership inside a land-expanding nation where property might be obtained but also economic opportunity that was mostly independent of the state. Many people didn't own property, but Westward expansion held the promise of potential wealth in new lands.

By contrast, European traditions of feudalism, aristocracy and social class had opposed equality of economic and political opportunity for centuries. A person's fortunes were mediated through the state and through inherited privilege. Europeans have never believed in the political option of keeping the politic and economy separate in terms of practical policy because it's been outside European experience and was prevented by existing European political institutions. Europe also had limited property availability with property held in large estates and defended by aristocratic families with political influence. Classical liberalism in America expanded liberal political ideas that had been innovated in England under the Magna Carta (1215), the English Petition of Rights (1628) and the English Bill of Rights (1687)[7]. Americans wanted even greater individual independence from state interference under an even more limited government.

After the U.S. Constitution was ratified, grassroots politics withered because the nexus of political action had moved.

Classical liberals sought to become free from government interference in their society. Political freedom depended on economic freedom. Property owners under this system became politically organized to protect private property and wealth. Property owning citizens with the vote would use it to elect legislators who would support their interests. Colonial communication depended on physical travel and electing a representative made sense. But representative government wasn't the same kind of grassroots political involvement as the town hall meeting had been. And as representative government in a more powerful federal government became the norm under the U.S. Constitution, grassroots political involvement declined[8]. This may have been the greatest weakness that developed during classical liberalism—the loss of a public space for direct political activism after town halls and local politics had already greatly contributed to the design of the Constitution[9]. The loss of the town hall political meeting meant that some of the political vigor that contributed to nationhood was gone from the Constitutional Republic.

In 1785, Gabriel Bonnet Abbe de Mably (1709-1785), wrote a letter to John Adams in which he warned that a "commercial elite" might gain political power in the U.S. to aid their commercial interests at the expense of the Republic: "If feeble laws have not the power to hinder the commercial bodies from seizing upon all authority; if the public morals present no succors to the people; but, strive, in vain, to set some limits to the rage of avarice, I must tremble at the prospect of the final rupture of all the bonds of your confederation."[10] Just after the birth of the United States as a nation, Mably had already seen a potential weakness in the U.S. design of the politic. Nowadays, political favoritism of the neoliberal commercial elite has led to advantages for them that have been counterproductive to the wider commonwealth.

The decline of the town hall as a political force left a power vacuum that was eventually filled by special interest politics. Special interest politics grew powerful under modern liberalism when the regulatory state and tax base expanded. That expansion provided money for special projects. Special interest factions have taken political change from a public concern among individuals to one monitored and directed by private interests through organizations[11]. Nevertheless, the political policy combination of classical liberalism and economic liberalism created a strong social commonwealth until the Civil War. The politic and economy were people-powered with economic incentives where property owning people kept most of the wealth that their work built up in their improved lands. Economic liberalism incentivized production and made the American colonies and American Republic grow. And constant property expansion within the United States created a value base to grow new wealth. Tariffs supported government and protected new American production enterprises. Political support from property owners for the legislature and other government branches rested on the idea that good politics and economic prosperity went together. Without prosperity, political policy can't be called successful in the United States.

Some elements of classical liberalism.

During the colonial period, private entrepreneurs in chartered companies and joint stock companies invested in ventures that would establish colonies in America. Some ventures failed. Economic production power from workers, property owners who hired others to work and shopkeepers and trades people sent money, goods and services cycling virtuously to create wealth in the economy. The power of the politic to represent people's political interests and the power of an emerging land based economy were kept separate to thrive synergistically. The commonwealth without a federal income tax allowed people to develop their property gradually. Small local property taxes supported local poor people without a trade and without property but gave them less than they could earn if they could acquire a situation in work as a laborer or tradesman[12, 13].

Politicians didn't tax as much and the economy was free of large burdens after the Revolutionary War debt payments were funded by a payment plan with money raised from tariffs and a whiskey tax[14]. Alexander Hamilton, the Secretary of the Treasury during the administration of George Washington, consolidated state Revolutionary War debt along with federal debt onto federal accounts[15]. He then helped to organize the establishment of the First Bank of the United States. By doing that, he made the first political power-play in the United States to take a portion of state power into the federal government. His bold move was opposed by Thomas Jefferson.

Alexander Hamilton, George Washington and John Adams were Federalists and Thomas Jefferson, James Monroe and James Madison were Democratic Republicans[16]. These were opposing political factions vying for power in early America. Federalists favored more federal power, and Democratic Republicans, also known as Anti-Federalists, favored state empowerment and an agricultural economy. Hamilton wanted to fund the Revolutionary War debt with a payment plan linked to a national bank. The idea of consolidating the war debt proved to be an incentive that motivated Alexander Hamilton. Hamilton expanded federal power and he stretched congressional power somewhat outside assigned constitutional borders of "necessary and proper" in creating the First Bank of the United States (1791-1811). Besides paying down the debt, Hamilton saw a national bank as providing investment money to would-be developers at busy locations along the Atlantic seaboard that would circulate American monies.

Alexander Hamilton also contributed in part to an economic plan that has been called "the American System". Hamilton invented a practical outline for American Commerce in his 1791 "Report on Manufactures." In this report, he avoided policy extremes. He advocated neither the extreme of a full blown laissez faire trade economy with absolutely open trade, nor the extreme of an exclusively agricultural economy. He advocated in favor of some tariff protection imposed by Congress on imports in order to further the development of new American industries in both agriculture and manufacturing.[17, 18]

Hamilton wanted to protect American industries at home, allowing them to grow inside domestic markets without being crushed through competition with European nations that could offer cheaper products. Tariffs could not only protect American production opportunities by allowing new ventures to prosper, they could also raise revenues for the fledgling state and stimulate employment by helping fledgling businesses to survive[19]. In 1818, Henry Clay proposed to utilize Hamilton's protective tariffs in order to fund infrastructural improvements by building roads or canals. Clay's system, influenced in part by Hamilton, has been called "the American System"[20].

Though controversial, the founding of the First Bank of the United States allowed the federal government to organize the total Revolutionary War debt in order to act as pay-agent so that the new nation could pay European countries, like France, which had loaned Americans money when American patriots needed it to win the war. With the Revolutionary War debt under a credible payment plan, business could resume in the U.S. commonwealth and the new United States could begin to gain recognition of nation state status among the cadre of European nations. One of the big jobs of the new American government was to arrange economic circumstances to enable prosperity. Tariffs charged for trade between states were ended and state economies prospered side by side.

Tariffs that protected American industries against European competition were maintained and were a principle source of revenue for the new United States. National bank branches facilitated money circulation. People who owned property were big winners under classical liberalism. The First Bank of the United States could lend money to investors and accept deposits from anyone who wanted a bank to place their money into. Bank branches made banking accessible in many port cities[21]. The interest rate at the First Bank of the United States was near 5%, which is close to the average interest rate of 5.18% for the span of U.S. history[22]. Current very low interest rates are uncommon in U.S. history, although Treasury Bills were pegged at a low 0.375% interest rate after WWII.[23]

Property expansion at the expense of indigenous peoples was widespread and was rationalized to remove the terrible consequences of that political and economic choice. Americans tried to avoid awareness of how they caused tragedy for Native Americans despoiled of their land. Echoes of that hardship still reverberate in today's post-modern politics. Thomas Paine, wrote about the English influencing Native Americans to fight against Americans during the Revolutionary War[24]. But Native Americans had become embroiled in the conflicts between European transplants before then. For instance, Native Americans fought on both sides, for the British and for the French during the French and Indian War (1754-1760).[25]

George Washington recognized that Native Americans could provide an advantage to either side during the Revolutionary War[26]. Native Americans in conflict with each other and with Europeans provided a justification for later aggression against Native American interests, for example to justify General Custer's violence in 1868 against Native Americans.[27] But Europeans coveted Native American property no matter what Native peoples did politically. They were seen as external to laws that would have protected a European's property rights. Externalizing political opponents in new lands was common-place in the

European colonial system. And Native Americans spoke a foreign language and were unfamiliar with the Western legal system. Land conflicts made many Americans into battle-seasoned warriors.

Because so much undeveloped land was taken by European newcomers, classical liberalism provided opportunities for many new Americans to better their economic situation through work and careful resource accumulation on small farms or inside small towns. Property ownership and its use weren't freely available to most common people in Europe. In America, even without property ownership, people could harvest wood, or food from the land. Slavery was also part of the Republic. It provided English second-son transplants, especially in the South with a kind of social hierarchy that made them superior to others through the whole economic system set up on slavery plantations. Their own embedded economic advantage through slavery was as much similar to the English system of social hierarchy as the Southern plantation owners could make it.[28] But slavery, which led to terrible brutality, had many negative effects. For example, slavery kept wages lower wherever it existed.

Native Americans, women, slaves, indentured servants and those without the means to hold property were disadvantaged and denied political empowerment because they didn't have a right to vote.[29] And all or at least part of their earnings were not their own. Property based voting restrictions didn't end in New York State until 1821, after the Anti-Rent Wars.[30] This meant that money and property determined the voting population in early America. Classical liberalism was idealistic, however, because it valued liberty and looked favorably on economic advancement, allowing many people to keep what they could produce in terms both of money and property.

A desire to have liberty came from persecuted people during the Protestant Reformation and endured.

Liberty as a political objective was rooted in the Protestant Reformation. And the classical liberal liberty-concept appreciated harms that freedom could cause others. Liberty free from license and laws that penalized harms were an integral part of the liberty system. Liberty was a political policy out of respect for people's consciences, choices and beliefs. But liberty in terms of access to money was harder to come by. Money wasn't easy to come by in colonial America, and many people purchased on credit. But if you lived in America and you could work, you could improve by paying off credit purchases with labor.[31] Freedom of choice in religion, in where a person lived and how a person lived were other happy features in many colonial communities. Labor discrimination based on a person's religion or reputation was a part of early America, but state persecution for these reasons was not. Classical liberalism in combination with economic liberalism offered a better life in the new commonwealth than could be had at that time in Europe except among the privileged classes.

Labor law during classical liberal times included "master servant laws". As industry and capitalism began to replace feudalism, land-tied feudal obligations to work began to lessen. Master servant law was drafted to regulate relations between laborers outside the professions and the people who hired them. These laws protected labor contracts by enforcing them in the case of contract breach by either the employer or the employed. But by far the employee was disadvantaged in a contract dispute because he could be sent to prison for not working by being absent or finding a better job, whereas employers who didn't fulfill their agreements were only fined. Master servant law allowed for a variety of unfair working conditions at low pay to persist and accounts for why most colonial people disliked wage labor.[32, 33]

Political competition between the nations of Europe inside the nation state system eventually undermined tax freedoms in America. Tax freedom was based on a politically conscious choice favoring economic productivity over war. During America's provoked entry into the War of 1812, Americans were unable to avoid military conflict. Later, the expenses of the Civil War and Reconstruction encouraged the growth of a more centralized federal government. The Civil War itself diminished states' rights against federal power. President Lincoln declared the states' right to secede from the Union as unlawful. That declaration was controversial because state secession was widely debated prior to the Civil War. Many people before the Civil War believed that states' rights included the right to secede. The Union side passed the first income tax during 1861, beginning an economic conversion from economic liberalism to mixed economy.[34]

Modern liberalism came about during the Civil War when the Union side began to tax incomes to pay for the war.

The Civil War erupted partly out of ongoing economic change under the policy of land expansion to the West. New technologies from the first wave of industrialization were having an effect in both the North and the South. New milling machinery in the North expanded the fabric industry. Invention of the cotton gin, also expanded cotton cultivation in the South. The gin could process more cotton species varieties which expanded cotton cultivation onto marginal Southern agricultural lands.[35] This was a further incentive to expand slavery. Transportation and communication improvements were forging new economic ties between distant regions. The lure of new opportunity called to those with the imagination to see what might be possible.

But slavery was disliked in the North and controversial in the West. Controversy about slavery generated a political and economic strain. The North and South rival economies were uneasy about how the expanding Western territories would impact their differing economic strategies. The economic question was whether the North would gain Western customers or whether slave holding agriculturists would spread into the West and emulate the Southern economic strategy. Industrialization was proceeding more rapidly in the North with transportation improvements such as the Erie Canal and more rail. When the North wanted federal money to expand rail further to the West, the South voted against the Pacific Railway Bill of 1860, because it wouldn't help the Southern economy.[36]

Before the Civil War, the South and North were already facing off on issues of economic development because each followed a different economic strategy. And at the time of the Civil War, England had already outlawed slavery in the British colonial system. The U.K. ended the slave trade in 1834, when the Slavery Abolition Act went into effect,[37] so global political tides were moving against slavery. An inability to reconcile differing economic strategies precipitated the conflict which led to losses of life and property during the Civil War. The economic value held in slaves, at that time legally owned in the South, was perhaps greater than three billion dollars.[38] Money invested in slaves and the tremendous labor production that the cotton gin made possible under slavery represented a financial obstacle to change.

After the Civil War, the government's policy to exterminate buffalo herds was an act of violence against Native American interests, extending the policy of taking their lands and property to be used in accord with strategies of land development that went with farming and subsequent urban development. Political policy to ignore the natural rights of Native Americans was a contradiction to neoclassical liberty principles. But the vanquished-hero imagery of Native Americans resonated with Greek and Roman classical texts that extolled heroic war. Instead of seeing Native Americans as politically marginalized, they were imagined as a people that was becoming extinct. But they weren't really dying out. It was just a strategy that sought to avoid guilt over land expropriation. People rationalized that if Native Americans were mostly gone, then they could never occupy their former lands. Land expropriation wasn't the only classical liberal contradiction to liberty principles. Slavery was another source of tension. The Civil War erupted on the one hand out of the contradiction of slavery in a system that emphasized natural rights. But on the other hand, the Civil War was motivated by economic changes associated with rail and it made way for economic policies that would expand the market economy. The Civil War also emphatically provided a preview of what industrialized war-making was like. Technology enhanced war was tragically more fully realized during the twentieth century.

The second political ideology of the United States, modern liberalism, can be recognized through a change of economic strategy from economic liberalism to mixed economy. Mixed economy was a mixture of public and private ownership and oversight of business concerns. The government's oversight of commerce grew during the modern liberal period. Modern liberalism and mixed economy were paired to give the federal government more power so that it could improve public life. Under modern liberalism, the government through Congress and the Court system expanded positive law to require certain actions of businesses and individuals. The government got into the economic driver's seat to decide national economic strategies.

As the voting franchise was broadened, Americans got the universal vote. Many thought that their votes would allow them to direct the federal government to attend to the needs of ordinary people. They imagined more government power would give the government a better chance to serve them. But many new voters weren't educated in classical or neoclassical traditions. They didn't realize that a power-increased government might not serve them as they imagined. Three approaches propelled the change toward a larger and more powerful federal government.

The first was German Idealism. It extolled power above other political attributes. The second was American spiritualism which reached beyond rational causes into the hidden world beyond physical reality. Third was American pragmatism which sought ends above means to solve practical problems by ignoring history and trying novel approaches. These new ways of thinking moved against Enlightenment rationalism to embolden a faith-based certainty that modernity required new methods. Liberty, with its roots in the Protestant Reformation, was no longer a foremost consideration of American politics. Social justice was extolled above liberty and tolerance. And the growth of newspapers during modern liberalism brought more social problems to people's attention. Suddenly, it wasn't ok to allow new social problems to fester. No longer would it be "live and let live." Political machinery would now be put into place to fix problems.

People were afraid that liberty as an avenue to social justice had failed. It had not protected Americans from the terrible consequences of the Civil War or forms of civil labor strife that came both before and after. After the Civil War, long-term strife over workers' rights had erupted: the 1886 Haymarket strike and executions, 1892 Homestead strike, an 1890 Depression, and New York work strikes. The conditions in the Chicago meatpacking plants described by Upton Sinclair in *The Jungle* (1906) shocked readers, as did the immigrant slums of New York photographed by Josef Riis, in *How the Other Half Lives* (1890). Labor violence appalled the American heart during the 1913 Ludlow Massacre.[39] A burgeoning newspaper industry told sensational stories to a wider audience than media had ever reached before. Many of these problems happened in the context of the growth of the market economy—an economic revolution. They weren't due to a failure of classical liberalism. They were just an outgrowth of increased population, new technologies and growth in the transportation system.

Modern liberalism expanded the federal government's purse and power.

Modern liberalism and mixed economy came about because of the Civil War. They carried on under the Progressive policies of the Wilson administration, and the New Deal policies of Franklin Delano Roosevelt during the Great

Depression. Political urgency was triggered as a consequence of new technologies that increased competition between nation states. The second wave of industrialization meant harnessing energies like steam and technologies like radio and telegraph as well as development of fossil fuel refineries, state sponsored expansion of rail accompanied by changes in local commodity markets, immigration, growth of cities and fewer agricultural jobs because of new farm machinery. Higher taxes and government social welfare programs were characteristic of this ideology. Some call it managed capitalism. It was a mild form of socialism and its socialist character was so opposite in philosophy from classical liberalism that its progression was uneasy and controversial. Some Americans across several generations opposed and continue to oppose modern liberalism but it clearly displaced classical liberalism under the industrialization challenge of the late nineteenth and early twentieth century. Government policies regarding the economy, regulation and taxation changed radically to create the mixed economy.

The Industrial Revolution, starting in the 18th century, had provided jobs and an incentive for people to come to cities. The market economy became the U.S.'s economic engine after land expansion into the West had ended. About a hundred years before the Industrial Revolution, the Scientific Revolution began advancing a better standard of living. It had broadened medical and scientific knowledge which eventually improved life in the city. Better sanitation and public health helped populations to grow. People came to the cities, some immigrated, worked, became more educated and the population increased in Europe and America. Greater populations had an effect on politics. One way that more people affected politics was because of increased tax revenue. This tax revenue in the U.S., funded a permanent war economy that became stubbornly established after WWI and WWII. Industrial warfare increased competitive pressures under the nation state system. And political pragmatists who wanted to win wars adopted mixed economy to fund war and welfare. Through war and welfare, modern liberal politicians had greater foreign and domestic political influence. People who had moved from an agrarian lifestyle to life in the city lived under increasing federal economic and political management.

In addition to war funding, part of what propelled modern liberalism during the early twentieth century was continued pressure from ideological competitors within the nation state system. Communism and fascism presented new military challenges. Economic nationalism developed in Germany and took form. Power hungry ideologies became manifest as politicians tried to politically control their economy and divert money into political projects in order to dominate globally in competition with other states for global control of land or other resources. Communism's promise of worker utopia encouraged the development of social welfare under U.S. modern liberalism in order to compete with the idea of communist worker paradise, which promised to provide a more secure family lifestyle.

Aggressive nationalistic forces were stopped through united political opposition to them during the World Wars. But WWI and WWII destroyed most of the infrastructure wealth that had been created during the Industrial Revolution in Europe. At the end of WWII, 70% of European industrial infrastructure had been destroyed. In the USSR, because of the "scorched earth policy", the destruction was even worse, more than 30,000 factories destroyed, 70,000 villages, 1700 urban areas.[40] Rebuilding presented an economic and political challenge. Mixed economy policies diminished economic profits by cycling money out of the economy and funding political projects instead. After the peak of industrialization was over and industrial production began to decline, social welfare became less affordable. Social welfare became a later point of political contention after modern liberalism gave way to neoliberalism. Neoliberal politicians since President Carter have reduced social welfare programs but they have increased spending on military technologies and corporate welfare.

Modern liberals adapted to social changes and new technologies.

Technology and industry reshaped society starting in the 18th century. Higher productivity during the Industrial Revolution under new machine processes starting with the Newcomen Steam Engine had moved industrialization from England to the rest of Europe and to America starting in 1704.[41] The cotton gin was invented in 1790.[42] Gaining momentum, the Industrial Revolution was a juggernaut by the time of the early twentieth century. It gave birth to enormous social changes that replaced ordinary customary experience with new experiences and new demands on people to "change with the times".

The wave of productivity under new energy from steam, gas and oil, rail expansion and better communications had provided so much economic growth that it was unparalleled in history. What that means is that no one in human history had ever seen growth like it. So people struggled with changes that galloped across people's livelihoods. Almost nothing in society remained as it had been. With new technologies and larger populations, the economy became as complex as the politic. But eventually the growth rate slowed. Economic inefficiencies exacerbated diminished demand in already-developed markets. Manufacturing provided less surplus tax under falling demand. Labor unions continued to fight for higher wages and benefits. Taxes were high and that diverted money out of the economy and into politics. After WWII, undeveloped markets abroad seemed to provide better new opportunities for a new political ideology called neoliberalism and that is the third U.S. political ideology.

Neoliberals were opportunists, desperate to out-compete collectivist ideologies.

Neoliberalism has been an opportunistic political ideology. It grew rapidly as the Industrial Revolution's advanced economies experienced falling demand after post- WWII's Europe was rebuilt. But its foundations began at 1944's Bretton Woods United Nations Conference, when 44 Allied nations met and decided to end economic nationalism by uniting global economies. It has been an alliance between transnational corporations and government. A global political ideology that has allied Congress and corporations to develop economic opportunities around the world, it benefits global corporations more than any other group. Some have called neoliberalism predatory capitalism[43] or economic imperialism.[44] Corporatists in the U.S. utilized mobile capital to initiate widespread political, economic and cultural change.

Changes in the U.S. politic and economy were enabled through the use of direct lobbying, media, think tanks and education. Neoliberals have influenced congressional legislation, getting laws passed that provide multinationals with tax savings and other political advantages. This has allowed global corporatists to take advantage of economic opportunities in developing international economies outside legal structures. Neoliberal trans-nationalists inside corporations operate between legal contexts. Without national or global legislation there's been insufficient legal oversights to protect workers, investors or the environment.

This enhances riskiness for global enterprises. But it also has usually provided a cost savings to transnational corporations by preventing litigation in most cases of wrongdoing. Developing nations with cheaper wages and raw materials have provided global corporatists savings on production costs. Controlling these economic markets by offering them easy access to credit has provided political leverage by way of debt. Imposition of the Washington Consensus[45] economic model as a follow-up to debt insolvency has provided a further cost savings by reducing expensive social programs and stopping the progress of other kinds of economic strivings that would otherwise lead to greater economic independence. If these new markets achieved independence, they could curtail their supply of raw materials or finished products and raise their export prices.

Neoliberalism substituted consumerism for market economy and has outsourced most factory production. This benefited corporatists operating globally. Financialization has been an important feature of the neoliberal period. Financialization began with the Big Bang in London in 1986 that deregulated British banking. It was advanced by internationalizing bank branches into more market locations which was made possible through new computer technologies. Financialization has used easy credit to increase debt and debt interest payments.[46] It fueled the hostile takeover environment in American business that manifested in the 1990's. And trading market volatility has been enhanced through new financial products that are exchanged by algorithm directed computer trading. Some traders have advantages based on their superior access to trading information.

International universal banking and new banking technologies have loosened-up and increased money flow. Milton Friedman supported monetarization, or an increased money supply. Money flow increased from both legal and illegal sources.[47] This is partly due to lax monitoring policies in financial markets. Manufacture outsourcing in piecemeal production lines scattered across the globe also has characterized a neoliberal strategy to move money into the hands of a corporate elite that can take advantage of cheaper factors in those markets through their access to capital. Neoliberalism has been a stealthy political ideology when compared with classical liberalism and modern liberalism.[48] Few opportunists who gain advantages under government sponsors have discussed publicly how their business was subsidized. This reticence has allowed neoliberals to avoid a moral evaluation of public costs for corporate advantages. Neoliberals imagine they have achieved yet another good deal because of their skillful cultivation of political and economic opportunity.

Wages in the U.S. have experienced downward pressure and poverty in the U.S. has grown under neoliberalism, which concentrates economic wealth into the hands of a corporate elite, as Mabry warned could happen back in 1785. Manufacturing centers in the Midwestern U.S. have been abandoned because American jobs have gone overseas and U.S. workers have lost the opportunity to remain employed. Prisons have grown in size to jail people who can't find a job in a shrinking economy.[49] Taxes have remained high in the context of expensive military costs and government debt along with social welfare programs like Social Security, Medicaid and Medicare left over from modern liberalism and new corporate welfare. Falling real demand, inflation, high taxes, declining living conditions, and growing poverty have been well known characteristics of neoliberal policy. Multinational corporatists have continued to expand their economic opportunities under tax subsidy to the detriment of domestic small businesses in the United States and potentially competitive businesses in developing nations. Public policies of tailored tax subsidies have given multinational corporatists a competitive advantage and encouraged them to use debt financing.

Even though neoliberals give lip service to free markets, their political habits have increased mega-corporate monopoly power to distort markets. Another market distortion in trading markets has been HFT, or high frequency trading. Commodity price inflation or deflation under artificial demand has been created by high frequency traders and it has distorted the price of commodities for the real market. Many HFT bids are later cancelled after they have already affected the market price in a process called "quote stuffing". Also, if derivatives that short a commodity are purchased in large quantities they can drive the price down. Or HFT bets can inflate the price of goods such as agricultural goods. Market distortions can cut the profit margin for domestic small business selling under the two alternating adversities of commodity inflation or commodity deflation and falling demand in manipulated markets. This hurts small business survival, further destroying opportunities for people outside the corporatist system to become employed as these businesses fail.

Multinationals respond to small business failures by viewing them in terms of Social Darwinism, "only the big firms survive". Neoliberal accelerationist policy[50] supports this view. Infotainment press, under five or six main corporatist news services, has failed to inform a frustrated and confused public about real issues. Congress has appeared combative between political parties but mostly over trivial matters. Congress has continued to support neoliberal policies that have been under development by the U.S. government since the end of WWII and it has failed to admit policy failures. Congress has never openly declared the neoliberal nature of foreign or domestic policies it has implemented during successive presidential administrations since Eisenhower. A relentless drive to globalize under open trade and mobile capital bears witness to neoliberalism's advance. This globalization has been different from global trade at other times in history.

Different kinds of global trade happened under each political ideology.

Global trade under early classical liberalism was trade in products from one nation to another inside the colonial mercantilist system. Banking capital centers were able to lend outside their nations but most investment was at the national or state level. People who wanted freer trade, like Adam Smith (1723-1790) during classical liberalism opposed the mercantilist system because it had protection-ist trading tariffs on goods such as corn. Goods traded between nations during mercantilism were finished manufactured goods and commodities such as sugar or salted fish. Textiles were traded all around the world during colonial times.[51]

As the U.S. began to pursue modern liberalism, global trade expanded because wars had increased international connections. Nations undergoing industrial development intensified their own production and competed for whatever raw materials they needed but couldn't produce. Economic competi-tion increased concurrently with political competition. Nations began preparing for war. World War II cemented alliances between Allied powers and ended colo-nialism as a way to get raw materials.

International globalization changed its character starting with GATT treaties organized at the UN Bretton Woods conference. GATT regulated manufactured goods trading. John Maynard Keynes (1883-1946) attended Bretton Woods and some have said that his presence indicated the continuation of modern liberal-ism and mixed economy in Europe and America after the war.[52] But managed economies under mixed economy policies transformed gradually as open trading agreements altered global markets from managed capitalism of domestic corpo-rations to state sponsored transnational global corporatism.

Before mobile capital, local banks made loans to local companies for local development that paid local wages in a virtuous money cycle that benefitted many groups in the community. But neoliberal banks with access to increas-ingly mobile capital, took money out of locally virtuous circulation, subtracting money from the community. Gradual change began as a step-by-step neoliberal process. Loans were made to underdeveloped nations from non-local banks, the IMF and World Bank, for example. Infrastructure was built under deals that employed European and American infrastructure builders in developing economies where local builders could have been employed instead. Developing nations got new roads and infrastructure but the money didn't help local people to become employed. Debt was owed by the developing nation. And that debt was a political lever. It could be used to leverage Washington Consensus policies onto the developing nation if it defaulted on the debt it owed. Since loans were sometimes short term maturity loans for long term projects, default was likely at some later point in time. Or if the economy was an export economy and its primary exports lost value, that nation's debt would go into default. And prices were not under the control of small developing nations but were influenced instead by larger economies that bought from them.

After the electrical and plumbing infrastructure was built, factories had just the infrastructure that they needed. Global multinationals built factories in developing economies which were by then under a debt obligation that provided political leverage. Third world nations were made vulnerable through these infrastructure debts. Their political and economic policies were controlled into a neoliberal format. They were oppressed by debt obligation away from what might have been an opportunity toward economic evolution. They became trapped in export economies. In this way, multinational American companies have colonized economic opportunities abroad.[53, 54]

Congressional policy to support transnational corporations has harmed the domestic economy.

Congress's support for multinationals not only leverages multinational success against the success of small local business in the developing world. It also leverages multinationals against small local businesses in the United States. Small business can't compete with the advantages possessed by the large transnationals under U.S. trade and tax policy. Congressional legislation in the U.S. has favored the global economy instead of the domestic economy for decades-long spans of federal policy. One indication of this is that the Democrats took full employment out of their political plank more than two decades ago. And American labor unions can't negotiate in favor of better wages in the U.S. because American firms have relocated their operations to take advantage of cheaper sources of labor abroad.

Workplace benefits such as healthcare stop making sense in the labor marketplace when labor without healthcare can be bought cheaply abroad. The Affordable Care Act was written in part to get American corporations out of paying for healthcare. Labor safety suffers from the same global malady. American companies that afford a safety investment for their workers are at a disadvantage when foreign competitors don't spend money to enhance their worker's safety. Global pressures that have led to lower American wages, less concern over worker safety, fewer labor benefits and "low road" employment policies have caused unhappiness in the United States' labor force. Diminished American labor productivity because of labor non-participation[55] has been a sign of growing labor dissatisfaction. There has been a trend of fewer jobs and especially since the Great Recession, far fewer high paying jobs. Outsourcing work to factories abroad has been negotiated by American treaties. Outsourcing promotes transnational industries even though it has increased domestic unemployment. Political favors go to neoliberal elites who bought political influence with global capital to open the doors of economic expansion abroad even at the expense of the domestic U.S. economy and other developed nation's domestic economies.

Understanding the politic by recognizing government policies that affect people's economic opportunities can provide clearer analysis of American life.

As you learn about them, your recognition of these three American political ideologies can clarify the politic and economy. U.S. political speech can be flavored by all three ideologies or it can substantially favor one of them. Without insight into what has characterized each American political ideology, politicians can sound confusing whenever they speak about politics. And some political speakers confuse their political audience anyway because the politician fails mean anything in particular based on any political policies. Their speech doesn't refer to what politicians can really do. A political speech should be about who gets what and it should nest inside ideological principles for one of the three political ideologies.

For example, if the speaker favors classical liberal principles, she should avoid invading people's private lives with more regulations and she should repeal regulations that already interfere with people's lives. She would favor less taxes. If the speaker is a modern liberal, he would want to regulate the economy, tax heavily and elaborate the nanny state. He would advocate for a mixed economy under the belief that it would encourage more equal political and economic opportunity for everyone. If the speaker is a neoliberal, she would blame everyday Americans for political and economic problems, reduce taxes most of all for corporations, and provide multinational corporate welfare in order to get better access to economic opportunities abroad. When a politician doesn't say who gets what and why, they make a political speech that has no substance. Or worse, speaks nonsense to get out of being more politically accountable for political problems. Until you recognize ideological formats, it can be difficult to sort out what a political speaker is saying. But when you sort out the different ideologies, politicians finally make sense. Then you can evaluate them. It's helpful to know the political context for what they are saying as an aid to evaluating their policies.

Recognizing dominant political factions or special interest factions competing in the context of today's mostly neoliberal politics can also be illuminating. For example, when a politician says that he supports liberty, whose liberty? Is he supporting a multinational corporatist's liberty abroad to get the best international trading circumstances at the expense of small businesses domestically and at the expense of worker safety abroad and lower wages at home? When a politician says that social welfare programs like Obamacare are important to the American people, which Americans will benefit? The ACA brings most Americans higher taxes inside a shrinking economy during a jobless recovery in order to support a government subsidized health program that breaks every proper business standard of equal and fair pricing, privacy and access. The ACA isn't helping most Americans. It's a monster tax increase written by insurance companies who were defending their opportunity to profit by selling a government mandated product. When a neoliberal businessman declares that government deregulation at specialized economic zones will help businesses prosper, it could be that he advocates for unregulated trade for multinational corporatists while small businesses are heavily regulated. You can see through these rhetorical political declarations once you learn about the three American political ideologies and the factional interests that are served under them. Neoliberals come out of their camouflage when you know how to recognize their politics.

Historical quotes, in each of three chapters, and abundant references will add rhetorical and empirical flesh to this outline and aid further exploration of these three ideologies and their contribution to history and to our current American political environment and economy. Examination of the relationship between the politic and the economy of a nation provides insights into the greatest individual or group beneficiaries of each political and economic pairing and those people whose troubles aren't addressed. History reveals the circumstantial urgency that motivated change and the ideas that provided a new structure to accommodate change.

People continue debating the relationship of the politic to the economy.

The politic and the economy respond to different social influences and logically can be viewed as separate even though they act synergistically. Under classical liberalism, when the U.S. Constitution was written, the Founding Fathers separated the economy and the politic to create new liberty for individuals and to limit the power of government. Whether the economy and the politic should be treated in policy as separate is the most contentious philosophical disagreement between classical liberalism, modern liberalism and neoliberalism. Classical liberals wanted liberty in both the politic and economy. They wanted to protect economic opportunities and they didn't want to enhance the power of the federal government beyond a minimum required to govern a free republic. Modern liberal socialists wanted to put the wealth of society into political programs and political influence in war and social welfare. Neoliberals have wanted the government to provide corporations with tax subsidies and to use military resources to make business opportunity more accessible globally in order to generate more capital for international business elites.

The amount and kind of political regulation of the economy is what most distinguishes the political and economic power of each ideology and also what characterizes the complications brought about by that power. But economies are complex and have limited resources. Siphoning money out of the economy to fund politics or to strengthen global business at the expense of domestic businesses weakens the grassroots economy and can eventually undermine both the politic and economy as has been seen under communist regimes and now under neoliberalism. Both modern liberalism (socialism) and neoliberalism (international corporatism), centralize economic opportunity such that economic inefficiencies become a built in part of their economies, leading eventually toward economic failure.

The Law, banking and warfare affect both the politic and economy.

Both the politic and economy under any circumstances are changing and evolving, strengthening or weakening. Whatever affects both the economy and the politic offers greater potential to maintain or to undermine each policy pairing of politic and economy. Three active disciplines can be recognized that affect both the economy and the politic. They are the law, banking and war. All three can substantially apply pressure towards economic and political change. Each of these disciplines can provoke change or by contrast, society can achieve social stability through the way that it designs and regulates the law, banking and war. Viewing war, banking and law under each ideology supplies insight into the ideology's stability and staying power.

Specific actors and ideas affect the politic but the sometime intention of people to control political outcomes through a political ideology has remained impossible for anyone to achieve. Constructivism is the idea that certain social developments can be arranged through political and economic manipulation when without this interference, they will not happen naturally. Constructivism has been tried by neoliberals and socialists. But unintended consequences show the limits of any political ideology to affect outcomes that shape human destiny. An appreciation for complexity, adaptation and unpredictable evolution distinguishes the post-modern era of the present from the modern period (see complex adaptive systems in the prelude's appendix). The classical liberal view of the politic and economy as a machine that could be controlled if only it were understood has been proven to be an inaccurate modeling. The arc of history shows that events happen on a contingency basis. Events proceed based on what came before and they affect what will happen later. Complex adaptive systems like the economy and the politic will adapt unpredictably to events.

While policy can influence outcomes in the politic and economy, policy can't determine political or economic outcomes independent of society's choices. But good policies can help the politic and economy adapt peacefully to changing circumstances.

A new American political brew may be forming.

What new political ideology is forming in Post-Modern and Post-Industrial Age America remains to be seen. The relationship between the politic and the economy, the evolving opportunities realized by our society remain in a state of flux. As the economy, when considered as a whole, has grown weaker under neo-liberalism, a new political ideology and economy may take its place. President John F. Kennedy famously said, "Those who make peaceful revolution impossible make violent revolution inevitable", or again, somewhat differently, said, "The best road to progress is freedom's road."[56, 57] Knowing more about the politic and knowing more about the economy, recognizing how they interact to create winners and losers, may lead you to an understanding of how to create greater happiness and success through good policies. Americans, like you, can utilize the political tools in our representative government under the 1789 Constitution. That's what leaders who implemented the other three ideologies all have done. American ideologies begin with the notion of government by the people and for the people. The 'people' can be anyone who learns how to assemble and participate in political organization that will move the levers of power.

In the twenty first century more than fifty per cent of American voters opt out of political participation by refusing to vote. Media commentators seem to think that this large non-participatory segment indicates that people in the U.S. don't care about politics. Others call it a form of protest, even though it doesn't change politics. But they're wrong to see only that. A politically savvy observer would recognize growing political potential for a new political ideology if it could mobilize and represent the interests of that non-participatory group—the group ready for change.

They could be a readymade majority if a new political ideology could unite them. This new ideology probably wouldn't be neoliberalism or modern liberalism or even classical liberalism. It probably wouldn't be promoted by either the Democrat or Republican parties, which mostly follow neoliberal policies. But it could be the ideology that can create new opportunities and organize non-participants into the next American political force empowered to enable changes that partake of new possibilities. A new American political ideology could perhaps capture energy in the politic that reflects people's values and regulate the economy to capture their productive energy. It could better enable Americans to be politically active and to do economically important things.

Or another possibility is what no one wants: a breakdown of civility under a collapsing politic and economy. Civil coherency depends on orderliness in law, banking and conflict management. If neoliberalism fails and no new organizing political and economic structure emerges, society could teeter on the brink of a collapse. Many challenges face America but the most important one is civility during a process of change. Three political ideologies prove that Americans can reorganize the politic and economy under the pressure of change. This may be the time for a new political and economic format. The new American polity could embody the next historical step in our American journey.

Fast Car Analysis: Prelude

"the politic": the action arena that decides "who gets what".
"the economy": set of all markets for goods and services where people negotiate prices and values in order to make mutually beneficial exchanges.

A limited government has **more concentrated political power** than a politic that has become distracted by many regulatory tasks.

rationalism + humanism = **liberalism**
liberalism + double entry bookkeeping = **capitalism**

Three reasons to analyze and view the politic and economy separately:
first, because political freedom requires economic freedom;
second, because powerful market economies can harm "the people" when economic power is used in the politic to oppress others;
third, because the politic has a moral dimension and is judged by whether people are happy while the economy works instead by profit vs. loss in a system of negotiated exchange.

Three disciplines that affect both the politic and economy and for which policy considerations are most important: finance, war, and law

How to identify the three American political ideologies:

Classical liberalism: had the least federal government interference in economic life. It had land based economic wealth, states powers balanced with federal powers, individual freedom from government coercion for some, slavery and indentured servitude for others, population growth, tariffs, and the American System. The Revolutionary War showed that Americans recognized American interests as separate from British interests and it removed American colonial land and wealth from British taxation and control. The War of 1812 exemplified an unavoidable engagement originating from nation state conflict. There were many bloody battles to claim land from Native Americans, other Europeans and to fight against tax schemes. Private life was separated from public life and was protected from government interference.

Modern liberalism: began the federal government's intervention in the U.S. economy through greater taxation and regulation. Income taxes helped win The Civil War for the Union side. After the Civil War, the federal government gained greater power than state governments had. Improved transportation and communication linked up the nation, while improved sanitation, and chemical fertilizers led to population growth. A wider voting franchise included black men, women and the propertyless. The market based economy grew when immigration brought impoverished people to work in factories. Newspapers and magazines informed the public about social problems. But federal money incentivized the growth of more political factions than before. Labor strife increased. The intercontinental railroad connected the nation by providing easier overland travel. Implementation of warfare and welfare after the Great Depression undermined profit reinvestment in the economy. The market economy encouraged the formation and growth of the regulatory state. Keynesian strategies after the Great Depression failed to create economic recovery of the nation's markets. There was more federal government interference in private property and private life.

Neoliberalism: has shown the most federal government intervention in the economy. Promotion of corporate trans-national business and corporate concentration into fewer larger corporations has created titans that distort the market. Increased numbers of political factions and the growth of organizations that have become active in the politic on behalf of corporate power has led to excessive multiplication of laws, reduced social welfare, increased public taxes, increased corporate welfare, reduced corporate taxes, and less political accountability to the public. Monopolies have concentrated corporate power as evidenced by fewer companies in healthcare, finance, media, energy, and agriculture. Government empire-seeking for corporate development, and increased war budgets have depleted the treasury. Justice has become more transactional. Corporate personhood has made corporations more powerful, and a judicial legal vacuum in foreign nations has permitted transnational corporations to operate without international legal oversight. Public and private debt have increased. Private life has become invaded by government surveillance and excessive regulations. Corporations allowed into the economic driver's seat have sought short term gains by the self-interested.

Prelude Appendix

The Nation State System

The nation state system has operated since the end of the Thirty Years' War, and was enacted by European states who agreed to do so in the Peace of Westphalia in 1648. The Protestant Revolution had torn European communities apart, and the Thirty Years' War was the worst that Europe had seen. It was fought with mercenary armies, mostly on what would later become German soil, as ruling aristocrats brought religion and politics into the war arena. At the closing of the tumult and bloodshed of the Protestant Reformation, European aristocrats modeled the nation state system after the diplomacy that had already been invented by Renaissance Italian city states. Most aristocrats also reduced the number of binding declarations about the state's religion that had forced religious commitments that offended people's own religious consciences and that had caused social unrest.

During the Renaissance, Italians had discovered a new way to balance power through diplomacy in the city states. Other European communities admired diplomacy because in addition to a peace dividend, it enabled trade between city states that was profitable. Diplomacy was a new tool that encouraged negotiation before battle. Nation states could pursue their own interests by whatever means including warfare, but diplomacy lessened the frequency of wars. Colonialism and capitalism spread the nation state system around the world after 1648 and nation state diplomacy has negotiated the trade and treaty agreements that now encircle the globe. Although some see neoliberal politics as a challenge to the nation state system, it remains a crucial part of everyday global politics.

Nation State Features:
Balance of power diplomacy between nations:

A political treaty network has been validated by nation state partners in order to preserve their power constructs. Each nation makes its own rules and has its own politics. The most powerful nations dominate by making alliances with equally powerful nations that contribute to maintaining the nation state system. Nations can have a variety of political ideologies and modalities.

Tiered/unequal power relationships:

When nations of different economic and political power form alliances with each other, trade between nations will not be equally profitable for both parties because the dominant power will negotiate to its best advantage and under the principle of reciprocal demand, the nation with the greater demand will tend to set the price of goods.

State interests are sovereign:

Nation states oppose the existence of international bodies that would oversee global enterprise and constrict nation state power. Nations compete with each other for natural resources, treaty partners and other potential advantages.

International global legal anarchy:

Under a system of sovereign nations, no higher international power can form that would disrupt nation state power. This has become problematic in the twenty-first century because it blocks global legal oversight of transnational banking and business operations that have become commonplace. Instead of global legal oversight, trade is conducted under treaty obligations that are limited and often lack clear jurisdictional rules for court proceedings in the case of harms. Clear international rules of penalty and oversight are luxuries outside the system of nation states. But legal oversight has always been a necessity to trade. Global trade is therefore harmed and nations often disagree about how to repair damages when harms occur.

Territorial boundaries:

Nation states have a physical territory with a border. Planning for conservation of a natural resource whether to utilize it sustainably or to preserve it for the future can be harmed by the nation state system of land parceling into political territories. Biomass regions that comprise regions of natural diversity in animal and plant species are harder to protect when nations differ about how to use them. Some transnational companies have been eager to negotiate for their access to fragile regions in order to harvest their saleable resources. Poor nations can be incentivized to abandon natural resource protection and the region can suffer irreparable harms. An example of this problem, has been the unwillingness of many coastal nations to negotiate treaties that would limit fishing in nearby territorial and extra-territorial waters. The broad ocean, away from national borders has never benefitted from a global conservation treaty and for this reason, many fisheries have become depleted.

No tolerance of empire:

Any nation striving for single state hegemony, for example, Hitler's Germany and Napoleon's France, were aberrations that offended the nation state system which doesn't allow for empires that take territory from other European nations. Nations became united to oppose these ambitious men. Despite unipolar U.S. political dominance after the end of the Cold War, aggressive actions by the U.S. have not involved invasion followed by territorial expansion. Even though the U.S. military has operated in order to stop communist trade networks from forming during the Cold War, and it has defended neoliberal trade networks, the U.S. has stayed within the broad power and territorial guidelines established by the nation state system.

Stability:

The nation state system adapts to diversity and this creates stability through the system of diplomacy. But it also makes some changes which could be advantageous, such as international commerce laws hard to achieve. It continues to be the system that keeps global politics heterogeneous. Although global trade has become established as a means of political positioning, diverse kinds of governments exist in the global world of nation states. Monarchies, aristocracies, federal republics, communist nations, constitutional governments, parliamentary governments, theocracies and tribal networks remain. The hope of ever uniting these groups to cooperate in forming an international legal system remains small, though some progress has been made toward identifying international standards for transnational corporate behavior. The sooner a legal system that oversees international trade and business operations can form, the better will it be able to protect public and private interests.

(Appendix endnote sources listed after Prelude Endnotes.)

Complex Adaptive Systems

Complex adaptive systems or CAS have been described since the mid twentieth century. When observation-based modeling failed to account for the behavior of large weather systems, people became aware that with enough complexity, systems can possess adaptive components that can evolve and change in an unpredictable way that is contingent on a set of possible variables. Earlier in history, during the nineteenth and early twentieth century, scientists had believed and hoped that systems could be analyzed into parts that could be fully understood. They imagined that scientists taking a system down to a model of its components would be able to predict and control the system's behavior in response to a stimulus. That was inside the context of Newtonian Physics and before the Heisenberg Uncertainty Principle. In the past, linear cause and effect kinds of arguments modelled a world that could be controlled if only scientists knew enough about the system. But large aggregates of independently acting agents can influence any CAS into new capacities that are surprising and that can't be predicted. Complex adaptive systems can evolve. That viewpoint differs from the earlier view of scientists.

Features of CAS:

(1) Large numbers of actors.
(2) Additive behaviors that create large effects.
(3) Energy exchanges with nearby systems to contribute to maintaining greater stability.
(4) New opportunities created because of flexible alternatives.
(5) Small changes can create a large sudden effect on the system.

A CAS can be examined under equilibrium conditions or when undergoing a change in conditions. CAS's can be stable or experience sudden change. The development of tipping points can be an element of CAS study, or alternatively, resilience can be studied. Resilience happens because independent segments of adaptable components can help the system to remain stable. A tipping point can be reached when enough of the system is put into states of transition and an unpredicted state of change remodels the entire set of contingent elements. Some examples of CAS include the immune system, the weather, stock markets, commodity markets, the politic, the economy, language development, genetic evolution, elements that are part of pathogenic infection, and adaptation to and within the urban environment. As the politic and economy have grown with expansion of the world's population, they have become more complex and more adaptive. This brings greater resilience but also the potential of enormous and perhaps sudden change.

Timeline of historical influences that affected Americans before and after the U.S. existed:

1204 Sack of Constantinople; ancient Greek and Roman books were brought back to the territory of what would later become Italy; also double entry bookkeeping was in use as shown by bookkeeping documents of Giovanino Farolfi and Company.

1215 The Magna Carta was signed by King John at Runnymede in England and it supported the rule of law: "No free man shall be taken or imprisoned or dispossessed, or outlawed, or banished, or in any way destroyed, nor will we go upon him, nor send upon him, except by the legal judgment of his peers or by the law of the land".

1350 Beginning of the Renaissance.

1360 Approximate birth of Hans Fugger, the founder of a weaver's guild and patriarch of the Fugger Banking Firm; his son, Jacob Fugger and his grandson Jacob Fugger II became the first capitalists. Clocks invented around 1300 spread into use.

1450 Gutenberg's movable typesetting printer changed how information could be shared. Cosimo de Medici founded the Platonic Academy in Florence to study classical sources of information, especially Plato.

1453 Sack of Constantinople; ancient Greek and Roman books were brought back to pre-Italy; secret radicals that wanted an alternative to the partnership between the church and state became fascinated by Roman and Greek ideas.

Around 1500 mariners began to use the north pointing magnetic compass (a Chinese invention) and the astrolabe (from the Islamic world) and navigators made detailed charts of the world's seas. This led to greater exploration outward from Europe. Serfdom ended in most of Europe as money replaced services and goods as the unit of exchange. War-technology spread of cannons and development of firearms (gunpowder invented in China; modified by Europeans to be used in firearms). One thousand printing firms were making books in Europe.

1503 Michaelangelo Buonarroti began working on the Sistine Chapel.

1513 Niccolo Machiavelli wrote *The Prince* and dedicated it to Lorenzo Medici. It was the first book of realist politics but it wasn't translated into English until more than 100 years later, in 1640. Machiavelli never acquired the Medici's favor because he had opposed Platonism in favor of liberal rationalism. In *The Discourses*, Machiavelli wrote a longer and more detailed political work. It was the background and foundation from which Machiavelli wrote *The Prince*.

1517 Martin Luther's "Ninety-five Theses".

1520 End of the Renaissance; Protestant Reformation began (Latin Church).

1536 King Henry VIII left the Catholic Church and began the Church of England, or the Anglican Church.

1543 After the death of Copernicus, his book, *Concerning the Revolutions of the Celestial Bodies*, was published. It eventually changed the Catholic Earth-centered world-view. The Scientific Revolution was launched when the sun became the center of the universe as proven by empirical observation.

1589-1613 Shakespeare wrote most of his plays.

1607 The founding of Jamestown, Virginia happened.

1620 The founding of Plymouth, Massachusetts happened.

1628 The English signing of the Petition of Right by King Charles I limited the King's power, rejected the divine right of Kings, made law supreme over the king and allowed taxation only under the support of Parliament.

1642-1660 The English Civil War and the Interregnum under Puritan leader Oliver Cromwell. The first "citizen army" in the "era of revolutions" was a Protestant army.

1648 -1650 The Peace of Westphalia ended the Thirty Years' War and brought the Protestant Reformation toward closure. The nation state system carried on by inventing diplomacy to change the political options of Europe.

1687 The beginning of the Enlightenment.

1689 The English Declaration of Rights supported the 1628 Petition of Right and outlined thirteen rights that Parliament recognized as part of English heritage. These rights became the basis of later liberty protections developed under the influence of English law in the American colonies.

1700 Thomas Newcomen invented the Newcomen Steam Engine to remove water from coal mines in England. This invention began the first wave of the Industrial Revolution.

Prelude Endnotes

1. Library of Congress Researchers, "Primary Documents in American History," last modified Mar 19, 2013, www.loc.gov/rr/program/bib/ourdocs/articles.html, accessed 2012.

2. "Socialism vs. Liberalism," www.differencebetween.net/miscellaneous/politics/difference-between-socialism-and-liberalism, accessed 2014.

3. Simon Black, Sovereign Man Blog, "I for inevitable", posted by Tyler Durden, www.zerohedge.com/news/2012-11/guestpost-i-inevitable Durden, 11-05-2012, accessed 2013.

4. Hannah Arendt, "What Is Authority?" from *The Portable Hannah Arendt*, ed. Peter Baehr, (New York: Penguin Group, 2003), 485.

5. Bill Still, *No More National Debt*, (St. Petersburg: Reinhardt and Still Publishers, The Still Foundation, Inc, 2011), 88-89.

6. The Federal Reserve Bank of Philadelphia, "The First Bank of the United States," www.philadelphiafed.org/publications/economic-education/ firstbank.pdf, accessed 2013.

7. Akhil Reed Amar and Les Adams, *The Bill of Rights Primer*, (Birmingham: Palladium Press, 2002, 3-12.

8. Hannah Arendt, "The Revolutionary Tradition and Its Lost Treasure", from *The Portable Hannah Arendt*, ed. Peter Baehr, (New York: Penguin Group, 2003), 508-516.

9. Hannah Arendt, "The Revolutionary Tradition and Its Lost Treasure", from *The Portable Hannah Arendt*, ed. Peter Baehr, (New York: Penguin Group, 2003), 508-516.

10. Gabriel Bonnet Abbe de Mably, The Online Library of Liberty, A Project of Liberty Fund, Inc, www.oll.liberty fund.org/?option=com_staticxt&staticxt &staticfile=full-quote.php%3Fquote=224&itemid=275, last modified 5 Oct, 2009, accessed 2013.

11. Hannah Arendt, "The Revolutionary Tradition and Its Lost Treasure", from *The Portable Hannah Arendt*, ed. Peter Baehr, (New York: Penguin Group, 2003), 508-516.

12. Joseph Postell, "The Right Kind of Regulation: What the Founders Thought About Regulation," in *Rediscovering Political Economy*, eds. Joseph Postell and Bradley C.S. Watson, (Plymouth, UK: Lexington Books, 2011), 211-214.

13. Soss, Joe, Fording, Richard and Sandford Schram, *Disciplining the Poor: Neoliberal Paternalism and the Persistent Power of Race*, (Chicago: University of Chicago Press, 2011), 85-86.

14. "Economic History of the United States," enwikipedia.org/wiki/economic history of the United States, accessed 2013.

15. Larry Schweikart, "American Banking from Birth to Bust, And All Points in Between," in *Rediscovering Political Economy,* eds. Joseph Postell and Bradley C. S. Watson, (Plymouth, UK: Lexington Books, 2011), 233.

16. Howard Zinn, *A People's History of the United States, 1492 to Present*, (New York: Harper Collins Publishers, Harper Perennial Modern Classics, 2005), 97.

17. Alan Levine, "The Idea of Commerce in Enlightenment Political Thought," in *Rediscovering Political Economy*, eds. Joseph Postell and Bradley Watson, (Plymouth, UK: Lexington Books, 2011), 76-77.

18. Timeline of American Planning History. Source, www.taxplanning.org/media/files/page/ Planning History 1785 -2000.pdf, accessed Dec, 2013.

19. Roger Ransom, *Coping With Capitalism: The Economic Transformation of the United States 1776-1980*, (Englewood Cliffs, NJ: Prentice-Hall Inc, 1981), 162.

20. Timeline of American Planning History. Source, www.taxplanning.org/media/files/page/ Planning History 1785 -2000.pdf, accessed Dec, 2013.

21. The Federal Reserve Bank of Philadelphia, "The First Bank of the United States," www. philadelphiafed.org/publications/economic-education/firstbank.pdf, 2013, accessed 2013.

22. Lawrence Lewitinn, Talking Numbers-CNBC/ Yahoo Finance, "Here's 222 years of interest rate history on one chart", finance.yahoo.com/blogs/talking-numbers/222-years-interest-history-one-chart-173358843.html, Sept 18, 2013, accessed 2013.

23. Wikipedia, "1951 Accord", enwikipedia.org/wiki/ 1951 accord, accessed 2013.

24. Thomas Paine, "Common Sense," ed., Howard Fast, *The Selected Work of Tom Paine and Citizen Tom Paine*, (USA: Random House, Inc., 1945), 30.

25. Frances Pohl, *Framing Art: A Social History of American Art*, (New York: Thames and Hudson, 2002), 69.

26. Richard Bradshaw and Sarah Percy, "Mercenaries and Military Manpower", mercenarymatters.wordpress.com/2009/02/10/mercenaries-in-the-american-revolution., Jan and Feb 2009, accessed 2013.

27. Frances Pohl, *Framing Art: A Social History of American Art*, (New York: Thames and Hudson, 2002), 226.

28. David Hackett Fischer, *Albion's Seed: Four British Folkways in America*, (New York: Oxford University Press, 1989), 388.

29. Marianne Doezema and Elizabeth Milroy, eds., *Reading American Art*, (New Haven and London: Yale University Press, 1998), 81-82.

30. Marianne Doezema and Elizabeth Milroy, eds., *Reading American Art*, (New Haven and London: Yale University Press, 1998), 82-86.

31. Meyer Weinberg, *A Short History of American Capitalism*, USA, 2003, Chapter 3, "Colonial Economy", www.allshookdown.com/newhistory/CH03.pdf, accessed 2013.

32. Suresh Naidu, Noam Yuchtman, Web Appendix to "Coercive Contract Enforcement: Law and the Labor Market in 19th Century Industrial Britain, Appendix 1A: Enactment and Enforcement of Master and Servant Law", www.aeaweb.org/aer/data/feb2013/20100770_ app.pdf, accessed Aug 19, 2013.

33. Wikipedia, "Master and Servant Act," enwikipedia.org/wiki/Master and Servant Act, accessed 2013.

34. Roger Ransom, "The Economics of the Civil War," posted Feb, 2010, eh.net/encyclopedia/ article/ransom.civil war.us, accessed 2013.

35. Roger Ransom, *Coping With Capitalism: The Economic Transformation of the United States 1776-1980*, (Englewood Cliffs, NJ: Prentice-Hall Inc, 1981), 37.

36. Roger Ransom, "The Economics of the Civil War, posted Feb, 2010, eh.net/encyclopedia/article/ransom.civilwar.us, accessed 2013.

37. Wikipedia, "Abolition of Slavery Timeline," enwikipedia.org/wiki/abolition-of-slavery-timeline, 2014.

38. Roger Ransom, "The Economics of the Civil War", posted Feb 2010, eh.net/encyclopedia/article/ransom.civilwar.us, accessed 2013.

39. Howard Zinn, *A People's History of the United States, 1492 to Present*, (New York: Harper Collins Publishers, Harper Perennial Modern Classics, 2005), 355-357.

40. Wikipedia, "Aftermath of World War II," enwikipedia.org/wiki/Aftermath of World War II, accessed 2014.

41. Thomas Greer and Gavin Lewis, *A Brief History of the Western World, Eighth Edition*, (Orlando: Harcourt College Publishers, 2002), 556.

42. Roger Ransom, *Coping With Capitalism: The Economic Transformation of the United States 1776-1980*, (Englewood Cliffs, NJ: Prentice-Hall Inc, 1981), 37.

43. Ravi Bhandari, "Rise of the Global Corporatocracy: An Interview with John Perkins, Sept 17, 2012, monthlyreview.org/2013/03/01/rise-of-the-global-corporatocracy-an-interview-with-john-perkins, accessed 2013.

44. Phillip Mirowski, Dieter Plehwe, eds., *The Road From Mont Pelerin: The Making of the Neoliberal Thought Collective*, (Cambridge, MA, Harvard University Press, 2009), 324, (public choice theory, Gordon Tullock).

45. Manfred Steger and Ravi Roy, *Neoliberalism: A Very Short Introduction*, (New York: Oxford University Press, 2010), 19-20.

46. Thomas Palley, F*inancialization: The Economics of Finance Capital Domination*, (New York: Palgrave Macmillan, 2013), 69.

47. Alan Block and Constance Weaver, *All Is Clouded By Desire: Global Banking, Money Laundering and International Organized Crime*, (Westport, CT: Praeger Publishers, 2004).

48. Manfred Steger and Ravi Roy, *Neoliberalism: A Very Short Introduction*, (New York: Oxford University Press, 2010), preface.

49. Soss, Joe, Fording, Richard and Sandford Schram, *Disciplining the Poor: Neoliberal Paternalism and the Persistent Power of Race*, (Chicago: University of Chicago Press, 2011), Soss, Fording, Schram, 83-111.

50. Kent Weaver, *The Politics of Industrial Change: Railway Policy in North America,* (Washington, DC: The Brookings Institution, 1985), 1-25.

51. Marianne Doezema and Elizabeth Milroy, eds., *Reading American Art*, (New Haven and London: Yale University Press, 1998), 1-11.

52. Manfred Steger and Ravi Roy, *Neoliberalism: A Very Short Introduction*, (New York: Oxford University Press, 2010), 6.

53. John Perkins, *Confessions of an Economic Hitman,* (New York: Plume, Penguin Group, 2004).

54. Richard Peet, *Unholy Trinity: The IMF, World Bank and WTO,* (New York: Zed Books, 2003).

55. Steve Hargreaves, "Labor Participation Lowest Since 1978," money.cnn.com/2013/09/06/news/economy/labor-force-participation, Sept 2013, accessed 2014.

56. Robert F. Kennedy, BrainyQuote, "John F. Kennedy Quotes," www.brainyquote.com/quotes/authors/j/john_f_kennedy.htmlBrainyquote.com, accessed 2013.

57. Robert F. Kennedy, BrainyQuote, "John F. Kennedy Quotes," www.brainyquote.com/quotes/authors/j/john_f_kennedy.htmlBrainyquote.com, accessed 2013.

Prelude Appendix References

The nation state system

1. Thomas Greer and Gavin Lewis, *A Brief History of the Western World, Eighth Edition,* (Orlando: Harcourt College Publishers, 2002).

2. Immanuel Wallerstein, *World Systems Analysis: An Introduction,* (Durham and London: Duke University Press, 2004).

3. Theodore Couloumbis, James Wolfe, *Introduction to International Relations: Power and Justice, Third Edition,* (NJ: Prentice Hall, Inc., 1986), 64-84, also 42-64.

4. Jennifer Zerk, *Multinationals and Corporate Social Responsibility: Limitations and Opportunities in International Law,* (New York: Cambridge University Press, 2006).

5. Fritz Machlup, *A History of Thought On Economic Integration,* (New York: Columbia University Press, 1977), 219.

Complex Adaptive Systems

1. Wikipedia,"Complex System," enwikipedia.org/wiki/Complex System, accessed 2012.

2. Wikipedia,"Complex Adaptive System," enwikipedia.org/wiki/ Complex Adaptive System, accessed 2012.

3 William Frej and Ben Ramalingam, 2012, "Foreign Policy and Complex Adaptive Systems: Exploring New Paradigms for Analysis and Action", www.santafe.edu/media/working papers//11-10-022.pdf, accessed Feb 2013.

4 Peter Fryer, "What Are Complex Adaptive Systems? A Brief Description of Complex Adaptive Systems? A Brief Description of Complex Adaptive Systems and Complexity Theory", www.trojanmice.com/articles/complexadaptivesystems.htm, accessed Feb 2013.

5. Nonlinear Systems, http:www.globalcomplexity.org/ NonlinearSystems.htm, accessed Dec 2012.

6. Ricard Sole, *Phase Transitions;* (New Jersey: Princeton University Press, 2011).

7. Scott Page, *Diversity and Complexity,* (New Jersey: Princeton University Press, 2011).

Historical timeline sources:

1. Thomas Greer and Gavin Lewis, *A Brief History of the Western World, Eighth Edition,* (Orlando: Harcourt College Publishers, 2002).

Prelude

2.   Niccolo Machiavelli, *The Prince And the Discourses*, with Max Lerner, (New York: The Modern Library, Random House, 1950).

3.   Wikipedia, "Constantinople," enwikipedia/wiki/Constantinople, accessed 2014.

4.   Akhil Reed Amar and Les Adams, *The Bill of Rights Primer*, (Birmingham: Palladium Press, 2002.

5.   Frances Pohl, *Framing Art: A Social History of American Art*, (New York: Thames and Hudson, 2002), 57.

6.   Wikipedia, "Werner Sombart," enwikipedia.org/wiki/Werner_Sombart, accessed 2013.

Time cuts down all,
Both great and small.

Classical Liberalism
American Revolution (1776), until the Civil War 1861.

Origins of classical liberal ways of political thinking.

Classical liberalism developed from several powerful origins. The first was the energy of the cultural movement called the Enlightenment. The second was accord brought about by the European exploration of rationalism and humanism. Both showed the influence of long-gone early civilizations in Greece and Rome. A third influence was a willingness to experiment beginning with a rational model. A fourth was tolerance, from the Protestant Reformation. This tolerance was respect for people's interior beliefs and conscience. Humanism and rationalism convinced people that humans could choose a better life for themselves and their children. Also that mankind's well-being is a good ruler for measuring the good that society can embody. This approach was an alternative to church faith in Providence and leaving everything to God. A respect for people's religious choices led to respect for individuals. Liberalism partnered up with capitalism and they gradually unleashed forces that began to change Europe.

The economic conversion from feudalism to capitalism shaped many of the choices that happened during classical liberalism. Capitalism was a new way of doing business that maneuvered around feudalism and led to social changes. These social changes caused by capitalism created new political tensions that erupted into revolutions. Certain hoped for Enlightenment expectations regarding politics differed from prior political experiences under earlier political systems in Europe. This difference led to political experimentation at the same time that scientists were progressively modeling the natural world differently than church clerics had during the feudal past. The American Revolution was radical in its approach to building the government of the new Republic.

The American Revolution initiated into play a new political experiment in the way the U.S. Constitution organized government and limited governmental power. Many classical liberal voices expressed unique ideas that influenced the politics of classical liberalism. Conceptual placement of human liberty at the top of a hierarchy of political values changed both the politic and the economy.

Classical liberalism's liberty concept respected people's need to shape their own life free from governmental oppression but with restraint in order to avoid causing harm to other people. This promoted social peace and justice within society's embrace except for excluded classes like indentured servants, Native Americans and slaves. Classical liberals didn't agree with each other about every idea that each of them wrote, but they were interested in considering many points of view as potential selections inside a rich intellectual diet. Learning contributed to experimentation with rational approaches. American society adopted political philosophies of classical liberalism until the politics of nation state competition encouraged a political move back towards big government.

Nation state competition eventually convinced people that power in government was needed more than liberty was needed. War decided the political contest between individual power and government power in favor of governmental power. Nevertheless, classical liberalism advanced social respect for individualism and for innovation. Despite the social failings of political policies regarding Native Americans, women and slaves, classical liberalism's experimentation with a new government format bore fruit that was good for those in a position to enjoy it. New technologies like the cotton gin and rail, farm and industrial machinery, petroleum for energy, initiated a change regime that advanced the economy of classical liberalism but helped destabilize the classical liberal politic. The historical exhaustion of Westward land expansion also meant that a new kind of economy would be needed that would no longer depend on opening new lands to European immigrants. Political policy and economic policy had to adapt to a changing world. Fast population growth also helped to undo the political arrangements of classical liberalism which had been part of an agricultural world that contained fewer people who were more spread out.

Quotes from classical liberal political thinkers can bring the past alive with the hopes that people had for a better political future.

Historical quotes, recognized contributors, and political works in the context of their own time is where we can discover the ideas of classical liberalism. Classical liberal ideas germinated into an appreciation for liberty and limited government in the United States. Classical liberalism in Europe didn't function or develop in the same way because aristocracy and later, bureaucracy was so much a part of the European experience. In Europe it wasn't possible to seriously imagine a separation between the politic and economy. Europe had an extensive feudal, manorial, scholastic, monarchic and aristocratic set of traditions where class inequality was endemic and class distinctions mattered more. The American experience was more egalitarian, risky, innovative and radical. But classical liberalism in American political practice only lasted until the Civil War. The quotes listed here besides contributing to the formal structure of classical liberalism and economic liberalism also influenced subsequent political ideologies even into the present. These visionary ideas remain worthy of attention. If you are an American, their rhetoric can bring classical liberal visions for a better tomorrow to you as part of your American heritage.

Thomas Hobbes's (1588-1679), *Leviathan, or the Matter, Forme and Power of a Commonwealth Ecclesiasticall and Civil,* was published in 1651, or about two years after the end of the Thirty Years' War. This was just after the English Civil War and also at the genesis of the European nation state system, near the end of the Protestant Reformation. The energy of all that conflict was enormous. People in disagreement over religious matters fought until violence made religious tolerance the only option. People's heartfelt longing to end violence through a new political system caused them to invent formal diplomacy as an alternative to warfare. Differences between nation states were revealed as diplomacy brought about the dramatic individuation of nations. New technologies brought an urgent need to modify political arrangements between nations. Thomas Hobbes has been compared to Bernard Shaw as a beloved witty Englishman and people of his time enjoyed his writings and commentary.[1] But some say that his defense of absolute sovereignty initiated a subsequent political cascade towards totalitarianism in the twentieth century.[2] His writings both defend the sovereign and undermine the idea of infinite or infallible kingly power. Quotes below are from *Leviathan*.[3] Considering that Hobbes lived long before the twentieth century, he probably never deserved to be blamed for the bloody twentieth century's experiments with totalitarian government.

> *"I authorize and give up my right of governing myself, to this man, or to this assembly of men, on this condition, that thou give up thy right to him, and authorize all his actions in like manner.* This done, the multitude so united in one person, is called a COMMONWEALTH, in Latin, CIVITAS. This is the generation of that great LEVIATHAN, or rather to speak more reverently, of that *mortal god*, to which we owe under the *immortal God*, our peace and defense."[4]

> "the felicity of this life, consisteth not in the repose of a mind satisfied. For there is no *finis ultimus*, utmost aim, nor *summum bonum*, greatest good... which ariseth partly from the diversity of passions, in divers men; and partly from the difference of knowledge, or opinion each one has of the causes, which produce the effect desired."[5]

> "LIBERTY, or FREEDOM, signifieth, properly, the absence of opposition.... a FREEMAN, is he, that in those things, which by his strength and wit he is able to do, is not hindered to do what he has a will to."[6]

"The obligation of subjects to the sovereign, is understood to last as long, and no longer, than the power lasteth, by which he is able to protect them."[7]

"No man therefore can conceive any thing, but he must conceive it in some place; and endued with some determinate magnitude;"[8]

"The use and end of reason, is not the finding of the sum and truth of one, or a few consequences, remote from the first definitions, and settled significations of names, but to begin at these, and proceed from one consequence to another. For there can be no certainty of the last conclusion, without a certainty of all those affirmations and negations, on which it was grounded and inferred."[9]

"Competition of riches, honour, command, or other power, inclineth to contention, enmity, and war: because the way of one competitor, to the attaining of his desire, is to kill, subdue, supplant, or repel the other."[10]

In writing *Leviathan*, Thomas Hobbes wrote the first authentically liberal political book in post Reformation Europe under the influence of his own positive regard for Euclid's geometrical proofs.[11] That Hobbes was inspired by Euclid underscores the influence of classical studies in his analysis. In *Leviathan*, he systematically wrote verbal formulas not unlike Euclid's geometric proofs. These described political concepts like freedom, sovereignty, happiness, commonwealth, honor, and competition. He wrote about the power of rhetoric and the use of reason. Writing just at the close the Protestant Reformation and at the end of the English Civil War, he supported absolute sovereign rule and worried that a person's loyalty to their own conscience or to their religion could disrupt peace in a sovereign realm as he had experienced in his own England.

More than his specific opinions about absolute sovereignty, what was valuable about *Leviathan* for classical liberalism, was Hobbes recognition of the power of political organization to accomplish greater tasks than individuals are capable of accomplishing alone. Organizations have been even more important in the U.S. since the twentieth century. Hobbes's willingness to analyze politics as affairs of finite identifiable character and finite identifiable kinds of power also helped people to better cope with political power. Hobbes saw importantly that different people want different things and argued against a political objective to attain a single greatest good. That encouraged people to think beyond what a king could do in terms of a single set of good political acts. He also recognized natural limits in the power of sovereigns. His ability to parse out basic political concepts allowed others who came later to advance more rational ideas about politics. Rational politics recognized the power both of individuals and of groups in a finite way that could be characterized. Hobbes helped people to stop feeling overpowered by the concept of an infinitely empowered state as they recognized the sovereign's natural limits.

John Locke, (1632-1704) contributed in two important ways to political arguments that eventually formed classical liberalism. The first was by articulating the idea of modern empiricism and the second was by describing and declaring in favor of popular sovereignty. His idea that ordinary reason and the natural senses could reveal natural truths was important to people who had sometimes rudimentary educational backgrounds because he described the world as a place that ordinary people could understand. Locke's empirical reasoning contrasted with Plato's idea of inborn knowing and with the Catholic idea of divine inspiration. Empiricism placed politics into the mental grasp of those who were able to read and to reason for themselves and with friends. Locke persuaded people with ordinary common sense kinds of argument.[12] His *"Essay Concerning Human Understanding"* from 1690, contributed the idea of philosophical empiricism. Another Lockean work, *Two Treatises of Government* also from 1690, articulated the idea of "popular sovereignty", or the idea that people have a right to change a government that doesn't meet its moral obligations. He wrote about natural rights and natural law, expanding Roman ideas about sovereignty into the right to rebel against an improper government should it trespass against those rights.[13, 14]

The following quotes are from *Two Treatises of Government* (1690).[15] The timing of this work was after the English Interregnum (Cromwell's rule as Protector), right after the English Glorious Revolution, when Parliament asserted its power against the English King James. It did this by bringing forward the monarchic reign of William and Mary in his place. King James' politics had been unpopular and he left England. Parliament also passed the English Bill of Rights in 1689. This document encouraged the English toward representational government by recognizing the right of Englishmen to possess arms, to petition the King and to enjoy legal due process while it proscribed the King's powers to suspend laws, lay taxes or raise an army to only when Parliament approved of it.

Along with the Magna Carta, the English Bill of Rights inspired political convictions found in the American Constitution. The Glorious Revolution also maintained the religious primacy of the English Anglican Church in opposition to a return to Catholicism.[16] American government differed from English government in that Americans separated church and state. Locke's writings were clearly influential in the language of the Declaration of Independence. That is a testament to Locke's importance to Thomas Jefferson, the main author of the Declaration of Independence. Locke may have been the most influential classical liberal thinker to affect early American politics.

"The great and chief end, therefore, of men's uniting into commonwealths, and putting themselves under government, is the preservation of their property."[17]

"The end of government is the good of mankind; and which is best for mankind, that the people should be always exposed to the boundless will of tyranny, or that the rulers should be sometimes liable to be opposed, when they grow exorbitant in the use of their power, and employ it for the destruction, and not the preservation of the properties of their people?"[18]

"When any one, or more, shall take upon them to make laws, whom the people have not appointed so to do, they make laws without authority, which the people are not therefore bound to obey;"[19]

"Where-ever law ends, tyranny begins, if the law be transgressed to another's harm; and whosoever in authority exceeds the power given him by the law, and makes use of the force he has under his command, to compass that upon the subject, which the law allows not, ceases in that to be a magistrate; and acting without authority, may be opposed"[20]

"in well ordered commonwealths, where the good of the whole is so considered, as it ought, the legislative power is put into the hands of divers persons, who duly assembled, have by themselves, or jointly with others, a power to make laws, which when they have done, being separated again, they are themselves subject to the laws they have made; which is a new and near tie upon them, to take care, that they make them for the public good."[21]

"The legislative cannot transfer the power of making laws to any other hands; for it being but a delegated power from the people, they who have it cannot pass it over to others."[22]

"But if a long train of abuses, prevarications and artifices, all tending the same way, make the design visible to the people, and they cannot but feel what they lie under, and see wither they are going; it is not to be wondered, that they should then rouze themselves, and endeavour to put the rule into such hands which may secure to them the ends for which government was at first erected;"[23]

Locke was born to Puritan parents. So it seems likely that his life was caught up in the politics of the Protestant Reformation. He kept his writings encoded for privacy and was cautious about timing the publication of his work. He was influential in showing people a simpler way to think by using their own experiences to examine life. His philosophical conjectures influenced other philosophers such as Immanuel Kant (1724-1804), David Hume (1711-1776) and George Berkeley (1685-1753).[24] Locke revolutionized people's thinking both in politics and philosophy. He changed the way that people conducted their analysis of the law and of politics by moving the analysis from language based rhetorical analysis to experience based observation. That shifted the ground significantly for how arguments have been made in the twenty-first century as compared with the period before Locke (see the appendix).

The next classical liberal contributor was Charles de Secondant Baron de Montesquieu (1689-1755). It seems amazing that Charles de Secondant Baron de Montesquieu would be an aristocrat in the middle of classical liberal rebellion against aristocracy and that he was innovating toward its destruction. But he inherited the title of Baron from his uncle late in life after growing up outside of wealthy circumstances.[25] He lived in France as a lawyer for his local community. He was important to the U.S. because he articulated ideas about the separation of powers in liberal governments that influenced the governmental design outlined by the U.S. Constitution in 1789. His *Spirit of the Laws* (1748)[26] was his effort to design a government's structure that would serve freedom without an overgrowth of power that would destroy freedom. He was seeking the correct balance of power in politics, imagining that a perfect form for freedom could exist if only it could be described.

"Before laws were made, there were relations of possible justice."[27]

"The united strength of individuals…constitutes what we call the body politic."[28]

"In republican governments, men are all equal; equal they are also in despotic governments; in the former, because they are everything; in the latter, because they are nothing."[29]

"If a republic be small, it is destroyed by a foreign force; if it be large, it is ruined by an internal imperfection…It is therefore, very probable that mankind would have been, at length, obliged to live constantly under the government of a single person, had they not contrived a kind of constitution that has all the internal advantages of a republican, together with the external force of a monarchical, government. I mean a confederate republic."[30]

"Political liberty is to be found only in moderate governments; and even in these it is not always found. It is there only when there is no abuse of power. But constant experience shows us that every man invested with power is apt to abuse it, and to carry his authority as far as it will go. Is it not strange, though true, to say that virtue itself has need of limits? ... To prevent this abuse, it is necessary from the very nature of things that power should be a check to power. A government may be so constituted, as no man shall be compelled to do things to which the law does not oblige him, nor forced to abstain from things which the law permits."[31]

"There would be an end of everything, were the same man or the same body, whether of the nobles or of the people, to exercise those three powers, that of enacting laws, that of executing the public resolutions, and of trying the causes of individuals."[32]

"As all human things have an end, the state we are speaking of will lose its liberty, will perish. Have not Rome, Sparta, and Carthage perished? It will perish when the legislative power shall be more corrupt than the executive."[33]

Mercantilism was the economic formula being pursued by nation states as they became more nationalized after the Peace of Westphalia 1648, which initiated the nation state system after the Thirty Years' War, beginning a process of gradual nation building and statist competition. Under mercantilist policy, nations tried to keep a positive balance of trade with other nations by exporting more than they imported so that their own national treasury had more gold. Gold represented wealth that could be used to buy commodities or to pay for war or colonial expansion. Colonialism, imperialism and global trade by sea were all part of the classical liberal period. Economic protectionism was under frequent debate during mercantilism. Several people spoke in favor of open trade during the classical liberal period and afterward. Adam Smith (1723-1790), David Ricardo (1772-1823) and Richard Cobden (1804-1865) were all influential speakers advocating for opening trade relations with other nations. In advocating for open trade they were opposing mercantilism.

There have been several important differences between global trade in classical liberal times and global trade now. Classical liberal global trade was between agriculturalists, textile manufacturers and fishermen, for example, which were groups that occupied a nation's territory. Finished products were exchanged in merchant trading between nations. Piecemeal production lines in numerous locations across nations, such as that practiced in modern global value-added factories, wasn't invented then because it took too long to move money from place to place and it was so much more difficult for distant locations to communicate. Merchants made money buying in one market and selling in another where they could make more money through arbitrage (taking advantage of price differences). Profits stayed mostly inside nations as long as their balance of trade was positive—more money received from products they exported than was spent on imports.

Trade balance was only one aspect of trade between nations. There was also trade volume and prices. J.S. Mill wrote in 1830 that a trade advantage differential between partners in trade would be determined by the **principle of reciprocal demand**. This idea wasn't published until 1844.[34] Mill was thinking about prices and how they are determined in trade. The nation with higher demand would influence prices more than a nation that possessed lesser demand. Therefore, trading advantages would not be equal.

Banks were located within home nations though some had branches in other nations. How profits circulated or became invested was different then compared to now. Regional economies mattered more then. And both then and now, nations were competing against each other and also making alliances of advantage in order to get more political and economic power. Looking further back in history, a nation's border and its territory mattered differently under the nation state system, than it had before 1648, because of the nation state system of formal diplomacy. Looking forward from classical liberalism to neoliberalism, the trading boundary that a border represents still matters. It matters today under neoliberalsm's bilateral treaties and other trade arrangements, but people's travel is more regulated, now. Today's mobile capital is different from the past as well.

Today's advanced communication technologies have supplied tools to make the most of more open trading borders. Transportation and communication improvements have made piecemeal assembly of products possible, where parts are produced and put together in many nations. Also, corporate legal protections were different during classical liberalism. Mercantilist corporations were sometimes granted exclusive trading rights to certain regions which they opened for a sovereign nation. These were regional trade monopolies. Limited liability has existed since classical liberal times, but today, corporations have modern legal advantages that define their rights differently than under classical liberalism. Fourteenth Amendment protections in the U.S., have expanded legal and political protections for American corporations. Holding companies where assets and liabilities can be hidden, provide corporations with investment camouflage and there are more investment opportunities in financial markets under international banking.

Adam Smith, a Scotsman, wrote *The Wealth of Nations*,[35] in 1776, the same year as the American Declaration of Independence was issued. Perhaps his great contribution besides writing about the economy of a commonwealth in the first place, is to have advocated for specialization of labor in industrial manufacturing processes. But even though he supported specialization, Smith worried that it would harm people by making their life too routinized. He also wanted more open trading arrangements with other nations. According to Andrew Skinner, Smith's education gave him a wide view of society because as well as economics, he studied history, philosophy and politics. His cultural wide-view apparently led him to advocate for government sponsorship of education despite its cost.[36]

"The greatest improvement in the productive powers of labour, and the greater part of the skill, dexterity, and judgement with which it is anywhere directed, or applied, seem to have been the effects of the division of labour."[37]

"The word VALUE, it is to be observed, has two different meanings, and sometimes expresses the utility of some particular object, and sometimes, the power of purchasing other goods which the possession of that object conveys. The one may be called 'value in use'; the other, 'value in exchange'."[38]

"The subsistence of the labourer, or the real price of labour, as I shall endeavour to show hereafter, is very different upon different occasions; more liberal in a society advancing to opulence than in one that is standing still; and in one that is standing still than in one that is going backwards."[39]

"The interest of the dealers, however, in any particular branch of trade or manufactures, is always in some respects different from, and even opposite to, that of the public. To widen the market and to narrow the competition, is always the interest of the dealers...The proposal of any new law or regulation of commerce which comes from this order ought always to be listened to with great precaution, and ought never to be adopted till after having been long and carefully examined, not only with the most scrupulous, but with the most suspicious attention. It comes from an order of men whose interest is never exactly the same with that of the public, who have generally an interest to deceive and even to oppress the public, and who accordingly have upon many occasions, both deceived and oppressed it."[40]

"In order to put industry into motion, three things are requisite; materials to work upon, tools to work with, and the wages or recompence for the sake of which the work is done."[41]

"Both productive and unproductive laborers, and those who do not labour at all, are all equally maintained by the annual produce of the land and labour of the country. This produce, how great soever, can never be infinite, but must have certain limits."[42]

"It is not by augmenting the capital of the country, but by rendering a greater part of that capital active and productive than would otherwise be so, that the most judicious operations of banking can increase the industry of the country."[43]

"Great nations are never impoverished by private, though they sometimes are by public prodigality and misconduct. The whole or almost the whole public revenue, is in most countries employed in maintaining unproductive hands."[44]

"In general, if any branch of trade, or any division of labour, be advantageous to the public, the freer and more general the competition, it will always be the more so."[45]

Adam Smith was the Professor of Logic at Glasgow in 1751, and wrote *The Theory of Moral Sentiments* in 1759, long before he addressed topics in economics. He argued in favor of economic efficiency in *Wealth of Nations*, partly in order to encourage greater levels of employment and less poverty. David Ricardo's (1772-1823) background and training were completely different from Adam Smith's. He was trained to trade in the English stock market by his father, at the early age of fourteen. So his insights into economics grew out of practical experiences in business speculation from which he became wealthy. He also became a member of the English Parliament.[46]

Ricardo published *Principles of Political Economy and Taxation* in 1817. His most famous contribution to economics from this text was his use of the **law of comparative advantage**. Although Robert Torrens (1780-1864), has been recognized as the first person to formulate the law of comparative advantage, he was not a proponent of open trade, while David Ricardo advocated for open trade.[47] Under Ricardo's interpretation, this law says that absolute advantage has less bearing on profitable production than comparative advantage. According to Ricardo, whichever nation can produce a product most cheaply should produce exclusively this product in order to trade it for everything else it needs so as to create greater prosperity. Like Adam Smith, Ricardo advocated for the specialization of labor in industry and for freer trade.

In the twenty first century, Ricardo's law of comparative advantage doesn't produce the same local outcomes of advantage when profits go outside national borders as in the past when they stayed within a producing nation's borders. Jobs have moved from developed nations to developing nations where production factors, labor as one example, are cheaper. Mobile capital in the twenty first century can dominate capital negotiations by bringing in foreign money that rewards foreign banks. By setting low wages and minimizing capital rewards to producers, mobile capital can reduce capital rewards for production. The manufacturing labor community gains less under this arrangement because capital doesn't circulate virtuously in the production community. The mobile capital of today doesn't work to the community's advantage the way that it did in Ricardo's time. In Ricardo's time, the law of comparative advantage provided the greatest advantages when certain conditions were met.

They were: cheap transportation, widespread accurate product information, competitive markets without oligarchy, markets without monopoly domination and open trade.[48] Some of the conditions for best comparative advantage aren't met under neoliberal development strategies. For example, transportation costs may increase under conditions of higher demand for petroleum products in developing nations, although containerization and large powered shipping vessels instead of sailing vessels save shipping costs as compared with shipping in Ricardo's time. Modern advertising and marketing distorts product information in favor of selling, increasing costs. China has a communist oligarchy that favors some industries over others with easier financing and the U.S. has greater multinational corporate tax advantages for global companies as compared to domestic companies.

American policy favors big international corporations. But government subsidy provides an exception to market influence. Very large firm size distorts the market and reduces competition. And modern advertising distorts product information. All of these influences create market inefficiency that can shrink the size of the overall economy. For all these reasons, trading under the law of comparative advantage works out differently now than in Ricardo's day. The quantity of local economic power represented by profit also has changed because manufacturing profit often leaves a region of production after large multinationals have used their access to capital advantages to out compete local businesses.[49] This pulls production incentives away from laborers. Here are some quotes from David Ricardo.

"The produce of the earth—all that is derived from its surface by the united application of labour, machinery, and capital, is divided among three classes of the community, namely, the proprietor of the land, the owner of the stock or capital necessary for its cultivation, and the labourers by whose industry it is cultivated…But in different stages of society, the proportions of the whole produce of the earth which will be allotted to each of these classes, under the names of rent, profit, and wages, will be essentially different; depending mainly on the actual fertility of the soil, on the accumulation of capital and population, and on the skill, ingenuity, and instruments employed in agriculture."[50]

"No extension of foreign trade will immediately increase the amount of value in a country, although it will very powerfully contribute to increase the mass of commodities, and therefore the sum of enjoyments."[51]

"Under a system of perfectly free commerce, each country naturally devotes its capital and labour to such employments as are most beneficial to each. This pursuit of individual advantage is admirably connected with the universal good of the whole. By stimulating industry, by rewarding ingenuity, and by using most efficaciously the peculiar powers bestowed by nature, it distributes labour most effectively and most economically; while, by increasing the general mass of productions, it diffuses general benefit, and binds together, by one common tie of interest and intercourse, the universal society of nations throughout the civilized world."[52]

"every dimunition in the wages of labour raises profits, but produces no effect on the price of commodities. One is advantageous to all classes, for all classes are consumers; the other is beneficial only to producers; they gain more, but every thing remains at its former price."[53]

"The same rule which regulates the relative value of commodities in one country, does not regulate the relative value of the commodities exchanged between two or more countries."[54]

"The demand for money is regulated entirely by its value, and its value by its quantity."[55]

"The real price of a commodity is here properly stated to depend on the greater or less quantity of labour and capital (that is accumulated labour) which must be employed to produce it."[56]

"it is the natural price of commodities in the exporting country, which ultimately regulates the prices at which they shall be sold, if they are not the objects of monopoly in the importing country."[57]

"To alter the money value of commodities, by altering the value of money, and yet to raise the same money amount by taxes, is then undoubtedly to increase the burthens of society."[58]

Richard Cobden (1804-1865) was neither an intellectual like Smith nor a stock market trader like Ricardo. Instead, he worked as an English diplomat to negotiate freer trade between England and France. He favored more open trade because he believed that it could transform enemies into neighbors who favored their trading partnership over war. He thought trade could moderate the jealousy of neighbor states. This idea has been influential ever since. After WWII, 44 Allied nations met to discuss the project of repairing the world as soon as fighting ended. Diplomats at Bretton

Woods, in 1944, at one of the first meetings of the United Nations, met and advocated an elimination of economic nationalism in favor of opening global trade. For diplomats, greater peace between nations and greater prosperity were some of the rhetorical incentives to open trade.[59] Here are some Cobden quotes.[60]

"Free Trade! What is it? Why, breaking down the barriers that separate nations; those barriers, behind which nestle the feelings of pride, revenge, hatred, and jealousy, which every now and then burst their bounds, and deluge whole countries with blood; those feelings which nourish the poison of war and conquest, which assert that without conquest we can have no trade, which foster that lust for conquest and dominion which sends forth your warrior chiefs to scatter devastation through other lands, and then calls them back that they may be enthroned securely in your passions, but only to harass and oppress you at home."[61]

"We advocate the abolition of the Corn Law because we believe that to be the foster-parent of all other monopolies; and if we destroy that—the parent, the monster monopoly—it will save us the trouble of devouring the rest."[62]

"How can protection, think you, add to the wealth of a country? Can you by legislations add one farthing to the wealth of the country? You may, by legislation, in one evening, destroy the fruits and accumulation of a century of labour; but I defy you to show me how, by the legislation of this House, you can add one farthing to the wealth of the country. That springs from the industry and intelligence; you cannot do better than leave it to its own instincts."[63]

Smith, Ricardo and Cobden hoped that opening global trade would reduce the likelihood of nations going to war to obtain resources possessed by rival nations. They recognized the jealousy of nations within the nation state system. Nevertheless, it is doubtful that Smith would have endorsed the deregulation of corporations and finance that has occurred over the last thirty years, since he gave a specific warning that recognized the opposing interests of businessmen and society. And Ricardo recognized that the combination of inflation in a climate of increasing taxes can burden society, and since 2008 both are in evidence. Cobden, believed that opening global trade would encourage a peaceful exchange of goods. But twentieth and twenty-first century wars have been ongoing under a variety of excuses since the end of WWII. After WWII, the CIA was created to act covertly within the global political and economic arena during the expansion of global trade. Whether a more uniform global economy would be possible or would eventually encourage peace under increasing disparities of income in every nation practicing neoliberalism has become doubtful. And whether a more homogenized world economy would become a lasting circumstance also has remained in question since the politic and economy have always existed under a regime of change.

The American Revolution's loudest promoter may have been Thomas Paine (1737-1809), an Englishman. He stayed the course of the American Revolution for seven years, publishing a variety of encouragements in the form of books and pamphlets until the end of the war. After the war, he went to France and wrote about the French Revolution, spending some of his time in jail. He also wrote about the plight of the English working class commoners and considered what their rights might be. His most famous publications were: "Common Sense" (1776), *The Rights of Man* (1792), and *The Age of Reason* (1794).[64] As a skilled propagandist, he encouraged hope in liberty but justified by practical considerations. He sacrificed whatever popularity he had achieved during the American Revolution when he continued to make arguments advocating legal and political change in the interest of every common person's greater prosperity. He became an author devoted to the rational cause of liberty from the time he read the American Declaration of Independence, until the end of his life.[65]

"Society in every state is a blessing, but Government, even in its best state, is but a necessary evil; in its worst state an intolerable one: for when we suffer, or are exposed to the same miseries *by a Government,* which we might expect in a country *without Government,* our calamity is heightened by reflecting that we furnish the means by which we suffer."[66]

"A government of our own is our natural right: and when a man seriously reflects on the precariousness of human affairs, he will become convinced, that it is infinitely wiser and safer, to form a constitution of our own in a cool deliberate manner, while we have it in our power, than to trust such an interesting event to time and chance."[67]

"We ought to reflect, that there are three different ways by which an independency may hereafter be effected, and that one of those three, will, one day or other, be the fate of America, viz. By the legal voice of the people in Congress; by a military power, or by a mob: It may not always happen that our soldiers are citizens, and the multitude a body of reasonable men; virtue, as I have already remarked, is not hereditary, neither is it perpetual. Should an independency be brought about by the first of those means, we have every opportunity and every encouragement before us, to form the noblest, purest constitution on the face of the earth. We have it in our power to begin the world over again."[68]

"O! ye that love mankind! Ye that dare oppose not only the tyranny but the tyrant, stand forth! Every spot of the old world is overrun with oppression. Freedom hath been hunted round the Globe. Asia and Africa have long expelled her. Europe regards her like a stranger, and England hath given her warning to depart. O! receive the fugitive, and prepare in time an asylum for mankind."[69]

"There never did, there never will, and there never can, exist a Parliament, or any description of men, or any generation of men, in any country, possessed of the right or the power of binding and controlling posterity to the *"end of time,"* or of commanding for ever how the world shall be governed, or who shall govern it; and therefore all such clauses, acts or declarations by which the makers of them attempt to do what they have neither the right nor the power to do, nor the power to execute, are in themselves null and void. Every age and generation must be as free to act for itself *in all cases* as the ages and generations which preceded it."[70]

"I believe in one God, and no more; and I hope for happiness beyond this life…I believe the equality of man; and I believe that religious duties consist in doing justice, loving mercy, and endeavoring to make our fellow creatures happy…My own mind is my own church…All national institutions of churches, whether Jewish, Christian, or Turkish, appear to me not other than human inventions, set up to terrify and enslave mankind, and monopolize power and profit."[71]

Two Utilitarians gave arguments in support of classical liberalism and they were Jeremy Bentham (1748-1832) and his younger protégé, John Stuart Mill (1806-1873). Law was a profession practiced by many of Bentham's forebears and also became part of his training. But the law wasn't the only thing Bentham was interested in. He also enjoyed a kind of practical philosophy. Bentham was the inventor of Utilitarianism. Utilitarians take a philosophical position that advocates in favor of social happiness. The Utilitarian Principle is also called the 'greatest happiness principle'. Their position was that laws should be written or people should choose to do whatever creates the greatest happiness for the greatest number of people. Bentham believed that happiness was even quantifiable and that people could make life choices by weighing the potential happiness outcome of each possible avenue of choice for everyone who could be affected. His quantification-of-happiness idea is mostly forgotten now. But in Bentham's day, it led him to argue beneficially for the replacement of old English laws that caused people unnecessary suffering and unhappiness. The Reform Bill of 1832 contained revisions of laws, many of which were suggested by Bentham and his followers. He was also an inventor and acknowledged eccentric.[72]

J.S. Mill, began as Bentham's acolyte as a young person but rebelled as an adult into becoming someone who forged his own philosophical opinions. J.S. Mill's father, James Mill, was a journalist and one of Bentham's assistants. The son, J.S. Mill, wrote on a variety of topics in the following works: *A System of Logic* (1843), *Principles of Political Economy* (1848), *On Liberty* (1859), *Utilitarianism* (1861), *Considerations on Representative Government* (1861), and *The Subjection of Women* (1869). He was following in his father's footsteps when he worked for the East India Company a few years before it was abolished. He was also a member of the English Parliament. Mill's facts and quotes were taken from *On Liberty* and *The Subjection of Women*.[73] Bentham quotes were obtained from wikiquote.[74]

"The principle of utility judges any action to be right by the tendency it appears to have to augment or diminish the happiness of the party whose interests are in question…if that party be the community the happiness of the community, if a particular individual, the happiness of that individual." Jeremy Bentham[75]

"Nature has placed mankind under the governance of two sovereign masters, *pain*, and *pleasure*. It is for them alone to point out what we ought to do, as well as to determine what we shall do." Jeremy Bentham[76]

"It is with government, as with medicine. They have both but a choice of evils. Every law is an evil, for every law is an infraction of liberty: And I repeat that government has but a choice of evils: In making this choice, what ought to be the object of the legislator? He ought to assure himself of two things; 1st, that in every case, the incidents which he tries to prevent are really evils; and 2ndly, that if evils, they are greater than those which he employs to prevent them….There are then two things to be regarded: the evil of the offence and the evil of the law; the evil of the malady and the evil of the remedy." Jeremy Bentham[77]

"Secresy is an instrument of conspiracy; it ought not, therefore, to be the system of a regular government." Jeremy Bentham[78]

"The great writers to whom the world owes what religious freedom it possesses, have mostly asserted freedom of conscience as an indefeasible right, and denied absolutely that a human being is accountable to others for his religious belief." J.S. Mill[79]

"Over himself, over his own body and mind, the individual is sovereign." J.S. Mill[80] "the peculiar evil of silencing the expression of an opinion is, that it is robbing the human race; posterity as well as the existing generation; those who dissent from the opinion, still more than those who hold it. If the opinion is right, they are deprived of the opportunity of exchanging error for truth: if wrong, they lose, what is almost as great a benefit, the clearer perception and livelier impression of truth, produced by its collision with error." J. S. Mill[81]

"Our merely social intolerance kills no one, roots out no opinions, but induces men to disguise them, or to abstain from any active effort for their diffusion. With us, heretical opinions do not perceptibly gain, or even lose, ground in each decade or generation; they never blaze out far and wide, but continue to smoulder in the narrow circles of thinking and studious persons among whom they originate, without ever lighting up the general affairs of mankind with either a true or a deceptive light." J.S. Mill[82]

"the absorption of all the principal ability of the country into the governing body is fatal, sooner or later, to the mental activity and progressiveness of the body itself." J.S. Mill[83]

"a State which dwarfs its men, in order that they may be more docile instruments in its hands even for beneficial purposes—will find that with small men no great thing can really be accomplished; and that the perfection of machinery to which it has sacrificed everything, will in the end avail it nothing, for want of the vital power which, in order that the machine might work more smoothly, it has preferred to banish." J.S. Mill[84]

"the only unfailing and permanent source of improvement is liberty, since by it there are as many possible independent centres of improvement as there are individuals." J.S. Mill[85]

Frederic Bastiat (1801-1850), also contributed to the set of writings and commentary about classical liberalism. A French lawyer who lived somewhat after the Baron de Montesquieu (b.1689), he made valuable contributions to classical liberal thoughts regarding the proper social purpose of law and against socialism. His famous and brief work, *The Law* (1850),[86] lucidly explained the proper use and application of the law from the classical liberal perspective. Bastiat contrasted classical liberal uses of law and socialism's use of law.

His declarations about the proper applications of law also provided a contrast between what he thought in 1850 and the ideas of modern legal justices such as Justice William Rehnquist and Justice Antonin Scalia who have complained about too-activist interpretations of law according to politics instead of according to legal language.[87] Whereas Hobbes' *Leviathan* was published right after the beginning of the nation state system, Bastiat's life ended just a decade and a half before the end of the American Civil War. It was after the Civil War that Americans started to pay income tax and increased the size of the federal government. Modern liberalism arrived then to regulate the market economy. Modern liberalism was a version of socialism that was more about regulating productive businesses than nationalizing them, although government owned utilities became common. They were called natural monopolies because of their high start-up costs. If he'd lived to see the changeover from classical liberalism to modern liberalism, Bastiat probably would have warned Americans about socialist pitfalls that could eventually cause harm to private ownership and economic prosperity.

"As long as it is admitted that the law may be diverted from its true purpose—that it may violate property instead of protecting it—then everyone will want to participate in making the law, either to protect himself against plunder or to use it for plunder....It is indeed impossible to imagine, at the very heart of society, a more astounding fact than this: *The law has come to be an instrument of injustice.* And if this fact brings terrible consequences to the United States—where the proper purpose of the law has been perverted only in the instances of slavery and tariffs—what must be the consequences in Europe, where the perversion of the law is a principle; a system?"[88]

"Socialists desire to practice *legal* plunder. Socialists, like all other monopolists, desire to make the law their own weapon. And when once the law is on the side of socialism, how can it be used against socialism?"[89]

"it is impossible for me to separate the word *fraternity* from the word *voluntary*. I cannot possibly understand how fraternity can be *legally* enforced without liberty being *legally* destroyed, and thus justice being *legally* trampled underfoot."[90]

"Socialism, like the ancient ideas from which it springs, confuses the distinction between government and society."[91]

"How did politicians ever come to believe this weird idea that the law could be made to produce what it does not contain—the wealth, science, and religion that, in a positive sense, constitute prosperity?"[92]

"is not liberty the freedom of every person to make full use of his faculties, so long as he does not harm other persons while doing so? Is not liberty the destruction of all despotism—including, of course, legal despotism?

Finally is not liberty the restricting of the law only to its rational sphere of organizing the right of the individual to lawful self-defense; of punishing injustice?"[93]

"As long as these ideas prevail, it is clear that the responsibility of government is enormous. Good fortune and bad fortune, wealth and destitution, equality and inequality, virtue and vice—all then depend upon political administration. It is burdened with everything, it undertakes everything, it does everything"[94]

Bastiat disliked the growth of government that he had come to recognize at the time he lived and published *The Law*. And the U.S. Constitution was designed in 1789, under classical liberalism, to operate a limited rather than an expansive government. The contrast between limited law under classical liberalism and the later expansion of the modern liberal regulatory state has accounted for Congress's modern-day inefficiency. Congressional representatives were organized by the U.S. Constitution to create legislation that would benefit the general public under a limited government. Governmental powers expanded first under modern liberalism and more under neoliberalism.

Nowadays under neoliberalism, Congress legislates for special interests. Congress is influenced by lobby representatives paid for by corporatists. Lobby donations also influence elections. And a regulatory mountain of concerns distracts Congress. For today's Congress, every regulation can be a political deal in the making. But writing legislation that would take a larger viewpoint into account, that would balance American economic interests better evades Congress altogether. The regulatory job of Congress expanded under modern liberalism and grew even larger during the neoliberal period under regulatory reforms. The role of government under modern liberalism and mixed economy expanded beyond the American Constitution's design. And this expansion of the government's role has worsened under neoliberalism because neoliberals intervene in the economy to help the largest corporations (see accelerationist policy). This leads to monopoly and inefficiency. The Congress of today, how it operates, what occupies its attention, would be unfamiliar to the Founders.

Classical liberals practiced a variety of occupations. The people who were quoted above came from either Britain or France, the preeminent powers of the day.

If you notice the variety of occupations practiced by those whose quotes we have examined, you can see that different kinds of thinkers and thinking helped make up the idea-set that organized classical liberalism. Note the variety of nations and occupations: Hobbes, English witty writer, Locke, English philosopher, Montesquieu, French lawyer, Smith, Scottish academic and writer,

Ricardo, English stock trader and member of Parliament, Cobden, English diplomat, Paine, English propagandist, Bentham, English lawyer and inventor, Mill, English writer and businessman, and Bastiat, French lawyer. None of them were from Germany.

That's because Germany was a nation late to flower in the nation state system. And Germany's delay to develop was partly due to its location at the center of the fighting during the bloody Thirty Years' War roughly at the end of the Reformation. The Peace of Westphalia ended that conflict and erected the nation state system. But it took Germany a longer time to recover from the mostly mercenary fighting that happened in what would later become the German nation state. Germany later generated the philosophical ideas that spawned the collectivist wave of socialism and communism. And France contributed other collectivist thinkers, such as Rousseau, of whom Bastiat complained. Perhaps of greater importance, statist competition between nations in the nation state system stimulated the economic switchover to income taxation to pay for wars. War-ready footing combined with modern transportation to birth the mixed economy under modern liberalism in the United States. When combined with industrial age productivity, war led to unparalleled growth in the size of government bureaucracy.

A few more quotes from the underclasses.
A few additional quotes from notable underclass persons of classical liberalism are offered below. The experience of Native Americans, African Americans, indentured servants and women show classical liberalism's brutality and cold-heartedness toward less powerful people. Instead of political favoritism or class advantages, these people relied on their clever resourcefulness.

Mary Wollstonecraft (1759-1797), was unconventional, a writer, a rationalist arguing for female educational opportunities and greater independence. Her most famous feminist book was *A Vindication of the Rights of Women* (1792). Women had already entered the political arena in Europe even before the nation state system was established in 1648. And of course some entered politics under the nation state system. England's Elizabeth I, began her reign as Queen in 1558. Christina of Sweden, reigned from 1633-1654, Russia's Elizabeth I, from 1741 until 1762, and Russia's Catherine II, from 1762-1796.[95]

Women political activists were guillotined in France during the French Revolution, for speaking against aristocracy and in favor of women's equality.[96] The transformation of ordinary women's roles began partly due to economic and political changes that happened when capitalism undermined feudalism, establishing a changed economy. Wollstonecraft pointed out that the arguments that had kept society stratified, and that had kept women under the dominion of men had stopped making sense. Absolute sovereignty and patriarchy shared "similar arguments" and "similar rebuttals". More importantly, old hierarchies held back economic opportunity and intellectual development that could benefit larger society. Society increasingly needed educated people to cope with new developments that increased cultural complexity. The education of both sexes eventually became indispensable. Here are some quotes from Wollstonecraft.[97]

> "How many women thus waste life away the prey of discontent, who might have practiced as physicians, regulated a farm, managed a shop, and stood erect, supported by their own industry, instead of hanging their heads surcharged with the dew of sensibility that consumes the beauty to which it first gave lustre."[98]

> "Till women are more rationally educated, the progress in human virtue and improvement in knowledge must receive continual checks."[99]

> "The endeavor to keep alive any hoary establishment beyond its natural date is often pernicious and always useless."[100]

> "Should it be proved that women is naturally weaker than man, from whence does it follow that it is natural for her to labor to become still weaker than nature intended her to be? Arguments of this cast are an insult to common sense, and savour of passion. The *divine right* of husbands, like the divine right of kings, may, it is hoped, in the enlightened age, be contested without danger, and though conviction may not silence many boisterous disputants, yet, when any prevailing prejudice is attacked, the wise will consider, and leave the narrow-minded to rail with thoughtless vehemence at innovation."[101]

> "Virtue can only flourish amongst equals."[102]

Mary Wollstonecraft, gave birth to an illegitimate child and offended social mores of her time by never marrying and having sex with men who were not her husband. She died of complications due to pregnancy after publishing several books but was not regarded positively until later generations learned about her through her writings. Feminists admired her for forging a new path for women both in her public and private life—one that she couldn't enjoy without opprobrium at the time that she lived.

African Americans have played activist roles under every American political ideology and also have served as American soldiers in every political conflict. It isn't the case that they contributed politically only around the time of the Civil War. And slavery was legally practiced in the North until 1820, so the consequences of slavery weren't only part of Southern history.[103] The difference was that the Southern economy relied on slavery whereas the North was able to pursue its mostly small scale agriculture and other sources of productivity without it.

Frederick Douglas (1818-1895) and Harriet A. Jacobs (1813-1897), both wrote emotionally moving slave accounts witnessing slavery's injustice and brutality. These people endured and described slavery. Their writings resisted inaccurate social illusions about slavery and helped people to emotionally and conscientiously recognize crimes being committed against other human beings instead of rationalizing them into unconcern. In the earliest colonial period, when the American colonies were founded, slavery resembled other kinds of class oppression that were common in Europe because of lingering feudalism and aristocracy. But as society continued to change from feudalism to capitalism, slavery grew out of step with modernizing influences.

Capitalism and industrialism were remodeling society and slavery didn't fit into the new pattern of work and wages. Both slavery and Master and Servant Laws that penalized labor organization kept wages low for workers outside bondage. And the old methods of the whip and chain resisted progress toward industrialization. Legal sanction for both white bondage and black bondage eventually became relics of the past. Frederick Douglas wrote several slave accounts and he was an eloquent writer. He used a variety of arguments to persuade readers that slavery should end. He expressed dismay at the brutality of slavery so well that his readers changed their mind sometimes and took the side of emancipation. He showed that slaves who could read and write could express themselves rationally. And after a slave achieved literacy, he didn't easily accept that slavery should be permitted to rob him of his opportunities.

Teaching slaves to read was illegal in the South and it took luck and determination for a slave to get a chance at literacy. Although community education was widespread among the Puritans in the North, it wasn't in the South. Only private tutors were available in the South and they only taught children of wealthy plantation owners. Education wasn't available to the poor white or black Southern people. When Douglas became literate, and wrote about his slavery experiences, he showed himself to be capable of having a dialogue with white culture. His arguments transformed slavery experiences from "slaves as socially oppressed outsiders" to "persecuted slavery insiders who understood their ill treatment in society to be unjust". This gave literate slaves rhetorical common ground with abolitionists and non-slave owners.

Douglas showed that slavery led to a variety of social ills. One example was the reality of slave owners fathering children with their women slaves in order to get greater numbers of tragically enslaved progeny. Another was desperately poor and uneducated white non-slave owners bitter over their own poverty who experienced a lower wage and standard of living under the influence of slavery. Poor non-slave owners sometimes violently attacked slaves. Also, slave mothers were separated from their children and children from their mothers spreading grief for lost loved ones among slave families. And the hardship of slavery to lesser masters was brought to heart by stories that told about inadequate food, shelter and medicine. When comparing the wealth of the North and the South, Douglas expressed surprise at higher wages in the North than at home in the South where slave labor kept wages lower.

He had mistakenly believed that the North would be poor like non-slave owning whites in the South and his narrative showed that slavery was to blame as an economic system that created economic disparities and lasting poverty. Slaves worked long hours but their labor only helped their masters whereas labor in the north produced higher wages that also went farther to circulate virtuously within the community. Harriet A. Jacobs bore witness against sexual exploitation and described her struggles to free herself and her children from slavery both before and after the Fugitive Slave Act of 1850. This Act made it possible for Southerners to go to the North and capture fugitive slaves. She described the hardship and worry she and her children experienced as Southerners refused to allow her family members to buy their freedom or even cheated them after their freedom was purchased in a system that was bent on relentless human exploitation. Here are quotes from Frederick Douglas's *Narrative of the Life of Frederick Douglas, an American Slave*, 1845,[104] and Harriet Jacobs, *Incidents in the Life of a Slave Girl*, 1861.[105]

"He would at times seem to take great pleasure in whipping a slave. I have often been awakened at the dawn of day by the most heart-rending shrieks of an own aunt of mine, whom he used to tie up to a joist, and whip upon her naked back till she was literally covered with blood. No words, no tears, no prayers, from his gory victim, seemed to move his iron heart from its bloody purpose....It was the first of a long series of such outrages, of which I was doomed to be a witness and a participant." Frederick Douglas[106]

"There were no beds given the slaves, unless one coarse blanket be considered such, and none but the men and women had these. This, however, is not considered a very great privation. They find less difficulty from the want of beds, than from the want of time to sleep; for when their day's work in the field is done, the most of them having their washing, mending, and cooking to do, and having few or none of the ordinary facilities for doing either of these, very many of their sleeping hours are consumed in preparing for the field the coming day; and when this is done, old and young, male and female, married and single, drop down side by side, on one common bed,—the cold damp floor, each covering himself or herself with their miserable blankets; and here they sleep till they are summoned to the field by the driver's horn." Frederick Douglas[107]

"The whisper that my master was my father may or may not be true... slaveholders have ordained, and by law established, that the children of slave women shall in all cases follow the condition of their mothers... such slaves invariably suffer greater hardships....the master is frequently compelled to sell this class of his slaves, out of deference to the feelings of his white wife; and, cruel as the deed may strike any one to be, for a man to sell his own children to human flesh-mongers, it is often the dictate of humanity for him to do so; for, unless he does this, he may not only whip them himself, but must stand by and see one white son tie up his brother...and ply the gory lash to his naked back" Frederick Douglas[108]

"But to the slave mother New Year's day comes laden with peculiar sorrows. She sits on her cold cabin floor, watching the children who may all be torn from her the next morning; and often does she wish that she and they might die before the day dawns. She may be an ignorant creature, degraded by the system that has brutalized her from childhood; but she has a mother's instincts, and is capable of feeling a mother's agonies." Harriet Jacobs[109]

"On condition of paying his mistress two hundred dollars a year, and supporting himself, he was allowed to work at his trade, and manage his own affairs. His strongest wish was to purchase his children; but though he several times offered his hard earnings for that purpose, he never succeeded." Harriet Jacobs[110]

"He told me I was his property; that I must be subject to his will in all things. My soul revolted against the mean tyranny. But where could I turn for protection? No matter whether the slave girl be as black as ebony or as fair as her mistress. In either case, there is no shadow of law to protect her from insult, from violence, or even from death; all these are inflicted by fiends who bear the shape of men." Harriet Jacobs[111]

"If the secret memoirs of many members of Congress should be published, curious details would be unfolded. I once saw a letter from a member of Congress to a slave, who was the mother of six of his children. He wrote to request that she would send her children away from the great house before his return, as he expected to be accompanied by friends. The woman could not read, and was obliged to employ another to read the letter. The existence of the colored children did not trouble this gentleman, it was only the fear that friends might recognize in their features a resemblance to him." Harriet Jacobs[112]

Virginia had adopted labor indenture historically in 1620.[113] Usually young people in their teens and early twenties without transportation money to come to the Americas had their transport paid in exchange for work. The condition of indentured servants could be better than or as bad as that of a slave. A master would pay the boat transport and a fee and then have the indentured person at his disposal for a period of time contracted out in an agreement. People who possessed skills in demand usually got better contracts. Conditions were severe enough in the colonial South that many indentured people didn't live to the end of their service term. Indenture in the colonies was common until slavery became comparatively cheaper economically during the 1680's.[114]

After the 1820's, industrialization had reduced poverty so well in Europe that European passengers could pay their own fair when they emigrated to the United States.[115] Indenture lasted in the U.S. into the nineteenth century. Indenture during the 1840's was used by Asian immigrants to Cuba and South America on sugar plantations but the workers also received wages and could buy out their remaining contract or get a different employer if they didn't like their circumstances.[116] Asian indentures working in mining and laying rail were known in California in the 1850's and also in Hawaii until its annexation.[117] The British government began to prohibit Indian migration to the West Indies as indenture to pay off economic debts in 1917.[118] Here are a few quotes from indentured servants. The first is from a letter written to a family member left behind in England and the second comes from a memoir.

> "What we unfortunate English People suffer here is beyond the probability of you in England to Conceive, let it suffice that I one of the unhappy Number, am toiling almost Day and Night, and very often in the Horses drudgery, with only this comfort that you Bitch you do not halfe enough, and then tied up and whipp'd to that degree that you'd not serve and Animal, scarce any thing but Indian Corn and Salt to eat and that even begrudged nay many Negroes are better used, almost naked no shoes nor stockings to wear, and the comfort after slaving during Masters pleasure, what rest we can get is to rap ourselves up in a Blanket and ly upon the Ground, this is the deplorable Condition your poor Betty endures, and now I beg if you have any Bowels of Compassion left to show it by sending me some Relief, Clothing is the principal thing wanting."[119] Elizabeth Sprigs[119]

> "My master employed me in the Business: I continued satisfied with him for sometime; but being desirous to settle at *Philadelphia*, during the rest of my servitude, I declared to him, I would sta no longer, and desired him to dispose of me to some other Master, and insisted upon it, agreeably to the Tenour of my Indenture. This Demand made him cross to me, and I

attempted an Escape, but was taken, and put into Prison; but was soon released, with a promise to satisfy my Demand. About a Fortnight after, we went to the Mayor of *Philadelphia*, his Name was *Griffith*, a Man of exact Justice, tho' an *Irishman*, who reconciled us; so I returned back to *Burlington*, and continued with him three Years, he forgiving me the other Two; I was ever after perfectly pleased with my Master's Behavior to me, which was generous." William Moraley[120]

The last group of quotes come from Native Americans and these quotes won't capture the full sweep of calamity that befell them. Not only were their lands stolen but they were also afflicted with new diseases that gave them little chance to resist unwanted changes or to recoup their growing losses. Of all Americans, Native Americans are possibly the most resilient because Native American cultures have suffered from two terrible maladies: disease and invasion. Some groups have died out, but many tribes have retained a sense of social cohesion. Poverty remains common on the Reservation. But the economic and political changes that enveloped Native Americans and their resilience shows how people can choose to adapt to catastrophic change.

Native Americans at the time of European settlement, had an oral history tradition rather than a written one, so quotes were usually statements made by Native Americans but recorded in a non-native language after passing through a Native translator who knew a European language. The quotes may lack some of the character that they would have had to a native speaker who heard the quote spoken in the context of the personality and language of the speaker. Nevertheless, the quotes are effective and moving even though expressed in English. Taken from *Bury My Heart at Wounded Knee*, by Dee Brown,[121] they are quotes from Western Tribes later in the history of Native American oppression. Though overlapping in time from classical liberalism into modern liberalism, attacking Native Americans was a long standing policy of the U.S. government. Also included, three presidential quotes about Native Americans show that Presidents were ruthless in their determination to sweep Native Americans out of the way of the American political empire.

"I did not know then how much was ended. When I look back now from this high hill of my old age, I can still see the butchered women and children lying heaped and scattered all along the crooked gulch as plain as when I saw them with eyes still young. And I can see that something else died there in the bloody mud, and was buried in the blizzard. A people's dream died there. It was a beautiful dream…the nation's hoop is broken and scattered. There is no center any longer, and the sacred tree is dead." Black Elk[122]

"They made us many promises, more than I can remember, but they never kept but one; they promised to take our land, and they took it." Mahpiua Luta, or Red Cloud[123]

"Where today are the Pequot? Where are the Narragansett, the Mohican, the Pokanoket, and many other once powerful tribes of our people? They have vanished before the avarice and the oppression of the White Man, as snow before a summer sun…Will we let ourselves be destroyed in our turn without a struggle, give up our homes, our country bequeathed to us by the Great Spirit, the graves of our dead and everything that is dear and sacred to us? I know you will cry with me "Never! Never!" Tecumseh of the Shawnees[124]

"Whose voice was first sounded in this land? The voice of the red people who had but bows and arrows…What has been done in my country I did not want, did not ask for it; white people going through my country… When the white man comes in my country he leaves a trail of blood behind him…I have two mountains in that country—the Black Hills and the Big Horn Mountain. I want the Great Father to make no roads through them. I have told these things three times; now I have come here to tell them the fourth time." Mahpiua Luta, or Red Cloud[125]

"Indians and wolves are both beasts of prey, tho' they differ in shape." George Washington[126]

"If ever we are constrained to lift the hatchet against any tribe, we will never lay it down till that tribe is exterminated, or driven beyond the Mississippi…in war, they will kill some of us; we shall destroy them all." Thomas Jefferson[127]

"My original convictions upon this subject have been confirmed by the course of events for several years, and experience is every day adding to their strength. That those tribes cannot exist surrounded by our settlements and in continual contact with our citizens is certain. They have neither the intelligence, the industry, the moral habits, nor the desire of improvement which are essential to any favorable change in their condition. Established in the midst of another and a superior race, and without appreciating the causes of their inferiority or seeking to control them, they must necessarily yield to the force of circumstances and ere long disappear." Andrew Jackson[128]

Classical liberal quotes show rational examination of good government amid conditions of political and economic disparity.

Quotes from intellectuals that organized classical liberalism's rational discourse and those from an underclass that benefited least from classical liberalism hint at wide differences in the hopes and failures of the ideology. But change was afoot during classical liberalism. Limiting government was a kind of radical experiment. Economic prosperity was a goal but some people were excluded from the economic benefits of classical liberalism. Capitalism and the first wave of industrialization created social change and the nation state system's political tendency towards competition and warfare between states continued to impinge on the American experiment. These pressures eventually caused the United States' Civil War which marked a permanent change in American politics and economics. But population growth, economic expansion, and a stable government bore witness to success in the political experiment of limited government. Classical liberalism succeeded in important ways. One way to measure classical liberalism's success was in population growth. In 1790, the U.S. population was 3,929,214 and by 1860 it was 31,443,321.[129] Classical liberalism supported a vast increase in the number of persons participating in American society.

Viewing the politic and economy as separate creates controversy, but there are three good reasons to do so.

Controversy over how the economy should be regulated, whether the power of the politic should be kept separate from or combined with the power of the economy, has led to heated arguments and strong differences of opinion among political ideologies. Another way to look at the problem is to imagine how politicians could utilize money taken out of the economy to benefit themselves, their associates and a variety of political goals. Another consideration could be whether the economy works better when profits cycle back virtuously into economic production where people use and produce the products of the marketplace under fewer regulations and taxes. Should economic productivity be diverted into achieving political goals? How and in what amount can production profits within a market be diverted into politics without destroying the incentive to produce? Tension between these positions has been part of modern politics and the energy of that tension stimulates an opportunity for several rhetorical arguments to be made.

The first argument made by classical liberals was that ***political freedom would require economic freedom***. The Protestant Reformation led to a greater appreciation for individual conscience but also wariness about focused political power bent on ordering people's individual life choices to create political advantages that rulers might desire. Many people died during the Thirty Years' War and the death and destruction caused by religious disagreement convinced people to try tolerance, and power limitation. Two other arguments can be seen to underlie the idea that the politic and economy should be considered as separate.

The second argument can be related to Montesquieu's plan for establishing a **balance of power** in society, where power was kept diffuse in order to prevent abuses of power. Society has only so much power and keeping the power of production separate from the power of governance keeps society safer from abuses of power that can lead to tragic social losses. Governance isn't perfect as can be seen from bloody historical conflicts. Keeping government smaller and power more diffuse in the politic on one hand and allowing the economy to be productive for markets instead of for politics on the other hand, might avoid focused political violence in its largest threat dimension. A more productive commonwealth can result from limited political power, because productivity creates wealth instead of warfare.

The balance of power argument starts with the idea of good government. Good government is accountable to constitutional rules that put people's interests in common. Also, successful governments make people feel happy and safe. When people are unhappy and unsafe, the government isn't successful. Accountability among those who serve in government is important so that when a government isn't good, it can be improved by recognizing problems and fixing what's wrong. Corruption shouldn't reward those who abuse public power.

John Adams (1735-1826), the first Vice President and second President of the U.S., wrote a letter to John Wythe in 1776, and he described how to evaluate government. He wrote, "We ought to consider what is the end of government, before we determine which is the best form. Upon this point all speculative politicians will agree, that the happiness of society is the end of government, as all Divines and moral Philosophers will agree that the happiness of the individual is the end of man. From this principle it will follow, that the form of government which communicates ease, comfort, security, or in one word, happiness, to the greatest number of persons, and in the greatest degree is best."[130] Utilitarians also articulated a similar connection between happiness and good government.

The connection of good governance with happiness was well accepted in 1776. People worried, however, about abuses of power like the ones that Montesquieu's warned about. The separation of the politic and economy in classical liberalism was a strategy to prevent abuses of power. While governments functioned to protect people's property and happiness, the economy functioned to make commodity exchanges possible for the purpose of making a living and under more fortunate circumstances, building wealth. Montesquieu's suggestion about separation of powers guided the founders who wrote it into the design of U.S. government under the Constitution. The separation of powers was a key design feature. Having an executive to enforce law, a legislature to write law and an independent judiciary to interpret law was essential in the constitutional design to prevent abuses of power in politics. Corporate abuses of power were also known to the founders from chartered companies, the forerunners of modern corporations. These mercantile corporations sometimes held sovereign licensed monopoly enterprises that were permitted to utilize force to protect their economic interests. They could bring their own army, develop a newly encountered territory by subduing resistance, claim the territory in the name of the King and sometimes enslave the inhabitants. Conceptualizing the power of the politic and the economy as separate was another way to check power's advance and to keep power from concentrating into only a few hands.

A third argument can be made based on *the functional difference between government and economy*. Society has two strong arms, the politic and the economy. The energy of the politic differs from the energy of the economy and each follows different cues from society. Because they operate by following different social cues, they operate best when they operate separately. The power of governance is inappropriate to the economy just as the power of the market is inappropriate to governance. Neither can take on the other's role and continue to succeed in its own role. But together their energy can direct society to prosperity.

The functional argument that distinguishes good politics from good economy is based on how these two spheres of action are distinguished as working by different kinds of cues from society. Good government under a constitution functions to protect people's property and natural rights and can be evaluated by whether people are happy and whether government is accountable to what people expect of good governance. But the economy doesn't become organized through a document like a constitution. Its power is diffuse. In contrast to the politic, the way that the economy functions is different. An economy is the aggregate of various markets. Although markets require legal protections of property and the enforcement of contracts, markets function by profit and loss.

According to Thomas Sowell (b. 1930), "While markets coordinated by price movements—"capitalism" as it is called—may seem like a simple thing, markets are misunderstood more often than some other things that are considered more complex. Although a free market economic system is sometimes called a profit system, it is in reality a profit-and-loss system—and the losses are equally important for the efficiency of the economy, because losses tell producers what to stop producing."[131] Putting the quotes from Adams and Sowell together, we can see that government coordinates its power through a constitution and is evaluated on the happiness principle and the economy works by diffuse interactions in a profit and loss marketplace where sellers adapt to demand by changing their product to suit the market. These are functionally distinct ways of discipline in the politic and the economy.

Economic conflict can erupt between the interests of individuals and those of organizations in the marketplace.

Just as individuals band together in the politic to form political factions, they can band into guilds and monopolies inside an economy. When a product sells and makes a profit, it benefits the seller, providing a profit and allowing him to stay in business selling more of that product. If a product sells at a loss then the seller should stop selling that product and change production to something else that can make a profit. Although this process of winnowing out the unprofitable isn't efficient for sellers because it makes them constantly change their inventory according to demand, it is the best possible market strategy to meet buyer's demand because it makes sellers in the marketplace efficient at providing what people want. Fickle demand which changes all the time can be hard on sellers but it helps markets to meet people's needs. Constant change, however, puts pressure on sellers and can encourage the development of monopolies, guilds and cartels.

Guilds have played a role in history since before the Renaissance. The first capitalist guild in Europe, was assembled as a weaver's guild set up by Hans Fugger in 1380, in Augsburg, Germany. Timing for the enterprises of the Fugger family stretched almost into the Italian Renaissance. Hans was succeeded by sons who enlarged the business until it grew from the cloth trade to banking and mining.[132] Fugger business acumen allowed their enterprises to survive for generations. They coexisted with monarchs and aristocrats with whom they eventually made money deals loaning money in exchange for mining rights. During the Fugger's businesses, the politic operating under kings and aristocrats was constantly pillaging profit out of the economy and out of the Fugger family enterprises.

In the Digital Age, high capital investments into complex production factories scattered across multiple nations for complicated manufactures can make changing products expensive and monopoly more tempting than when simpler products were manufactured. But monopolies work against market efficiency for buyers by slowing down change in the marketplace in order to reduce the cost of change to sellers. And sellers have less incentives to innovate through research or to address business shortcomings such as ineffective or dysfunctional management. The two-sidedness of economic relationships between buyers and sellers can make a buyer's advantage seem like a seller's disadvantage. And at all times, an economic deal has two sides in an exchange and two kinds of outcomes. It is the ubiquity of binary outcomes in economic exchanges that makes economics look complicated. But the overall health of the market depends on buyers and sellers meeting together to negotiate in order to establish the value of commodities. That idea is simple. If they are prevented from negotiating the best value based on the production cost and what people want, need, and can afford to buy, then the market won't be efficient. Healthy exchanges create a win for both the buyer and the seller.

A political ideology that can interfere with markets is socialism. While monopolists try to slow the rate of market change and enhance profits by controlling the supply of goods and limiting the number of producers, socialists try to predict and control the market to make money for politics. While monopolists sometimes get exclusive market advantages through governments, socialists are the government. They move market profits into the politic and try to control markets by centralizing their own oversight and control of markets. Efforts to slow change in the market or to control prices, amounts and kinds of goods reduces the overall wealth of an economy by reducing market efficiency and/or by robbing its profits. Stealing the energy of the marketplace by making it serve monopolists or socialists instead of everyone together drains vitality out of the economy. Reduced incentive to trade eventually undermines the profitability of centrally manipulated and controlled markets. The energy of trade requires freedom to negotiate for fair trade.

The political rules of taxation and regulation affect markets and the economy as do relationships between political and economic actors.

The way that markets are regulated and taxed by governments creates a relationship between the economy and the politic. During the classical liberal period, regulations were part of the government's relationship with the economy but they were different from the kind of regulation that happened in the other ideological periods of modern liberalism and neoliberalism. In the prologue, the American System was mentioned that used tariffs on foreign goods to encourage developing domestic industry and infrastructure to improve transportation to everyone's benefit. The Constitution created economic interests in common among states. And domestic economic regulation during classical liberalism was different from today's economic regulation.

Joseph Postell wrote an essay, "The Right Kind of Regulation,"[133] about classical liberal economic regulations and how they were in step with economic liberty. He wrote that there were two kinds of regulations. One was to provide public services such as delivering mail by creating post offices and post roads. These services were a public-wide benefit. The other kind of regulation was to enforce and protect contracts. Enforcing and protecting contracts might include, for instance, the inspection of meat or the licensing of a doctor. These kinds of regulations were seen as being protective of the value in contracts and private property because they helped to ensure that people got what they paid for. These were regulations to enhance a person's chance to get a fair deal.[134] Since people were free to come and go from trading arrangements after contracts were filled, people were seen as free economic agents negotiating their own best deals within the oversight of the law.

Richard Wagner, in his essay, "Promoting the General Welfare,"[135] made observations about the entanglement between political actors and economic actors. He postulated that alliances between actors in the politic and actors in the economy would multiply in conjunction with growth in the size of the federal government. That's why he saw the limited federal government of the classical liberal period as being less entangled with the economy than later administrations in more recent times. He saw entanglement as the result of spontaneous interactions between actors in the politic and economy and he envisioned that entanglement was innate under the freedom design of the U.S. Founders.[136]

In *Who Rules America? Power, Politics, and Social Change*, William Domhoff[137] chronicled contemporary connections between government and business. Those connections have formed an extensive network of relationships between people who think alike because they share similar social training. Such connections begin with social interactions and only later spread into political and economic networks. They start with an association between elite families through schools and private clubs. Elite property owning families wielded political and economic influence also during colonial times and during the classical liberal period.[138] These associations, likewise, came with property ownership, wealth and education.

Increasing fiscal debt became an accepted policy after the classical liberal period.

Economic liberalism ended when mixed economy started. Income Taxes began in 1861, when the Congress of the Union forces passed the Revenue Act of 1861. Prior to the Civil War, tariffs had supplied federal monies. By taxing income directly, the individual's liberty to keep earnings declined. Income taxes reduced political freedom and economic freedom because the government got the power to spend more of other people's money. Eventually regulation produced the "nanny state". This nanny role of government gave politicians even more power to interfere in the marketplace and to oversee the kinds of industries that would exist. Higher taxes took profits from the economy and moved them into government projects, like funding NASA or the CIA, during the neoliberal period. Government expenses were partially offset by taxes levied from profits during the end stage of the Industrial Revolution. But with higher taxes there was pressure to make more money in order to pay the tax and pressure to invest in technologies that would make a larger profit possible. Wars also created more debt. Debt was substantial after the two World Wars. Costs of repair in European nations was also high to pay for the rebuilding.

During the classical liberal period, a payment plan to pay off government debt was part of political policy. Carrying permanent government debt wasn't considered economically prudent during early U.S. history. But that hasn't been true later under the other two political ideologies. Debt has played a prominent role in twentieth and twenty-first century nation state economics. Under late modern liberalism, Keynesianism advocated more federal deficit spending in order to stimulate the economy. Monetarism, printing more cash or creating cash substitutes has been seen under neoliberalism. Keynesianism and monetarism in an atmosphere of easy credit access have led to greater debt as part of government policy to stimulate economic buying.

Increasing sovereign debt happens when too much of the economy is being used by the government to fund government projects. Profit motivates economic activity and higher taxes eat up profits and discourage productivity. Government debt reaches the stage of "too much" when government spending exceeds the ability of the economy's production profits to pay for the cost of doing business and the cost of taxation for debt. But it can also be too much when it wastes economic resources that have better possible uses. Politicians don't have spending restraint unless legal steps are taken to make them accountable for political expenditures. The pattern of overspending for political projects repeats many times in the historical record. Politicians most value their ability to influence others. And giving government a bigger purse, as happened in the modern liberal period and as has continued under neoliberalism, can lead to power investments that enhance political power but don't provide an economic return.

Presently, during the neoliberal period, as the Industrial Revolution has given way to the Digital Age, government has become a booster and sponsor of multinational globalization through open trading treaties and tax rebates or delays. Congressional legislation has provided tax benefits to those who invest abroad. This has put global market businesses ahead of domestic business. Also, the federal government under neoliberalism has provided a tax subsidy to specific industries and that created a stimulus in IT for those industries. IT development accelerated in banking, the military and media. These areas have enhanced political power but they extracted more wealth than they created.[139, 140, 141,142]

Under neoliberalism, monetary expansion under monetarism has been pushed further and another financial strategy has been born: financialization. When there is a gap in demand for products because people make less money in a less active economy, greater debt can temporarily provide money to extend consumption. This has fueled financialization, under neoliberal monetarist policy. According to Krippner, financialization is "the increasing role of financial motives, financial markets, financial actors and financial institutions in the operation of the domestic and international economies."[143] Financialization will be discussed with neoliberalism.

Modern debt has been used to increase interest payments under financialization and to decrease investment in production. Debt between the IMF and World Bank and third world nations in the mid twentieth century created political leverage that favored first world national interests. The combination of indebted domestic corporations and indebted American families can also create a kind of political weakness where people can't innovate a new economy even if the old economy is performing poorly. This causes problems inside a shrinking economy with increasing unemployment where innovation may be the only remedy for lackluster economic performance. Debt can contribute to political malaise because it can make politicians less accountable to long term goals. Sovereign debt motivates government policy toward support for debt finance rather than toward building wealth or solving political problems. And as people become economically weaker, they have less political power to challenge the government's failings. Strong governments avoid fiscal debt and that helps to maintain a strong economy.

Classical liberalism showed that rational consideration of the politic and economy can lead to better governance strategies.

Enlightenment philosophers tried to describe the nature of governments. They warned about enlarging a government's power. Describing the nature of governments and of markets reveals a difference between these sectors. Because happiness is the goal of good governance, the politic has moral repercussions. American politicians who occupy high offices take oaths to obey and to defend the Constitution. These are promises to act within the bounds of constitutional law. Political accountability both to the law as it is written and to the public welfare helps to keep good government operating to benefit society. In contrast, the market isn't primarily about moral obligations. Instead, its goal is profit and efficiency. Laws operating in the marketplace keep business transactions fair so that producers can benefit from their work and profit can circulate virtuously to create wealth and production opportunities. Profits keep incentives in the marketplace to encourage production.

Corruption can disrupt the performance of the politic and the economy. It can destroy society's health when government stops being accountable to happiness and when the economy benefits only a few socialists or monopolists, disrupting exchanges for everyone else. Whenever this disruption occurs harm is done. Then the two arms of society, the politic and economy, stop serving society. And sometimes harm can't be undone. Then that pairing strategy between the politic and the economy comes to an end and a new one replaces it. The need for change can accumulate like a coiled spring until it can no longer be resisted. When the Age of Revolutions began near the end of the Enlightenment, tension caused by new economic opportunities interacting with old economic strategies reorganized power relationships. As society reorganized from feudalism to capitalism, beginning in the Renaissance, laws were also rewritten. Sometimes changes in the law happened in response to social unrest. Just laws can be like a pressure release valve to lessen social strife. People prefer to live in a just society.

The vast scope of the law over history has included a major shift in the approach to legal analysis.

The pursuit of law study across its historical scope, causes a person to cross a philosophic boundary between two methods of analysis, one from antiquity and the other which arose in the modern period. Greek rhetorical methods from the Greek dialectic informed early law analysis and modern empirical methods have informed later law. The first is language based and allows legal rhetorical analysis to characterize aspects of legal practice as good or bad, as proper or improper to human society. By contrast, empirical methodology has used observation to analyze law. It has considered evidence regarding what law practice does or fails to do. Because the law extends from antiquity to the present, the two methods of analysis both pertain to today's law.

The change in methodology from rhetorical legal analysis to empiricism can be jarring. The rhetorical method seems to rationalize the law, even idealize the law, using language analysis, definitions and reasoning. Empiricism based on direct observation, although pragmatic, describes but doesn't throw out bad legal practices. Reading about law, leads the reader into both strategies of law analysis. Both methods of talking about law are valid for their times and they don't necessarily contradict each other except in terms of method and intellectual flavor. Looking into descriptions of law from ancient to modern cultures reflects a change in the methodology of analysis from language based rhetorical reasoning to observation based reasoning and shows that each reasoning method has had different strengths.

Rhetorical arguments set out first causes, definitions and basic principles and under this technique, when the law deviates, it is called perverted. This legal reasoning method doesn't stop perversions though it can recognize failure of the law to be legitimate and it can suggest likely consequences or possible improvements. But there are no perversions of law under empirical methods of observation based reasoning; only description. Evidence of harm can be presented and better possible alternatives can be considered. In either case, law isn't static and is only as useful as society's value system can make it. The law under either system of description has had the same job to do. That job is to create relationships of civility, making civilizations and civil accomplishments possible.

Law operating in the politic and the economy acts in two ways. First, the law outlines and maintains the boundaries within which healthy government and robust markets operate. Legal boundaries encourage the politic and economy to operate fairly and in socially useful ways. The law defines and defends normal social interactions in government and economy to prevent opportunism that would infringe natural rights or rob material assets. This encourages a healthy commonwealth. Second, the law prevents waste and corruption by creating avenues for accountability. Accountability has involved identification of harms and compensation or penalty.

In government, constitutions act to limit the power of government. They do this in order to prevent abuses by setting up a design that is power-limited and politically non-predatory. Constitutions can change political competition into political cooperation. In markets, laws that enforce contract agreements and that protect property from theft keep the market safe from would-be pillagers so that there will be mutually beneficial exchanges that efficiently move products to where they are needed. But when the law comes to represent the interests of powerful special interests over society in opposition to social interests, both governments and markets can become wasteful and corrupt. Adam Smith warned about this when he wrote about applying a "suspicious attention" to business's advice on commerce regulations. History has sad examples of corrupt governments and marketplaces that fail to serve society and eventually expire after their laws have stopped serving the public. The law impacts both the politic and economy and many observations can be made about the role of law under classical liberalism.

The law has crossed historical eras, diverse cultures, has utilized many written languages and understanding it in your culture requires focused study. But a briefer analysis can clarify its scope and potential to civilize society by limiting harms.

Understanding the law well, requires historical study, learning about legal precedents, learning legal language and years of discovery and dedication because it spans human society across all literate civilizations. But a basic outline can be put forward, anyway, at least for the West. Broadly speaking, there are three branches of Western law: common law, civil law, also known as Roman law, and Scholastic law or Cannon Law, also known as law under the Catholic Church that originated mostly during the Manorial period and continued until the Protestant Reformation.

Most Europeans follow predominantly Roman law based on Roman statute from the time of the Roman Empire (not from the Roman Republic, which had a different concept of the law) but also some laws from other traditions. Emperor Justinian, in the fifth century, codified Roman law in the *Corpus Juris Civilis*.[144] European law has relied heavily on the *Corpus*. The English and American system of law has been mostly a common law system but there have been influences from the other two kinds of law. Common law has been the law of the community recorded to show community values and legal precedents. It comes from the idea that laws are more than a political declaration supported by force. Law, according to common law traditions, has been what the people support and believe in. It is related to the phrase "consent of the governed".

Rule of law is also an essential part of the American legal system. It predates American liberty law. Civilizations that possessed a written language have been found to also develop a rule of law. Rule of law was part of Chinese history, history of the Middle East and European history, for example. Rule of law was what someone meant when they said "a nation of laws and not of men". Rule of law has recognized the sovereignty of law over all persons, so that everyone would be subject to the same legal rules. It has prohibited arbitrary fiat political declarations enforced by police action. Rule of law has been published so that everyone can obtain access to law and can know what the law requires. This has been so that commission of a crime would reflect a guilty mind and so that those in power wouldn't have any exclusive knowledge of law and gain an inappropriate power through the law to destroy others.

Law practice among legal specialists has involved federal law, state law, city ordinance, public prosecutions, civil torts, and contract law. There are so many kinds of law. Law has overseen most kinds of human exchanges and should encourage fairness. There has also been positive law that requires a certain action and negative law that prohibits actions. The American system under classical liberalism was a system of negative law. Americans under classical liberalism's limited government, had a Congress that legislated mostly to protect property and stayed out of people's everyday lives.

Personal sovereignty, as described by John Locke, was an important part of classical liberalism and so was natural law. Natural law has had ancient roots and has recognized people's dignity in the real context of a natural human lifespan. Natural law has seen human life as being affected by necessity, or what life requires of us as human beings, and reciprocity, or "pay-back", and also what can be understood by reason, or people's ability to understand justice. Natural law has been the law that is obvious because it makes sense to a rational mind. Because of the idea of natural law, it has been unlawful to require by law what isn't possible in real world experience.

Natural law has been the rational measure for man-made laws; a kind of pure and rational form that can serve as a model for drafting laws that make sense. Locke expanded on natural law and Roman concepts of individual sovereignty to write about natural rights and personal sovereignty. Natural rights, he declared are innate to all persons, equal among all persons and not granted by governments because they precede government. Proper governments respect these natural rights. The phrase "We hold these truth to be self-evident" from the American Declaration of Independence referred to natural law. The phrase "that all Men are created equal, that they are endowed by their Creator with certain unalienable Rights, that among these are Life, Liberty, and the Pursuit of Happiness" referred to natural rights. The phrase "That to secure these Rights, Governments are instituted among Men, deriving their just Powers from the Consent of the Governed." expressed the idea of popular sovereignty.

Some differences are obvious between classical liberal law and law practices from modern liberalism and neoliberalism.

Randy E. Barnett (b. 1952), in his book *Restoring the Lost Constitution: The Presumption of Liberty*,[145] wrote that to early Americans, natural rights were liberty rights.[146] He wrote that "natural rights are the set of concepts that define the moral space within which persons must be free to make their own choices and live their own lives if they are to pursue happiness while living in society with others."[147] He identified six basic natural rights: the right to worship according to conscience, the right to speech, the right to emigrate, the right to self-defense and property ownership, the right to alter or abolish an unjust government, the right to assemble.[148]

Barnett also wrote about "necessary and proper" as a standard for legislation. The "necessary and proper" clause can be found in the enumerated powers of Congress, in Article One, Section Eight of the U.S. Constitution. It is in the last part of Section Eight and after listing other powers, it reads that Congress has the power... "To make all Laws which shall be necessary and proper for carrying into Execution the foregoing Powers, and all other Powers vested by this Constitution in the Government of the United States, or in any Department or Officer thereof."

The clause embodied the idea that legislation should be necessary to allow the government to do the job that is specified in the Constitution but also proper in that wherever possible, it should not infringe on liberty or trample on natural rights. The Constitution's Bill of Rights has listed specific natural rights under the American legal system. The Ninth and Tenth Amendments of the Constitution refer to other natural rights not specifically described for individuals in the Ninth and for states in the Tenth Amendment.[149] The Ninth and Tenth Amendments were written to satisfy the Anti-Federalists who wanted unspecified rights to be respected so that the Bill of Rights wouldn't be an exhaustive list but would instead be seen as a partial listing of rights. From these amendments Barnett argued for a normal American "presumption of liberty" as the classical liberal legal standard. But he observed that the U.S. government in the present day continues to invade the space of liberty as it was defined during classical liberalism under the U.S. Constitution. Unless a right has been specifically described in the Bill of Rights, the Supreme Court has ignored it. The unspecified rights in the Ninth and Tenth Amendments have been mostly ignored.[150]

Barnett recognized a change of judicial interpretation and of executive and legislative power, expanding governmental powers since classical liberal times at the expense of liberty. Enumerating congressional power was a strategy of limitation. And bypassing necessary and proper was a way to expand federal power. Randy Barnett and others have called the new standard a "presumption of constitutionality."[151] He recognized it as originating in The New Deal Era, under Justice Brandeis.[152] In tracing the interpretive change to Justice Brandeis, Barnett described the change from "presumption of liberty" to "presumption of constitutionality" that happened during the political course-change from classical liberalism to modern liberalism. Under a "presumption of constitutionality", congressional legislation has been considered by the Supreme Court to usually conform to the U.S. Constitution without the earlier constraints of "necessary and proper". This has allowed the government to implement social programs that would not have been permissible under a strict liberty scrutiny. It also allowed for expansion of the military industrial complex into covert actions.

Most Americans trust that the law and how it works in America has been consistent across political eras. But the law has been practiced differently during the classical liberal, modern liberal and neoliberal periods. For example, as mentioned, classical liberalism mostly utilized negative law to protect private property. It followed a policy in favor of a "presumption of liberty"[153] instead of a presumption that people wielding political power would probably follow the Constitution. And the constitutional recommendations for a balance of power within a limited government was acceptable to classical liberals. Later, modern liberalism used positive law to require certain behaviors, and to justify the development of government agencies paid for by taxes to regulate American life.

Amendments that were added to the Constitution during modern liberalism repaired some of the political inequality experienced by emancipated slaves and women, granting them voting rights. The Eleventh Amendment was added during classical liberalism as was the Twelfth Amendment. The Thirteenth, Fourteenth, Fifteenth, Sixteenth, Seventeenth, Eighteenth, Nineteenth, Twentieth and Twenty-first Amendments were all added during modern liberalism. The Twenty Second, Twenty Third, Twenty Fourth, Twenty Fifth, Twenty Sixth and Twenty Seventh Amendments were added during the neoliberal period. Income taxes (Sixteenth Amendment) made subsistence living impossible and pressured people to make more money. Modern liberals increased taxes and diminished support for natural rights in the context of an expanded government which reduced individual rights in favor of social welfare and political power.

Neoliberals have modified laws through regulatory reform and these laws favor corporate interests. Modern liberal regulations had to be changed in order for neoliberals to enhance corporate advantages. Congress tailor-made legislation in favor of global corporate interests doing business abroad in order to incentivize globalization in high risk settings. Neoliberal politicians have supported political operations under the CIA and U.S. military to expand economic opportunities for multinational corporations. Some neoliberal politicians have opposed natural rights such as the right to *habeus corpus*. Lobbies and think tanks have influenced legislators to deregulate so that large corporations could acquire advantages and re-regulate in order to burden competitors. Corporate interests have used capital to influence Congress to enact legal deconstructions to remake political landscapes to the advantage of multinational corporatists.

Under both the modern liberals and the neoliberals, the federal government has grown in power relative to state government. The interruption of the right to *habeus corpus*, or the right to be charged of a criminal offense if held by authorities, has created concern about present-day protections for individual American freedoms. Neoliberals regard the liberty of multinational corporations at a higher value than individual liberty. They have expanded policing powers at every level of government and developed the surveillance state. These political developments have contrasted sharply with liberty concepts of the classical liberal period. In classical liberal times, before the "nanny state," "trial by jury" included the jury member's evaluation in a criminal court of whether a law's application would result in justice. In the case jurists believed that the law's use would be unjust, they could end the trial. In modern day criminal courts, jurists aren't instructed to evaluate justice broadly but rather they are expected to evaluate whether a specific law can be applied according to evidence provided in court. And prosecutors instead of juries determine penalties in most criminal court proceedings because of the prevalence of plea bargains. In the event of a plea bargain, the case won't be overseen by a judge and jury at all.[154] This is a narrower approach as compared with the earlier standard of jurors as gatekeepers of justice under classical liberalism.

Another change in law practice between classical liberalism and today is how justices interpret law. Judicial review is when the Supreme Court uses constitutional law to evaluate other legislation. Constitutional law is the most powerful law. If a legal statute conflicts with constitutional law it can be struck down by the courts. Judicial review was an accepted idea in classical liberal America. Alexander Hamilton wrote about it in *The Federalist Papers* (1777-1778): "The interpretation of the laws is the proper and peculiar province of the courts. A constitution is, in fact, and must be regarded by the judges as, a fundamental law. It therefore belongs to them to ascertain its meaning as well as the meaning of any particular act proceeding from the legislative body." and also, "No legislative act, therefore, contrary to the Constitution, can be valid."[155] Although judicial review was written about in *The Federalist Papers*, the way judicial review is done now has changed.

Classical liberal legal interpretation was based on legal language found in preceding cases. To remain true to that standard in the present-day after more than a hundred years have passed occasionally requires historical research into language meanings at the time a statute was written. Alternatively, some Justices have chosen to characterize the meaning of law based on other standards besides textual analysis. During classical liberalism, greater emphasis was put on understanding legal language. Justices rarely modified their interpretation outside the language of the law. Justice Rehnquist (1924-2005) in 1990 wrote, "Judges must be aware today that there are currents of ferment in the legal world that seek to revise or even overthrow traditional notions of judicial interpretation."[156]

Today there is a conflict between textualism and other means of interpreting the Constitution that offer greater flexibility to interpret outside of legal texts. Although Justice Scalia, a textualist, will research the authentic meaning of legal text at the time that it was written which may require historic investigation, he believes that greater flexibility outside the textual meaning that is authentic to history can give justices too much discretion. It can cause them to revise laws outside their proper function as legal interpreters who are supposed to maintain legal fidelity.[157] Greater flexibility in judicial interpretation may endanger the political independence of the judiciary and the accuracy of legal interpretation. Justices aren't supposed to enlarge their own political power through judicial interpretation.

Landmark judicial cases can act to establish a new legal standard for subsequent judicial cases.

When a judge writes a ruling it can establish a new legal standard that will be used in subsequent cases. Case law can change a social trajectory by defending a cause that had been previously neglected. Landmark cases are the ones that move future cases in a new direction. Some landmark cases that have affected liberty include the following instances. *Marbury v. Madison (1803)*, a classical liberal case,[158, 159] was an early example of judicial review, when Justice John Marshall used judicial review but under both jurisdictional controversy and conflict of interest circumstances. There was greater legitimate controversy over the circumstances of conflict of interest than over the use of judicial review. Another landmark case was *McCulloch v. Maryland (1819)*, a classical liberal case.[160] In this case, Justice John Marshall ruled that the "necessary and proper" clause had expanded rather than limited the power of the court, an interpretation that differed from earlier statements made by James Madison. Marshall also ruled in this case that states couldn't tax the profits of central banks.

Santa Clara County v. Southern Pacific Railroad (1886), a modern liberal case,[161] was a landmark case ruling under Justice Morrison Waite. It worked to change legal precedent by combining with another case, *Dartmouth College v. Woodward (1819)*, a classical liberal case,[162] ruled on by Justice John Marshall. The two rulings have been used somewhat indirectly to support personhood rights granted to corporations which has caused modern day controversy in the United States. In *Texas v. White (1869)*, a modern liberal case,[163] Justice Salmon P. Chase ruled in the Supreme Court that states are not legally allowed to secede under the U.S. Constitution. This ruling ended further states' rights arguments regarding the right to secede.

In *O'Gorman & Young, Inc. v. Hartford Fire Insurance Co. (1931)*, a modern liberal case,[164] Justice Louis Brandeis, during the era of Progressive political legislation used an argument of presumption of constitutionality for the first court ruling of this kind. Presumption of constitutionality ended liberty protection scrutiny for new legislation by the earlier standard of necessary and proper. Eight years later in another landmark case, *United States v. Carolene Products Co. (1938)*, a modern liberal case,[165,166] Justice Harlan Fiske Stone, in footnote four, referred to and further defined the "presumption of constitutionality" which by this time had essentially replaced the earlier standard of "necessary and proper".

These cases particularly show how legal interpretation can change how well or poorly the U.S. Constitution works to protect individual liberty. But these rulings also provided a political advantage. They created interpretive flexibility in the courts, ushering in political changes as the political ideology of the nation changed from classical liberalism to later modern liberalism and neoliberalism. Flexibility in law has changed the political landscape across the span of American history. Changes in the law have been the force that has enabled the advance of modern liberalism and now neoliberalism. This is obvious when you remember added regulations in the modern liberal period and deregulation and regulatory reform in the neoliberal period.

Land was the basis of wealth and land expansion served as the economic engine of the classical liberal period.

Under classical liberalism, land was the basis of wealth. Daniel Webster, a U.S. Senator in 1838 gave a speech to the Senate in which he said, that land "became property, to be bought and sold for money; whereas in the hands of government, it called for no expenditure, formed the basis of no transactions, and created no demand for currency."[167] Native American lands were taken to provide a new source of revenue creation for government. Land was a commodity that could be exchanged for money by the government during the colonial period. It also became the new currency of a landed elite in America.

Land grants were sought by people in high office and many received grants in the thousands of acres.[168] As the United States continued growing, land speculation for the frontier lands continued to be a mainstay of wealth building until somewhat before the Civil War. Credit in large quantities wasn't available to everyone and early land grants were usually among elites. This led to wealth concentration among elite families, a feature of political importance.[169] People who could use family money or acquire a grant could make more money when the land was sold. But most people living in America both before and after the Revolution didn't possess wealth or property in large acreage.[170]

Surveying American Lands was an important part of nation planning. The earliest surveys happened before the United States existed as a nation. Early surveys that served as a description for land grants often used a physical landmark to mark one boundary like a mountain or river. As colonies became more settled, surveys were refined to show latitudinal and longitudinal boundaries. A young George Washington learned the profession of survey in the 1740's in order to advance his personal interests in land survey and to produce more than one hundred maps. His experience as a surveyor helped him to acquire land and speculate in land sales.[171]

In 1763, Charles Mason and Jeremiah Dixon conducted a survey of Pennsylvania. [172] They were trained in England and used instruments imported from there. In 1774, the Continental Congress declared that the survey of lands west in relation to the colonies into 640 acre townships should proceed in order to facilitate their sale.[173] In 1785, the survey of the "Old Northwest" was "the largest single act of national planning" in American history.[174] Land survey was and remains an essential step for property identification and exchange in a land based capitalist economy. Land survey was an important political project to establish ownership and local property taxation.

From the classical liberal viewpoint, property protection was a form of justice.

According to Thomas G. West, in his essay, "The Economic Theory of the American Founding", in classical liberal times, elite property owners were convinced of three policies for defending property rights. These were the right to own and use property, the right to sell property and the governmental responsibility to "support sound money."[175] West also identified two ways of seeing property during the early founding era. They were first, property ownership as utility and second, property ownership as a form of justice. Property ownership as a utility regarded favorably the efficient uses of property to produce wealth. According to West this view of property dominates now. But property protections for individuals as a form of justice was also an essential belief held by property owners during classical liberal times. Modern day people seldom discuss property ownership in the context of individual justice for property owners.

Classical liberal persons with political connections, family connections or access to credit had a natural right and the economic means to acquire property and to retain it after they acquired it. Depriving a person of their property was seen as an injustice.[176] Tension during classical liberal times centered on the contest between private and government ownership of property. Few expected equality in property among all Americans because the opportunity to acquire property was different for different classes. Class property distinctions had long been a part of European culture shaped partly by feudalism. Attitudes from that period persisted, though changing, in Europe even at the time of the American Revolution. Class economic inequality in terms of the ability to acquire land wasn't as worrisome culturally as government ownership of property instead of private ownership. The modern day erosion of property ownership as a form of justice and as a protected natural right has changed present day concepts about both money and property.

The concept of property as utility and not as justice has led legislators and justices to remove some legal restraints that once protected private property and money. Property and money are less protected now as compared to the classical liberal period. For example, the Supreme Court ruling, in *Kelo v. City of New London (2004,)*[177] allowed a private neighborhood to be condemned through the city's eminent domain power to make way for a new housing development that people in government believed would increase tax revenues.[178] People living in New London were to be evicted from their old homes and a new development was to be constructed by a private company using a city-supplied investment stipend of eighty million dollars.[179] Bidding for the project wasn't open to the public and it wasn't competitive. After the ruling, the project went forward. But it was never finished and therefore it was unprofitable. The city also failed to obtain the increased taxes that were predicted for which it had advanced the stipend. The city's treasury therefore was pilfered by developers, the neighborhood was destroyed and the project failed. This example showed a cost-benefit argument that replaced a natural rights argument. What's worse, the projected profits were never realized though many people lost their homes. A neighborhood was destroyed for nothing. This emphasis of property utility over property rights wouldn't have happened in classical liberal times.

Owning shares in joint stock companies was a risky way to make money during classical liberalism but these were the enterprises that brought settlement to the English colonies.

How could a speculator make money during classical liberal times? After all, not everyone was a laborer, a farmer or craftsperson. A private investor from Europe or the U.S. could become an investor in a joint stock company, where he could obtain a share of a profit in any sort of entrepreneurial venture. The East India Company, for example, was a joint stock company founded in 1600. Or an investor could invest in a chartered company, often under a sovereign sponsored monopoly of trade inside a specific region. Some chartered companies had their own navy and army and behaved like "a state within a state". The English Royal African Company monopolized the slave trade from 1672-1698.[180]

Chart of English History:

Here's a chart of English history that will provide a context to events happening concurrently in the colonies and the United States during classical liberalism.[181, 182, 183] Until the American Revolution, of course, English politics and economics were American politics and economics. Even after the Revolution, many Americans thought of themselves in terms of having English ancestry and English traditions. And England's history was important to classical liberal period colonists and later citizens of the United States. American trading had been primarily with the English. So, this English history pertains directly to American economic and political history. It also mattered both in terms of how the events were perceived by Americans, how events set a precedent for later American political thought, and how they became the point of departure for specific reasons set out in the Declaration of Independence.

Chart of English History:

1215 Magna Carta signed by King John;

Stuart English Dynasty included James I (1603-1625)

Charles I (1625-1649), (tyrant who dismissed Parliament and persecuted Puritans);

1625-1630 Anglo Spanish War;

1627-1629 Anglo French War;

1628 The English Petition of Rights;

1642 English Civil War. **The Interregnum** (1649-1658) was the period of time where Oliver Cromwell (1599-1658) ruled England as the Puritan Protector. Richard Cromwell (1626-1712), succeeded him but only ruled for a year (1658-1659). He was replaced by the English King Charles II, ending the Interregnum.

Stuart English Dynasty included Charles II (1660-1685), and James II (1685-1688);

1689 English Glorious Revolution and the English Declaration of Right, William III and Mary II ruled (1689-1694), William III only (1694-1702), Anne (1702-1714);

Hanoverian/Windsor Dynasty

Included George I, who ruled (1714-1727) and George II, who ruled (1727-1760)

1756-1763 French and Indian War, or also known as the Seven Years War George III ruled from (1760-1820);

1812-1815, War of 1812, also known as the Anglo American War George IV (1820-1830).

Money from Europe turned the wheels of the future nation as it was founded, as it was born into independence and as it obtained more territory for expansion.

Modern historical events of huge importance that involve human agency involve ambition and money. Funding for three classical liberal political or economic ventures shows some of what entrepreneurial or government deal making was like in classical liberal times. All three ventures had one foot in America and the other in England or in Europe. Global money circulation can be seen in all three ventures. The timeline in the previous section shows the political context of early colonial development.

The first historical venture was an economic one, the Massachusetts Bay Colony founding in 1630. This venture shows how private funding accomplished so much in classical liberal times. But the funding was a long term investment in a project of uncertain outcome. The second venture was war, the American Revolution, a political venture that required economic funds. A third venture, the Louisiana Purchase, was the political acquisition of territory through money exchanged by treaty. Both the American Revolution and the Louisiana Purchase required public funding that was generated initially through European bank loans that were paid off afterwards.

Joint stock companies had two sides, according to materials sourced from the Mayflower founding[184] which happened in 1620, ten years earlier than the Massachusetts Bay Company's colonization effort in America in 1630. According to the Mayflower document, the first half of the joint stock gamble was sponsored by "the Adventurers", and the second half by "the Planters". Two vessels were bought for the Mayflower venture. It was planned to last only seven years after which time the gains would be split and the partnership ended.[185] The later Massachusetts Bay Company venture included several vessels including, *Arabella*, in 1630. It was different from most other joint stock company ventures because it had greater financial and social advantages.

It was sponsored by organized Puritans that came over from the middle classes rather than the poorest classes, in family groups with a power hierarchy through faith and church leadership. They were escaping from Charles I's persecution of Puritans just before the English Civil War. Between 1629 and 1640, eighty thousand Puritans left England and twenty one thousand of them came to Massachusetts.[186] Three quarters of them paid their own passage. At a time in history when the average husbandman could only make twenty pounds per year and save about four pounds out of expenses, the fare was between fifty and eighty pounds for a family of six to ship to America. Puritans could afford to pay.

Once the colony was established, it took years to bring any profit and the investors of the Massachusetts Bay Company eventually sold their shares to the colonists. Some of the investors joined the expedition later during the transfer of shares. A land grant to the Massachusetts Bay Company was issued by English King James I, but replaced by Charles I, in 1629, by a Royal Charter. This Royal Charter was revoked in 1684. English political squabbling, including the English Civil War and after events involving the Anglican Church, caused political tension in the Colony until political issues were resolved by the English Glorious Revolution in which Parliament gained more power over a new King and the Anglican Church prevailed as the English state religion. Meanwhile, the Puritans who had moved to America and bought their Massachusetts Bay Company shares had more independence from the English King, just as they desired.

England won the contest among European powers to settle North America in part because private funding for colonization was less affected by European warfare contests. The Puritan migration shows how religious persecution inspired by the Protestant Reformation continued creating trouble in England. Unlike the American strategy of separating church and state, England combined politics and religion by adopting the National Anglican Church. Massachusetts Bay Colony also shows the lengths to which people will go to practice their own beliefs inside a like-minded religious community. In 1691, King William III wrote a new colony charter and unified several small communities including Massachusetts Bay, Martha's Vineyard, Plymouth, Nova Scotia, Nantucket, Maine, and New Brunswick. The new community was called the Province of Massachusetts Bay. The charter also extended voting rights outside the Puritan religion.[187] This separation offered a further hindrance to the domination of religion in political matters.

The second economic investment to consider is the American Revolution. Accomplishing a victory in the American Revolution was expensive and funding the war seemed nearly impossible to achieve at the time. There wasn't money to feed the army nor to pay for armaments nor uniforms nor equipment nor wages. As a colony, America didn't have her own army or navy. England had the most powerful navy in the world at that time and an experienced military. Motivating people to fight a war to sever the American colonies from the English parliamentary monarchy wasn't easy. The war wasn't universally supported by everyone in America. Violence between those loyal to England and the Revolutionaries was a fight over both politics and land ownership. Merchants in arms sales could gain but other merchants who exported primarily to European nations would lose money. And the Revolutionary War was complicated by other European powers that didn't stay out of it. But their involvement mostly helped the colonists to win.

Prussians, the French and Spanish supported the American liberty cause, and Britain, which had allied with German troops during the Seven Years War (from 1754-1763, also called the French and Indian War) employed German troops again in the Revolutionary War. Americans called these soldiers mercenaries, but lured them into joining the American forces whenever they could. The fledgling American government, the Constitutional Congress, in 1775, printed two hundred forty two million Continentals to serve as wartime currency but it wasn't backed by gold or silver specie because the entire colonies had only twelve million in gold specie.[188]

Because the Continental wasn't backed by specie it deflated in real purchasing value almost immediately. Self-sufficient farmers were less harmed at first by the bad currency but the deflation undermined wages for the army, the group most harmed under the Continental currency scheme. The first issue of Continentals was followed by the second issue of Continentals unbacked by specie which also became almost worthless in a short time. Some states began to issue their own currency. These various debts from many sources encouraged squabbles among states after the Revolutionary War.

A contributing cause of the Revolution before it happened had been the "Intolerable Acts". These Parliamentary Acts were in favor of English interests at the expense of American ones. After the French and Indian War, England had begun to restrict westward expansion, under the Quebec Act, with an eye toward developing the fur trade for England.[189] But colonists had begun to see their interests as separate from England's. The Revolutionary War was fought in part to support American interests as distinct from English ones and to allow westward American expansion to continue.

After France lost to England in the French and Indian War (1754-1763, the Seven Years War), France harbored a grudge. In 1776, France started loaning money and war supplies to Americans to help them keep on fighting toward a victory against England. Later, high sovereign debt in France, in part from helping the Americans, contributed to the French Revolution in 1789. Banks in Amsterdam and Paris also loaned money to finance the Revolutionary War. Eventually, according to one source, the U.S. Revolutionary War cost the United States sixty six million in precious metal specie.[190] Alexander Hamilton, as mentioned, created the First Bank of the United States to consolidate the federal and state debt and to create a payment plan. The whiskey tax and tariffs on imports paid down the debt.

Observations of the Revolutionary War show that it was international in terms of national powers and national interests. Also, England's aggressive navy had created competitive animosity with other European powers who joined America's revolution in order to thwart a rival nation. Funding for the war was also international. The newly assembled nation couldn't fund her military needs and relied on Europe's banks and treasuries for monetary resources. After the Revolution, Americans wanted to push westward. The Louisiana Purchase made Western expansion possible. It is the third financial deal to consider under classical liberalism.

The Louisiana Purchase happened under Thomas Jefferson's presidential administration. He was surprised by the opportunity to buy the huge land acquisition from France, which nearly doubled the size of the United States, because at the time he was offered the large territory, he was bidding through his diplomatic emissaries only to obtain a smaller property, the Port of New Orleans or the perhaps the city of New Orleans. Jefferson had been content when New Orleans was a Spanish possession. He had a treaty with Spain that allowed him to use the port to export American goods like tobacco and cotton. He was alarmed when Spain gave it back into French possession under Napoleon's rule. A large amount of American exports left out of the New Orleans' port and Jefferson wanted to keep the negotiated right to store and ship American goods out of New Orleans. That portage right was denied shortly after the territory was reacquired by France, which alarmed American exporters.[191, 192]

Napoleon, who knew that Britain would harass French interests if France combined American territorial expansion with European territorial expansion surprised Jefferson by offering the entire portion for fifteen million dollars. Congress approved the deal quickly, in 1803. Jefferson paid three million in gold from the U.S. Treasury as a down payment, and borrowed the balance from two banks: Francis Baring and Company of London, and Hope Company of Amsterdam.[193] Jefferson issued bonds and monetized the debt by inflating American currency.

People who bought American bonds were paid their bonds in currency that had less real buying power. Wealth generation in the early period of nationhood was still tied to land expansion. Land speculation, especially during westward expansion, was an opportunity to get more cash when property appreciated in value. The Louisiana Purchase generated wealth in the American economy because it provided more land for westward expansion. Different regions of the new United States made money producing different exports. In order to make money there had to be a surplus amount of something that could be sold. People in the northeast could make money in fishing and shipping exports, and after the American Revolution in clock-making, gunsmithing, and textile milling. The middle of the nation had the fur trade and the South, agricultural exports of cotton and tobacco, indigo and rice. Economic expansion because of industry and better transportation would later change the nation's economy. But for the classical liberal period wealth was made in land exploration and sale and whatever surplus production could fetch in local or international markets.[194, 195, 196]

After land expansion into new territories, there was land speculation.

Later, after new lands were exhausted, ongoing investments in land speculation continued and land titles changed hands. After the early years of settlement, after the period of land grants provided by sovereign European powers to incentivize discovery, after second son large land purchases, sometimes through joint stock companies, came nationhood. And under nationhood, the U.S. could annex new states, an ongoing process after the Louisiana Purchase. When a new state was brought into the Union it would give some of its territory to the federal government. The federal government would sell those lands to generate revenue. If a land speculator had money or could obtain credit, he would buy lands from the U.S. federal government and resell them to immigrants at a higher price than the government charged. This process pushed up the value of land.

During periods of easy credit, speculators could sell a lot of land deeds. But these deeds weren't paid for; they were only backed by debt. When credit tightened, some debtors defaulted. Then several land ventures would collapse and some speculators would end up in debtor's prison. Insurance sales could also make money during classical liberal times by insuring company ventures and banks. The failure of the Ohio Life Insurance Company helped cause The Panic of 1857. In that case, insurance coverage exceeded the expected loss pay out for agricultural products when agricultural exports to Europe declined after the Crimean War.[197]

The First Bank of the United States and the Second Bank of the United States both had limited eras of operation because different groups wanted banks to serve different purposes.

Two federally sponsored banks existed during classical liberalism: the First Bank of the United States (1791-1811), mentioned earlier, and the Second Bank of the United States (1817-1836). The First Bank of the United States was founded by Congress during the administration of George Washington at the urging of Alexander Hamilton, as mentioned in the prologue. Understanding the controversy that attended the founding of this bank is important to understanding other bank controversies over American history including the one that developed around the Second Bank of the United States, founded during the administration of James Madison and controversially undermined during the administration of Andrew Jackson. The key is to realize that banks were used for different purposes by different economic groups. Both banks had a twenty year charter and neither bank's charter was renewed after the first twenty years.

Bank controversies involve factions of interests that differ. Listening to one side in a bank controversy tends to show only that one point of view—a solidly defensible case in someone's interest—while the other side's interests are made to seem less important or even immoral. Banking serves a social purpose and a variety of individual interests because of the social and individual utility of money in all kinds of economic transactions. Money has served various different goals, even during the classical liberal period when Adam Smith and David Ricardo lived. Adam Smith wanted more specialized labor in order to increase efficiency in production and produce more capital for investments that would create more jobs and reduce unemployment and poverty. Here, money was used to create jobs. And Ricardo saw investments in the stock market as a challenging and worthwhile way to increase capital by undertaking a series of educated investment risks with other financial associates. Investing harnessed the power of money to transform fleeting opportunity into realizable gains that could be invested again.

Money also has existed as a store of value and a way of comparing values between commodities. Capital in the form of money can be used by a farmer to buy his seed for example or in real estate to buy a property in the hopes that its value will increase or by a corporation striving to make a profit under limited liability where only a person's shares in a company are at stake. Money can be collected as a tax on a person's property, or can be utilized to enable the purchase of a property in order to build a house or a factory. Persons who use money come from every walk of life and a bank acts as the institutional repository for people's money intentions and uses, or "the productive stream". Solvency, for this reason is a social good. But care for solvency sometimes can rub investors the wrong way when they want to harness as much money as possible to leverage an opportunity.

If you look at the historical controversy between the uses of the First Bank of the United States and the Second Bank of the United States, there were several discordant interests. During classical liberalism there were state banks and federal banks. There were conflicts of interest about how to utilize the bank between European owners of federal bank shares and American owners of state bank shares. There were also conflicts of interest regarding how much financial risk the bank should engage in. Investment interests wanted more risk and commercial interests wanted less risk. There were also competitions between state banks and federal banks for customers; each group wanted more customers. There was a class conflict between wealthy investors that wanted to conduct risk mostly in land speculation and agricultural interests that wanted to cultivate profits mostly by working and developing the land. Each group engaged in a different lifestyle in a social hierarchy where they interacted with each other rarely and on unequal terms.

The First Bank of the United States was founded to serve eventually, a variety of interests, but it began in connection with the Funding Act of 1790, in order to exchange federal securities for Revolutionary War debts that were held in different amounts by the thirteen states. These state incurred debts, in the amount of twenty one and a half million dollars, according to one source, were consolidated with federal debt and administered thereafter by the federal government.[198] Consolidating this debt, as mentioned in the Prelude, was useful as an essential financial-housekeeping function of the federal government after the U.S. gained independence from England.[199]

The Second Bank of the United States was founded to pay the debt for the War of 1812; again, an essential financial housekeeping function of the federal government. A source of controversy regarding the federal banks happened because the interests of state banks seemed in conflict with federal banks when the federal banks received part of their capitalization by the federal government. To state bankers this seemed like an unfair advantage. Both federal banks also kept a leash on state banks by holding their bank notes on account. The First Bank of the United States would accept state bank notes and hold them. And when the First Bank of the United States wanted to slow down state bank credit issuance it would present state bank notes to state banks for payment in gold. This allowed the federal bank to have an effect on the amount of state bank notes in circulation.[200]

Too many notes in circulation could cause inflation. Federal banks were owned in part by foreign investors and this created another conflict between U.S. domestic state bank investors and European federal bank investors. For example, twenty per cent of the Second Bank of the United States was owned by European investors.[201] Much later in history, during the Great Depression, FDR's regulation of banking, under the Banking Act of 1933, helped to sort out these disparate interests by separating commercial banking and investment banking and by creating the FDIC (Federal Deposit Insurance Company) to insure commercial bank deposits. Bank insurance protected "the everyman's" contribution to the productive stream of bank savings deposits, for example people's retirement savings or wages.

Controversy involving the First Bank of the United States started with the topic of congressional authority to create a bank as an alternative to direct issuance of money under Article I, Section 8: "The Congress shall have Power To lay and collect Taxes, Duties, Imposts and Excises, to pay the Debts and provide for the common Defense and general welfare of the United States; but all Duties, Imposts and Excises shall be uniform throughout the United States; To borrow money on the credit of the United States…To coin Money, regulate the Value thereof, and of foreign Coin, and fix the Standard of Weights and Measures; To provide for the Punishment of counterfeiting the Securities and current Coin of the United States;" and in Section 10: "No State shall enter into any Treaty, Alliance, or Confederation; grant Letters of Marque and Reprisal; coin Money; emit Bills of Credit; make any Thing but gold and silver Coin a Tender in Payment of Debts; pass any Bill of Attainer, ex post facto Law, or Law impairing the Obligation of Contracts, or grant any Title of Nobility."

Even today, protestors over the creation of the First Bank of the United States have claimed that the Congress had no power to establish a federal bank because of Article 8 providing that Congress should coin money directly, rather than delegate the responsibility. Another protest against founding the First Bank of the United States has argued that a fiat currency without a metal backing can't be legal tender in state financial dealings because of Article 10. The necessary and proper clause was controversially stretched to establish the First Bank of the United States. But Alexander Hamilton believed in "implied powers." And the issue of fiat currency without a metal exchange guarantee happened variously during American history, for instance when Greenbacks were issued by Abraham Lincoln to pay for the Civil War.

Controversy under the Andrew Jackson administration regarding renewal of the Second Bank of the United States charter was fueled by suspicion regarding foreign owners of the bank and class conflict between farmers and investors, and between state banks and federal banks.[202] These controversies show how banks play a varied role in financial exchanges that are needed by different groups in the economy, and they also show that people's financial interests may conflict over the various possible uses of money. Balancing interests among different groups, as shown in this discussion, can be an important part of bank regulation. Insufficient balancing of diverse interests motivated the end of the First and Second Bank of the United States' charters.

Betting on the future sometimes leads to financial failure both during classical liberalism and today.

Another look at classical liberal financial dealings leads to insurance instruments of 1857 that caused financial losses similar to derivative engineered losses of 2007-2008. An insurance policy is different from a derivative investment because it only protects against downside loss without rewarding for an upside gain. But both offer avenues of speculation against undesirable future outcomes and both can create losses when the scope of change is larger than expected. Modern derivatives rely on securitization, which was only invented in the U.S. during the twentieth century starting with veteran's mortgage securities. Securitization turns an asset like a mortgage from a fixed physical asset on a payment plan in a bank to an asset that can be bought as an investment in a financial firm. Derivatives are bets on those securities investments which require a counter-party buyer and usually a financial institute as seller. They are rated by a ratings agency and priced according to risk.

The Ohio Insurance Company failed in 1857 when it couldn't cover financial losses in agricultural products because the demand for American agricultural exports declined. Likewise, in the sub-prime mortgage market of 2007-08, the derivative bets on securitized assets exceeded demand for those products when they were shown to be high risk instead of low risk, causing the market to collapse and those investments to lose value. Several largest financial firms would have failed except for government loans, and many smaller banks closed down. Derivatives had declined rapidly in value after the ratings were proven to be faulty.

Classical liberal money losses sometimes happened because of bank failures, or a change in money's value.

Several ways that people lost money during the classical liberal period included bank runs and panics, inflation and speculative market collapses. People who had money in the bank lost it all if the bank failed, because of no FDIC insurance for commercial accounts before the Banking Act of 1933. Even in the classical liberal period, governments around the world borrowed from banks in other countries. So, international banking existed even during classical liberal times. But classical liberal international banking differed from modern international banking for several reasons.

Modern-day deregulation combined with computer technologies that speed international transfers of money and assets is part of what distinguishes international banking then and now. During the period of classical liberalism, the politics of Europe could influence banking in the U.S. especially when it was a new nation. Bank failures in the U.S. were sometimes due to a sudden European restriction of credit to America such as happened in 1837, under the Bank of England. A need to pay for U.S. war debt such as the War of 1812 led to monetization of the debt through printing extra dollars such that war bonds were paid to American citizens in inflated, or devalued currency (money loses its value if it is printed and circulated in excess of economic productivity). Overspeculation in Western land expansions under the Monroe Doctrine also caused bank failures. Too much debt on paper that wasn't backed by real assets expanded to displace real asset transactions and unbalanced bank accounts with promises instead of capital.

Banks in the classical liberal period used fractional lending and lent out more money than they kept in gold and silver reserves. This has been customary for centuries, ever since double entry bookkeeping changed the way people think about how to put money to work in an economy. But when money in circulation exceeded actual gold or silver reserves, banks could become insolvent if there was a run and the bank ran out of gold or silver to exchange for paper. A run could be triggered by a European policy change affecting credit or a single bank failure that would spread. Sometimes a commodity price decrease could cause a run on banks. Twenty first century central bank policy has been shaped by historical bank runs. Moving money to wherever a run is happening in today's international banking system can help to defend the large central bank system. Back in the classical liberal period, bank runs could destroy a bank because it wasn't possible to transfer money quickly from a solvent bank to an insolvent one. Restriction of gold or silver specie could also cause a panic as it did in 1857 under President Jackson's executive order known as the Specie Circular. The Specie Circular was a requirement that people pay for land purchases with coin. It was meant to reduce land speculation and land price inflation. There were several financial panics during classical liberalism: The Panic of 1772, The Panic of 1785, The Panic of 1792, The Panic of 1819, The Panic of 1837, The Panic of 1857.

Although the First Bank of the U.S. was established in 1791, its charter wasn't renewed in 1811. It wasn't a Central Bank exactly like the Federal Reserve because it didn't control or regulate other banks though it did cooperate with the Treasurer, Alexander Hamilton, during a few crises from the bank's early years. It was "the government's bank", capitalized with federal funding of two million dollars with an additional eight million from private investors. It was larger than the three other major American banks together, but had only a twenty year charter.[203] The First Bank of the United States circulated currency in excess of economic productivity in order to monetize the Louisiana Purchase.

The Second Bank of the U.S. was chartered in 1816 but its charter wasn't renewed after twenty years either. Both of these banks were controversial, for the reasons mentioned. Madison and Jefferson believed that it wasn't constitutional to create them. After political negotiation, Washington allowed the 1st BUS to be created to help pay the Revolutionary War debt that was owed both by states and the federal government to European governments and banks. Financial pressures led American Presidents by expediency, rather than according to constitutional principle, toward the creation of the First and Second Bank of the United States.

Inflation of the dollar beyond economic productivity hurt savers and made the economy weaker, but it offered an advantage. It helped to fund entrepreneurial ventures and Westward land expansion by paying off earlier debt more cheaply with value deflated currency. Under a growing economy, people's employment opportunities were expanding, and production efficiency tended to increase. Even though early America had a cyclic boom and bust personality, the U.S. recovered quickly from economic losses. More people, working in more businesses, producing more in a growing market led to economic vitality. But debtors who couldn't pay went to debtor's prison. Congress made such prisons illegal in 1833. Famous financiers, such as William Morris, were arrested and placed into debtor's prison. Today, prisons set aside specifically for debt are gone. But people can still be imprisoned for failure to pay court assigned fees even when they are indigent.

"The past is never dead. It's not even past." –William Faulkner[204]

Looking back at classical liberal America can distort our perceptions like looking through the wrong end of a telescope. Every part of that history is over and "safe". It seems small, less colorful than today, sorted into historical categories and contexts. But what happened then is connected to what happened later and to what is happening now. Happenings were risky at the time, vibrant, tense with competing ideas about government and individual power, people's striving and readiness to grab a better future but not for everyone's gain. Everyone did gain freedom to worship under separation of church and state. And people had enough freedom to prosper by working but only if a person wasn't an indentured servant—working whites in bondage to a contract—or a slave or a woman. Native Americans were outside legal protections and subjected to political genocide. Native Americans and members of the underclass had little autonomy and no vote.

Americans of any class had access to fishing, hunting, and forests to harvest as common property and to subsidize their living expenses. Constant growth by land acquisition and population meant expanding opportunities in an expanding economy. Along with the Louisiana Purchase in 1803, there were land acquisitions through treaties with England, Spain, Mexico and Texas in 1818, 1819, 1839, 1845, 1846, 1848, and 1853. Literacy during the classical liberal period was highest among Puritans in the North, 80% for men and 50% for women and lowest in the South, 50% for men, and 25% for women.[205] Many of the classical liberal population were not aware of the ideas that influenced and motivated the Founders. People were separated by where they lived, by their economic circumstances, their opportunities and their education. Before the Civil War that started in 1861, the United States had already acquired the territory of the lower 48 states and money making through land acquisition was ending. The expansion of rail had begun and spread more in the North but some rail was also in the South. This rail gained greater strategic importance during the Civil War.

The classical liberal period began in the Age of Revolutions, a time of political upheaval inside nations, but also during sea contests for sea trading superiority between nations, and European land wars for territorial dominance. There were contests to subdue or drive away Native peoples occupying their own lands in colonial territories and between European would-be colonizers. Conflicts at this time were mostly territorial, punctuating political and economic change based on land acquisition in the classical liberal period. Some political conflicts were regarding taxation.

Numerous conflicts with Native Americans included at least twenty one examples of battle campaigns in North America, according to one source, as listed before the Civil War: 1622-1644 Powhatan Wars, between Jamestown colonists and Powhatan Indians, 1637 Pequot War, in the Connecticut River Valley, Pequot Indians fought Puritans, 1675-1676, King Phillip's War, New England Indians pushed back against European land expansion onto their territories, 1676 Bacon's Rebellion, Nathaniel Bacon organized settlers against local Native Americans, 1689-1697 King William's War, allied French and Native American forces attacked British forces in New York, New Hampshire and Maine, 1702-1713, Queen Anne's War, British soldiers won Acadia from allied French and Native American forces, 1711-1713, Tuscarora War, North Carolina conflict between settlers and Native Americans, 1715-1716, Yamasee War, South Carolina conflict with Native Americans, 1744-1748, King George's War, Britain battled Spanish, French and Native American forces "from French Canada to the Caribbean", 1754-1763, The French and Indian War (also known as the Seven Years War), British captured Quebec and France's American colonies, 1760-1762, Cherokee Uprising, British fighting Native Americans in Tennesee, Virginia, and the Carolinas, 1763-1766, Pontiac's War, several Native American tribes tried to expel the British from former French Canadian lands, 1763-1764, Paxton Boys Uprising, Conestoga Indians attacked by settlers, 1774 Lord Dunmore's War, expansion into the Appalachian mountains caused violence between Native Americans and Virginia settlers, 1790-1812, Ohio Valley Campaigns, U.S. forces fought Native American tribes, 1817-1818, First Seminole War, runaway slaves were recaptured from Native American communities, 1832, Black Hawk War, state militia and federal army attacked five Native American tribes, 1835-1842, Second Seminole War, refusal of Seminole tribe to relocate, 1838-1839, Trail of Tears, four thousand Cherokee deaths during relocation to Oklahoma territory, 1855-1858, Third Seminole War, relocation out of Florida, 1860-1900 Plains and Western Indian Wars, U.S. settlers and U.S. army fought Native Americans for their land.[206]

The great number of violent clashes and conflicts tends to be overlooked in modern times. Native Americans survived not just an armed invasion but also a germ invasion when new Europeans germs were first encountered by them. Native Americans have struggled to tell about their experiences. The National Museum of the Native American opened in Washington D.C. in 2004 and shows Native American artifacts as precious objects that reflect cultures of the past[207] that still influence Native American cultures of today. The 2010 U.S. Census report counted 2.9 million Native Americans in the United States.[208]

Struggle in the colonies regarding territorial administration or taxation, according to one source, included: 1677-1679, Culpepper's Rebellion, where Carolina settlers imprisoned the governor and replaced the legislature, 1689-1691, Leisler's Rebellion, Jacob Leisler, the militia grabbed the governor's office and invaded French Canada, 1765-1766, Stamp Act Revolt, England's revenue building strategy was resisted by Americans, 1768-1771, Regulator War, North

Carolina settlers fought local bureaucracy, 1773, Boston Tea Party, a demonstration against direct shipping of tea to America by the British East India Company under an exemption for the Navigation Acts that restricted direct tea traffic by colonists, and undercut American tea smugglers, and also against the Tea Act of 1773, 1775-1783, The American Revolution, a war fought for independence that first requested repeal of thirteen "Intolerable Acts" enacted without colonial Parliamentary representation, 1786-1787, Shay's rebellion, Massachusetts march against harsh economic measures during an economic downturn, 1794 Whiskey Rebellion, Pennsylvanian protest against the Whiskey Tax enacted by Congress to help pay for the American Revolutionary debt, 1839-1846, Anti-Rent War, a protest in New York against an unfair Dutch land "incomplete sale" system that set up feudal based obligations for land use, under land ownership voting requirements that excluded most people, 1842, Dorr Rebellion, clashes because of land ownership voting requirement.[209] Some of these revolts changed politics but with attending losses and violence. Americans were fighting for political self-determination that decided their political obligations and economic opportunities.

Consequences that have accrued from these battles were extensive. Some groups won a greater chance at opportunity and some groups were harmed. Native Americans lost their land rights and many were killed in the intersection of European and Native cultures, some from battles and others from disease. North American tribal descendants had to survive hardships that scarred their cultures and destroyed parts of them. As Native American lifestyle has adapted, many tribes have lost their languages. According to the 2010 Census, only 29% of Native Americans speak a language other than English at home.[210] European powers competed with each other in the struggle for American territories only to lose those territories in the American Revolution and the end of colonialism. Long distance bureaucracy proved unable to cope with new transplants striving for independence. The aggression between European powers over territory during colonial contests continued in Europe into the First and Second World Wars. Economic and political nationalism flourished within the nation state system, making war a political option.

Classical liberalism embodied the fertile intersection of the ancient classical world and early modern periods in human history. The tension between the Catholic Church and the Scientific Revolution led to the Protestant Reformation. And the nation state system that tolerated disparate forms of government provided an opportunity for classical liberal experiments in governance and economy. Colonialism, invention, mercantilism, and nation state competition were expansionary forces. Winners were people who could acquire property and who could gamble and win to take advantage of new opportunities. Losers were the exploited people who lacked property and also lacked education and the chance to improve their lives in order to gain new opportunity. Classical liberalism established an ideology that put liberty at the apex of political values and because of it, respect for personal freedom grew within the Western culture set of social values.

Freedom helped technologies to develop and created a cultural dividend, from the cotton gin to trains and rail to the telegraph. Technologies continued to expand opportunities as a new industrial economy took shape. Banking was international but regulated by nations. It was hampered by the limitations of communications before the Digital Age. The law during classical liberal times was more respectful of rhetoric but an earlier tradition that respected language based logic gave way during the modern liberal period to pragmatic empiricism. Hegelian dialectical methods came to replace Greek dialectic methods of reasoning (see the appendix for a clear distinction). Violence in war changed property ownership among competitors and altered the character of North American culture. As land expansion ended, the Industrial Machine Age began and classical liberalism changed its spots by changing its economy from economic liberalism to mixed economy.

Fast Car Analysis for Classical Liberalism

Opportunity is what connects the politic and economy; political policies affect people's opportunities.

Thomas Hobbes recognized that sovereigns weren't all-powerful and that different people could want different outcomes in their life. These early insights brought greater rationalism to the politic.

John Locke changed philosophy and politics. He recognized that people could use their ordinary faculty of reason to understand the politic and talk with others about it. He didn't think that only certain classes could grapple successfully with political issues. He also expanded the Roman idea of sovereignty from Roman law to the idea of personal sovereignty. This pushed the recognition of martial power in society that could rebel against improper government toward Puritan ideas regarding religious conscience which could recognize government immorality and call for reform. Reforms can make peaceful transitions possible.

Economic and political disparity was part of everyday life before and during the classical liberal era.

The Protestant Reformation and respect for people's inner consciences brought liberty protections into the American political system. People's respect for the inner life motivated tolerance.

The Anglican Church was the Church of England. Puritans had escaped England in order to practice their religion without government penalties. Conflict between the English Anglican Church and other Protestant churches in the colonies led Thomas Jefferson to call for **separation between church and state**. The American Revolution led Americans to abolish Anglican churches and reclassify them as Episcopalian.

Liberty was concerned not only with freedom from coercion but also with tolerance and refraining from license; people were expected to avoid causing harm to others. If harm was caused, a judgement for restitution to repair the harm might follow. But different social classes experienced different levels of protection from harm. Some were not protected such as slaves and indentured servants and women. Native Americans were outside of legal protections.

The American **Constitution** was written to prevent power abuses and governmental oppression but also to encourage economic and political freedom by putting people's political and economic welfare under common legal protections based on natural rights. Natural rights have been recognized in the U.S. since colonial times.

Mercantilism and colonialism happened during the classical liberal period; global shipping connected ports around the world; merchant ships carried goods from port to port; navies protected merchant ships. Tariffs were enacted to protect vested interests at home. International loans were part of early American history to fund the Revolutionary War and the Louisiana Purchase.

Fractional lending was an accepted part of classical liberalism and it had been practiced for centuries of time. Bank overreach and government debt can both lead to economic recessions or regime failures.

Judicial review has been an accepted power of the Supreme Court since colonial times. Landmark judicial rulings create judicial precedents that guide future rulings.

According to J.S. Mill, **the principle of reciprocal demand** states that gains from trade between trading partners will be unequal; they will be influenced by reciprocal demand.

The social co-evolution of finance through the Italian innovation of double entry bookkeeping and Ancient World rationalism and humanism gave birth to liberalism and capitalism which ended feudalism. The **partnership of liberalism and capitalism** changed the outcome of combining classical rationalism and humanism in Renaissance Europe as compared with the Ancient World. It may be what accounts for the dynamic partnership between the politic and economy in the present-day.

Classical Liberalism Appendix

The historical development of the rule of law has happened repeatedly in various societies after they develop the technology of writing.

People seem to have an innate sense of fairness, something that they acquire for at least two reasons. First, all people even very young children, have a sense of property— a notion that some things belong to them. Their right to exist within the span of a mortal life, to have privacy, a safe space to occupy and the right to protect themselves is related to ideas about property of self, objects, and place. This is probably a necessary trait with a biologic basis. The second reason that people have a sense of fairness may be based on the fact that harms can cause suffering and everyone is vulnerable to suffering.

Communities with writing usually develop a guideline for preventing harms in the community. This is the written rule of law. The rule of law is nourished by people's sense of fairness and justice and their willingness to write rules down to protect people. The rule of law is moral. Some have put the rule of law into consideration with ideas about human dignity, mortal necessity and political reciprocity. Rule of law helps societies to prosper because it makes the law apply equally to all persons regardless of their social status. It has always opposed the political or economic consolidation of power based on arbitrary force. It makes the law supreme over all people, but it remains true to the community by having characteristics that resist corruption.

Those characteristics include several. One characteristic is that of being written down so that the rule of law doesn't become arbitrary. And legal precedent held in a public record nests the rule of law inside a set of community values. As a recorded tool of civilization, the rule of law is available for anyone to know and understand. By being a public record, persons won't accidentally transgress against the law or become an excluded group not protected by the law. The rule of law relies on simplicity so that the rule of law can be known after it is published. To be guilty should require a guilty mind. The multiplication of laws during the neoliberal period has contradicted the goal of having a limited number of legal norms that can be comprehended by everyone. Some believe that neoliberal laws are too numerous and that staying within the law has now become impossible. To the extent that there are too many laws to know and enforce equally, the rule of law can't be utilized under neoliberalism to maintain civility.

Another characteristic of the rule of law is that everyone is subject to the rules that it outlines no matter what their social position. As will be seen in the following chapter on modern liberalism, the influence of money in civil litigation provided a way for the wealthy to obtain or escape from damage awards without facing proceedings for harms in a criminal court. But a poorer person often couldn't afford civil litigation. This has led to imbalances of justice. Obtaining justice under modern liberalism became ever more expensive. Under neoliberalism the option to seek justice in court has been further curtailed by the high costs and terrible complexity of litigation. And corporate personhood has provided a timeless opportunity for corporations to appeal court decisions with which they disagree. Money, plus grossly unequal power positions, plus growing legal complexity plus inconsistent methods of court interpretation of law and inconsistent executive enforcement of law have made social oversight by rule of law hard for many Americans to obtain at present. This interruption of rule of law endangers civility in the United States.

The rule of law comes before liberty law. Liberty law came about when the U.S. Constitution with its Bill of Rights was adopted in 1789 and 1791. Natural rights are to be respected in the U.S. along with the rule of law. The rule of law and liberty law stand on a foundation of humanism that recognizes that people have an innate inalienable value and that both the individual and society should be protected from harms. A respect for individual freedom without causing harm to others is part of the liberty concept that grew strong during classical liberalism. The rule of law has always been an inclusive promise to protect all people rather than an exclusive deal that is made to protect only those with greater political or economic power. It is an ancient-world social technology that is completely needed in the present-day.

When a nation claims to be a rule of law nation, what it claims is that all of its laws are enforced equally for all persons and are published fairly and openly in an understandable manner and that they are adjudicated fairly as well. A disruption in any part of this set of expectations can lead to a breakdown of social trust and cooperation. A breakdown in the rule of law doesn't bode well for maintaining order and it can also lead to financial losses that undermine a healthy economy. In the U.S., as set out in the U.S. Constitution, Congress drafts laws which are adjudicated by an independent and impartial judiciary and enforced by the federal, state and municipal police forces. The Executive, Congress and Justice departments are independent bodies with limited power respectively to enforce, write and to maintain the fidelity of law toward society's best interests for peace and justice. According to some, recent political events since passage of the PATRIOT Act have exceeded both constitutional and rule of law boundaries. No authority or power can authentically justify ignoring the rule of law. Rule of law remains an essential social ingredient that makes civilization possible.

(Appendix endnote sources listed after Classical Liberalism Endnotes)

Ways of thinking: comparing rhetoric vs. empiricism and Greek dialectic vs. Hegelian dialectic.

People living at different times in different cultures have always needed to examine each possible choice to determine what choice is best. Rhetoric is a way to do this. Rhetoric is "the realm in which things may always be otherwise, the realm in which belief stands open to change"[1] Rhetoric doesn't determine a single doctrine or fixed opinion. Instead, a topic is explored by asking, for example, three kinds of questions: "What is the case?", "How should we judge?", and "What should we do?"[2] Three measures can be taken to help evaluate the questions: "Is it ethical? (Does it cause harm?), "Is it aesthetically pleasing?" (Is it beautiful?), "Is it practical?" (Does it work and what are its advantages and disadvantages?).[3] Regarding the kinds of choices that might be considered there are "policy issues" about the future, "definitional issues" about the present and "evaluative issues" about the past.[4]

During the Middle Ages the idea of "One Church, One Doctrine" contributed to violent clashes between church factions. When liberalism brought humanism and rationalism into religious discussions the Protestant Reformation became inevitable. But the Greek dialectic was never about choosing one doctrine. Instead it was a process of elimination through discursive argument to reach conclusions about what policy would be best. Or rhetoric could be how to understand a present day problem through a variety of descriptions that could be examined by several people until the most truthful description would be decided upon. Or rhetoric might be how to understand a past event based on a variety of descriptions about circumstances until a clearly better description could be proved to be the best one. Rhetoric can still be a way to examine arguments in order to consider a variety of viewpoints and arrive at a clearer understanding based on the freedom to explore whatever makes the most sense. Rhetoric isn't about expertise. Instead it is a willingness to explore and make a reasoned determination that is contingent on the available information. That determination can change if a better reasoned argument comes along later. Rhetoric isn't dogma. But it can rely on persuasion through sympathy, patriotism, a person's character or logic.

The dialectic is "the art or practice of logical discussion as employed in investigating the truth of a theory or opinion."[5] Dialectic is the comparison of at least two reasoned arguments to determine which is best by supporting one position and as compared with an alternative one. The Greek dialectic was practiced by Plato (428-347 BC) and Socrates (470-399 BC). Socrates and Plato were famous for winning contests of argument against an opponent by discovering a flaw in their opponent's reasoning. But the Greek way of conducting dialectic in order to throw out an inferior argument has changed during modernity. The Hegelian dialectic can be employed instead of the Greek dialectic and the goal of the Hegelian dialectic is different. It comes from Georg Hegel (1770-1831) and begins with a thesis, then an antithesis and finally a synthesis of argument. It uses a spiral of sequential arguments in order to relate to a sequence of viewpoints without picking one that is better than another. Hegel thought the spiral of argument would bring a person closer to infinite Godlike understanding. But Hegel wasn't using his dialectic to decide everyday questions of public policy. He was striving for a spiritual instead of a practical understanding.

Many have found Hegel's dialectic to be a pointless exploration without a practical end. But Hegelian discussion has been commonplace when media presents multiple points of view without choosing sides in a controversy. When the 2008 financial collapse happened, Hegelian dialectic arguments in the press would present possible explanations but fail to describe policy failures that had caused harm to the public. Since the politic is about who gets what, the Greek dialectic would be more advantageous when judging the effectiveness of a public policy like financial deregulation, for example. The Greek dialectic would be capable of describing the goals of neoliberal regulatory reform and then following through with an evaluation of policy effectiveness and a description of unintended harms. Finally, under Greek dialectic methods a route to policy improvement could be charted. But the Hegelian dialectic would fail to offer any practical determinations at all. Infotainment employs something like the Hegelian dialectic, flooding the mind with entertaining alternative snippets of information but never choosing what would be a good policy based on an exploration of available information.

Platonism progressed during the Renaissance and some Platonists held a belief that caused controversy during the classical liberal period among rational philosophers such as John Locke (1632-1704). Platonists held that there was an innate human understanding of certain real world types but Locke believed instead that people were born unencumbered by understandings. He believed in the *tabula rasa*. He thought that people learned from their own experiences and their observations and by what others might teach them. In Locke's "Essay Concerning Human Understanding", Locke described empiricism as observation and description. He thought of empiricism as a method to increase human understanding. Empiricism analyzed how people learned. And it brought the possibility of understanding to every rational mind through education and discovery.

This idea eventually inspired other philosophers to write about human understanding. But it also gave birth to philosophical skepticism. Kant and Hegel imagined limitations in human understanding based on our finite abilities of viewing and understanding the world imperfectly. Empiricism changed the way that reasoned experience was examined by modern people. By comparison, in the ancient world understanding had proceeded based on rhetorical argument, definitions, first causes and a goal to reach an ideal. Herodotus believed that "man is the measure of all things" and that through reason people could understand what mattered most compared to lesser alternatives.

In ancient Greece mankind was the best judge of arguments. After Locke, the world increasingly relied upon empiricism, or observation of what was already happening. And at first this gave people encouragement to understand their world through empirical exploration and education. But after Kant and Hegel, man was seen as having a limited ability to understand. It was thought that mankind could err when making judgments about the better course of action. While Greek rhetoric could throw out a bad argument for moral reasons or reasons of practicality, empiricism would only describe what was already happening without judging it morally, or practically. After empiricism and philosophical skepticism took hold philosophers began to doubt man's ability to understand and make a better choice. Some philosophers doubted philosophy could understand truth. And some philosophers abandoned truth as an achievable goal and left philosophy. Hegel has been considered outside philosophy by some philosophers because he abandoned seeking truth in order to substitute a kind of spiritual quest for God-consciousness.

Empiricism, or the observation of happenings, has slowed reforms because it doesn't use a moral ruler to suggest policy changes. By failing to use mankind's judgment or any external standard of value as a consistent measure of rightness or wrongness empiricism hasn't facilitated policy comparisons. And avoiding policy comparisons has served political interests because their policies can then remain uncharacterized and unquestioned. Both Greek rhetoric and empiricism have influenced the way that the law is understood and shaped in the present day. The method of rhetoric uses definitions and qualifications to evaluate law within a specific legal and moral guideline of legal norms. Empiricism uses observation to make qualifications about how law is being used but approaches law more as a phenomenon that serves a variety of competing interests without picking a moral measure of propriety. Both offer valid ways to view the law but these different approaches aren't equal in their fervor to reform the law.

Essential characteristics of Classical Liberalism:
1. Classical liberals had a belief rooted in the Protestant Reformation that respected religious differences because they were differences of conscience. This was tolerance. Private life was thought to be separate from public life and the government had no influence over many areas of private life. Unlike England where the Church of England existed as a state church, in the U.S., there was separation between church and state.
2. Classical liberals held a belief that limited government was better for society. They wrote the U.S. Constitution in order to limit the power of government through a legal document. Such a document created political interests in common and stopped some forms of political competition. The Bill of Rights extended formal protections for natural rights and the Anti-federalist's fought for its incorporation. But natural rights existed in classical liberal rhetoric independently of a formal document. A limited government could limit potential harms that a more powerful government could cause such as tyranny and tax oppression. Governments were seen as a necessary evil that required power limitation.

3. Liberty was the highest political ideal and the liberty-without-license pairing meant that, in principle, people avoided causing harm to others while exercising the greatest individual freedom. Courts enforced reparations for harms. Good government was judged by people's happiness.

4. International banking lent capital to fund large payments for war debt, or land acquisition. The First and Second Bank of the United States existed amid controversies involving disparate interests among disparate groups. They both lost their charter after twenty years of operation. Fiscal policy expectations were for debt to be paid off by the federal government.

5. The government's job was to protect property and wealth; there was little positive law. Law's function was protective of contracts and not regulatory regarding behaviors.

6. Classical liberals were willing to externalize some groups from wealth and power depending on class and land ownership. These exclusions came from European cultural habits. People in the "wrong class" such as indentured servants, Native Americans, slaves, and women didn't vote or possess political power and people without property also couldn't vote.

7. Classical liberalism had a land based economy that relied upon land sales, land speculation and land development for wealth building. When land changed hands, its value often increased.

8. Classical liberal courts were newly formed and relied upon rule of law, common law colonial records, English legal norms and liberty law as a basis of legal proceedings. Classical liberals supported an end of primogeniture and entail. Colonial communities were able to experiment by building local governance structures in town-hall meetings. Colonial governance strategies and English governance strategies combined when the U.S. Constitution was written.

9. Classical liberal founders were political experimenters, familiar with classical models of the ideal state. They were willing to remodel the state away from European political norms. They tried to balance powers in government to prevent tyranny.

10. Classical liberals appreciated the warrior mentality and they had a willingness to engage in battle to obtain land access and land holdings. Violence entered into contests for land and against taxes. Elites didn't do as much fighting, although they contributed in leadership roles. The common poor battled for the new nation.

Classical Liberal Timeline:

1651 Thomas Hobbes published *Leviathan: Or the Matter Forme and Power Of A Commonwealth Ecclesiasticall and Civil.* It was the first liberal analysis of politics.

1690 John Locke's *Two Treatises of Government* and *An Essay Concerning Human Understanding* were published; the first argued in favor of "consent of the governed" and natural rights and was influential in the drafting of the "Declaration of Independence." *An Essay Concerning Human Understanding*, held an explanation of empiricism which has changed the cultural method of how knowledge is gained and proven.

1712 The Newcomen Steam Engine was invented by Thomas Newcomen (1663-1729) in partnership with Thomas Savery (1650-1715). It was the new workhorse of the Industrial Age that got people thinking about machine power instead of people or animal power.

1776 The Declaration of Independence was signed by representatives from each colony, "with a firm reliance on the protection of divine Providence, we mutually pledge to each other our Lives, our Fortunes and our sacred Honor." and sent off to King George III.

1791-1811 This was the era of the First Bank of the United States. It was the bank sponsored by the federal government that made payments from tariff collections such as the whiskey tax to European nations such as France that had loaned the colonies money during the U.S. Revolutionary War.

1793 Ely Whitney's cotton gin was invented and it made slaves more valuable and increased cotton production by opening up marginal land for cultivation.

1798-1802, 1803-1816 Two spans of time where England began using income tax in order to fund warfare.

1800-1850 Romanticism's peak in visual art, music and literature. Romanticism dared to cultivate an awareness of the sublime. Admiration for the sublime may have contributed to later political nationalism. The Romantic Period also departed from Enlightenment Era rationalism, preferring feelings and insights at a personal level.

1807 Robert Fulton invented and developed the Hudson River steamboat transportation enterprise.

1803-1815 The Napoleonic Wars of Europe; The Louisiana Purchase; Lewis and Clark expedition to the West.

1812 War of 1812, a battle in the U.S. against England and to expand American territory on Native American lands.

1815-1917 Strict Gold Standard held together by British Sterling Pound System. This was the modern era of global currency supporting international global trade.

1816-1836 The Second Bank of the United States; acted as finance agent to pay for the War of 1812.

1825 The Erie Canal opened linking inland wheat producers to New York Harbor.

1827 The first railroad, the Baltimore and Ohio Railroad opened. Rail changed local communities into national ones and people became interested in novelty because new opportunity and experiences became widely available.

1829 Joseph-Nicephore Niepce formed a partnership with Louis-Jaques-Mandes Daguerre to begin inventing what would become the daguerreotype. After Neipce died, Louis-Jaques-Mandes succeeded in 1837, and produced a single positive image for each exposure process.

Mid 1830's U.S. cotton accounted for more than half of U.S. exports.

1839 William Henry Fox Talbot invented the calotype. It was the first image-capturing method that produced a negative. It became the forerunner of photography.

1840 Trans-Atlantic steamship provided by Samuel Cunard, a British-Canadian shipping magnate from Halifax.

1846-1848 Mexican War; annexation of 40% of Mexico's territory including Texas, California, Nevada, Arizona, New Mexico and Utah.

1856 Bessemer converter blast furnace for steel production was invented by Henry Bessemer.

1857 Jean Francoise Millet's painting *The Gleaners. Dred Scott V. Sandford (1857).*

1859 First commercial oil well drilling began in Pennsylvania.

1860 The dollar value of slaves if the government had bought them to end slavery was 2.7 billion dollars—a prohibitively high cost that non-slave owners were not prepared to pay to slave owners. The Homestead Act was vetoed. The Pacific Railway Bill was voted down by Southern Congress members.

1861-1865 The Civil War; cost of the Civil War estimated in 1860 dollars was 6.7 billion dollars.

1863 Edouard Manet's painting, *Olympia.*

How the *Dred Scott v. Sandford (1857)* case increased tension between pro-slavery and anti-slavery political factions:

Slavery was introduced to Virginia in 1620, on large plantations that were labor intensive. But by the time of 1857, when the *Dred Scott* case ruling happened the political forces to end slavery had already changed the slave trade. Virginia, the first state to import slaves onto plantations was the first to ban further imports of slaves in 1778, partly to protect its own internal slave trade. Denmark banned slave trading in 1792. The Atlantic Slave Trade was forbidden in England in 1807 and by an act of Congress in 1808, in the United States. The Slavery Abolition Act of 1833 had abruptly ended the institution of slavery inside England. But after 1808, even though the Atlantic slave trade was banned by Congress, slaves continued to be imported to the U.S. by smugglers and also slaves that were already in the South were traded between states. Slavery went on in the U.S. well after it had been banned in England. The Missouri Compromise of 1820, admitted Missouri as a slave state and Maine as a free state and it seemed that some parts of the U.S. territory would allow slavery while others would ban it. But the Kansas-Nebraska Act repealed the Missouri Compromise. Then the Dred Scott decision came about wherein the Supreme Court overruled any Congressional legislation that would ban slavery.

Having some free and some slave areas in the U.S. interfered with the ownership of slaves as property when slave owners sought to relocate. In thinking of the U.S. as one territory under the U.S. Constitution, the issue of slavery was one that was creating division for decades ahead of the Civil War. In the *Dred Scott v. Sandford (1857)* case, Dred Scot wanted freedom and he tried to use the Supreme Court to get it. He had been purchased by Dr. John Emerson in 1833. Doc Emerson was a surgeon in the U.S. Army and he moved to an army base in Wisconsin, a free state, where Scott resided with the Emerson family for ten years. The Doctor was often away on army business and while he was gone, Dred Scott would hire out his labor. Hiring out was a way to make some money for the owner but also motivate a slave to work for himself for a reduced wage. Scott tried to buy his freedom after Doc Emerson died but Mrs. Emerson refused to allow it. Also, the Emersons owed Scott back wages and didn't want to pay him. Dred Scot sued for his freedom in court in Wisconsin until his case came to the Supreme Court.

But in 1857, the Supreme Court ruled three ways which gave little room for political compromise on the slavery issue. First they ruled that African Americans couldn't be citizens. The Court also ruled that Congress didn't have the power to legislate for the abolition of slavery, nullifying the Missouri Compromise or any other legislative effort to moderate slavery. Finally the Court ruled narrowly that Fifth Amendment protections served slave owners, and that slaves as non-citizens were outside of all legal protections.

This decision ignored the Declaration of Independence that said, "All Men are created equal", it ignored the fact that slavery was brought to the U.S. but hadn't always existed there. It ignored the Article One, Section Nine, in the Constitution which declared that "The Migration or Importation of such Persons as any of the States now existing shall think proper to admit, shall not be prohibited by the Congress prior to the Year one thousand eight hundred and eight...", after which Congress had made the Atlantic Slave Trade illegal in 1808. It ignored Amendment One, Section Nine, "The Privilege of the Writ of Habeas Corpus shall not be suspended, unless when in Cases of Rebellion or Invasion the public Safety may require it." The Supreme Court ruling of *Dred Scott v. Sandford (1857)*, only worsened slave issue tension and made the Civil War more likely. After the Civil War, the 13th, 14th and 15th Amendments corrected the *Dred Scott* ruling.

The Thirteenth Amendment, Section One reads: "Neither slavery nor involuntary servitude except as a punishment for crime whereof the party shall have been duly convicted, shall exist within the United States, or any place subject to their jurisdiction."

The Fourteenth Amendment, Section One reads, "All persons born or naturalized in the United States and subject to the jurisdiction thereof, are citizens of the United States and of the State wherein they reside. No State shall make or enforce any law which shall abridge the privileges and immunities of citizens of the United States; nor shall any State deprive any person of life, liberty, or property, without due process of law; nor deny to any person within its jurisdiction the equal protection of the laws."

The Fifteenth Amendment, Section One reads, "The right of citizens of the United States to vote shall not be denied or abridged by the United States or by any State on account of race, color, or previous condition of servitude." Unfortunately, civil rights after Reconstruction reverted to Jim Crow. Only the Civil Rights Movement in the 1960's eventually changed the South, after many people fought to see political equality more fully realized. In the meantime, the Supreme Court made other rulings that were as disastrous for African Americans as Dred Scott had been. One was the case of *United States v. Cruikshank (1876)*, in which the court failed to prosecute white Southerners who had murdered one hundred African Americans participating in local politics. In *United States v. Cruikshank (1876)*, the Supreme Court also ruled to allow vigilante groups to persist that persecuted African Americans in states that failed to prosecute vigilante crimes. The use of the Fourteenth Amendment to apply the Constitution's Bill of Rights at the state level began after the Reconstruction era, under the "doctrine of incorporation." It was a slow selective process that applied the Bill of Rights protections to states as court cases came up that gave the Supreme Court an opportunity to apply them. Instead of using the Fourteenth Amendment's "privileges and immunities" clause, the Supreme Court used the Fourteenth Amendment's "due process" clause. The first case that used the incorporation doctrine was *Gitlow v. New York (1925)*, a First Amendment case.

Classical Liberalism Endnotes

1. Richard Peters, introduction to Thomas Hobbes, *Leviathan: Or the Matter, Forme and Power of a Commonwealth Ecclesiasticall and Civil*, Michael Oakeshott, ed., with Richard Peters, (New York: Macmillan Publishing Company, 1962), 7-16.

2. J.M. Kelly, *A Short History of Western Legal Theory*, (New York: Clarenden Press, Oxford University Press, 1992), 172.

3. Thomas Hobbes, *Leviathan: Or the Matter, Forme and Power of a Commonwealth Ecclesiasticall and Civil*, Michael Oakeshott, ed., with Richard Peters, (New York: Macmillan Publishing Company, 1962).

4. Thomas Hobbes, *Leviathan: Or the Matter, Forme and Power of a Commonwealth Ecclesiasticall and Civil*, Michael Oakeshott, ed., with Richard Peters, (New York: Macmillan Publishing Company, 1962), 132.

5. Thomas Hobbes, *Leviathan: Or the Matter, Forme and Power of a Commonwealth Ecclesiasticall and Civil*, Michael Oakeshott, ed., with Richard Peters, (New York: Macmillan Publishing Company, 1962), 80.

6. Thomas Hobbes, *Leviathan: Or the Matter, Forme and Power of a Commonwealth Ecclesiasticall and Civil*, Michael Oakeshott, ed., with Richard Peters, (New York: Macmillan Publishing Company, 1962), 159.

7. Thomas Hobbes, *Leviathan: Or the Matter, Forme and Power of a Commonwealth Ecclesiasticall and Civil*, Michael Oakeshott, ed., with Richard Peters, (New York: Macmillan Publishing Company, 1962), 167.

8. Thomas Hobbes, *Leviathan: Or the Matter, Forme and Power of a Commonwealth Ecclesiasticall and Civil*, Michael Oakeshott, ed., with Richard Peters, (New York: Macmillan Publishing Company, 1962), 32.

9. Thomas Hobbes, *Leviathan: Or the Matter, Forme and Power of a Commonwealth Ecclesiasticall and Civil*, Michael Oakeshott, ed., with Richard Peters, (New York: Macmillan Publishing Company, 1962), 42.

10. Thomas Hobbes, *Leviathan: Or the Matter, Forme and Power of a Commonwealth Ecclesiasticall and Civil*, Michael Oakeshott, ed., with Richard Peters, (New York: Macmillan Publishing Company, 1962), 81.

11. Richard Peters, introduction to Thomas Hobbes, *Leviathan: Or the Matter, Forme and Power of a Commonwealth Ecclesiasticall and Civil*, Michael Oakeshott, ed., with Richard Peters, (New York: Macmillan Publishing Company, 1962), 7-16.

12. Thomas Greer, Gavin Lewis, *A Brief History of the Western World, Eighth Edition*, (Orlando: Harcourt College Publishers, 2002), 477.

13. Thomas Greer, Gavin Lewis, *A Brief History of the Western World, Eighth Edition*, (Orlando: Harcourt College Publishers, 2002), 502-503.

14. Edward Corwin, *The Doctrine of Judicial Review: Its Legal and Historical Basis and Other Essays*, (Clark, NJ: The Lawbook Exchange Ltd., 2011), 28.

15. John Locke, *Two Treatises of Government And A Letter Concerning Toleration*, (New York: Classic Books International, 2010).

16. Thomas Greer, Gavin Lewis, *A Brief History of the Western World, Eighth Edition,* (Orlando: Harcourt College Publishers, 2002), 501-502.

17. John Locke, *Two Treatises of Government And A Letter Concerning Toleration,* (New York: Classic Books International, 2010), 75.

18. John Locke, *Two Treatises of Government And A Letter Concerning Toleration,* (New York: Classic Books International, 2010), 135.

19. John Locke, *Two Treatises of Government And A Letter Concerning Toleration,* (New York: Classic Books International, 2010), 126.

20. John Locke, *Two Treatises of Government And A Letter Concerning Toleration,* (New York: Classic Books International, 2010), 120.

21. John Locke, *Two Treatises of Government And A Letter Concerning Toleration,* (New York: Classic Books International, 2010), 88.

22. John Locke, *Two Treatises of Government And A Letter Concerning Toleration,* (New York: Classic Books International, 2010), 86.

23. John Locke, *Two Treatises of Government And A Letter Concerning Toleration,* (New York: Classic Books International, 2010), 132.

24. Jeremy Stangroom, James Garvey, *The Great Philosophers,* (New York: Barnes and Noble, Arcturus Publishing Limited, 2006, 48-51.

25. Baron de Montesquieu, www.rjgieb.com/thoughts/ Montesquieu/ Montesquieubis.html, accessed July 9, 2013.

26. Charles de Secondat Baron de Montesquieu, *The Spirit of the Laws,* (New York: Prometheus Books, 2002).

27. Charles de Secondat Baron de Montesquieu, *The Spirit of the Laws,* (New York: Prometheus Books, 2002), 2.

28. Charles de Secondat Baron de Montesquieu, *The Spirit of the Laws,* (New York: Prometheus Books, 2002), 6.

29. Charles de Secondat Baron de Montesquieu, *The Spirit of the Laws,* (New York: Prometheus Books, 2002), 74.

30. Charles de Secondat Baron de Montesquieu, *The Spirit of the Laws,* (New York: Prometheus Books, 2002), 126.

31. Charles de Secondat Baron de Montesquieu, *The Spirit of the Laws,* (New York: Prometheus Books, 2002), 150.

32. Charles de Secondat Baron de Montesquieu, *The Spirit of the Laws,* (New York: Prometheus Books, 2002), 152.

33. Charles de Secondat Baron de Montesquieu, *The Spirit of the Laws,* (New York: Prometheus Books, 2002), 161-162.

34. Fritz Machlup, *A History of Thought on Economic Integration,* (New York: Columbia University Press, 1977), 219.

35. Adam Smith, *The Wealth of Nations Books I-III*, with Andrew Skinner, (London, UK:

Penguin Books, 1987).

36. Adam Smith, *The Wealth of Nations Books I-III*, with Andrew Skinner, (London, UK: Penguin Books, 1987), 1-82.

37. Adam Smith, *The Wealth of Nations Books I-III*, with Andrew Skinner, (London, UK: Penguin Books, 1987), 110.

38. Adam Smith, *The Wealth of Nations Books I-III*, with Andrew Skinner, (London, UK: Penguin Books, 1987), 131.

39. Adam Smith, *The Wealth of Nations Books I-III*, with Andrew Skinner, (London, UK: Penguin Books, 1987), 138.

40. Adam Smith, *The Wealth of Nations Books I-III*, with Andrew Skinner, (London, UK: Penguin Books, 1987), 358-359.

41. Adam Smith, *The Wealth of Nations Books I-III*, with Andrew Skinner, (London, UK: Penguin Books, 1987), 392.

42. Adam Smith, *The Wealth of Nations Books I-III*, with Andrew Skinner, (London, UK: Penguin Books, 1987), 431.

43. Adam Smith, *The Wealth of Nations Books I-III*, with Andrew Skinner, (London, UK: Penguin Books, 1987), 419.

44. Adam Smith, *The Wealth of Nations Books I-III*, with Andrew Skinner, (London, UK: Penguin Books, 1987), 432.

45. Adam Smith, *The Wealth of Nations Books I-III*, with Andrew Skinner, (London, UK: Penguin Books, 1987), 429.

46. J.R. McCulloch, ed., *The Works of David Ricardo: With a Notice of the Life and Writings of the Author*, (Honolulu: University Press of the Pacific, 2002), xv-xxiii.

47. Fritz Machlup, *A History of Thought on Economic Integration*, (New York: Columbia University Press, 1977), 217-218.

48. Theodore Couloumbis, James Wolfe, *Introduction to International Relations: Power and Justice Third Edition*, (Englewood Cliffs, NJ: Prentice Hall, Inc., 1986), 331.

49. Theodore Couloumbis, James Wolfe, *Introduction to International Relations: Power and Justice Third Edition*, (Englewood Cliffs, NJ: Prentice Hall, Inc., 1986), 375.

50. J.R. McCulloch, ed., *The Works of David Ricardo: With a Notice of the Life and Writings of the Author*, (Honolulu: University Press of the Pacific, 2002), 5.

51. J.R. McCulloch, ed., *The Works of David Ricardo: With a Notice of the Life and Writings of the Author*, (Honolulu: University Press of the Pacific, 2002), 72.

52. J.R. McCulloch, ed., *The Works of David Ricardo: With a Notice of the Life and Writings of the Author*, (Honolulu: University Press of the Pacific, 2002), 75-76.

53. J.R. McCulloch, ed., *The Works of David Ricardo: With a Notice of the Life and Writings of the Author*, (Honolulu: University Press of the Pacific, 2002), 75.

54. J.R. McCulloch, ed., *The Works of David Ricardo: With a Notice of the Life and Writings of the Author*, (Honolulu: University Press of the Pacific, 2002), 75.

55. J.R. McCulloch, ed., *The Works of David Ricardo: With a Notice of the Life and Writings of the Author*, (Honolulu: University Press of the Pacific, 2002), 114.

56. J.R. McCulloch, ed., *The Works of David Ricardo: With a Notice of the Life and Writings of the Author*, (Honolulu: University Press of the Pacific, 2002), 250.

57. J.R. McCulloch, ed., *The Works of David Ricardo: With a Notice of the Life and Writings of the Author*, (Honolulu: University Press of the Pacific, 2002), 227.

58. J.R. McCulloch, ed., *The Works of David Ricardo: With a Notice of the Life and Writings of the Author*, (Honolulu: University Press of the Pacific, 2002), 257.

59. Wikipedia, "Richard Cobden," enwikipedia.org/wiki/Richard_Cobden, accessed May 2013.

60. Wikiquote, "Richard Cobden," enwikiquote.org/wiki/Richard_Cobden, accessed July 2013.

61. Richard Cobden, "Speech at Covent Garden, September 1843," Wikiquote, "Richard Cobden," enwikiquote.org/wiki/Richard_Cobden, accessed July 2013.

62. Richard Cobden, "Speech in London, February 1844," Wikiquote, "Richard Cobden," enwikiquote.org/ wiki/Richard_Cobden, accessed July 2013.

63. Richard Cobden, "Speech in the House of Commons, February, 1846, Wikiquote, "Richard Cobden," enwikiquote.org/wiki/Richard_Cobden, accessed July 2013.

64. Howard Fast, *The Selected Work of Tom Paine Including: Common Sense, Crisis Papers, Rights of Man, The Age of Reason, And Citizen Tom Paine, A Historical Novel of America's Spokesman for the Revolution*, (New York: The Modern Library, Random House, 1945).

65. Thomas Paine, "The Last Crisis," in *The Selected Work of Tom Paine Including: Common Sense, Crisis Papers, Rights of Man, The Age of Reason, And Citizen Tom Paine, A Historical Novel of America's Spokesman for the Revolution*, Howard Fast, (New York: The Modern Library, Random House, 1945), 86.

66. Thomas Paine, "Common Sense," in *The Selected Work of Tom Paine Including: Common Sense, Crisis Papers, Rights of Man, The Age of Reason, And Citizen Tom Paine, A Historical Novel of America's Spokesman for the Revolution*, Howard Fast, ed., (New York: The Modern Library, Random House, 1945), p6.

67. Thomas Paine, "Common Sense," in *The Selected Work of Tom Paine Including: Common Sense, Crisis Papers, Rights of Man, The Age of Reason, And Citizen Tom Paine, A Historical Novel of America's Spokesman for the Revolution*, Howard Fast, ed., (New York: The Modern Library, Random House, 1945), 30.

68. Thomas Paine, Wikiquote, "Thomas Paine, appendix comments to the third edition," http://en.wikiquote.org/wiki/Thomas_Paine, accessed 2011.

69. Thomas Paine, "Common Sense," in *The Selected Work of Tom Paine Including: Common Sense, Crisis Papers, Rights of Man, The Age of Reason, And Citizen Tom Paine, A Historical Novel of America's Spokesman for the Revolution*, Howard Fast, ed., (New York: The Modern Library, Random House, 1945), 31.

70. Thomas Paine, *Rights of Man*, in *The Selected Work of Tom Paine Including: Common Sense, Crisis Papers, Rights of Man, The Age of Reason, And Citizen Tom Paine, A Historical Novel of America's Spokesman for the Revolution*, Howard Fast, ed., (New York: The Modern Library, Random House, 1945), 99.

71. Thomas Paine, *Age of Reason*, in *The Selected Work of Tom Paine Including: Common Sense, Crisis Papers, Rights of Man, The Age of Reason, And Citizen Tom Paine, A Historical Novel of America's Spokesman for the Revolution*, Howard Fast, ed., (New York: The Modern Library, Random House, 1945), 285.

72. Jeremy Stangroom, James Garvey, *The Great Philosophers,* (New York: Barnes and Noble, Arcturus Publishing Limited, 2006), 84-87.

73. John Stuart Mill, *On Liberty and the Subjection of Women*, Alan Ryan, ed., (New York: Penguin Books, 2006).

74. Wikiquote, "Jeremy Bentham," enwikiquote.org/wiki/Jeremy Bentham, accessed 2011.

75. Jeremy Bentham, *An Introduction to the Principles of Morals and Legislation*, 1789 edition, Wikiquote, enwikiquote.org/wiki/Jeremy Bentham, accessed 2011.

76. "Jeremy Bentham," *An Introduction to the Principles of Morals and Legislation*, 1789 edition, Wikiquote, enwikiquote.org/wiki/Jeremy Bentham, accessed 2011.

77. Jeremy Bentham, *Principles of Legislation,* Wikiquote, "Jeremy Bentham," enwikiquote.org/wiki/Jeremy Bentham, accessed 2011, chapter ten.

78. Jeremy Bentham, *On Publicity*, Wikiquote, "Jeremy Bentham," enwikiquote.org/ wiki/Jeremy Bentham, accessed 2011.

79. John Stuart Mill, *On Liberty and the Subjection of Women,* Alan Ryan, ed., (New York: Penguin Books, 2006), 14.

80. John Stuart Mill, *On Liberty and the Subjection of Women,* Alan Ryan, ed., (New York: Penguin Books, 2006), 16.

81. John Stuart Mill, *On Liberty and the Subjection of Women,* Alan Ryan, ed., (New York: Penguin Books, 2006), 23.

82. John Stuart Mill, *On Liberty and the Subjection of Women,* Alan Ryan, ed., (New York: Penguin Books, 2006), 39.

83. John Stuart Mill, *On Liberty and the Subjection of Women,* Alan Ryan, ed., (New York: Penguin Books, 2006), 127.

84. John Stuart Mill, *On Liberty and the Subjection of Women,* Alan Ryan, ed., (New York: Penguin Books, 2006), 129.

85. John Stuart Mill, *On Liberty and the Subjection of Women,* Alan Ryan, ed., (New York: Penguin Books, 2006), 80.

86. Frederic Bastiat, *The Law*, Dean Russell, trans., (New York: The Foundation for Economic Education, Inc., 1990).

87. Antonin Scalia, Bryan Garner, *Reading Law: The Interpretation of Legal Texts*, St. Paul, MN: Thompson/West, 2012, quotes on facing page after title page, and 1-46.

88. Frederic Bastiat, *The Law,* Dean Russell, trans., (New York: The Foundation for Economic Education, Inc., 1990), 18-19.

89. Frederic Bastiat, *The Law,* Dean Russell, trans., (New York: The Foundation for Economic Education, Inc., 1990), 22-23.

90. Frederic Bastiat, *The Law,* Dean Russell, trans., (New York: The Foundation for Economic Education, Inc., 1990), 25.

91. Frederic Bastiat, *The Law,* Dean Russell, trans., (New York: The Foundation for Economic Education, Inc., 1990), 32.

92. Frederic Bastiat, *The Law,* Dean Russell, trans., (New York: The Foundation for Economic Education, Inc., 1990), 33.

93. Frederic Bastiat, *The Law,* Dean Russell, trans., (New York: The Foundation for Economic Education, Inc., 1990), 51.

94. Frederic Bastiat, *The Law,* Dean Russell, trans., (New York: The Foundation for Economic Education, Inc., 1990), 65.

95. Jane Slaughter, Melissa Bokovoy, *Sharing the Stage: Biography and Gender in Western Civilization, Volume Two*, (USA: Houghton Mifflin Company, 2003), 65.

96. Jane Slaughter, Melissa Bokovoy, *Sharing the Stage: Biography and Gender in Western Civilization, Volume Two*, (USA: Houghton Mifflin Company, 2003), 86-118.

97. Wikiquote, "Mary Wollstonecraft," enwikiquote.org/ wiki/Mary_Wollstonecraft, accessed 2013.

98. Mary Wollstonecraft, *A Vindication of the Rights of Women*, Wikiquote, "Mary Wollstonecraft," enwikiquote.org/wiki/Mary Wollstonecraft, chapter nine, accessed 2013.

99. Mary Wollstonecraft, *A Vindication of the Rights of Women*, Wikiquote, "Mary Wollstonecraft," enwikiquote.org/wiki/Mary_Wollstonecraft, chapter three, accessed 2013.

100. Mary Wollstonecraft, *The French Revolution*, Wikiquote, "Mary Wollstonecraft," enwikiquote.org/wiki/Mary_Wollstonecraft, accessed 2013.

101. Mary Wollstonecraft, *A Vindication Of the Rights of Women*, Wikiquote, "Mary Wollstonecraft," enwikiquote.org/wiki/Mary_Wollstonecraft, chapter three, accessed 2013.

102. Mary Wollstonecraft, *A Vindication Of the Rights of Women*, Wikiquote, "Mary Wollstonecraft," enwikiquote.org/wiki/Mary_Wollstonecraft, accessed 2013.

103. Molly McGarry, *Ghosts of Futures Past: Spiritualism and the Cultural Politics of Nineteenth Century America*, (California: University of California Press, 2008), 81.

104. Frederick Douglas, *Narrative of the Life of Frederick Douglas, an American Slave,* of the *Early African American Classics*, Anthony Appiah, ed., (New York: Bantam Classics, Random House, Inc., 2008).

105. Harriet Jacobs, *Incidents in the Life of a Slave Girl*, of the *Early African American Classics*, Anthony Appiah, ed., (New York: Bantam Classics, Random House, Inc., 2008).

106. Frederick Douglas, *Narrative of the Life of Frederick Douglas, an American Slave,* of the *Early African American Classics*, Anthony Appiah, ed., (New York: Bantam Classics, Random House, Inc., 2008), 21.

107. Frederick Douglas, *Narrative of the Life of Frederick Douglas, an American Slave,* of the *Early African American Classics*, Anthony Appiah, ed., (New York: Bantam Classics, Random House, Inc., 2008), 26.

108. Frederick Douglas, *Narrative of the Life of Frederick Douglas, an American Slave*, of the *Early African American Classics*, Anthony Appiah, ed., (New York: Bantam Classics, Random House, Inc., 2008), 19-20.

109. Harriet Jacobs, *Incidents in the Life of a Slave Girl*, of the *Early African American Classics*, Anthony Appiah, ed., (New York: Bantam Classics, Random House, Inc., 2008), 151.

110. Harriet Jacobs, *Incidents in the Life of a Slave Girl*, of the *Early African American Classics*, Anthony Appiah, ed., (New York: Bantam Classics, Random House, Inc., 2008), 137.

111. Harriet Jacobs, *Incidents in the Life of a Slave Girl*, of the *Early African American Classics*, Anthony Appiah, ed., (New York: Bantam Classics, Random House, Inc., 2008), 153.

112. Harriet Jacobs, *Incidents in the Life of a Slave Girl*, of the *Early African American Classics*, Anthony Appiah, ed., (New York: Bantam Classics, Random House, Inc., 2008), 285.

113. David Galenson, *The Journal of Economic History*, Cambridge University Press, www.colorado.edu/lbs/eb/alston/econ8534/SectionIII/Galenson_The_Rise_and_Fall_of_Indentured_Servitude_in _the_Americas.pdf, Mar 1984, accessed 2013.

114. David Galenson, *The Journal of Economic History*, Cambridge University Press, www.colorado.edu/lbs/eb/alston/econ8534/SectionIII/Galenson_The_Rise_and_Fall_of_Indentured_Servitude_in _the_Americas.pdf, Mar 1984, accessed 2013.

115. David Galenson, *The Journal of Economic History*, Cambridge University Press, www.colorado.edu/lbs/eb/alston/econ8534/SectionIII/Galenson_The_Rise_and_Fall_of_Indentured_Servitude_in _the_Americas.pdf, Mar 1984, accessed 2013.

116. David Galenson, *The Journal of Economic History*, Cambridge University Press, www.colorado.edu/lbs/eb/alston/econ8534/SectionIII/Galenson_The_Rise_and_Fall_of_Indentured_Servitude_in _the_Americas.pdf, Mar 1984, accessed 2013.

117. David Galenson, *The Journal of Economic History*, Cambridge University Press, www.colorado.edu/lbs/eb/alston/econ8534/SectionIII/Galenson_The_Rise_and_Fall_of_Indentured_Servitude_in _the_Americas.pdf, Mar 1984, accessed 2013.

118. David Galenson, *The Journal of Economic History*, Cambridge University Press, www.colorado.edu/lbs/eb/alston/econ8534/SectionIII/Galenson_The_Rise_and_Fall_of_ Indentured_Servitude_in _the_Americas.pdf, Mar 1984, accessed 2013.

119. Isabel Calder, ed., *Colonial* Captivities, *Marches, and Journeys*, (New York: Macmillan Company, 1935), 151-52, historymatters.gmu.edu/d/5796, accessed Sept 2013, Elizabeth Sprigs serving a Maryland indenture 1756, accessed 2013.

120. William Moraley, *The Infortunate: or, the Voyage and Adventures of William Moraley*, 1743 Newcastle, England, reprinted *The Delaware County Republican*, 1884, historymatters. gmu.edu/d/6229, accessed Sept 2013.

121. Dee Brown, *Bury My Heart at Wounded Knee: An Indian History of the American West*, (New York: Henry Holt and Company, LLC., 1970).

122. Dee Brown, *Bury My Heart at Wounded Knee: An Indian History of the American West*, (New York: Henry Holt and Company, LLC., 1970), 446, Black Elk quote.

123. Dee Brown, *Bury My Heart at Wounded Knee: An Indian History of the American West*, (New York: Henry Holt and Company, LLC., 1970), 449, Mahpiua Luta or Red Cloud quote.

124. Dee Brown, *Bury My Heart at Wounded Knee: An Indian History of the American West*, (New York: Henry Holt and Company, LLC., 1970), 1, Tecumseh of the Shawnees quote.

125. Dee Brown, *Bury My Heart at Wounded Knee: An Indian History of the American West*, (New York: Henry Holt and Company, LLC., 1970), 103, Mahpiua Luta or Red Cloud quote.

126. Levi Rickert, ed., Native Currents, Native News Network: Connecting Native American Voices, www.nativenewsnetwork.com/us-presidents-in-their-own-words-concerning-native-american-indians.html, George Washington quote, accessed 2013.

127. Levi Rickert, ed., Native Currents, Native News Network: Connecting Native American Voices, www.nativenewsnetwork.com/us-presidents-in-their-own-words-concerning-native-american-indians.html., Thomas Jefferson quote, accessed 2013.

128. Levi Rickert, ed., Native Currents, Native News Network: Connecting Native American Voices, www.nativenewsnetwork.com/us-presidents-in-their-own-words-concerning-native-american-indians.html, Andrew Jackson quote, accessed 2013.

129. United States History, "U.S. Population, 1790-2000: Always Growing," www.u-s-history.com/pages/h980.html, accessed May 2013.

130. John Adams, "Letter to John Wythe," Wikiquote, "Letter to John Wythe," wikiquote/wiki/Letter_to_John_Wythe," reference to: http://www.britannica.com/eb/article-9116853/Document-John-Adams-The-Foundation-of-Government, accessed 2013.

131. Thomas Sowell, *Basic Economics: A Common Sense Guide to the Economy, Third Edition*, (New York: Basic Books, A Member of the Perseus Books Group, 2007), 15.

132. John Flynn, *Men of Wealth: The Story of Twelve Significant Fortunes From the Renaissance to the Present Day*, (New York: Simon and Schuster, Kessinger Legacy Reprints, 1941), 8-9.

133. Joseph Postell, "The Right Kind of Regulation: What the Founders Thought About Regulation," in *Rediscovering Political Economy*, Joseph Postell, Bradley Watson, eds., (Lanham, Maryland: Lexington Books, a division of Rowman and Littlefield Publishers, Inc., 2011).

134. Joseph Postell, "The Right Kind of Regulation: What the Founders Thought About Regulation," in *Rediscovering Political Economy*, Joseph Postell, Bradley Watson, eds., (Lanham, Maryland: Lexington Books, a division of Rowman and Littlefield Publishers, Inc., 2011), 209-230.

135. Richard Wagner, "Promoting the General Welfare: Political Economy for a Free Republic," in *Rediscovering Political Economy*, Joseph Postell, Bradley Watson, eds., (Lanham, Maryland: Lexington Books, a division of Rowman and Littlefield Publishers, Inc., 2011), 135-157.

136. Richard Wagner, "Promoting the General Welfare: Political Economy for a Free Republic," in *Rediscovering Political Economy*, Joseph Postell, Bradley Watson, eds., (Lanham, Maryland: Lexington Books, a division of Rowman and Littlefield Publishers, Inc., 2011), 135-157.

137. William Domhoff, *Who Rules America? Power, Politics, and Social Change,* (New York: McGraw Hill, 2006.

138. Allan Wallach, "Thomas Cole and the Aristocracy," in Marianne Doezema, Elizabeth Milroy, eds., *Reading American Art*, (New Haven: Yale University Press, 1998), 78-108.

139. Kent Weaver, *The Politics of Industrial Change: Railway Policy in North America*, (Washington D.C.: The Brookings Institution, 1985), see accelerationist policies, 1-25.

140. Andrew Bacevich, *The New American Militarism: How Americans Are Seduced By War*, (New York: Oxford University Press, 2005), p21-23.

141. Rajiv Sethi, "James Tobin's Hirsch Lecture," Economist's View, economistsview.typepad.com /economistview/2010/05/james-tobin-hirsch-lecture.html, from *Lloyd's Bank Review*, 1984, 2010, accessed 2014.

142. Edward S. Herman, Noam Chomsky, *Manufacturing consent: The Political Economy of the Mass Media*, (New York: Pantheon Books a division of Random House, Inc., 1988).

143. Greta Krippner, quoted in Thomas Palley, *Financialization: The Economics of Finance Capital Domination*, (New York: Palgrave MacMillan, 2013), 1.

144. Thomas Greer, Gavin Lewis, *A Brief History of the Western World, Eighth Edition*, (Orlando: Harcourt College Publishers, 2002), p140.

145. Randy E. Barnett, *Restoring the Lost Constitution: The Presumption of Liberty*, (Princeton, NJ: Princeton University Press, 2004).

146. Randy E. Barnett, *Restoring the Lost Constitution: The Presumption of Liberty*, (Princeton, NJ: Princeton University Press, 2004), 52-86.

147. Randy E. Barnett, *Restoring the Lost Constitution: The Presumption of Liberty*, (Princeton, NJ: Princeton University Press, 2004), 80.

148. Randy E. Barnett, *Restoring the Lost Constitution: The Presumption of Liberty*, (Princeton, NJ: Princeton University Press, 2004), (quoting Rosen, and other sources), 257-258.

149. Randy E. Barnett, *Restoring the Lost Constitution: The Presumption of Liberty*, (Princeton, NJ: Princeton University Press, 2004), 52-86.

150. Randy E. Barnett, *Restoring the Lost Constitution: The Presumption of Liberty*, (Princeton, NJ: Princeton University Press, 2004), 52-86.

151. Randy E. Barnett, *Restoring the Lost Constitution: The Presumption of Liberty*, (Princeton, NJ: Princeton University Press, 2004), 252.

152. Randy E. Barnett, *Restoring the Lost Constitution: The Presumption of Liberty*, (Princeton, NJ: Princeton University Press, 2004), 224-252.

153. Randy E. Barnett, *Restoring the Lost Constitution: The Presumption of Liberty*, (Princeton, NJ: Princeton University Press, 2004), 26.

154. Jed S. Rakoff, "Why Innocent People Plead Guilty," *New York Review of Books,* www. nybooks.com/articles/archives/2014/Nov/20/Why-innocent-people-plead-guilty-/?utm_ medium=email&utm_campaign=nyr+plea+bargains, accessed 2014.

155. Alexander Hamilton, James Madison, and John Jay, *The Federalist Papers*, with Clinton Rossiter, (Chicago: Signet Classics, 1961), essay by Hamilton, #78, 467.

156. Justice Rehnquist, in *Reading Law: the Interpretation of Legal Texts*, Antonin Scalia, Bryan Garner, (St Paul, MN: Thomson/West, 2012), post title page quotation.

157. Antonin Scalia, Bryan Garner, *Reading Law: the Interpretation of Legal Texts*, (St Paul, MN:

Thomson/West, 2012), xxii-xxx.

158. Wikipedia, *"Marbury v. Madison, (1803)"* enwikipedia.org/wiki/Marbury_v_Madison, accessed 2013.

159. Edward Corwin, *The Doctrine of Judicial Review: Its Legal and Historical Basis and Other Essays,* (Clark, NJ: The Lawbook Exchange Ltd., 2011).

160. Wikipedia, *"McCulloch v. Maryland (1819)",* enwikipedia.org/wiki/McCulloch_v_Maryland, accessed 2013.

161. Wikipedia, *"Santa Clara County v. Southern Pacific Railroad (1886),* enwikipedia.org /wiki/ Santa_Clara_County_v_Union_Pacific_Railroad, accessed 2013.

162. Wikipedia, *"Dartmouth College v. Woodward (1819)"* enwikipedia.org/wiki/ Dartmouth_College_v_Woodward, accessed 2013.

163. Wikipedia, *"Texas v. White (1869)"* enwikipedia.org/wiki/Texas_v_White, accessed 2013.

164. Wikipedia, *"O'Gorman & Young, Inc. v. Hartford Fire Insurance Co. (1931)"* enwikipedia. org/wiki/0%27Gorman%26_Young_inc_v_Hartford_Fire_Ins_Co, accessed 2014.

165. Wikipedia, *"United States v. Carolene Products Co. (1938),* enwikipedia.org/ wiki/United_States_v._Carolene_Products_Co., accessed 2014.

166. Randy E. Barnett, *Restoring the Lost Constitution: The Presumption of Liberty,* (Princeton, NJ: Princeton University Press, 2004), 229.

167. Meyer Weinberg, "A Short History of American Capitalism," www.allshookdown.com/ newhistory/CH03.pdf, last updated 2002, accessed 2013.

168. Meyer Weinberg, "A Short History of American Capitalism," www.allshookdown.com/ newhistory/CH03.pdf, last updated 2002, accessed 2013.

169. Meyer Weinberg, "A Short History of American Capitalism," www.allshookdown.com/ newhistory/CH03.pdf, last updated 2002, accessed 2013.

170. Meyer Weinberg, "A Short History of American Capitalism," www.allshookdown.com/ newhistory/CH03.pdf, last updated 2002, accessed 2013.

171. Edward Redmond, "George Washington: Surveyor and Mapmaker," memoryloc.gov/ ammem/gmd.html/gwmaps.html, accessed 2013.

172. Silvio Bedini, "Reprint: Early American Surveyors: Mapping the Wilderness," Professional Surveyors Magazine, www.profsurv.com/magazine/article.aspx?i=2038, accessed, 2013.

173. *Continental Congress and Constitutional Convention, 1774-1789*, Library of Congress Teachers, "The New Nation, 1783-1815: Policies and Problems of the Confederation Government, Disposing of Lands in the Western Territory," www.loc.gov/teachers/classroom-materials/presentationsandactivities/presentation/timeline/newatn/confed/docsoc.html, accessed 2013.

174. Timeline of American Planning History, www.taxplanning.org/media/files/page/Planning_History_1785_to_2000.pdf, accessed 2013.

175. Thomas West, "The Economic Theory of the American Founding," in *Rediscovering Political Economy*, Joseph Postell, Bradley Watson, eds., (Maryland: Lexington Books, a division of

Rowman and Littlefield Publishers, Inc., 2011), 159-160.

176. Thomas West, "The Economic Theory of the American Founding," in *Rediscovering Political Economy*, Joseph Postell, Bradley Watson, eds., (Maryland: Lexington Books, a division of Rowman and Littlefield Publishers, Inc., 2011), 161-162.

177. "Kelo v. City of New London (2004)," www.oyez.org/cases/2000-2009/2004/2004-04/108, accessed 2013.

178. Thomas West, "The Economic Theory of the American Founding," in *Rediscovering Political Economy*, Joseph Postell, Bradley Watson, eds., (Maryland: Lexington Books, a division of Rowman and Littlefield Publishers, Inc., 2011), 170.

179. Injustice for Justice, *"Kelo v. New London,* Lawsuit Challenging Eminent Domain Abuse in New London, Connecticut," www.ijorg/kelo, accessed 2013.

180. Wikipedia, "Chartered Company," enwikipedia.org/wiki/ Chartered_Company, accessed 2013.

181. John W. Wright, *The New York Times 2010 Almanac*, (New York: Penguin Reference, 2009), 456-457.

182. Akhil Reed, Les Adams, *The Bill Of Rights Primer: A Citizen's Guidebook to the American Bill of Rights*, (Birmingham: Palladium Press, 1998), 1-23.

183. Thomas Greer, Gavin Lewis, *A Brief History of the Western World, Eighth Edition*, (Orlando: Harcourt College Publishers, 2002), chapter nine.

184. Azel Ames, Project Gutenberg's The Mayflower and Her Log, Complete, http://www.gutenberg.org/files/4107/4107-h/4107-h.htm#linkappendix, 2006, last update, 2012, accessed 2013.

185. Azel Ames, Project Gutenberg's The Mayflower and Her Log, Complete, http://www.gutenberg.org/files/4107/4107-h/4107-h.htm#linkappendix, 2006, last update, 2012, accessed 2013.

186. David Hackett Fischer, *Albion's Seed: Four British Folkways in America*, (New York: Oxford University Press, 1989), 13-17.

187. Wikipedia, "Massachusetts Bay Colony," enwikipedia.org/wiki/ Massachusetts_Bay_Colony, accessed 2013.

188. Wikipedia, "Economic history of the United States," enwikipedia.org/ wiki/ Economic_history_of_the_United_States, accessed 2013.

189. Ben Baack, "The Economics of the American Revolutionary War," eh.net/encyclopedia/the-economics-of-the-american-revolutionary-war-2/, accessed 2013.

190. Wikipedia, "Economic history of the United States," enwikipedia.org/ wiki/ Economic_history_of_the_United_States, accessed 2013.

191. Jesse Greenspan, History in the Headlines, "8 Things You May Not Know About the Louisiana Purchase," www.history.com/news/8-things-you-may-not-know-about-the-louisiana-purchase, accessed 2013.

192. Wikipedia, "Economic history of the United States," enwikipedia.org/ wiki/ Economic_history_of_the_United_States, accessed 2013.

193. Wikipedia, "Economic history of the United States," enwikipedia.org/wiki/Economic_history_of_the_United_States, accessed 2013.

194. The U.S. Economy: A Brief History, usa.usembasy.de/etexts/oecon/chap3.htm, accessed 2013.

195. U.S. History: Pre-Columbian to the New Millennium, "The Middle Colonies," www.ushistory.org/us/4.asp, accessed 2013.

196. Section Two, New England and the Middle Colonies,amin.bhbl.neuc.org/ ~mmosal/ushistorytextbook/Chapter%203%20Colonial%20Way%20of%20Life…, accessed 2013.

197. Paul Gu, "Ohio Life Insurance and Trust Company," www.ohiohistorycentral.org/w/Ohio-life-insurance-and-trust-company, accessed 2013.

198. Wikipedia, "The Funding Act of 1790," enwikipedia.org/wiki/Funding Act of 1790, accessed 2013.

199. Wikipedia, "The Funding Act of 1790," enwikipedia.org/wiki/Funding Act of 1790, accessed 2013.

200. "The First Bank of the United States, A Chapter in the History of Banking," philadelphia.org/publications/economic-education/first bank.pdf, Dec 2013, accessed 2013.

201. Wikipedia/ "Second Bank of the United States," enwikipedia.org/wiki/Second Bank of the United States, accessed Dec 2013.

202. Wikipedia/ "Second Bank of the United States," enwikipedia.org/wiki/Second Bank of the United States, accessed Dec 2013.

203. Peter McNamara, "Hamilton and Jefferson: Two Visions of Democratic Capitalism," Joseph Postell, Bradley Watson, eds., *Rediscovering Political Economy,* (Lanham MD: Lexington Books, of Rowman and Littlefield Publishers, Inc., 2011), 187-207.

204. Dave Itzkoff, "The Past Is Never Dead: A Faulkner Quote in 'Midnight in Paris' Results in a Lawsuit," *The New York Times*, artsbeat.blogs.nytimes.com/2012/10/26/ the-past-is-never-dead-a-faulkner-quote-in-midnight-in-paris-results-in-a-lawsuit/?_php=true&_type=blogs&_r=0, accessed 2014.

205. David Hackett Fischer, *Albion's Seed: Four British Folkways in America*, (New York: Oxford University Press, 1989), 813.

206. Timeline of US Military Conflicts, niagarageneology.org/pdfs/timeline_of_us_military_conflicts.pdf, accessed 2013.

207. Antonio Zamora, Scientific Psychic, www.scientificpsychic.com/alpha/travel/Indianmuseum.html, accessed 2013.

208. American Indians by the Numbers, www.infoplease.com/spot/aihmcensus/html, accessed 2013.

209. Timeline of US Military Conflicts, niagarageneology.org/pdfs/timeline_of_us_military_conflicts.pdf, accessed 2013.

210. American Indians by the Numbers, www.infoplease.com/spot/aihmcensus/html, accessed 2013

Appendix References:

Rule of law and the technology of writing.

1.   Dr. Mark Cooray, "The Rule of Law," www.ourcivilization.com/cooray/btof/chapter/80. htm, accessed 2013.

2.   "Rule According to Law," legaldictionary.thefreedictionary.com/ Rule+of+Law, accessed 2013.

3.   Wikipedia, "Rule of Law," enwikipedia.org/wiki/Rule-of-law, accessed 2011.

4.   J.M. Kelly, *A Short History of Western Legal Theory*, (New York: Clarendon Press, Oxford University Press, 1992).

5.   Antonin Scalia and Bryan A. Garner, *Reading Law: The Interpretation of Legal Texts*, (St. Paul, MN: Thomson/West, 2012).

6.   Dabcanboulet, "Dicey's Views On the Rule Of Law and the Supremacy of Parliament, sourced to 2002, everything2.com/title/Dicey%2527s+views +on +the +rule +of+law +and+the +supremacy+ of+parliament, accessed 2013.

Rhetoric vs. Empiricism and Hegelian dialectic vs. Greek dialectic.

1.   Jeffrey Walker, Glen McClish, *Understanding Arguments: Readings for College Writings*, (Boston: Houghton Mifflin Company, 1991).

2.   Jeffrey Walker, Glen McClish, *Understanding Arguments: Readings for College Writings*, (Boston: Houghton Mifflin Company, 1991).

3.   Jeffrey Walker, Glen McClish, *Understanding Arguments: Readings for College Writings*, (Boston: Houghton Mifflin Company, 1991).

4.   Jeffrey Walker, Glen McClish, *Understanding Arguments: Readings for College Writings*, (Boston: Houghton Mifflin Company, 1991).

5.   *Random House Webster's Unabridged Dictionary, Third Edition*, (New York: Random House Inc., 2001), p547.

6.   Jeffrey Walker, Glen McClish, *Understanding Arguments: Readings for College Writings*, (Boston: Houghton Mifflin Company, 1991), 3-49.

7.   Jeremy Stangroom and James Garvey, *The Great Philosophers: From Socrates to Foucault*, (New York: Barnes and Noble Publishing, Arcturus Publishing, 2005), 48-51, 76-79, 88-91.

8.   The Daily Bell, http://thedailybell.com/619/Hegelian-Dialectic, accessed, 2012.

9.   Kevin Knight, ed., "Dialectic," http:// www. newadvent.org/cathew /04770ahtw, accessed 2012.

10.   American Expose, "Hegelian Dialectic," http//www. amerikanexpose.com/hegel/, accessed 2012.

11.   Wikipedia, "Dialectic," enwikipedia.org/wiki/Dialectic, accessed 2012.

Classical liberal timeline sources:

1. The Web Chronology Project: Western and Central Europe Chronology, "The Industrial Revolution," www.thenagain.info/webchron/westeurope/indrev.html, 2013

2. Roger Ransom, "The Economics of the Civil War," ehnet/encyclopedia/article/ransom. civilwar.us, accessed 2012.

3. Pearson Education Inc., "Military Conflicts in U.S. History," www.infoplease.com/ipa/ A0931831.html, accessed 2013.

4. Filippo Cesarano, *Monetary Theory and Bretton Woods; The Construction of an International Monetary Order*, (New York: Cambridge University Press, 2006.)

5. Deepak Lal, *In Praise of Empires: Globalization and Order*, (New York: Palgrave MacMillan, 2004.

6. Howard Zinn, *A People's History of the United States: 1492-Present*, (New York: Harper Collins Publishers, 2005) 127.

7. Toke Aidt, Peter Jensen, Journal of Public Economics, "The taxman tools up: An event history study of the introduction of the personal income tax," www.econ.cour.ac.uk/faculty/aidt/papers/web/taxman.pdf, accessed 2013.

8. Wikipedia, "Romaniticism", enwikipedia/wiki/Romanticism, accessed 2013.

9. Marilyn Stokstad, *Art History, Second Edition, Vol. II*, (Upper Saddle River, NJ: Prentice Hall, Inc., 1995.

Dred Scott v. Sandford

1. Alex McBride, The Supreme Court: Supreme Court History: The First Hundred Years, "Dred Scott v. Sandford (1857)," www.pbs/wnet /supremecourt/antebellum /landmark_ dred.html, accessed 2014.

2. U.S. Supreme Court Media, IIT Chicago Kent College of Law, "Dred Scott v. Sandford," www.oyez.org /cases /1851-1900/1856 /1856_0, accessed 2014.

3. Primary Documents in American History, "Missouri Compromise," www. loc.gov /rr/ program/bib /ourdocs/Missouri.html, accessed 2014.

4. Wikipedia, "Atlantic Slave Trade," enwikipedia.org /wiki/Atlantic_slave_trade, accessed 2014.

5. Wikipedia, "United States v. Cruikshank," enwikipedia/org/wiki/United_States_v_Cruikshank, accessed 2014.

6. ACLU of Massachusetts, Rights Matter, "The Story of the Bill of Rights," www.rightsmatter.org / teachers /chapter9.html, accessed 2014.

7. David Gans, Constitutional Accountability Center, Mar 2009, theusconstitution.org/texthistory/580, accessed 2014.

8. Incorporation Doctrine, legaldictionary.thefreedictionary.com/Incorporation+Doctrine, accessed 2014

Modern Liberalism
Civil War, 1861, until WWII, 1944 and Bretton Woods.

The Civil War era was both a political and an economic transition.

The Civil War era was not only a political transition but also an economic one. After the French and Indian War gave England victory over France and the English hegemony in America, after the Americans won independence from the English, after the War of 1812 and after Native American lands were repeatedly invaded and taken over by European transplants and then annexed into the future United States, the land boom was over. A new economic system that wasn't based on land acquisition was needed. Historically, the North and South had developed economies inside separate production systems where land ownership served as the foundation for most wealth building during the colonial period. But Northern lands and Southern lands possessed different advantages and required different development strategies to bring them to their most productive state.

The North, with lands that possessed marginal agricultural advantages, had self-sufficient farms that couldn't produce much of an agricultural surplus. Without a surplus, without the ability to sell an over-abundant amount, there could be little agricultural profit. So instead of developing farming as the only venture, Northerners also relied on timber for building ships. The ancient forests of the east coast were populated by huge trees the like of which can no longer be found. They were used to build sailing ships and houses. Northerners sold ships and salted fish and various whale products to make money in the shipping trade. Merchant shipping and then other industries like flour mills and textile mills became central to the Northern economy. The Middle colonies made a more robust agricultural living with fertile farms and a longer growing season. Wheat was a profitable cash crop for the middle colonies. The middle colonies also sold linseed to Irish flax farmers. The Northern and Middle colonies made money with timber sales, livestock killed and sold as meat, and furs obtained by trading with Native Americans.[1]

The South made the most of its remarkably fertile soils. Southern land owners did it under plantation based agriculture on large acreage that required a great deal of labor under harsh, sometimes deadly, conditions including brutal work and terrible humid heat. Malaria, once alien to the colonies, became established later with imported slaves. The early South put money into buying the contracts of indentured servants, often younger English people in their teens and twenties who didn't have money to pay their own trans-Atlantic passage. Indentured servants worked to pay their passage under a system where planters reimbursed transport merchants for their servant's passage fare while the servants worked for an agreed upon time span.

Later, when it was cheaper to buy slaves than to purchase indentures, planters bought slaves imported from Africa. This brought people into the South from many backgrounds. Three cultural and ethnically distinct groups were present, including the plantation owners of English second son aristocracy (driven by primogeniture to come to America), English people of less advantaged commoner families and African cultures, alien to the West. These groups together comprised a diverse mix. The Protestant North was more culturally uniform under its Puritan influence. The Middle colonies had some cultural diversity because of their tolerance for differences. Although these early cultural groups didn't remain the predominant ones in terms of the whole population as the population grew after the 1830's, their influence set each region apart from the other.[2, 3]

The strong willed people of the North and South each wanted a different kind of society to go with their different kind of economy.

Because the North and the South were settled by mostly English people that came from different demographic sets, these regions had strongly different views about the society they wanted to build and to strengthen. The North was settled by Puritans, Quakers and Dutch Protestants. The Puritans and Quakers put their religion at the center of their society. They were seeking religious freedom for their own group. Their aims were unlike those of Southern leaders, mostly Anglican second sons from wealthy aristocratic English families with their servants and slaves. In England, the English Civil War had been fought between the Anglicans and the Puritans and in the U.S. they continued to be rival political factions that sought different social ends. The English Civil War led to the English Interregnum, or period of Puritan rule in England. It lasted from 1642-1660. In colonial America, wealthy Southern plantation owners wanted to reproduce a class system like the one in England that would forever favor their families. Political groups in both the North and the South wanted their social system to prove superior to any other system. Both groups struggled for dominance. Because they differed in their economic and social approaches, they became political rivals. When circumstances began to change under new improvements in transportation, the economic interests of each region began to diverge even further. Their relationship became even more aggressively competitive.

Congress foresaw the nation's need for more engineers and authorized funding for West Point's Military Academy.

On the 16th of March, 1802, Congress looked ahead to the future and authorized funding for and establishment of the U.S. Military Academy, at West Point, New York. An engineering education for both war and geographical survey eventually prepared graduates for dual service in the military and the construction of railways.[4] Britain's Liverpool and Manchester Railway, a short line linking two English cities that opened in 1830, blazed a path for rail development of longer railway lines and of rail outside of England.[5] But canals were built before rail was. France's Canal du Midi (1681), Britain's Bridgewater Canal (completed, 1769), Eiderkanal, Denmark (1784), all demonstrated canal usefulness before rail was developed,[6] probably because rail was more expensive to build than canals. And railroads required greater technical investment in engines, rail and track. But despite its greater expense, rail could go more places than a canal system could.[7]

Improvements in transportation that got people thinking differently in the U.S. began with the Erie Canal. The Erie Canal, started in 1823, was originally 363 miles long. Several people wanted the Erie Canal and one of them was Joseph Ellicot. He wanted to increase the value of his New York state property holdings by improving transportation to his land.[8] President Monroe vetoed a congressional bill that would have funded the canal because he thought that federal funding would be unconstitutional.[9] Instead, New York State charged a toll to defray the cost of building the canal.

The canal cost seven million dollars to build because large diesel powered earth-moving machinery wasn't invented yet. But since the canal cut overland transportation costs by ninety percent, tolls were affordable and money could be easily made on the route once freight and passenger traffic took advantage of the shortcut the canal provided from New York's harbor to the Great Lakes. This route opened up the farming interior of the nation to the East coast.[10] The 1823 Erie Canal development persuaded people in the North to advocate in favor of government development of transportation but the South didn't see their own interests to be represented by such improvements. Southern products were shipped by Northern built ships from New Orleans either to Europe or to the Northern U.S. ports. The South didn't see its interests to be in common with the transportation interests of the North.

1860 was a disagreeable year that showed divergent interests between the Northern economy and the Southern economy.

1860 was a year of political disagreement between the North and the South on the issues of homestead size out West and rail expansion westward. The Homestead Act of 1860 would have aggravated the slavery issue by limiting government land parcels for sale to 160 acres, too small for plantations, so President Buchanan vetoed it. The Pacific Railway Bill would have expanded rail from coast to coast but Southern Congress members voted it down. Southerners didn't need transportation out West. This frustrated people in the North who wanted to expand their businesses into a larger market economy like the one made possible by the Erie Canal system. Land expansion was over but land speculators could get rich if lands they held were brought into communication with the rest of the nation. Much money could be made if only the South would get out of the way.[11]

The Civil War shows that competition won over compromise. The war contest would eventually remodel the nation away from evenly matched bickering between the North and South and also would lead to increased political domination of the South by the North for a long period. Southern tradition had looked to the European aristocratic class system of the past. It was conservative. The South had wealth in few hands, wealth to benefit mostly the richest families, wealth based on tradition and resistant to change. By contrast, the North was formed by religious radicals. Radical Protestants had escaped religious persecution, separating from European religious strife, away from aristocracy and toward a position that valued individual religious freedom where every person within the tradition of their own religious doctrine would act as a moral center. Surprisingly, even though the North and South were both determined to stay true to their own political and economic traditions, the North's economy was more flexible and amenable to change. Rail would be an advantage to the North just as the ship building trade had been.

Radical Northern ideas came to dominate American politics before and after the Civil War. Abolitionists came from the Protestant North. So did the people who later supported temperance and women's suffrage. The dominance of the North over the South would bring reforms in education, women's rights, abolition and temperance. History would change as Northern abolitionists led the United States to end slavery. Ending slavery and expanding transportation moved the nation toward industry under a national market economy and away from agriculture. This new economy no longer needed land expansion to keep it healthy. But it needed a new tax structure and a transition into income taxation moved the nation from classical liberalism to modern liberalism.

Income tax to pay for wars, and railroads to circulate people and goods.

In 1842, the United Kingdom adopted the permanent income tax. It had relied on a temporary income tax in the years 1798-1802 and 1803-1816. Paying for wars between nation states was what stimulated the development of this tax.[12] From 1799-1814, Napoleon Bonaparte I ruled in France and he stirred up expensive wars that required more tax money. Napoleon also encouraged the development of professional government bureaucracies. This motivated nations to charge a new kind of tax, income taxes to pay for wars and for growing a bigger bureaucracy. In the U.S., in 1861, the Union used a temporary income tax to fund the Civil War, and having this funding was part of the reason that the Union persevered to win against the Confederacy. Plantation owners didn't approve of income taxes and the Confederate army couldn't get the funding that it needed through voluntary donations during the Union blockade. Temporary income taxes continued in the U.S. during 1862-1872, 1894-1895. Permanent income tax was passed into law in 1913, during the Wilson Administration, under the Sixteenth Amendment.[13]

Economic financing for building railroads was mostly in the form of land grants. Millions of acres were given to rail companies. Some land was used to build track and other land was sold for funding rail expansion.[14] Rail bonds offered on Wall Street also made private money available to rail development in the late nineteenth century.[15] With a new mixed economy, taxes could fund an expansion of federal bureaucracy. Transportation regulation was the first agenda under the newly forming regulatory state. It would assert new taxes and new laws to direct the railroads for the sake of the market economy.

Railroads stirred up a lot of changes stimulated by goods and people circulation across the United States. One of the important changes was opening up the nation to strangers and making cities into places that grew so large with such varied and changeable populations that people could acquire anonymity by traveling. Railroads removed small communities from isolation and self-sufficiency and brought them into a newly competitive national marketplace. Overland travel was finally affordable and more convenient. Lecturers could give a public address in one city, take a train to the next city where they gave the same lecture and then leave by train for the following day's lecture. A lecturer in demand could make more money because of trains. The nation would now mix populations from different regions as people traveled. Newspapers also grew in importance. Traveling entertainers, church revivalists and spiritualists moved about the country and people began to see that life was always in motion: new people, new products to buy and new ideas. Consistent novelty became part of America's permanent makeup.

Post-Civil War Challenges.

After the War, economic losses in the South were not healed soon. The value of Southern slaves in 1860 has been estimated at $2,700,000,000.[16] Repairing the loss of money that had been invested in slavery or the loss of time and energy invested in producing a class system that couldn't work in the industrial age left scars on American culture both in the South and in the whole nation. Cultural racism has left a legacy of suffering and missed opportunities.

African cultural contributions to America have been of high value even without including their contributions to the agricultural South during slavery. In the arts, black Americans have dominated the shape of American jazz and blues music. They have enhanced and innovated in modern dance. And they have contributed widely in the visual arts. Black intellectuals like W.E.B. Dubois and

George Washington Carver, have made contributions to literature, and politics (Dubois) and agricultural science (Carver). After the Civil War, how to restore Southern agricultural wealth without slavery and after heavy financial losses was not an easy thing to understand. Northerners played a role but that also created more controversy. The high hopes of Southerners that their aristocratic culture would endure as part of America's legacy faded leaving bitter regret behind for a political and economic contest that they lost. The intertwined cultures of the South began to interact differently but in the wreckage of what had once produced wealth and now lay idle. The Southern economy after the war faced enormous uncertainty, insecurity and poverty.

Southerners have been Americans who survived military occupation and long lasting poverty along with their own lost hopes and failed intentions. Healing the South began by reuniting the three classes that formed Southern culture, second son aristocrats, African Americans and other English common folk under a changed economic structure. It was a slow process. After the war, and after Reconstruction, political leadership in the South would go mostly to men who had served honorably during the Civil War under the Confederate flag. But first, Reconstruction. Immediately after the Civil War ended, Republican Union forces that occupied the South supported African Americans into Southern government. Hiram Revels (1822-1901), an African American, served the Senate after he won his election to the office. Another black Senator, Blanche K. Bruce (1841-1898) served in Mississippi. Pinckney B.S. Pinchback (1837-1921) was Louisiana's Governor.[17] Military troops tried to force Southerners to accept equality among the races. But national patience didn't outlast Southern resistance to changes being enforced by the North. An application of federal force failed to produce social changes desired by the North in the South.

President Lincoln was elected under the Republican Party. The Southern Democrats lost to Southern Republicans for the first ten years of Reconstruction and then began stubbornly to regain political power. With their eventual regain of power they instituted Jim Crow, making black people a lower political caste in the South. Jim Crow showed the determination of the South to resist Northern interference in Southern society. The Civil Rights movement in the mid twentieth century eventually united multiracial political groups that insisted upon social change and that supported permanent court enforced institutional changes in recognition of the natural rights of African Americans. But this step was taken long after the war and also after military enforcement of racial integration had failed.

The new economy had a set of novel opportunities.

Whereas land acquisition was the basis of the classical liberal American economy, rail and the development of a national market economy shaped the U.S. after the Civil War. Before rail, local economies in the interior of the nation were mostly self-sufficient because it was expensive to bring goods overland. Early America used its waterways to great advantage but overland transport was so expensive that instead of moving goods from the center of the country to the coasts it was cheaper for people living on the coasts to either produce what they needed or to import shipped goods from Europe.[18] Grains were often converted into liquor because transporting spirits was easier than transporting grain. The expense of overland transport had closed off the center of the nation from the coasts and kept people rooted inside isolated communities because moving to a different community was too time consuming, expensive and risky.

The Erie Canal showed how important transportation was to formation of the market economy. People before rail who lived outside the reach of the Erie Canal relied on local businesses and local agriculture. When rail spread, it represented a new opportunity to travel and to export and import goods within the entire nation. A total national consciousness grew up in spite of regionalism for the first time. Of huge importance, rail gave the United States a new market economy that hadn't been possible before the railroad linked up the nation's producers and consumers. This created new problems including churn—changes in employment and in the business makeup of communities— because of competition. Some established businesses were closed because another manufacturer could make a product more cheaply and transportation was now affordable enough to bring it from far away. Local markets changed to be more accepting of goods from elsewhere instead of only relying on local production. Cities and regions began to specialize in certain goods and industries. Mixed economy within the context of income taxation was made permanent during Woodrow Wilson's administration in 1913. Income taxes gave increased political power to the federal government and funded changes that took better advantage of the economic dividends of industrial expansion during the second phase of industrialization.

Extra taxes put pressure on self-sufficient agriculturists to make money. It increased urban migration. But more money added to politics also meant more corruption and political deal making. And the growth of immigration both before and after the Civil War created new challenges in housing and labor. As the voting franchise increased to include people without property, and included African Americans and women, the idea of popular sovereignty changed. A wider voting franchise made people expand how they thought of popular sovereignty. Elections were not just for political representation but also for economic opportunity. People hoped that government elections from a wider voting franchise would get broad needs in the wider public more attention. People under the universal franchise began to believe that the government would be a better servant to meet their needs if it were more powerful. They imagined that each faction could get some of the public's money to get whatever it wanted.

German Idealism and American pragmatism were responses to growth in governmental power. Monopolies sprang up out of the market economy's wealth.

The warnings of the Founding Fathers about how government power should be limited weren't well appreciated or even understood in the new majority after everyone could vote. The altered voting demographic had changed from educated property owners to a wider spectrum of sometimes uneducated people. Power in government began to be longed for as the best palliative to meet people's multitude of needs. In Germany, Friedrich Nietzsche wrote about power as an end in itself. Max Weber wrote that government had a legitimate power to use violence against people inside its territory. Georg Hegel thought that people could have limitless understanding and limitless evolution towards human perfection. Karl Marx thought that historical materialism showed an inevitable class struggle for power dominance between classes. Everywhere in the political discussions of the age, people seemed to extol power above other attributes of government. Politicians began to promise that if their constituencies gave them more power they could deliver to them anything that was desired, security most of all. This was a march forward based on German Idealism.[19]

Classical liberal liberty concepts that had emphasized limited government gave way after the Civil War to expansion of the federal government. This expansion allowed investors to take advantage of new economic opportunity that would unify the nation differently and also make investors rich. Economic opportunity was the incentive for political change in this transition. But looking at modern liberalism's rhetoric makes the change look less like pragmatism and more like crazy political inconsistency. Americans moved from rationalism, humanism and neoclassical liberalism toward irrational spiritualism, socialism and constructivism. Constructivism is a belief that the politic can be controlled and directed to become something different than it had been before, even something outside of grassroots norms.

Instead of supporting individual liberty, people who wanted to help poor immigrants founded American pragmatism. This philosophy came about before women had the vote and gave people such as Jane Addams, an opportunity to be active within the community by performing public service. As a social philosophy, pragmatism called for personal action to help less advantaged Americans. Actions were to be evaluated on the basis of practical results instead of upon conservative philosophical principles. Pragmatism was forward looking and sought immediate improvements. National politics changed from supporting liberty and privacy based on a limited government to favoring an expanding government with positive regulations and subsidies. An active government also heated up the contests between political factions and grew their number because they were rewarded with government favoritism. More taxes in a bigger economy increased the value of the political prizes available for those who could gain government support.

Groups that benefited during the period of modern liberalism included some of the politically disempowered people who had lacked property under classical liberalism. Newly empowered people included women after they got the vote under the Nineteenth Amendment in 1920 and indentured servants who were replaced by immigrants without indenture as ship fares became cheaper and the industrial revolution advanced living standards and pay after the 1820's. Native Americans, who lost their lands, weren't among political winners. Instead, they were persecuted into the twentieth century. Former slaves under Jim Crow sometimes fared less well than people of color who fled the South. When African Americans migrated to the North they could sometimes find work in factories as did many new immigrants. But people of color encountered racism even in the Northern cities. The Gilded Age was rewarding for railway, steel, and oil tycoons. These monopolists vied for power with the government itself during the administrations of several presidents, first under Grant in the context of the Credit Mobilier scandal (with origins in the Lincoln Administration) and until FDR put a temporary slowdown on their takeover of politics.

On April 29th, 1938, President Roosevelt gave a speech entitled, "Message to Congress on Curbing Monopolies."[20] In it he said, "The first truth is that the liberty of a democracy is not safe if the people tolerate the growth of private power to a point where it becomes stronger than their democratic state itself. That, in its essence, is Fascism—ownership of Government by an individual, by a group, or by any other controlling private power. The second truth is that the liberty of a democracy is not safe if its business system does not provide employment and produce and distribute goods in such a way as to sustain an acceptable standard of living....This program should appeal to the honest common sense of every independent business man interested primarily in running his own business at a profit rather than in controlling the businesses of other men. It is not intended as the beginning of any ill-considered "trust busting" activity which lacks proper consideration for economic results...It is a program whose basic purpose is to stop the progress of collectivism in business and turn business back to the democratic competitive order."[21] In this speech he promised to increase government oversight of business and to break up monopolies. But while he warned against monopolists gaining too much power, he also expected American businesses to provide jobs. The power competition between governments and business to manipulate the economy towards different goals was obvious in this speech. This tension between the political goals of government that claimed to be acting in the public's interest and the political goals of monopolists striving to increase their political power through economic dominance gave a preview of neoliberalism.

New ideas for a new market society.

People's intellectual ideas were different in the U.S. during modern liberalism. The rationalism, humanism and liberalism of classical liberalism was left behind as an anachronism. During modern liberalism, Darwin and Freud's theories of evolution and the unconscious began to affect people's thinking. People thought about the mysterious unconscious instead of the conscious intellect. They became interested in spiritual mysteries. They became fascinated by hidden truths and interior perceptions. Darwin's theories led some to imagine that social contests should be brutal to eliminate rivals—Social Darwinism. Some people began to think about eugenics—the idea that scientific breeding could produce a better human to replace a flawed humanity—that man's sinful nature could be reworked. These attitudes opposed Greek humanism—the belief that human beings are essentially good and that they can make positive choices.

Others began to believe in the potential of humans to actively intervene in human affairs in order to prevent social harms or to change society. These were the Pragmatists. They ignored the Founding Father's warnings. Liberal thinking had started with first political principles found in Greek and Roman classics, and under classical liberalism had moved to second principles laid out by Locke, personal sovereignty and natural rights. But people now moved towards German Idealism, a political philosophy that was most interested in limitless power instead of in truth. German Idealism was based on the writings of four men.[22] Immanuel Kant (1724-1804), Gottlieb Fichte (1762-1814), Georg Wilhelm Friedrich Hegel (1770-1831) and Friedrich Wilhelm Joseph Schelling (1775-1854).[23] Nationalism began to loom larger, threatening all the accomplishments of industrialization. Conflicts between labor and industry punctuated the period. Crime increased. Prohibition became a constitutional experiment that proved that regulations could create instead of prevent social problems.[24, 25] Corrupt relationships between government enforcers taking protection money to look the other way and bootleggers showed that prohibition regulations stimulated crime. The World Wars took the shine off industrialization by showing the harmful effect of industrialized total-war under the huge war budget funded with income taxes. More taxes meant bigger wars.

Several groups have provided good insights into modern liberalism. The pragmatists, suffragists, abolitionists, prohibitionists, German Idealists, communists, labor rights activists, peace advocates and soldiers of wars, spiritualists, civil rights activists all offered a variety of comments on what brought this period of American history into great prominence and struggle worth writing about. All can't be included and many weren't trying to make a rational argument. They made emotional appeals instead. Many reasoned outside of conventional belief systems. Booker T. Washington, John Dewey, Jane Addams, Susan B. Anthony and Elizabeth Cady Stanton, Immanuel Kant, Georg Hegel, Charles Darwin, Karl Marx, Friedrich Nietzsche, Sigmund Freud, Jacob A. Riis, Major-General

Smedley D. Butler of the U.S. Marines, Walter Lippmann, and W.E.B. Dubois were people that can still speak to us about modern liberalism and whose voices may resonate with you as you begin to understand the world they described. Many were activists shaping a new politic inside a growing market economy. They made up new rules that couldn't be like the old ones. Rules that were based on entirely new contingencies.

Booker T. Washington's South.

The Reconstruction Period after the Civil War offered monster kinds of challenges. Challenges that would consume many lifetimes of focused effort. Whatever talents and insights a person could muster, they wouldn't run out of more work to do. Calamity of economy included poverty among every Southern class, lack of education in most, wartime destruction and the displacement of wealth from planters to other would be developers, many developers coming from outside of the South and causing resentment to fester. It wouldn't be true to say that the South was unimproved by the industrial revolution before the war, because the cotton gin's invention had hugely increased cotton production. In fact, the cotton gin had made slaves more valuable. But what the cotton gin could do on one hand to improve cotton production, the culture of slavery resisted on the other hand by making manual work a sign of inferiority. This delayed further industrial development. Idleness was admired instead of industry. The slave culture had kept the South from developing a modern economy. Booker T. Washington (1856-1915) explained this well.[26]

After the war, the South needed a training program to increase labor competency and to substitute personal initiative for the earlier system of slave labor exploitation. And it needed schools to educate people where no schools or basic skills training had existed before. Poverty after the war was widespread in the South because the earlier economy had been destroyed and a new economy hadn't yet replaced it. This meant that funding for schools came mostly from the North. Booker T. Washington was a Southern American freed from slavery during his childhood, who published, *Up from Slavery*, in 1901. He was heroic because of his determination to acquire an education against the long odds of his own poverty and to improve the lives of other African Americans through training and education.

His willingness to bring every talent he had to bear on solving problems in the South made him stand out and brought him into contact with people in the wealthiest classes of both Europe and America. He built social bridges between classes and between races and places. He utilized all his skill, education and training not only to teach and train but also to acquire donations and even to help in mending the wounded South by delivering speeches that famously reached out to people who were socially diverse, smoothing controversy and aiding social progress. His example of service was generous and inclusive of anyone who would help to mend the South, and most especially anyone who would help people of color. Decades later, well after Reconstruction, the South still had Jim Crow laws and this caused people like W.E.B. DuBois to criticize Booker T. Washington for his peaceful strivings. Reading quotes from *Up from Slavery*, may help readers to understand the challenges faced during Reconstruction and why Booker T. Washington's strategy was so different from later civil rights strategies.

"The whole machinery of slavery was so constructed as to cause labour, as a rule, to be looked upon as a badge of degradation, of inferiority. Hence labour was something that both races on the slave plantation sought to escape. The slave system on our place, in a large measure, took the spirit of self-reliance and self-help out of the white people....The slave owner and his sons had mastered no special industry. They unconsciously had imbibed the feeling that manual labour was not the proper thing for them. On the other hand, the slaves, in many cases, had mastered some handicraft, and none were ashamed, and few unwilling, to labour."[27]

"It was while my home was at Malden that what was known as the "Ku Klux Klan" was in the height of its activity. The "Ku Klux" were bands of men who had joined themselves together for the purpose of regulating the conduct of colored people, especially with the object of preventing the members of the race from exercising any influence in politics... Their objects, in the main, were to crush out the political aspirations of the Negroes, but they did not confine themselves to this, because schoolhouses as well as churches were burned by them, and many innocent persons were made to suffer. During this period not a few colored people lost their lives...The "Ku Klux" period was, I think, the darkest part of Reconstruction days."[28]

"General Armstrong had found out that there was quite a number of young colored men and women who were intensely in earnest in wishing to get an education, but who were prevented from entering Hampton Institute because they were too poor to be able to pay any portion of the cost of their board, or even to supply themselves with books. He conceived the idea of starting a night-school in connection with the Institute, into which a limited number of the most promising of these young men and women would be received, on condition that they were to work for ten hours during the day, and attend school for two hours at night. They were to be paid something above the cost of their board for their work....I gave them the name of "The Plucky Class"—a name which soon grew popular and spread throughout the institution."[29]

"My experience is that there is something in human nature which always makes an individual recognize and reward merit, no matter under what colour of skin merit is found. I have found, too, that it is the visible, the tangible that goes a long ways in softening prejudices. The actual sight of a first-class house that a Negro has built is ten times more potent than pages of discussion about a house that he ought to build, or perhaps could build."[30]

"One third of the population of the South is of the Negro race. No enterprise seeking the material, civil, or moral welfare of this section can disregard this element of our population and reach the highest success....Our greatest danger is that in the great leap from slavery to freedom we may overlook the fact that the masses of us are to live by the productions of our hands, and fail to keep in mind that we shall prosper in proportion as we learn to dignify and glorify common labour and put brains and skill into the common occupation of life....There is no escape through law of man or God from the inevitable:

The laws of changeless justice bind
Oppressor with oppressed;
And close as sin and suffering joined
We march to fate abreast.

...The wisest among my race understand that the agitation of questions of social equality is the extremest folly, and that progress in the enjoyment of all the privileges that will come to us must be the result of severe and constant struggle rather than of artificial forcing." —"The Atlanta Exposition Address"[31]

Changes in ideas during modern liberalism.

People's methods for conceptualizing the world around them innovated away from rationalism during the modern liberal period across Europe and America. Here's a partial list of intellectual contributors and their ideas that caused people to think differently during the modern liberal period:

Immanuel Kant (1724-1824)...mental attention reshapes life experience,
Georg Hegel (1770-1831)...Hegelian dialectic...desire for limitlessness;
Charles Darwin (1809-1886)...the ongoing process of evolution;
Karl Marx (1818-1883)...historical materialism...communism;
Friedrich Nietzsche (1844-1900)...power itself as achievement;
Sigmund Freud (1856-1939)...the hidden unconscious.

Locke's ideas influenced philosophers after the classical liberal period.

John Locke's life (1632-1704), during the classical liberal period, and more specifically his ideas about empiricism caused ripples in subsequent history. Locke's philosophical empiricism, or the method of learning by observation, contrasted with the rhetorical way of reasoning from first causes and carefully set-out definitions of objects and terms that had been followed from antiquity through the use of rhetorical argument. This created a rift between the reasoning method of the classical world and the reasoning method of the modern world. Modern liberal Pragmatists from Dewey to James to Addams to Oliver Wendell Holmes Jr., accepted no first causes or political rules that could alter their intention to change American politics. They argued against immovable principles of the past. Locke's empiricism caused repercussions in many social arenas where human thought could lead to social experiments in law and politics. Cultural reactions for and against empiricism that happened during the modern liberal period were probably unimagined by Locke during his lifetime.

Immanuel Kant (1724-1824) followed Locke's empiricism further. Kant decided that people couldn't be relied upon for perfect observation. He wrote about this in his book from 1781, *Critique of Pure Reason*.[32] His writings undid the confidence of empiricism. When he thought deeply about how we observe and think, he thought that we got in our own way, and failed to acquire a perfect understanding of the world around us. Georg Hegel (1770-1831), wrote *Phenomenology of Spirit*, in 1807. Here, he examined the span of all time to imagine the unfolding of Absolute Spirit in human history.[33] His Hegelian dialectic put a person's mind onto an endless spiral of conjecture in the hope of reaching ever more advanced questions that would lead to limitless realization of infinite understanding.

Hegel's prose has seemed impenetrable in many ways as compared with Locke's direct empiricism. Hegel wanted to obliterate limits and mortality by embracing limitlessness through a kind of God-consciousness. The Hegelian dialectic method differed from the Greek dialectic. The Greek dialectic would allow a person to argue against a bad idea and throw it out whereas the Hegelian dialectic could be only a sequence of conjecture that never decided anything. Hegel's desire for limitlessness also differed from Greek humanism. The Ancient Greeks had viewed people as limited because they had a mortal lifespan. But ancient Greeks also saw humanity as capable of heroic deeds that made life worthwhile.[34]

Hegel joined with other German thinkers to form German Idealism. Some discount German Idealism's qualification as any kind of philosophy for two reasons. The first reason is that many of the German idealists began their studies in theology rather than philosophy. And German Idealism reached back to spiritual faith based ways of substituting spiritual revelation for rational thinking. It also took the position that people can know by faith and without proof. This position particularly opposed Greek philosophy's way of seeking truth that can be proven through rhetorical or logical argument. The second reason to disqualify German Idealism as a kind of philosophy has been that German Idealism's embrace of limitlessness made power more important than truth. German idealists thought that an inner awareness could lead a person to possess hidden knowledge. These ideas may have encouraged Hitler's rise along with the rise of totalitarianism. The German idealists were not rationalists. They operated without epistemological justifications or rational proofs.[35]

Karl Marx (1818-1883) developed the idea of historical materialism and also the idea of class conflict that would lead inevitably to political revolution. He wrote *The Communist Manifesto* (1848). Historical materialism has been the belief that a sequence of political and economic forms pass through history in a maturation sequence that is inevitable. No one, according to this theory, can alter the process of deconstruction and reconstruction. Part of what made historical materialism scary to many was the idea that historical change would be irresistible and occur for hidden reasons by secret mechanisms instead of by laws or by rational choices. Marx made the argument that violent revolution was inevitable.[36]

New ideas reshaped the ways that people thought during modern liberalism. The hidden world of the unconscious, perhaps a limitless unknowable wellspring for the creative, or a well of secret motivation, made people think differently about intentions in society and among individuals. Constantly novel challenges made people feel even less rooted to the past. On the other hand, the idea of evolution made people think further than a single lifetime. After the tragic deaths that occurred during the Civil War, spiritualism in America became a strategy to reach toward people beyond death, to discover secrets held by the dead or to expand social boundaries by imagining greater sexual freedom in the spirit world. Spiritualism allowed people to explore social options beyond Victorian sensibilities.[37]

Mixed economy politics and the growth of bureaucracy created new money making opportunities funded by public monies and monopoly industry. Media opened people's awareness to scandal and new ideas in civil society and opened the world to advertising and propaganda. New products radically altered people's lives and their ideas about what might be possible with technology and industry. Factional politics under a wider voting franchise and a more powerful federal government led people to hope that the politic could make unlimited gains possible through greater political power. This approach couldn't be more opposite to classical liberalism's dedication to limiting government.

Quotes from modern liberal philosophers, scientists, and social thinkers.

Here are some quotes from modern liberal thinkers. They approached knowledge differently than people during the Enlightenment and during classical liberalism. Some of them, the German Idealists for example, rejected rationalism, epistemology or empiricism. Some of them, like Darwin or Marx or Hegel, looked beyond the span of a single person's life to try to understand hidden processes. Some, like Sigmund Freud or Friedrich Nietzsche rejected the external world for a new internal awareness. Here's a single quote from each of these contributors with an important idea or theory or phrase passed on to us by them. During modern liberalism, ideas spread from one place to another more quickly. A powerful idea could permeate all of Western culture to influence people in distant nation states at about the same moment. During classical liberalism, ideas had percolated more slowly. Sometimes decades would pass between the time that a writer could influence England as compared with France or Germany. See if you recognize any of these ideas as part of your cultural heritage.

"I term, therefore, an explanation of the manner in which conceptions can apply *a priori* to objects, the *transcendental deduction* of conceptions, and I distinguish it from the *empirical* deduction, which indicates the mode in which a conception is obtained through experience and reflection thereon; consequently, does not concern itself with the right, but only with the fact of our obtaining conceptions in such and such a manner. We have already seen that we are in possession of two perfectly different kinds of conceptions, which nevertheless agree with each other in this, that they both apply to objects completely *a priori*. These are the conceptions of space and time as forms of sensibility, and the categories as pure conceptions of the understanding. To attempt an empirical deduction of either of these classes would be labor in vain, because the distinguishing characteristic of their nature consists in this, that they apply to their objects, without having borrowed anything from experience towards the representation of them. Consequently, if a deduction of these conceptions is necessary, it must always be transcendental." Immanuel Kant, *Critique of Pure Reason*[38]

"Each stage is a specific realm of Nature and all appear to have independent existence. But the last is the concrete unity of all the preceding ones, just as, in general, each successive stage embodies the lower stages, but equally posits these, as its non-organic nature, over against itself. One stage is the power of the other, and this relation is reciprocal. Here can be seen the true meaning of *powers (Potenzen)*. The non-organic Elements are powers opposed to what is individual, subjective—the non-organic destroys the organic. But equally the organism, in its turn, is the power which subdues its universal powers, air, water; these are perpetually liberated and also perpetually subdued and assimilated. The eternal life of Nature consists in this: first, that the Idea displays itself in each sphere so far as it can within the finitude of that sphere, just as each drop of water provides an image of the sun, and secondly, that the Notion, through its dialectic, breaks through the limitation of this sphere, since it cannot rest content with an inadequate element, and necessarily passes over into a higher stage." Georg Hegel, *Introduction to the Philosophy of Nature*[39]

"Owing to this struggle for life, any variation, however slight and from whatever cause proceeding, if it be in any degree profitable to an individual of any species, in its infinitely complex relations to other organic beings and to external nature, will tend to the preservation of that individual, and will generally be inherited by its offspring. The offspring, also, will thus have a better chance of surviving, for, of the many individuals of any species which are periodically born, but a small number can survive. I have called this principle, by which each slight variation, if useful, is preserved, by the term of Natural Selection, in order to mark its relation to man's power of selection." Charles Darwin, *On the Origin of the Species*[40]

"In the social production of their life, men enter into definite relations that are indispensable and independent of their will, relations of production which correspond to a definite stage of development of their material productive forces. The sum total of these relations of production, on which rises a legal and political superstructure and to which correspond definite forms of social consciousness. The mode of production of material life conditions the social, political and intellectual life process in general. It is not the consciousness of men that determines their being, but on the contrary, their social being that determines their consciousness. At a certain stage of their development, the material productive forces of society come in conflict with the existing relations of production, or—what is but a legal expression for the same thing—with the property relations within which they have been at work hitherto. From forms of development of the productive forces these relations turn into their fetters. Then begins the epoch of social revolution…No social order ever perishes before all the productive forces for which there is room in it have developed; and new, higher relations of production never appear before the material conditions of the existence have matured in the womb of the old society itself." Karl Marx, *A Contribution to the Critique of Political Economy (preface)*[41]

"But how could we reproach or praise the universe? Let us beware of attributing to it heartlessness and unreason or their opposites: it is neither perfect nor beautiful, nor noble, nor does it wish to become any of these things; it does not by any means strive to imitate man. None of our aesthetic and moral judgments apply to it. Nor does it have any instinct for self-preservation or any other instinct; and it does not observe any laws either. There are only necessities: there is nobody who commands, nobody who obeys, nobody who trespasses. Once you know that there are no purposes, you also know that there is no accident; for it is only beside a world of purposes that the word "accident" has meaning….How could we drink up the sea? Who gave us the sponge to wipe away the entire horizon? What were we doing when we unchained this earth from its sun? Whither is it moving now? Whither are we moving? Away from all suns? Are we not plunging continually? Backward, sideward, forward, in all directions? Is there still any up or down? Are we not straying as through an infinite nothing? Do we not feel the breath of empty space? Has it not become colder? Is not night continually closing in on us? Do we not need to light lanterns in the morning? Do we hear nothing as yet of the noise of the gravediggers who are burying God? Do we smell nothing as yet of the divine decomposition? Gods, too, decompose. God is dead. God remains dead. And we have killed him…What after all are these churches now if they are not the tombs and sepulchers of God?" Friedrich Nietzsche, "The Gay Science"[42]

"The liberty of the individual is no gift of civilization. It was greatest before there was any civilization, though then, it is true, it had for the most part no value, since the individual was scarcely in a position to defend it. The development of civilization imposes restrictions on it, and justice demands that no one shall escape those restrictions. What makes itself felt in a human community as a desire for freedom may be their revolt against some existing injustice, and so may prove favorable to a further development of civilization; it may remain compatible with civilization. But it may also spring from the remains of their original personality, which is still untamed by civilization and may thus become the basis in them of hostility to civilization. The urge for freedom, therefore, is directed against particular forms and demands of civilization or against civilization altogether. It does not seem as though any influence could induce a man to change his nature into a termite's. No doubt he will always defend his claim to individual liberty against the will of the group. A good part of the struggles of mankind centre round the single task of finding an expedient accommodation—one, that is, that will bring happiness—between this claim of the individual and the cultural claims of the group; and one of the problems that touches the fate of humanity is whether such an accommodation can be reached by means of some particular form of civilization or whether this conflict is irreconcilable…At the same time we have been careful not to fall in with the prejudice that civilization is synonymous with perfecting, that it is the road to perfection pre-ordained for men." Sigmund Freud, *Civilization and Its Discontents*[43]

During the classical liberal period the voting franchise wasn't universal, as mentioned. Struggle for the vote included struggle among three groups. The first group was non-property owners, the second group was black men and the third group that struggled to get the voting franchise was women. An important modern liberal idea was that each member of society should have an equal opportunity to express his political opinions as well as have an equal opportunity for economic security. The struggle for a woman's right to vote, or suffrage, was begun long before the goal was achieved. It was begun in 1848, well before the Civil War but not achieved until 1920.[44] That's when the Nineteenth Amendment was finally passed, long after many of the women who worked on behalf of this political cause had died.

Susan B. Anthony (1820-1906) and Elizabeth Cady Stanton (1815-1902), were allies in the cause of women's rights including the right to vote and they worked for most of their lives to achieve a political change that neither woman lived long enough to realize. Their struggle moved the cause forward until women finally got the right to vote in 1920. The Nineteenth Amendment doubled the nation's voting franchise. And even though they lived and died before women got the vote, Anthony and Cady Stanton were politically able suffragists. They wrote speeches, founded a newspaper, visited politicians and spoke before crowds of people for decades, offending and inspiring by turns. Until finally, they changed people's minds. They also left a legacy of women's organizations and capable female political leaders who continued fighting for women's suffrage until the goal was finally achieved.

Susan B. Anthony came from a Quaker family in Massachusetts and Elizabeth Cady-Stanton came from a New York Dutch family that had once owned considerable property. Both women were brought into conversations in their families and communities where they heard about and spoke about abolition and prohibition as well as suffrage. Frederick Douglas (1818-1895) and Sojourner Truth (1797-1883), two famous African American abolition speakers, also supported women's suffrage and equal rights. During her own earlier time, Wollstonecraft's comments expressed something of women's frustration and desire for change. Later comments by Cady-Stanton and Anthony also reflected the woman's need for opportunity toward political and economic empowerment. But the struggle for suffrage was more than only a struggle for opportunity. These women had confidence that without the vote, a moral injustice was being done. In the nineteenth century patriarchal environment, achieving political empowerment for women was never an easy task.[45]

"Strange as it may seem to many, we now demand our right to vote according to the declaration of the government under which we live. We should not feel so sorely grieved if no man who had not attained the full stature of a Webster, Clay, Van Buren or Gerrit Smith could claim the right of elective franchise. But to have drunkards, idiots, horseracing rum-selling rowdies, ignorant foreigners, and silly boys fully recognized while we ourselves are thrust out from all the rights that belong to citizens, is too grossly insulting to…be longer quietly submitted to. The right is ours. Have it we must. Use it we will. The pens, the tongues, the fortunes, the indomitable wills of many women are already pledged to secure this right." Elizabeth Cady Stanton[46]

"All that distinguishes man as an intelligent and accountable being is equally true of woman; and if that government only is just which governs by the free consent of the governed, there can be no reason in the world for denying to woman the exercise of the elective franchise, or a hand in making and administering the laws of the land. Our doctrine is that "right is of no sex." Frederick Douglas, *The North Star*[47]

"The male element is a destructive force, stern, selfish, aggrandizing, loving war, violence, conquest, acquisition, breeding in the material and moral world alike discord, disorder, disease, and death….The idea strengthens at every step, that woman was created for no higher purpose than to gratify the lust of man….Society as organized today is one grand rape of womanhood under the man power." Elizabeth Cady Stanton, *The Revolution*[48]

"And now, at the close of a hundred years, as the hour-hand of the great clock that marks the centuries points to 1876, we declare our faith in the principle of self-government, or full equality with man in natural rights; that woman was made first for her own happiness, with the absolute right to herself—to all the opportunities and advantages life affords for her complete development; and we deny that dogma of the centuries , incorporated in the codes of all nations—that woman was made for man—her best interests…to be sacrificed to his will. We ask rulers, at this hour, no special favors, no special privileges….We ask justice, we ask equality, we ask that all civil and political rights that belong to the citizens of the United States be guaranteed to us and to our daughters forever." Susan B. Anthony[49]

The practical problems that accompanied industrialization and immigration included social and vocational education, housing and hygiene. Growth inside cities concentrated in the most affordable neighborhoods, closer to areas where people could get a job. According to the appendix at the end of Jacob Riis's book, *How the Other Half Lives*, written in 1890, New York City's population between the years of 1869 and 1880 grew from 468,492 in the tenements to 1,206,299 in the whole city. But population density studies showed a preponderance of population density and growth in the tenements. In 1880, there were 48.4 persons per acre in New York City; in Manhattan 92.6 persons per acre; in the Tenth Ward, 432.3 persons per acre; in the Eleventh Ward, 350.9 persons per acre; in the Thirteenth Ward, 353.2 persons per acre. By 1890, growth continuing, population densities were in New York City, 60.08 persons per acre, in Manhattan, 114.53 persons per acre, in the Tenth Ward, 522.00 persons per acre, in the Eleventh Ward, 386.00 persons per acre, in the Thirteenth Ward, 428.8 persons per acre.[50] The influx of freed slaves and European migrants from a variety of cultures and speaking various languages overwhelmed prior expectations for urban growth. Overcrowding led to bad and unsanitary housing. Tragic deaths occurred among people who had few economic or political resources to improve their material conditions.

Resources were eventually brought to bear on the problem of insufficient housing and sanitation but other challenges remained. One of them was integrating this diverse group of people into the culture of their new nation and getting the rest of the nation accustomed to them. Another challenge was one of education and vocational training. Many people were frightened by the size of the social problem as crime increased. Some people, like Jane Addams, wanted to gain what immigrants might bring from their early experiences, their cuisine, their music, the flavor of the exotic and far away. Jacob Riis (1849-1914), a reporter for the *New York Tribune*, was familiar with the slums because he was an immigrant who had lived there himself.[51] His descriptions as a reporter and photographer brought the slum problem into a more compassionate light that made city slums a-harder-to-ignore problem. He also gave fact based arguments that helped persuade people that intensive public or private spending in housing might be better than charity that would only take care of a momentary emergency without rectifying underlying causes. His long quotes paint word pictures that capture the place, people, times and problems very well.

"It was the stir and bustle of trade, together with the tremendous immigration that followed upon the war of 1812 that dislodged them. In thirty-five years the city of less than a hundred thousand came to harbor half a million souls, for whom homes had to be found…As business increased, and the city grew with rapid strides, the necessities of the poor became the opportunity of their wealthier neighbors, and the stamp was set upon the old houses, suddenly become valuable, which the best thought and effort of a later age has vainly struggled to efface. Their "*large* rooms were partitioned into *several smaller ones*, without regard to light or ventilation, the rate of rent being lower in proportion to space or height from the street; and they soon became filled from cellar to garret with a class of tenantry living from hand to mouth, loose in morals, improvident in habits, degraded, and squalid as beggary itself." It was thus the dark bedroom, prolific of untold depravities, came into the world."[52]

"The message came from one of the Health Department's summer doctors, last July, to the King's Daughter's Tenement-house Committee, that a family with a sick child was absolutely famishing in an uptown tenement. The address was not given. The doctor had forgotten to write it down, and before he could be found and a visitor sent to the house the baby was dead, and the mother had gone mad. The nurse found the father, who was an honest laborer long out of work, packing the little corpse in an orange-box partly filled with straw, that he might take it to the Morgue for pauper burial. There was absolutely not a crust to eat in the house, and the other children were crying for food. The great immediate need in that case, as in more than half of all according to the record, was work and living wages. Alms do not meet the emergency at all…It is estimated that New York spends in public and private charity every year around 8,000,000. A small part of this sum intelligently invested in a great labor bureau, that would bring the seeker of work and the one with work to give together under auspices offering some degree of mutual security, would certainly repay the amount of the investment in the saving of much capital now worse than wasted, and would be prolific of the best results. The ultimate and greatest need, however, the real remedy, is to remove the cause—the tenement that was built for "a class of whom nothing was expected," and which has come fully up to expectation. Tenement-house reform holds the key to the problem of pauperism in the city."[53]

John Dewey's (1859-1952) name goes forward from the past to our present as a defender of education's value to society and as a philosophical pragmatist who wanted to improve education by advocating kinds of educational emphases that would bring about greater social connection, imagination and innovation in a changing world. He was classified as a philosophical pragmatist along with others such as William James, Justice Oliver Wendell Holmes Jr., and Jane Addams. He complained about business confiscating the practical applications of science, controlling scientific information and using propaganda methods to interfere with society's better nature. He eventually taught at the University of Chicago, which was established in 1892 under a substantial financial donation from John D. Rockefeller with land donated by Marshall Field.[54] Dewey's ideas regarding individualism evolved over his long career to be more appreciative and less critical of individualism itself but insistent upon connecting individuals with their society. He appreciated that intellectuals relied on earlier ideas but wanted people's creative ideas to serve a purpose by going out into society to meet social needs. Connections and relationships, the way one idea or thing related to other ideas or things and the way it became enmeshed in the social whole interested John Dewey. Here are some quotes from Dewey's *The Public and Its Problems*, (1927).[55]

"Just as publics and states vary with conditions of time and place, so do the concrete functions which should be carried on by states. There is no antecedent, universal proposition which can be laid down because of which the functions of a state should be limited or should be expanded. Their scope is something to be critically and experimentally determined."[56]

"The smoothest road to control of political conduct is by control of opinion. As long as interests of pecuniary profit are powerful, and a public has not located and identified itself, those who have this interest will have an unresisted motive for tampering with the springs of political action in all that affects them."[57]

"Those still more inclined to generalization assert that the whole apparatus of political activities is a kind of protective coloration to conceal the fact that big business rules the government roost in any case...Most of those who hold these opinions would profess to be shocked if the doctrine of economic determinism were argumentatively expounded to them, but they act upon a virtual belief in it."[58]

"The use of science to regulate industry and trade has gone on steadily. The scientific revolution of the seventeenth century was the precursor of the individual revolution of the eighteenth and nineteenth. In consequence, man has suffered the impact of an enormously enlarged control of physical energies without any corresponding ability to control himself and his own affairs. Knowledge divided against itself, a science to whose incompleteness is added an artificial split, has played its part in generating enslavement of men, women and children in factories in which they are animated machines to tend inanimate machines. It has maintained sordid slums, flurried and discontented careers, grinding poverty and luxurious wealth, brutal exploitation of nature and man in times of peace and high explosives and noxious gases in times of war. Man, a child in understanding of himself, has placed in his hands physical tools of incalculable power."[59]

John Dewey's prose sometimes meandered. He rarely got to his point immediately and could be self-contradicting at times while at other times he disagreed with what was an accepted earlier view but without a thorough discussion. Sometimes Dewey's argument jumped so fast that his remarks seemed to have been made only for people who already had a classical education and who mostly agreed with him, anyway. On the other hand his comments regarding propaganda were more direct. The quotes having to do with unlimited government power showed that the modern liberal period challenged earlier classical liberal restrictions on government power. Dewey rejected the classical liberal political philosophy that advocated for limited federal power only to lament, in the last quote, the childlike nature of political rebirth during modern liberalism. He seemed to have abandoned the past wholeheartedly on the one hand and come to regret the shock of modern liberalism's contingent politics on the other hand. Modern liberals saw the economy and population grow and they imagined that new economic power would be better utilized by a bigger government. They didn't realize that a bigger government could use economic power to destroy as well as to build.

Jane Addams (1869-1935) was a pragmatist acting on society's behalf in the slum neighborhood of Chicago where she rented one whole floor of a building to provide educational services, calling her establishment Hull House. She founded Hull House with Ellen Gates Starr, three years before the University of Chicago was founded, in 1889.[60] She was acquainted with philosophical pragmatists such as Dewey, and James and eventually became interested in the social studies curriculum at the University of Chicago. She wrote on behalf of peace and in opposition to the U.S. entry into WWI. Addams began her community enterprise before women had the vote and before many women worked in the public arena.

Hull House gave educated women a community outlet for their talents by allowing them to become a social resource for the poor. She made a point to emphasize that both the women and the poor could benefit from their social intersection at the facility. But she also supported business concerns when she said that the purpose of educating immigrants was to create better factory workers rather than an educated public. She took this position while fighting to improve labor and living conditions for immigrants before labor laws. These were the days when children often worked in factories, and labor involved long hours often in unsafe conditions. Injury and even death were part of factory work. Families could be made destitute if a wage earning father were maimed or poisoned in doing factory work.

Slums filled cities like Chicago and New York and sanitation and disease was also a problem because of inadequate public sewage and infrastructure during massive population growth. Immigrant labor in huge quantities overwhelmed society's resources and Hull House offered a refuge and a place to begin the process of shaping the Chicago community newcomers in spite of crime, prostitution, undernourishment and other kinds of desperation. These quotes are from *On Education*, a book edited by Ellen Condliffe Lagemann, filled with selected Jane Addams quotes from her lectures and publications.[61] Many people in social work have been inspired by the actions that Jane Addams took at Hull House to fix problems in Chicago. Addams brought these problems to light in an effort to remedy lack of public resources in education and inadequate housing and sanitation especially for the immigrant poor but also for African Americans.

"If the shop constantly tends to make the workman a specialist, then the problem of the educator in regard to him is quite clear; it is to give him what may be an offset from the over-specialization of his daily work, to supply him with general information and to insist that he shall be a cultivated member of society with a consciousness of his industrial and social value."[62]

"The Hull House Theater is constantly besieged by children clamoring to "take part" in the plays of Schiller, Shakespeare, and Moliere, although they know it means weeks of rehearsal and the complete memorizing of "stiff lines"…one never ceases to marvel at the power of even a mimic stage to afford to the young a magic space in which life may be lived in efflorescence, where manners may be courtly and elaborate without exciting ridicule, where the sequence of events is impressive and comprehensible. Order and beauty in life is what the adolescent youth craves…"[63]

"The opportunity which the athletic field provides for discussion of actual events and for comradeship founded upon the establishment of just relationships is the basis for a new citizenship…The fifteen Small Parks of Chicago, equipped with clubrooms, poolrooms, drawing-rooms, refectories, reading-rooms, gymnasiums, swimming pools, and much other social paraphernalia, are, we believe, centers in which a higher type of citizenship is being nursed. Certainly the number of arrests among juvenile delinquents falls off surprisingly in a neighborhood where such a park has been established…"[64]

"The fact that in many European nations the socialists were among the major political parties, that a "Labor" Party had come to office in England was in itself an education in the use of words as they are current throughout civilization. Perhaps more important still the man of affairs began to contrast such attempts at political control of industrial situations with the associative business control which has been worked out in the United States…A mixed type of state with competitive and cooperative elements may have the greatest survival value and prove to be the most serviceable."[65]

In 1935, Major-General Smedley Butler (1881-1940), who had served in the Marines during WWI, wrote a pamphlet called *War Is a Racket*.[66] He was blowing the whistle on profiteers who made money during WWI, and calling for peace, hoping that the U.S. wouldn't enter WWII. Just as Jane Addams' efforts to prevent the U.S. entry into WWI failed, Butler was unable to stop the energy of nation-state conflict and the U.S. engagement in another catastrophic war. Wealth was destroyed in that war, much art and architecture, and many lives were lost or damaged. All of these losses motivated the Allied forces to dismantle economic nationalism by globalizing the economy in the neoliberal ideological changeover that happened after WWII. Even though Smedley Butler couldn't stop the war, his descriptions of how money was made by people who gained treasury access to fund militarization serves as a modern-day warning. Some people have made their money by unleashing war violence. And treasury money can motivate some to advocate for war. Butler brought attention to the profit side of warfare and the borderless corporate economy that was forming on a global scale.

"WAR is a racket. It always has been. It is possibly the oldest, easily the most profitable, surely the most vicious. It is the only one international in scope. It is the only one in which the profits are reckoned in dollars and the losses in lives…A racket is best described, I believe, as something that is not what it seems to the majority of people. Only a small "inside" group knows what it is about. It is conducted for the benefit of the very few, at the expense of the very many. Out of the war a few people make huge fortunes…In the World War a mere handful garnered the profits of the conflict. At least 21,000 new millionaires and billionaires were made in the United States during the World War."[67]

"Beautiful ideals were painted for our boys who were sent out to die. This was the "war to end wars." This was the "war to make the world safe for democracy." No one told them that dollars and cents were the real reason. No one mentioned to them, as they marched away, that their going and their dying would mean huge war profits. No one told these American soldiers that they might be shot down by bullets made by their own brothers here. No one told them that the ships on which they were going to cross might be torpedoed by submarines built with United States patents. They were just told it was to be a glorious adventure…Thus having stuffed patriotism down their throats, it was decided to make them help pay for the war, too. So, we gave them the large salary of $30 a month!…All they had to do for this munificent sum was to leave their dear ones behind, give up their jobs, lie in swampy trenches, eat canned willy (when they could get it) and kill and kill and kill…and be killed…But wait!…Half of that wage (just a little more in a month than a riveter in a shipyard or a laborer in a munitions factory safe at home made in a day) was promptly taken from him to support his dependents, so that they would not become a charge upon his community. Then we made him pay what amounted to accident insurance—something the employer pays for in an enlightened state—and that cost him $6 a month. He had less than $9 a month left…Then, the most crowning insolence of all—he was virtually blackjacked into paying for his own ammunition, clothing, and food by being made to buy Liberty Bonds at $100 and then we bought them back —when they came back from the war and couldn't find work—at $84 and $86. And the soldiers bought 2,000,000,000 worth of those bonds!"[68]

Walter Lippmann (1889-1979) was a journalist and propagandist who helped to sell the American public on enlistment and conscription for WWI, during the Wilson Administration. He was a gifted wordsmith. His eloquent prose persuaded his reader that whatever viewpoint he was selling was the one they should be buying. He didn't supply an academic analysis, relying instead on rhetorical reasoning based on common experience. His arguments sounded believable even when he sometimes distorted certain details like the economic difference between mixed economy and economic liberalism.

In 1937, he wrote *The Good Society*,[69] in which he tried to sell the American public on modern liberalism. *The Good Society* may be the best narrative for explaining the modern liberal period. Lippmann described modern liberalism as a modern improvement over classical liberalism. He wrote that liberalism was always the political philosophy that best supported specialized labor in the new exchange economy of expanding capitalism. He wrote that classical liberalism had gotten bogged down in laissez faire when it should have been responding to further developments that required political innovation in the nineteenth century period of the industrial revolution. For Lippmann the politic came before the market economy.

He distanced modern liberalism from collectivism in Europe under socialism and communism by stating that collectivists were against specialized labor and in favor of the earlier self-sufficiency economy of the feudal past. In this way he made American socialism seem progressive and European socialism seem antiquated. He wrote that American common law gradually improved American life by making legal changes respecting contracts and property. He said these changes were overseen by the American court system and Congress that operated through the opinions of judges and legislators seeking social justice. He contrasted the American common law system with European law which was based on Napoleonic adaptations of Imperial Roman law, writing that common law traditions have been part of a politically representative system vastly unlike fiat decrees made by centralized governments.

He made modern liberalism seem unlike socialism. So he failed to mention the fact that the innovation of mixed economy income taxes by the Union during the Civil War and made permanent by the Sixteenth Amendment was a reduction in economic freedom. He never said that growth of the regulatory state was only a milder kind of economic socialism. When he complained about the growth of monopoly, labor strife and immigrant slums he unfairly and inaccurately blamed classical liberalism. He didn't recognize that rail expansion had initiated a chain of events leading to expansion of the exchange economy, expansion of transportation, expansion of specialized labor in factories, expansion of immigrant populations that had caused the problems that became familiar to everyone during The Gilded Age. And economic expansion was a triumph of classical liberalism, not a failure. Technological progress led to these problems because technologies can bring change that isn't beneficial to everyone.

It would have been more honest for him to say instead that economic changes brought on by a national change from economic liberalism to mixed economy, from a land expansion economy to a commodity exchange economy required political adaptations undertaken in legislatures and courts. These political adaptations were made under the political ideology of modern liberalism. He might also have mentioned that nation state war contests had led nations to compete globally in both the economy and the politic. He might have said that these contests were irresistible for any nation seeking power. So much so, that enhancing political and economic power became the first objective of nation states.

Considering specific parts of *The Good Society*, reveals ideas in the context of modern liberalism. In chapter four, Lippmann wrote about how collectivism became fashionable in the generation of people living before WWI. But after seeing German, Russian and Italian collectivism in practice, people became afraid of the controlled economies and dictatorial politics. Nevertheless, even after most people had grown to doubt that collectivism was a better form of government, Lippmann noticed that collectivism was admired in academia.[70] In chapter two, Lippmann wrote about people's desire for an "omnipotent state" after they faced "machine technologies" during the industrial revolution. He saw this as a throwback to governance strategies from before the industrial revolution.[71]

But Lippmann wrote that he opposed collectivism, in chapter three, because a more powerful government with a more centralized and controlled economy wouldn't possess bureaucrats with any greater skill at knowing the future than a limited government would have. In a changing politic and economy, more control with no greater understanding, would lead to a government, Lippmann wrote, that would be "oppressive, reactionary, and corrupt". Lippmann still wanted liberalism to prevail as the mode of governance.[72] And Lippmann, in chapter five, wrote that every form of collectivism would only result in a state organized for warfare and conquest.[73] In chapter five, Lippmann wrote that socialism resembled "monopoly corporate capitalism."[74] This comment sounds like some modern day descriptions of neoliberalism. In chapter eleven, Lippmann wrote about holding companies and defined them as corporations that manage other corporations. He saw holding companies as collectivist businesses because they can interfere with market based pricing that happens under supply and demand. He also believed if an environment prevailed with an abundance of holding companies, they would eventually become nationalized. They would become "departments of the government."[75]

Modern holding companies can be used to hide assets or liabilities and they can be raided for capital by majority owners. Lippmann didn't seem to envision how greed could extinguish the existence of a holding company even if he did imagine their power making them more political.

Walter Lippmann's comments about the modern liberal legal system got interesting in chapter twelve. Lippmann used the phrase, "coercive authority of the state," an idea from German Idealism, in describing legal enforcement. He also wrote about the laws regarding "property, contracts and corporations" as an area where state intervention would be possible but also where customary considerations would hold some sway as law developed to accommodate what people found acceptable terms of obligation and rights. But Lippmann noted that rights would be protected non-uniformly.[76]

In chapter thirteen, Lippmann wrote about the use of civil court for private instead of criminal legal settlements so that legal dealings could become "transactional" instead of delivering a penalty.[77] Lippmann wrote in chapter fourteen about his vision of a world dominated by a system of common law that would allow people to govern their affairs without totalitarianism.[78] But in chapter thirteen, he wished to keep corporations under government control, under a "system of rights and duties" that would moderate corporate activities within the government's oversight.[79] Lippmann didn't realize that corporations might become the most powerful political faction and that they would utilize their personhood status under the fourteenth amendment to increase their immunity from prosecution or legal reprisal. Here's a quote from chapter fourteen that reflects Lippmann's preference for ends over means in his political analysis. This quote found Lippmann justifying colonialism and violence against other nations in the interests of promoting a new political solution to the economy and the politic that Lippmann thought would overcome disorder. This is a utopian kind of viewpoint right in line with collectivism's similar utopias. In this paragraph, Lippmann showed his own acceptance of violence against other political nation states.

"Though their work has been stained with blood, cruelty, and injustice, the men who open the world to economic development are completing the work of the explorers who set forth at the end of the fifteenth century... By advancing the regime of law and order throughout the globe, they have facilitated the world-wide division of labor and a stupendous improvement in the standard of life....Thus preemptive imperialism, the policy of the closed door, the attempt to make colonies a field of exploitation for special interests, must be regarded as a pathological disease, a reactionary but transient phenomenon, which has accompanied the progressive movement to open the planet to settlement and to a world-wide division of labor.... Thus there has indeed been enormous pressure from the capitalists to open territories to trade and investment and to establish law and order. But while this pressure may have been initiated by concession hunters, the sustaining motive to political expansion has been the need to overcome the disorder and insecurity which interrupt trade and imperil investments."[80]

Lippmann, along with other modern liberals, had no faith in cultural ideas that had been rooted in history and that had been the axis of classical liberalism. Modern liberals adopted contingent politics not founded upon a belief in liberty based on natural rights and natural law. Modern liberal pragmatism, contingent and separated from political principles, evolved into neoliberalism after WWII. Under neoliberalism, contingency politics became a politic of deconstruction/reconstruction and political opportunism. By accepting the "coercive power of the state" Lippmann helped the politic to become organized by power principles instead of moral principles. Real politik could then take the place of accountable politics where force mattered more than happiness.

W.E.B. Dubois (1868-1963) founded the Niagara Movement in 1905, which became the NAACP (National Association for the Advancement of Colored People) in 1910. This organization was more aggressive in identifying "institutional racism" than other individuals and organizations had been earlier. DuBois thought not just about racist individuals but also organizations that were racist. He worried about social racism practiced by non-blacks in government agencies and insurance companies and mortgage lenders and restaurant owners. This approach improved insights into the way racism happened in the United States. The NAACP's political efforts to stop racism were more "militant" in striving for social equity than the efforts of Booker T. Washington.[81] DuBois inspired many in the black community and he is credited with positively influencing the Harlem Renaissance. Despite DuBois's contributions, he alienated most black people when he joined the Communist Party in 1961. He moved to Ghana as an old man and died away from the United States. His essay "The White World" was published in 1940. Some have thought that it expressed bitterness against American racism and hope for a better society through collectivism.[82] Some of his comments seem also to echo those of Lippmann with regard to neocolonialism. Dubois' observations about neocolonialism foreshadowed the eruption of neoliberalism onto the global economic and political scene which began under GATT treaties in 1944.

"All our present frustration in trying to realize individual equality through communism, fascism, and democracy arises from our continual unwillingness to break the intellectual bonds of group and racial exclusiveness...Thus it is easy to see that scientific definition of race is impossible; it is easy to prove that physical characteristics are not so inherited as to make it possible to divide the world into races; that ability is the monopoly of no known aristocracy; that the possibilities of human development cannot be circumscribed by color, nationality, or any conceivable definition of race; all this has nothing to do with the plain fact that throughout the world today organized groups of men by monopoly of economic and physical power, legal enactment and intellectual training are limiting with determination and unflagging zeal the development of other groups; and that the concentration particularly of economic power today puts the majority of mankind into a slavery to the rest."[83]

"The democracy which the white world seeks to defend does not exist. It has been splendidly conceived and discussed, but not realized. If it ever is to grow strong enough for self-defense and for embracing the world and developing human culture to its highest, it must include not simply the lower classes among the whites now excluded from voice in the control of industry; but in addition to that it must include the colored peoples of Asia and Africa, now hopelessly imprisoned by poverty and ignorance. Unless these latter are included and in so far as they are not, democracy is a mockery and contains within itself the seeds of its own destruction....the quickest way to bring the reason of the world face to face with this major problem of human progress is to listen to the complaint of those human beings today who are suffering most from white attitudes, from white habits, from the conscious and unconscious wrongs which white folk are today inflicting on their victims. The colored world therefore must be seen as existing not simply for itself but as a group whose insistent cry may yet become the warning which awakens the world to its truer self and its wider destiny."[84]

Learning from modern liberal period thinkers and bringing their insights into present-day.

From John Dewey we learned that factions grew as the modern liberal government developed and grew in size. Factions competed for political advantages until they occupied the whole of modern liberal politics. Jacob S. Hacker and Paul Pierson, in their book, *Winner Take All Politics*, published in 2010, also wrote about factional politics.[85] They wrote that lobbies, and big money interests have more influence than public interest groups. In our current neoliberal period, multinational corporations and mega-financial institutions have formed the most powerful factions because they have the most money and because they can buy the favors of Congress. Favors installed inside congressional legislation, that is, which has provided savings on taxes, market niche, or other government backed advantages including non-prosecution as we saw in the financial industry after 2008. And Congress has developed a relationship with lobbies that often leads congressional members to join them after their terms in office.[86] Congress members actively seek financial support from PACs or Political Action Groups and from lobbies to fund their campaigns. They have a symbiotic power relationship that is more than a few favors owed. The reason that the public rarely sees that global corporate gains have been to the public's disadvantage is because multinationals operate out of the public's eye and somewhat outside U.S. regulations by doing business in developing nations. And also because corporate owned media held by five or six media companies fails to comment and elucidate the facts.

Lippmann, during modern liberalism, wrote about his unbelief in natural rights, and about flexibility in law that would change according to what was needed under common law principles. He imagined that common law would be more representative of the public's value set and that it would prevent tyranny as compared with Europe's Roman Codex. He hoped common law traditions would safeguard Americans. But modern liberals ignored natural rights. And without natural rights principles, in the atmosphere of deregulation and re-regulation, the re-sculpting of laws has made the public vulnerable. Higher taxes, lower wages and governmental trespasses against constitutional law have been one kind of outcome. But also treasury subsidy to corporations that has drained public resources. The failure to support natural law, and the failure to follow practices of legal consistency, have provided factional politics with the power to remodel the legal system in favor of the largest corporate interests.

The partnering of corporations and government, as seen for example in Fanny Mae and Freddy Mac, now nationalized, also can lead to the pillage of the treasury, in the amount of billions of dollars. This has been seen for example, in pairings between government regulators who failed to regulate bankers and realtors on multiple occasions since the S&L crisis in the 1980's and early 1990's. The process of undermining regulation is called **regulatory capture.** Major-General Smedley Butler, wrote about unreasonable quantities of public monies going to war contractors under modern liberal mixed economy but under neoliberalism the treasury's vulnerability has grown. The neoliberal public treasury has been vulnerable to pillage by war contractors, construction companies, mortgage companies, bankers and health insurance companies, among others. Access to treasury money has been a political perk routinely exploited by neoliberals.

Expanded government with a high tax base under both modern liberalism and neoliberalism has made money a target to be raided by opportunists. An early example of federal corruption happened during the Lincoln administration but wasn't discovered until the Grant administration. The Credit Mobilier Scandal occurred when members of Congress received bribes in exchange for supporting land grants and construction contracts made for the transcontinental railroad connection between the Missouri River and the Pacific by the American construction company Credit Mobilier. It was a front company founded to overcharge the government in rail construction. The Union Pacific Railroad's stock did very well from additional off-the-books profits until the stock lost value eight years later, after the fraud was exposed when *The Sun* discovered the impropriety and published a story.[87, 88, 89]

Dewey, DuBois and Lippmann, also wrote about propaganda's power over the public and its use by government and corporations. The First Amendment was written to protect free speech but how much value can anyone get from today's infotainment? During the twentieth century, after media deregulation, the largest media companies bought up all the smaller ones until only five or six media companies were left (see neoliberalism deregulation). Now media giants determine what Americans can read or hear about in the press. And neoliberal infotainment has moved far from providing relevant information and has even become boring with its empty content at moments of crisis. Press has become a Hegelian conversation that moves from topic to topic without taking a position with regard to what information is valuable or what tools might be applied to solve a problem.

To frustrated Americans, our U.S. Congress and President have seemed less accountable to the American people. Politicians have seemed too busy making political deals to deal with political problems and especially to stand and be accountable for them. Right now, even though the economy is shrinking, government statistics have insisted that it is growing because deficit spending pads GDP numbers. To use debt as GDP is to pretend that greater indebtedness to the future equals current production. What a misrepresentation that is. And the addition of "hedonic pricing"[90] and pricing for "intangibles"[91] to GDP numbers also has distorted the productivity estimate for the economy. These numbers aren't based on a transaction between a buyer and a seller but instead, have been made up out of thin air. This has hidden the true state of our shrinking economy. Political anxiety over budgetary debt ceilings has happened not just because of spending limitation but because without government spending, people would recognize that GDP has entered negative territory. Negative GDP would express obvious economic malaise and the failure of present day neoliberals to regulate the economy for positive growth.

Today's press is usually missing the story and has often ignored factual analysis which could be used by some to understand or even to solve problems. Issues aren't covered to connect underlying problems caused by bad policies. Each problem floats in a disconnected ocean of information. Even if facts are provided, it is usually for a short term span and not for an in-depth longer term. News coverage lacks newsy-ness. Distortions abound from lack of policy based coverage on topics like the government debt and the over printed U.S. dollar. Also under-reported, unemployment and underemployment that has hurt families, and labor non-participation. Inflation in healthcare because of its nature as a government subsidized industry under middle-men HMO's isn't covered and neither is the terrible costliness of Obamacare to individuals, or to small businesses. Transfers of money from the treasury to pay for the ACA or failures of care under the ACA haven't been mentioned either. Inflation in food and energy and deflation in wages and employment benefits also haven't been meaningfully dealt with by the U.S. press. Congress deregulated media decades ago. And the media now has no mandated responsibility to give "fair and balanced coverage" during news reporting over the public airwaves.[92]

The public-commons of bandwidth for broadcasting has been overwhelmed by entertainment-only instead of information content that would help people to understand better what is happening to the American commonwealth. Washington press coverage makes nonsense of what could be sensible and could be addressed if only opposite views weren't constantly presented as equally valid. Broadcasting empiricism in the twenty-first century lacks empathy or sympathy for the plight of American families facing economic problems. And modern day financialization has prospered under advertising that promises never-ending and ever-greater consumerism. People have been encouraged to buy what they can't afford. This has caused debt and has deep political roots and destructive outcomes for people living on less real income. Financialization has been a financial policy that has been destroying American economic vitality both for individuals and small business.

Ancient societies knew that usury could destroy a civilization. Interest rates shouldn't go much above 5% but credit card interest rates, student loans, payday loans and many other examples have interest rates that are many multiples higher than 5% and that qualify as usury. Under constant advertising many Americans take on more debt when they shouldn't. In the unhealthy economy with fewer good jobs people don't have much surplus to put into savings. Qualified individuals who have invested in a university education can't get work that pays enough to pay off student loans. And at very low interest rates that approach zero percent, and in an inflated economy, a savings account since 2008 has been losing money, anyway.

W.E.B. DuBois sounded bitter and hopeless when he wrote about white culture. He wrote about the willingness of white power to exploit others and his comments sounded like Walter Lippmann's when he wrote about colonialism. John Perkins, in his 2004 book, *Confessions of an Economic Hit Man,*[93] wrote about multinationals working with the IMF and World Bank to create debt dependency in the third world while building infrastructure under the direction of European or American construction companies. Debt dependency made third world countries vulnerable to political redirection under neoliberal tropes. This infrastructure was later utilized in factories partially owned by foreign multinationals. They profited at the expense of local social welfare programs and local wealth building opportunities.

The process of generating debt has been part of today's neocolonialism. It has been ruthless exploitation and deliberate installation of poverty to increase the pressure on local people to maintain low wage work. Poverty has improved arbitrage opportunity for would be exploiters. But returning now to a consideration of modern liberalism, it would seem that poverty wasn't a goal of the ideology. Instead, modern liberals wanted to regulate the economy to produce greater wealth for the entire public. Poverty wasn't what the American pragmatists were seeking when they established settlements like Hull House and rallied support to improve slum conditions in urban centers during modern liberalism. Modern liberal pragmatists advocated for labor unions and social programs. How could their better intentions turn within less than a century toward neoliberal exploitation?

Modern liberals undermined limited government and made abuses of power more likely.

The progression of neoliberalism out of modern liberalism happened because modern liberalism undermined limitations on American government that had prevented political expansion and predation upon public monies and interests. The growth of bureaucracy under the influence of greater funding through income tax increased the complexity of government and society. Monetarism began to alter the money economy to support greater sovereign debt and the conversion to fiat currency under the Nixon administration further expanded capital flows. Financialization and debt dependency under neoliberalism continue to remodel the economy.

Whereas modern liberals wanted an economy of plenty that operated by producing social wealth, neoliberalism's financialization has produced an impoverished economy run on debt. Too-Big-To-Fail banks speculate on Wall Street in commodity markets and financial markets to siphon more money out of the production economy. The increase of the federal government's size, the number of laws, the increasing scope of regulations, the deregulation of finance, the use of covert CIA operations or war to acquire economic advantages for corporations has expanded complexity in the politic and economy. Complexity has provided new opportunity for political evolution toward unintended political and economic changes.

Modern liberal Reconstruction after the Civil War, and Prohibition in the twenties provided lessons in the limits of law to reorganize society and on the vulnerability of society to regulatory abuse. They showed how wishful thinking backed by force can't immediately change society toward a politically intended social outcome. The relationship between the politic and the economy set out in the political policies of modern liberalism was soft socialism. This relationship has had consequences for economic wealth building and for social resources. Money pulled out of the economy in taxes has led to war's destruction, less money in production, more political factions seeking government favoritism and less political and economic freedom for individuals. Law, war and finance again have affected both the politic and economy and fully penetrate the possibilities of the political and economic pairing expressed by policies.

Modern liberal thinkers came mostly from the United States. Three Germans were included because of the importance of German Idealism. Germany and the U.S. were the most ascendant industrial nations during the Second Wave of the Industrial Revolution.

Here's a quick survey of the national origins of the people that were quoted in this chapter. Booker T. Washington, American educator and lecturer; Immanuel Kant, Prussian philosopher, Charles Darwin, English natural scientist (geology, biology); Sigmund Freud, Austrian psychologist; Karl Marx, German political historian; Georg Hegel, German philosopher; Friedrich Nietzsche, German philosopher, professor of classical studies at Basel and social critic; Jacob Riis, Danish-American immigrant and journalist; Susan B. Anthony, American political activist and lecturer; Elizabeth Cady Stanton, American political activist, writer and lecturer; John Dewey, American philosopher and professor; Jane Addams, American social activist; Walter Lippmann, American propagandist and writer; W.E.B. DuBois, American civil rights activist and writer.

Most of the people we have considered as persons who influenced modern liberalism in America were German or American. Germany and the United States were experiencing dramatic industrial growth during the modern liberal period. Inventions including the telephone, telegraph, rail expansion, oil and gas production, electricity and new industrial methods changed the life opportunities of everyone in the Western World. And capital made the germination and fruition of even more new ideas possible. Also at this time, communication improved so well that ideas could circle the world quickly. Darwin, Marx and Freud affected the whole Western world. The second stage of industrialization's technological and manufacturing improvements provided enough wealth for a variety of experimentation that happened during the period, including social welfare, and industrialized warfare—two kinds of political influence that grew.

The Post Civil War Judicial System adapted to market economy circumstances; the New Deal Era had even greater flexibility.

Lippmann wrote about a new kind of flexibility in law, especially regarding property. During classical liberalism, property deeds of ownership by individuals were protected by law and enforced by government power. During modern liberalism, property rights were segmented into categories and somewhat by the ability of the owner to afford legal representation. This gave less wealthy individual owners of property fewer legal protections. Lippmann wrote about the option to bypass the authority of the state by pursuing legal battles in civil court. But that meant by hiring legal representation for a civil lawsuit. The cost of legal representation could then, just as now, reduce a person's access to justice depending on what they could afford. Gilded Age monopolists could readily outbid small competitors in legal battles, for instance, and at other times monopolists subsidized other competitors who would undersell the underdog business.

Monopolies in rail, steel, gas and oil, shaped battles over market acquisition and power acquisition during the Progressive and New Deal eras between monopolists and their competition, and between monopolists and the government. Power was the great political ideal of the times. Economic profits were redirected by commerce regulations that were passed in Congress. This altered the financial performance of business enterprises in the marketplace. Also, monopoly and advertising raised prices beyond the influence of demand dynamics alone.[94] The American justice system changed, too.

According to Craig Green's essay, "An Intellectual History of Judicial Activism," the formal organization of the U.S. court system had to be worked out over time after the 1789 U.S. Constitution was enacted.[95] The early U.S. judicial of classical liberalism was vastly different from later court practices during modern liberalism and neoliberalism. The early court was less powerful because its organizational structure was still being worked out by Congress. The Judiciary Act of 1789, mostly written by Senator Oliver Ellsworth, developed the appellate system of court hierarchy and outlined a role for the Attorney General.[96]

In the early court system, the Justices of the Supreme Court participated as traveling judges on a "riding circuit" which allowed them to become familiar with legal practices in a variety of places, but their decisions often weren't published.[97] The Supreme Court's judicial home base was only established after Washington's capital was moved in 1800.[98] According to Green, the Reconstruction Era was bleak in terms of the kinds of court decisions that were rendered, including court deference to government military power over individual liberty and natural rights, and the undermining of equality under the law. The federal government held greater power than previously.

Oliver Wendell Holmes Jr., a philosophical pragmatist and Supreme Court Justice explained the justice system of his time.

Oliver Wendell Holmes Jr., who served on the Supreme Court, was a philosophical pragmatist and judge who wrote about how laws though necessarily rooted in history also had to change with the times. Reading some of his comments can help to show the changes that came about in the Supreme Court after the Civil War. Justice Holmes had served in the Civil War on the Union side, and witnessed the circumstances of wartime desperation, and the pressure of immanent destruction in combination with loyal military service even in circumstances where Confederate soldiers knew that they were serving a lost Southern cause. He observed that the Civil War had changed his generation saying, "in our youth our hearts were touched with fire."[99] The Civil War had put his life in dire peril, he'd been wounded on the battlefield and lost comrades in arms.

He said, "The law, so far as it depends on learning, is indeed, as it has been called, the government of the living by the dead. To a very considerable extent no doubt it is inevitable that the living should be so governed. The past gives us our vocabulary and fixes the limits of our imagination; we cannot get away from it. There is, too, a peculiar logical pleasure in making manifest the continuity between what we are doing and what has been done before. But the present has a right to govern itself so far as it can; and it ought always to be remembered that historic continuity with the past is not a duty, it is only a necessity."[100]

Holmes also said, "Life is a roar of bargain and battle, but in the very heart of it there rises a mystic spiritual tone that gives meaning to the whole. It transmutes the dull details into romance. It reminds us that our only but wholly adequate significance is as parts of the unimaginable whole. It suggests that even while living we are living to ends outside ourselves." These quotes show that Justice Holmes was aware of a growing social and cultural complexity that was a hallmark of the second surge of the industrial revolution. The demands of present circumstances were outweighing the demands of tradition and all within a social context that was too complicated to understand in terms of either its origin or its destination.

He also said, "A word is not a crystal, transparent and unchanging, it is the skin of a living thought and may vary greatly in colour and content according to circumstances and time in which it is used."[101] He wrote that, "The life of the law has not been logic; it has been experience…The law embodies the story of a nation's development through many centuries, and it cannot be dealt with as if it contained only the axioms and corollaries of a book of mathematics."[102] Holmes thought that judges' decisions in practice embodied law in fact.[103] In this way, judges could bridge the past into the present by considering precedent but also by judging what would be just in modern circumstances and then forging ahead with modifications.

Justice Holmes Supreme Court service involved many controversies and some of them involved competitive economic or political interests between factional parties which could be more contentious and controversial than a legal decision based on constitutional natural rights. According to Craig Green, the Court was changeable when the Constitution was new for developmental reasons—because the Court couldn't be itself until Congress and court practices brought the Court into familiarity with practices that became standardized over time.[104] Early Supreme Court Judges as well as appellate judges had more operational independence. Later, the court continued to change with changing social challenges.

The New Deal Era and FDR's threat to pack the court.

Legislative changes to American governing through federal congressional power became more aggressive from the end of the nineteenth century until about the middle of the twentieth century. There were landmark cases in the courts involving railroads, civil rights, First Amendment rights, Congress's power to regulate commerce, and the power of the Executive compared with Congress and the Judiciary. Some early modern liberal rulings were later changed, like *Plessy v. Ferguson (1896)*. During the New Deal, after the Supreme Court found FDR's National Recovery Administration (NRA) to be unconstitutional, Franklin Delano Roosevelt threatened to modify the court and "pack the court" with more justices that favored the New Deal executive decrees. He proposed judicial changes in the Judiciary Reorganization Bill of 1937. For every judge over seventy years of age, he proposed to add another one to a potential total of fifteen. This aggressive move on the part of the President alarmed people even in his own party, costing him political influence.[105] The Senate Oversight Committee stopped him by altering the proposed Bill and removing the portion that called for additional justices to be added.[106]

As the modern liberal economy grew, the government bureaucracy also grew. The regulatory apparatus required greater numbers of government employees and Congress expanded its powers by passing legislation that contested earlier power limitations. When the Supreme Court's constitutional interpretation supported the expanded powers, they became part of Congress's expanding operations model. During the Wilson administration, Emergency Powers were enacted by the executive branch expanding Presidential powers. The "presumption of constitutionality" also gave Congress more power. And, as mentioned in Chapter One, some Justices of the Supreme Court sometimes disregarded legal precedent by reinterpreting textual meaning. Judicial activism affected the court's rulings. All of these instances expanded the power of the federal government in new ways that were not part of the Constitution's guidelines as the Founders wrote them down.

In chapter one, the "necessary and proper" clause in Article One, Section Eight, of the Constitution was considered and the legislature's expansion into "presumption of constitutionality" was also mentioned. During the modern liberal period, other constitutional clauses were viewed in a way different from the founding period, expanding the power of Congress and of corporations. The "commerce clause" and the "due process clause" were reconsidered. The "commerce clause", like the "necessary and proper clause" can be found in the enumerated congressional powers in Article One, Section Eight. The modern expansion of powers denoted by the "commerce clause" has also been magnified by the "presumption of constitutionality" that was considered in chapter one. The "due process clause" is part of the Fourteenth Amendment. The "commerce clause", expanded Congress's regulatory power over most of the American economy. The "due process clause" which was written in order to protect the natural rights of African Americans was reinterpreted to classify corporations as having personhood rights. These reinterpretations of the Constitution led to a changed American way of life.

Congress's plenary power under the commerce clause expanded with the market economy.

Railroad development was costly and it was the first large industry in the modern liberal period.[107] When railroads charged inconsistent fees to customers, and states tried to regulate the fees, the Supreme Court recognized that railroads were part of a national market economy and therefore stopped the state regulation of rail fees in favor of federal regulation instead. Congress created the Interstate Commerce Commission in the Interstate Commerce Act of 1887.[108] The Supreme Court consistently ruled in favor of federal oversight for national markets in a series of landmark cases. The Commerce Clause was also used by the Supreme Court to expand Congress's control of labor environments. Regulating commerce was so well established in practice that it came to be considered a **plenary power** of the legislative branch.

One example of commerce expansion, probably the most dramatic case example to contrast judicial mores of the classical liberal and modern liberal period can be found in the case of *Wickard v. Filburn (1942)*.[109] Wheat prices had increased dramatically over the period of WWI. The federal government had guaranteed the price of wheat at $2 a bushel and "issued a proclamation to the plains: plant more wheat to win the war."[110] After the war ended, the price fell. After the Great Depression it fell more because of overproduction in the environment of economic failure.[111] As stocks fell, prices for wheat began to fall. During the Great Depression, President Franklin Roosevelt's administration tried to control agricultural prices by limiting the amounts of agricultural goods that came for sale in the marketplace under the Agricultural Adjustment Act. The overabundance of wheat that overfilled U.S. granaries also caused a glut of rail traffic trying to move the excess wheat to any American market that wanted it. It was thought by economists working in the government that less wheat would translate into higher prices. The idea was that too much agricultural production had created lower prices. Pursuant to the goal of reducing wheat production, the Agricultural Adjustment Act of 1938 limited the amount of acres that farmers could use in growing wheat.

Claude R. Wickard was an Ohio wheat farmer who grew more than double his allowed wheat acreage in order to produce more wheat for his own personal consumption. When he was ordered to pay a fine and to burn his excess wheat, he appealed to the Federal District Court which found in his favor. But when the government brought the case to the Supreme Court, it ruled against Mr. Wickard. In *Wickard v. Filburn (1942)*,[112, 113] the Supreme Court ruled that a farmer could not consume his own agricultural products in excess of a production quota because allowing farmers to do so could adversely affect the agricultural market and provide an exception to controlled quantities of agricultural goods. Instead of growing his own seed, the farmer should buy seed. This ruling disputed property protections of the classical liberal period by laying claim to the farmer's agricultural goods. Because the federal government was thought to be able to control the national market, whereas a single farmer could not do so, the Supreme Court granted Congress the power to regulate each farmer's production. But this ruling took away the farmer's ownership of his own produce and repurposed all of his production for the national wheat market.

The federal restriction of personal production and consumption by viewing it as part of the national market shows how the Supreme Court began to favor the welfare of social groups or markets over the immediate welfare of individuals or laborers. This ruling would have alienated the Founding Fathers because it made Mr. Wickard's agricultural production and labor subject to regulatory control by the government even though his production in excess was for personal use. The ruling also interfered with the farmer's liberty to produce and use his own production. It undermined his property rights. The commerce clause interpretation during the modern liberal period has led Congress to grow its power over commerce to an unlimited purview over private economic production even for products that would be grown or made for private consumption. And trying to regulate the entire American economy has been an enormous expansion of Congress's to-do list.

It goes far beyond the Constitution's design for congressional action. It has led to bureaucratic costs and undermines Congress's ability to act speedily to solve problems. It may be part of the reason for government snafus such as the problems Congress's Affordable Care Act implementation has encountered. Medical business made up 18.2% of the American economy in 2012 and coordinating and regulating that business is a monumental task.[114] *Wickard v. Filburn (1942),* also begs another question regarding Congress' ability to regulate markets. What would Congress do if a new domestic cottage industry sprang up that competed with American multinational manufacturing which has been favored by congressional policies under Congress' drive to globalize? Ping Fu, the founder of GeoMagic 3-D technologies has suggested in interviews that three dimensional printing might become a cottage industry that could replace large factory manufacturing. Would Congress disallow a new cottage industry that could produce goods for home consumption if such production would stop people from buying similar goods from transnational American corporations?

The Supreme Court ruled the first Agricultural Adjustment Act as unconstitutional but reinstated agricultural quotas under subsequent legislation.[115] Even though Roosevelt's pack the court scheme was foiled by the Senate Oversight Committee, it nevertheless caused a change in the court. Whereas the court had found Progressive labor legislation to be unconstitutional in the past going back to the Wilson administration, the Supreme Court, after 1937, became more favorable toward the Congress' and the President's New Deal inspired legislation. The Supreme Court took a new tack and considered the "ballot box" instead of the judiciary as the way to discipline legislation that might be against American constitutional traditions.[116] A similar "ballot box" argument was used by the Supreme Court when it ruled the ACA was allowed as a tax under the U.S. Constitution. After 1937, commerce legislation remained unhindered by the courts until *United States v. Lopez (1994)*, where the Supreme Court ruled against the United States. In this case the Court ruled against school zone anti-gun legislation written by Congress supposedly under the "Commerce Clause." The Court found that criminal regulation had nothing to do with commerce.

Summary of commerce clause applications that have been acceptable to the court.

Acceptable applications of the "Commerce Clause" in Supreme Court rulings have been summarized by the Court as follows:[117, 118, 119, 120]

First, Congress regulates flow of commerce between states, "channels of interstate commerce" (*Heart of Atlanta Motel v. United States (1964)*) (This power dates from classical liberal times).

Second, Congress protects persons and objects participating in commerce between states even in circumstances where trade doesn't cross a state border, for example in fare rates for intrastate freight movements (*Shreveport rate cases (1901-1939)*, (a modern liberal expansion of power).

Third, Congress has the power under the commerce clause only to regulate actions that have any relation to commerce (the first time this was proved in practice was not until 1994; in *United States v. Lopez (1994)* (see above).

When comparing the classical liberal and modern liberal concept of how the "commerce clause" was viewed before, and how the view changed, the change comes down to both circumstances and language. The language of the founding era used the word commerce less specifically, not to mean manufacture but rather more generally to mean the movement of goods across state borders.[121] Remember, from the prelude that one of the most egregious failures of the Articles of Confederation had been in failing to properly empower the federal government to regulate goods transport between states. The unintended consequence of this failure during the classical liberal period of the fledgling nation was state by state separation of economic interests in the United States. States were charging tariffs when goods were moved across their borders. Instead of being united in trade, they were competitors that were destroying mutual trade opportunities.

The U.S. Constitution in Article One, Section Eight, granted Congress powers "To regulate Commerce with foreign Nations, and among the several States, and with the Indian tribes." In Article One, Section Nine, the Constitution specifically forbade states to tax each other for interstate trade across their borders, "No Tax or Duty shall be laid on Articles exported from any State." This article was to prevent state to state economic competition and to encourage the mutual benefits that interstate trade would offer the new nation. The circumstance that changed the "commerce clause" interpretation during the modern liberal period was the economic change from a land expansion based economy to a market based economy where interstate trade grew and became more complex because of industrial manufacturing and transportation improvements. Several examples of congressional legislation regulating commerce can be found and also several landmark Supreme Court rulings regarding the constitutionality of these laws. The combination of legislation and judicial ruling expanded the "commerce clause" to eventually include the three expansive kinds of regulatory power listed above.

Wagner's Law predicted that increasing the size of the economy would increase the size of government bureaucracy.

Adolf Wagner (1835-1917), a German economist during the time of Otto von Bismark (1815-1898), stated that increasing the size of an economy would inevitably lead to an increase in the size of government. The increased size of the economy would drive nation states towards a larger government bureaucracy by providing an increase in funds collected in taxes and by increasing the complexity of economic transactions. More funds would allow the government to grow larger and increased complexity of transaction would lead to greater public demands for services that would help people adjust to new challenges.[122] Whether Wagner's Law can be applied in reverse for a shrinking economy has yet to be proven. But when an economy shrinks as may be happening under neoliberalism, it would seem that the size of its government should also shrink because revenues to support government bureaucracy would be shrinking. But what of public services in a shrinking economy with less jobs? How can public policy address public needs and a shrinking economy that can ill support government services? Perhaps in a shrinking economy, a change in regulatory policy that would stimulate domestic employment could provide more jobs instead of more programs.

The Interstate Commerce Commission stimulated regulatory expansion that spread from transportation to other areas of the economy over time.

The first independent regulatory agency in the U.S. was the Interstate Commerce Commission. It was created in 1887 by the Interstate Commerce Act, after the Supreme Court had ruled in *Wabash, St Louis & Pacific Railway Company v. Illinois (1886)* that states lacked authority to regulate railroads because they lacked authority over interstate commerce. This authority has been one of Congress's enumerated powers in Article One, Section Eight of the U.S. Constitution.[123, 124] Just as Railroads and transportation improvements had ushered in the market economy, their regulation brought about growth of the regulatory state.

During the modern liberal period, the slum problems described by Riis and

Addams improved under health and municipal regulations. In addition, labor became regulated under the Fair Labor Standards Act of 1938. This was the first federal regulation of labor that had survived the scrutiny of the Supreme Court for constitutionality. A labor census in 1900 had measured two million children at work in America at that time.[125] And many saw child labor as a permanent drain on society's future. As children got older they only knew the narrow life they had lived inside a factory. They couldn't offer much more to their family's life because they had missed the training and opportunity they needed to make the most of their individual potential and talent. Under the Fair Labor Standards Act, Congress reduced regular work hours, made overtime pay mandatory in excess of forty hours worked or with later time off to compensate, and eliminated child labor for most jobs. The Wagner Act, also known as the National Labor Relations Act of 1935, gave labor unions a legal right to exist and an opportunity to bargain for improvements. It created the National Labor Relations Board to ensure greater power equity between employers and unions. The NLRB acted as the authority that officially ruled over proceedings during labor disputes.[126]

The labor union movement grew until after WWII. Complicated political deal making between labor, the government and business created an improvement in the circumstances of work by providing a better balancing of competing interests after labor revolt and patriarchal industrial recalcitrance had already led to deadly confrontations, such as the Ludlow Massacre of 1914, and costly shut down strikes such as occurred in 1935, 1936 and 1937.[127] But under the Wagner Act, labor eventually had to give up its most potent weapon: the labor strike shut down. The decline of labor unions in the present time is partly due to the Wagner Act deal-making that took away labor's ability to fight back. Unions can't organize mass strikes.[128]

Nowadays, even when a business experiences high attrition of employees because of employee dissatisfaction, the loss of a single employee can't stop work and penalize an employer the same way as a work shut down could.[129, 130] Modern-day labor non-participation has grown as a greater number of individuals leave the workforce and reduce U.S. labor productivity. According to one source, labor participation has fallen to levels not seen since 1978.[131] Many possible explanations for the economic loss of employed contributors may include the lesser availability of employment, persons entering retirement, an increasing number of part-time jobs and reduced labor wages and benefits that provide less incentive to work. After 2008, many people stopped looking for employment because so many jobs offered minimum wage, which isn't a living wage standard.

Consequences of regulation.

The growth of the regulatory state since the establishment of the Interstate Commerce Commission has been breathtaking and has had unintended consequences. Some of the unintended consequences include: regulatory capture when regulators are rewarded when they look the other way instead of enforce regulations, conflicts of interest where government office holders are enticed out of elective politics into revolving door lobby influence, growth of political factions that compete by hiring lobbies to advocate for political favors, divisive Political Action Committees (PAC's), congressional focus on election politics and getting more wealthy sponsors instead of focusing on long term issues, time commitment for fund raising, the growth of think tank investigators that influence Congress and other groups in favor of specific viewpoints often from the perspective of a certain political ideology. All of these came about because of regulation.

According to one estimate, lobby spending in 2011 amounted to 3.32 billion dollars and involved more than twelve thousand lobbyists to reach 439 House of Representative office holders (with 2 vacancies) and 100 Senators.[132, 133] Many people have come to see lobbyists as too-successful political attention grabbers who displace ordinary American constituencies through their money, familiarity and access to our government officials. In the twenty first century, the American political scene has been captured by factional moneyed interests.

Growth of the regulatory state has led to a proliferation of regulations in a legal cacophony that defies the ability of even the well-meaning American citizen to comply with the law. So numerous are the laws that a person's ability to know the law has become impossible. And the proliferation of too many laws shows that the current legal system works improperly. The outcome of too many laws has become selective enforcement rather than rule of law oversight. How many regulations? According to one source, over the last twenty years, 81,883 new regulations have been written, costing taxpayers 1.8 trillion dollars a year.[134] "The number of specific regulatory restrictions listed in the *Code of Federal Regulations* (CFR) topped one million in 2010."[135] Too many laws are a sign of failure in the legal system.

The Goal of regulation was to create a better, safer marketplace.

Modern liberals had believed that more regulations would make people in the U.S. safer and lead to a better run national marketplace. It seemed at first that federal oversight of food and drug safety, of environmental cleanliness, of commerce and labor helped to prevent unnecessary death, illness and suffering. But the costs and confusions of over-regulating, and of bureaucratic regulation by un-elected public servants instead of by elected officials has now become extremely high. Accountability among bureaucratic regulators seems only to consist of certain protocols that must be followed in drafting new rules. Little has been done to dismantle regulatory mayhem that has been caused by over-regulation in Washington D.C. that affects everyone in the nation who wants to pursue either personal or public business in America.

A white paper entitled, "Counting Regulations: An Overview of Rulemaking, Types of Federal Regulations, and Pages in the Federal Register," takes the position that the number of new regulations might be over-represented. This, the author claims, is because deregulation amendments that dismantle earlier rules are counted as a new rule.[136] But, on the contrary, counting deregulation as regulation would be appropriate, since deregulation and regulation both require money and attention to be paid to the legislation that is flooding over America. Deconstruction and reconstruction of regulations into over a million rules (not an exaggeration, here), has harmed legal effectiveness and appropriate legal oversight. Over-regulation harms civilization itself. The technology of law can't operate properly in such an environment.

And the constant distraction of regulatory tsunamis and nagging special interests with their demands keeps Congress from taking a wider viewpoint of the entire nation's welfare. Congress has become less effective as a political body working towards writing legislation in the context of the whole commonwealth. Expansion of congressional power outside of the "necessary and proper clause," and expansion of the "commerce clause" have both harmed Congress's effectiveness by embracing power extension for Congress and the Courts instead of power limitation. The Constitution didn't design a government with such highly detailed regulatory goals. Now, the federal government tries to control the whole country's economy and politic. Hunger for ever greater political power and reach has changed the flavor of the American republic when either neoliberalism or modern liberalism are compared to classical liberalism. But Congress has become less powerful in terms of what it accomplishes. And the Courts rule more narrowly. The economy and politic seem out of control, veering from problem to problem.

Expansion of corporate power under the Fourteenth Amendment.

Also important, the expansion of the Fourteenth Amendment during the modern liberal period, extended the power and reach of corporations in America. The Thirteenth Amendment that forbade slavery was enacted on December 6th, 1865; the Fourteenth Amendment providing due process protections, on July 9th, 1868. Section One of the Fourteenth Amendment reads, "All persons born or naturalized in the United States and subject to the jurisdiction thereof, are citizens of the United States and of the State wherein they reside. No State shall make or enforce any law which shall abridge the privileges or immunities of citizens of the United States; nor shall any State deprive any person of life, liberty, or property, without due process of law; nor deny to any person within its jurisdiction the equal protection of the laws." Only five years later, the "due process clause" was cited to expand the power of corporations into personhood, even though its original purpose was to secure the natural rights of African Americans. And the natural rights of African Americans were abused until the civil rights movement of the mid twentieth century. Powerful railroad interests moved the law's application away from the legislature's intention.

Part of why this unintended application of the law could happen and could persist was because this way of using the law had fidelity with the preference of the American economy under classical liberalism for private instead of government power. Political struggle within the original colonies of early America was a contest, from the European perspective, between European monarchs who laid claim to colonial lands and private adventurers and investors who wanted to develop and own the same lands through land grants given in exchange for raw materials and other products that surviving colonists might one day produce. Death was a common early outcome of early American settlement. The personal cost of leaving familiar Europe, facing the unknown in America, early death for some but onward persistence by others made Americans determined to claim private ownership of the lands that were held by European monarchs. And "private" ownership could be by an individual or a corporation as long as it wasn't the monarchy.

Private ownership could be by corporations such as a joint stock company or by colonists. Today, corporations are still seen as private entities that are an alternative to government, but corporations can also be owned by government, like Fanny Mae and Freddy Mac. Even in colonial times, corporations could be granted military prerogatives to gain control of land assets for the crown. Under neoliberalism discerning various government and corporate interests in public private partnerships has become more difficult. Corporations can act as extensions of government that exist without political restraint under the U.S. Constitution. Corporations, such as private security services working in the Middle East, for example, have been seen by many as extensions of government that have possessed advantages in escaping public accountability that government operators would lack. During modern liberalism, the development of railroads led to expansion of the market economy—something that had wide political support by land owners and developers. Interest in expanding railroads gradually led to a wider interpretation of the Fourteenth Amendment in order to give rail its best chance to succeed without state tax predation.

Present-day Americans have started a movement to limit personhood rights for American corporations and some favor a constitutional amendment that would accomplish this goal. But the tradition of seeing corporations as private entities has been a longer tradition than the emerging one of seeing corporations as invaders that attack public interests. A difference in the public's attitude emerged after *Citizens United v. Federal Election Commission* (2010). Here's a list of important judicial cases that established personhood rights for American corporations:[137]

Trustees of Dartmouth College v. Woodward (1819), Supreme Court recognized corporate contract rights.

Santa Clara County v. Southern Pacific Railroad (1886) court reporter summary acknowledged equal protection of laws for corporations (this idea wasn't stated by the justices and the court reporter who wrote the summary inaccurately in order to advance corporate railway interests had been a past President of a railroad company).

Pembina Consolidated Silver Mining Company v. Pennsylvania (1888) Supreme Court recognized that the Fourteenth Amendment protections apply to corporations.

Northwestern National Life Insurance Company v. Riggs (1906) Supreme Court stated that Fourteenth Amendment protections apply to corporations but they remain under state regulatory authority.

Buckley v. Valeo (1976) the court ruled that corporate contributions in limited amounts for campaigns is a form of protected speech under the First Amendment.

Citizens United v. Federal Election Commission (2010) the court ruled that corporations can buy commercial air time to influence elections under First Amendment speech protections.

Western Tradition Partnership, Inc. v. Attorney General of Montana (2012) Supreme Court overruled Montana law that prohibited corporate election spending.

Corporate personhood has offered some protections and not others.

Corporate personhood rights refer mostly to protections of property, contract and speech. The right to vote and to have Fifth Amendment protections aren't part of corporate rights in the United States.[138] People who support the Corporate Social Responsibility Movement, hope that corporate personhood could lead to international court proceedings against corporations that cause harm to the public. Modern corporations can sometimes evade responsibility when they operate in foreign nations. In other nations laws and law regulation can be less stringent compared to U.S. law. They also evade accountability by possessing limited liability, and by creating holding companies and special purpose entities that move money out of a potential regulator's reach.

The recent outcry of Americans against corporate contributions to elections reflects people's awareness that they have been recent political losers in American politics since 2008's financial collapse. Many have come to believe that politics have become unfair and that their voices can't reach legislators because they are outbid in election politics by fat contributions that corporations can afford but that ordinary people can't. A book mentioned earlier that presents the idea that American politics has become determined by money is *Winner Take All Politics: How Washington Made the Rich Richer—And Turned Its Back On the Middle Class*, by Jacob S. Hacker and Paul Pierson.[139] Hacker and Pierson wrote about how modern media and polling has made money more important in election contests.

The authors also acknowledged that moneyed interests have always influenced American politics. This can be seen in railroad development, entry into the Civil War partly for economic reasons and American involvement in the two World Wars as will be considered in the next section. As Americans today become more frustrated and concerned that their political interests aren't being considered by Congress, the American political scene has come to be seen as out of control or out of touch with ordinary people's needs. More people are beginning to realize that politics in America isn't a perpetual motion machine that will always take care of their interests. Many interests compete for congressional favors under the umbrella of expanded powers that came about during the modern liberal period.

How war further changed the relationship between the politic and economy during the modern liberal period.

Warfare among nation states and the development of a growing market economy after the Civil War, have played a prominent role in encouraging Congress to regulate and tax the national economy differently in the U.S. under modern liberalism than under classical liberalism. Recall that classical liberalism embodied the confident belief that political freedom also required economic freedom. Income taxes changed the relationship of governments to their economies in Europe because of the costly Napoleonic Wars and in the U.S. because of the Civil War. The Civil War was the war that erupted out of the first phase of the industrial revolution in America. New inventions were part of the war. Trains, for example, transported Union troops and munitions to battle, and Union troops benefited from new kinds of guns, for example, the repeating rifle in 1864. Mortars led to trench warfare, some mortars as large as 13 inch caliber.[140] Rifled barrels for greater accuracy (invented at the time of the American Revolution) and the repeating rifle made Cavalry charges obsolete during the Civil War and the Cavalry changed from battle tactics to raiding tactics.[141]

The two World Wars erupted out of the second phase of the industrial revolution. Munitions inventions from the industrial revolution were tried in battle in the competition among nation states. For example, twenty ton Big Berthas were placed by the Germans during WWI, using nine tractors and a crane. They fired one ton missiles that left craters, uprooted trees, and altered the landscape from abundant life to one absent living landmarks. The long-comforting natural world was destroyed and made alien by the violent play of war across the battlefield.[142] WWII brought even worse armaments. The planes and tanks after WWI were bigger and flew faster. During WWII, they carried bigger bombs and bigger missiles.

Nuclear weapons decisively changed war and showed that war could accomplish global annihilation. That changed the way people saw the new technologies. After the World Wars, people saw technology's destructive capacity. At first they'd often benefitted from new technologies. The second phase of industrialization had provided positive economic returns. These were so amazing that their like had never been seen before. Many of today's Americans believe in constant economic growth because of technologies that stimulated growth in the past. Most

Americans see technology as a boon for economic growth. But positive economic returns have meant that the government could tax more of the economic surplus and utilize that money for greater influence in political programs and warfare. Post-industrial society has been less profitable and less productive. As IT has been diverted away from productivity and towards political advantages, technology hasn't spread advantages to as many people. And the impact of wars, that were bigger under bigger income tax budgets, was catastrophic to many.

According to Roger Ransom in *Coping with Capitalism: The Economic Transformation of the United States from 1776-1980,*[143] government spending in 1927 was 11.2 billion dollars or about "12% of GDP". After the Great Depression in 1940, government spending of U.S. taxes had risen to about 20.42 billion dollars. But taxes were increased to pay for the Second World War, and taxes stayed permanently higher after the war. By 1950 the government was spending 70.5 billion dollars or a quarter of the total U.S. economic production. This meant that economic production was diverted out of economic use and into the politics of warfare destruction and social welfare. By 1970, the government was diverting economic production for government spending in the amount of 333 billion dollars.

The number of government employees doubled between 1929 and 1980 in relative terms where in 1929, 10% of the population worked in government but in 1980, 20% worked in government.[144] When the federal government spent money taken in taxes it diverted that money from other uses in private investment and there was a steady government diversion of money out of the U.S. economy during the twentieth century. As the manufacturing boom ended after the second phase of the industrial revolution, there was less money in profits to spare for such politically motivated diversions. But after the World Wars, the military industrial complex had grown and it's appetite to spend tax money continued to grow throughout the Cold War. The size of the government bureaucracy had also increased.

The World Wars were so violent that they overwhelm our capacity to imagine them. What was destroyed has also been hard to imagine.

World War I and World War II were terrible, terrifying, inspiring of grief and bewilderment. Trying to understand them can feel like looking into a vicious sandstorm that has scoured away the gentle curves of organic civility and cultural faith retained from the pre-industrial past. Political and economic remnants of pre-capitalism were also destroyed. Aristocracy after the Second World War, suffered its last and fatal blow. Terrible death tolls resulted, maimed or shell shocked soldiers who could never work productively again, wasteful destruction of physical infrastructure, human and cultural wreckage that led to social alienation and increased cynicism about Western culture. After the wars, a residue of determination to carry on in the West remained in spite of ugly reminders that human life, once precious to Western Christian society, had been expendable in political contests. The consequences of the wars were horrible also for the world's monetary system. And finding a way to pay for them presented a challenge.

When tallied in total, the economic wastefulness of the World Wars combined with the Great Depression created an unmanageable storm of economic havoc. These lasting shocks to the world's economy eventually caused a change from a stable monetary system based on a strict gold standard to unstable fiat money.[145] The Bretton Woods Monetary System was the bridge between a strict gold standard and fiat money. The Bretton Woods Monetary System was based on a managed gold commodity system where the dollar defended gold at an agreed upon price instead of having the advantage of a market-set price for gold. The change from a strict gold commodity system to a managed gold commodity system altered the way the gold money system worked. Even though gold was part of both monetary systems, the way that gold worked inside the monetary system changed after gold prices were determined by diplomatic agreement instead of in the marketplace according to demand.

The costliness of the World Wars undermined the stability of the world's monetary system that had been sponsored by Great Britain. The "rules of the game" for the strict gold standard allowed the strict gold standard to be abandoned during wartime. And the "restoration rule" under the strict gold standard required the UK to re-value its currency relative to the price of gold at the same rate as before the nation had abandoned the strict gold commodity system in order to restore the strict gold standard's price and value structure. The strict gold commodity standard had been the most reliable money system because it kept sovereign governments on budget. David Hume's *price specie flow model* was used to understand and explain how gold established and maintained a stable economic system at equilibrium.[146]

Because the supply of gold has been mostly limited by scarcity, money that is valued under a strict gold standard can keep governments from expanding capital through the government's printing presses. If more money is printed it loses value relative to the market determined value of gold and this keeps government accounting balanced between debt and debt payments. Because the gold standard was accepted under UK auspices internationally, many nations collaborated on maintaining the gold standard because it kept values and prices constant. But the UK abandoned the strict gold standard during WWI. When the UK tried to reestablish it after the war, their reinstitution of the gold standard only lasted for six years. The UK had to abandon restoration of the strict gold standard because it would have required too much financial austerity to defend it.[147] Shocks to the twentieth century economy undermined economic discipline, price and value stability as will be further explored with neoliberalism.

Despite improvements in medical science and treatments, improvements in war machinery led to massive deaths and casualties. In WWI (1914-1918), one source lists 17 million deaths, 10 million military deaths and 7 million civilian deaths.[148] Another historical account lists much higher deaths in non-military populations of thirty million and an economic cost in the "trillions of dollars."[149] World Wars interrupted global food production and international shipping. So, starvation was part of the war legacy.

In WWII (1939-1945), the world suffered 60 million deaths, 22 to 25 million military deaths and 38 to 55 million civilian deaths.[150] Another historical account lists civilian deaths as 40 million and deceased combatants at 17 million dead.[151] These are shocking losses of human life. The embrace of limitlessness in warfare brought war to civilians. They weren't spared. But people grieving for the war dead didn't reach out toward them through spiritualism as they had after the Civil War in America where most of the Northern U.S. had been spared military occupation. Instead, vast cemeteries across the West were filled with crosses and monuments. The victorious and the vanquished dead, lost to their loved ones, populated many fields marked by crosses.

Civilian and military survivors carried on, bearing the burden of personal war experiences, especially in Europe. The war had swept over them and they couldn't stop it or change it. But Western art changed its face. After WWI, the cultural movement of Modernism swept global art. After WWII, until today, Postmodernism. Society's artists, writers, and architects realized and embodied cultural change as they felt it, imbibed it and put it into their work. Art both attacked and embraced culture by making social commentary, social criticism, social parody, acknowledgement of media in art, ugly art, art far from embellishment or pretty romantic views, art that strayed from impressionistic recordings of time and light or fundamental simple forms of modernism and entered the arena of social deconstruction. Sometimes this post-modern art has been hard to look at because it has reflected a non-ideal. The ugliness of mass destruction and mass suffering in world systems that embraced power was beyond anyone's ability to control or contain. Art testifies even though most people can't express war experiences in words. At other times, postmodern art has expressed superficiality or consumerism and put them in either a positive or a negative light.

During WWII, governments bought munitions and assembled war engines. Munitions incinerated Europe's and America's past social culture and political relationships. Destruction undermined older political and economic systems and made way for new global relationships to be constructed upon political and economic scaffolding that had been built specifically to further war aims. Munitions manufacturers profited. The English and Soviet Empires survived the Second World War, but declined and disintegrated afterwards.[152] The nations that were cut off from international shipping supply and that suffered shortages realized that trade was better than striving for self-sufficiency.[153] Colonialism by territorial invasion gave way to international trade for acquiring needed materials.

Technology has a dark side.

Economic building, destroying, and rebuilding was a catastrophic recycling that was frightening. It was, perhaps, an unintended outcome of Industrial Revolution technology on society and it served some interests and harmed others. Neil Postman, in 1998, wrote an essay entitled, "Five Things We Need to Know About Technological Change,"[154] in which he outlined the ways that technologies reach into society to modify it. The five ways include: (1) technology has a cost and a benefit; sometimes the costs outweigh the benefits (2) the effect of a technology will be uneven to people in a society; some may benefit while others may be harmed (3) making use of a technology changes the way that people experience and act in the world by changing the way people think and organize their energies and actions (4) technology brings consequences that can result in radical and "irreversible, unpredictable" changes to society and (5) people forget that technology isn't natural to existence; they imagine technology not as a choice but as something built-in to the human environment, like the sky is part of the natural environment. Industrial revolution technologies created a leisure culture with disposable income and creature comforts but eventually also led to social instabilities and losses like wars and economic instability. Specific examples have included destruction of the global monetary system when Britain abandoned the strict gold standard after WWI, the unwelcome atomic age of fear after WWII, and in between, the stock market's volatility and the Great Depression.

The economic machine assembled for the wars mattered after the war for some analysts only in terms of production not in terms of war's wastefulness. Not counting replacement costs, economic growth and per capita income after WWII showed economic progress. This was the approach of Mark Harrison in his discussion of war costs in "The Economics of World War II: An Overview."[155] But losses in terms of human lives and physical infrastructure mattered differently to ordinary people who lived after the war than it did to investors and bankers who kept business going even during periods of conflict. Ordinary people lost their community's wealth and people they loved, bankers and industrialists kept the war wheels turning and made sure that some wealth could be saved and reutilized during rebuilding. Investors found new opportunities in rebuilding. War destruction for investors represented a loss mostly to the past as long as restoration plans were implemented in the present that afforded new economic opportunities to build again.

Wars in Europe made way for the new. The First World War was the turning point away from liberalism for the West. The Second World War was a contest between fascism and modern liberalism which the fascists lost. And the wars made way for neoliberalism to replace modern liberalism in America. Communism exercised influence during the Cold War and communists vied for political mastery of nation states under the nuclear threat. Nuclear weapons made distance less relevant between aggressors and made interconnected diplomacy instead of isolationism a better political option. The politic and economy reorganized with survivor's guilt, fearfulness, and high taxes to support a war-ready state. Even under positive growth, the West had changed and optimism had faded.

The World Wars changed society in the West by making governments that engaged in the political contest more centralized. Government power increased along with governmental secrecy. Economic regulation increased and so did active economic interventions through tax and trade policy. Rationing was part of the United Kingdom's war plan during WWI. Price controls and rationing was a part of WWII in the United States.[156] Propaganda controlled the kind of information that was shared with the public during WWI and isolated people from military realities.[157] During WWII, the American Office of War Information (OWI) worked in tandem with the British Political Warfare Executive (PWE) to drop propaganda pamphlets on the front to dishearten enemy lines. And during the last year of WWII in the Pacific theater, "race hatred" was heard by defenders on public broadcasts to make their assault on the enemy as brutal as possible.[158] Of course, the Nazis were known to use media ingeniously to motivate popular support for the Third Reich. In the U.S., information provided to the public was tailored by a cooperative press to suit patriotic portrayals of U.S. foreign policy even after WWII. According to *Manufacturing Consent*, by Edward S. Herman and Noam Chomsky,[159] later twentieth century American military bodies have utilized American taxes to persuade Americans to support military programs and accept military viewpoints even outside of a state of war.[160]

Expansion of foreign policy from Allies in Europe to global diplomacy.

Expansion of U.S. diplomatic efforts onto a global stage happened during both WWI and WWII and as a permanent diplomatic policy after Bretton Woods agreements in 1944. These agreements opened global trading under GATT and created a political coalition of Allied governments that agreed to work together to rebuild Europe after the war and to cooperate under the influence of the United Nations. The power of the Executive Branch in the U.S. was affected by the expansion of the U.S. into global politics. Global political concerns have caused the Executive branch to expand its power. But in situations of controversy, congressional legislation has acted to restrict the President's power. Disagreements about the President's power over the U.S. budget, for example, under the 1921 Budget and Accounting Act, resulted in Congress's passage of the Congressional Budget and Impoundment Control Act of 1974 which established the Congressional Budget Office and prevented the President from impounding funds as President Richard Nixon tried to do.[161, 162] Budgetary conflicts continue to this day as has been witnessed repeatedly after the 2008 financial collapse.

Article One, Section Eight of the U.S. Constitution, in describing Congress's enumerated powers reads, "The Congress shall have Power....To define and punish Piracies and Felonies committed on the high Seas, and Offenses against the Law of Nations; To declare War, grant Letters of Marque and Reprisal, and make Rules concerning Captures on Land and Water; To raise and support Armies, but no Appropriation of Money to that Use shall be for a longer Term than two Years; To provide and maintain a Navy; To make Rules for the Government and Regulation of the land and naval Forces; To provide for calling forth the Militia to execute the Laws of the Union, suppress Insurrections and repel Invasions;"

Article Two, Section Two, of the U.S. Constitution, in describing the powers of the President reads: "The President shall be Commander in Chief of the Army and Navy of the United States, and of the Militia of the several States, when called into the actual Service of the United States; he may require the Opinion, in writing, of the principal Officer in each of the executive Departments, upon any Subject relating to the Duties of their respective Offices, and he shall have Power to grant Reprieves and Pardons for Offenses against the United States, except in cases of Impeachment...He shall have Power, by and with the Advice and Consent of the Senate, to make Treaties, provided two thirds of the Senators present concur; and he shall nominate, and by and with the Advice and Consent of the Senate, shall appoint Ambassadors, other public Ministers and Consuls, Judges of the supreme Court, and all other Officers of the United States, whose Appointments are herein otherwise provided for, and which shall be established by Law: but the Congress may by Law vest the Appointment of such inferior Officers, as they think proper, in the President alone, in the Courts of Law, or in the Heads of Departments."

These Constitutional articles limit and share the war powers between the executive and the legislature in accord with the balance of powers theory to prevent tyranny. Presidents have exceeded their constitutional prerogatives on more than one occasion. There have been several examples where a President used war aggression and got permission from Congress after-the-fact. For example, when President Truman called for a police action in Korea, when President Reagan supported CIA involvement in Nicaragua (but remember the Iran/Contra scandal that happened after Congress cut off funding) and when President Clinton used the U.S. military in Kosovo.[163]

When President Nixon and the military lied to Congress and secretly bombed Cambodia, he alienated the legislative branch. After the Vietnam War, Congress passed the War Powers Resolution Act of 1973 (also known as the War Powers Act). It created new executive obligations in case of international military conflicts away from U.S. territory. For instance, it reminded the President that Congress possesses the sole power of declaring War except in the case of a direct attack on U.S. soil. This takes war engagement out of the President's diplomatic tool kit except under the express permission of Congress and then triggers a sixty day time limit on deployment unless the President issues a written report describing the context of engagement of U.S. forces. Congress can also issue a

Concurrent Resolution calling for removal of American armed forces if it disagrees with their deployment.[164]

Executive orders have been issued by presidents since George Washington and usually they have not been politically controversial, but there are exceptions. For example President Lincoln's Emancipation Proclamation was an executive order that became effective in only the South on January 1st, 1863.[165] Executive orders can be issued by the President and they have the power of law unless the Supreme Court rules that the resolution is unconstitutional or a subsequent president revokes the order.[165] When President Truman, in Executive Order 10340 tried to nationalize steel mills, he was overruled by the Supreme Court in *Youngstown Sheet & Tube Co. v. Sawyer (1952)*. President Obama revoked President Bush's executive order that restricted access to presidential papers.[167] Executive orders can withdraw enforcement powers for controversial legislation or can call for government agency action to investigate a public issue or establish a government agency. President Truman issued an executive order to desegregate the military and President Eisenhower to desegregate the public school system. Beginning in 1907, the State Department began a numbering system for executive orders that was retroactive to 1862.[168]

Presidents also possess "emergency powers" and "executive privileges". Emergency powers have been used during the world wars but also for natural emergencies like hurricanes to activate FEMA (Federal Emergency Management Agency). Executive privilege limits access to "secret" papers of the president but there are limits outlined by the Supreme Court in *United States v. Nixon (1974)* and *Clinton v. Jones (1997)*, where presidents can't withhold information that could be useful in a criminal or civil case where they stand accused under trial proceedings.[169]

Modern liberal banking had three eras.

Banking during modern liberalism went through dramatic changes and controversies. Three main banking eras stand out. The first was the Civil War Era when Abraham Lincoln issued Greenbacks, promises to pay backed by the government without an exchange value in metals like gold or silver. The Second was twofold: Woodrow Wilson's signing of the Federal Reserve Act in 1913, establishing the current Federal Reserve System and passage of the Sixteenth Amendment that made income tax permanent, also in 1913. The third era was that of the Great Depression when Franklin Delano Roosevelt and his administration followed radical policies including a bank holiday, gold confiscation and stricter government oversight of bank operations under the Bank Act of 1933 to avoid further capital imbalances and mal-investment because of too much stock market speculation. This was the FDR era installation of Glass-Steagall that separated commercial and investment banking. The separation of the highest risk banking from commercial and savings banking made banking safer for non-bankers that used banks as the conduit of the production and profit stream.

Economic transactions have at least two sides, a party and a counter-party. A buyer and a seller, for instance. And markets are competitive, sellers who make the most of their opportunities to offer the best goods at the lowest price prosper more than those who are less adept at making profitable deals. A skilled business person knows prices, customers and what's new, so that the business person can accommodate new demand by fickle consumers at the best price. This serves the customer and serving the customer well serves society's interests well by creating the most efficient marketplace where fair transactions respond to buyer demand and the commonwealth gains wealth. Political competition in war between nation states has been destructive to economic wealth, though economic growth resumes after the war. Competition within markets can be constructive but competition between the market and society outside legal restraint or under oligarchies or monopolies creates market inefficiencies that can destroy society's wealth building opportunities.

In banking, alternative ways of thinking about money and utilizing money can clash as they did during the classical liberal period. Money serves diverse interests. Like the difference between how an investor uses money and a farmer or storekeeper uses it. Balancing financial interests serves society as a whole. The political choice not to re-charter the First Bank of the United States and the Second Bank of the United States revealed a clash of interests. Both banks lost their charter after the first twenty years, in part, because of state bank perception of the federal bank as an unfair competitor. Later, during the modern liberal period, another bank controversy involved President Lincoln's need of cash to fund the Civil War.

In order to avoid high interest charges between 24-36% that European banks would have charged him to get loans to fund the Union side, Lincoln had Greenbacks issued.[170] This was currency backed only by the promise-to-pay by the federal government and not backed by gold. Greenbacks stopped European banks from making an interest profit from loans to fund the Civil War, saving money for Lincoln but costing European banks. They lost the opportunity to charge Lincoln a fee for the use of their excellent specie backed money. In order to avoid the problems of inflation linked to the quantity of money that would be printed, like those experienced by Continental currency during the Revolutionary War, a limited quantity of controlled printing of Greenbacks was undertaken.

Their value fluctuated somewhat depending on how the Civil War was going, but they never lost their value the way that Continentals had. For example, their value in exchange for $100 in gold moved as low as $258 Greenback but gained ground after the Civil War to $150 Greenbacks/ $100 Gold.[171] Controversy after the Civil War erupted when Americans didn't want to give up their Greenbacks. Northeastern bankers couldn't manipulate the quantity of money as completely when Greenbacks were outside their metal backed control of the money supply.

People continued to circulate Greenbacks as money well after the Civil War. The history of Greenback circulation shows a conflict of money interests between Lincoln and European banks and between Northeastern bankers who preferred money with a metal backing and ordinary Americans, like farmers, using Greenbacks as currency to exchange goods freely among men like themselves, instead of gold backed bank notes.

The Administration of Woodrow Wilson brought two controversies. The first was controversy over the passage of the income tax amendment and this controversy stems from issues of legitimacy. The passage of the Sixteenth Amendment on February 3rd, 1913 has attracted controversy regarding whether the proper ratification steps were followed. The Sixteenth Amendment reads, "The Congress shall have power to lay and collect taxes on incomes, from whatever source derived, without apportionment among the several States, and without regard to any census or enumeration." Constitutional amendments can be ratified by two methods. Congress chooses the ratification method. Ratification occurs either by vote of the state legislature or by "a Constitutional Convention in each state."[172]

Secretary of State Philander C. Knox had the task of attesting to the proper ratification by a minimum of 36 states. He attested to the ratification. But researchers have disputed his claim. The Supreme Court has ruled that the Sixteenth Amendment is ratified according to Knox's testimony, and that it is law because of subsequent Court rulings that have accepted it as legal. The matter has been laid to rest as far as the Supreme Court is concerned. And today's taxpayers are considered to be a nuisance if they complain to the IRS. If a taxpayer makes any comment to the IRS contesting its right to tax, there is an immediate penalty of $5,000.[173]

Of course, the Sixteenth Amendment can be repealed, as the Eighteenth Amendment was repealed by the Twenty-first Amendment, but until then, the Supreme Court accepts it as a part of the U.S. Constitution. President Wilson's passage of the income tax amendment, led to an increase in the tax rate which expanded after the Second World War to a higher rate that has funded a permanent military expansion that happened during the Twentieth century.[174] It increased pressure on American citizens to make money so that they could pay their tax bill. Subsistence life on farms could no longer make ends meet under the new American tax requirement.

The other Wilson controversy was establishment of the Federal Reserve. This was to become another federal bank like the First Bank of the United States and the Second Bank of the United States but now a more powerful central bank with twelve branch banks and oversight of other banking institutions. National banks under national charter were required to buy stock in their regional Federal Reserve Bank and to provide a specified amount of bank reserves to the Federal Reserve Bank in their district. Both groups of bank's business interests were thus married by money according to a legal requirement.[175] The Congress wrote the

Federal Reserve Act and the President signed it into law on December 23rd, 1913. Although the Federal Reserve was supposed to prevent financial collapse, it failed to prevent the Great Depression in 1929, the third era of importance to banking during the modern liberal period.

Because money acts as a store of value, it is important that the amount of dollars that are in circulation are proportional to economic productivity. Other stores of value, like real estate or the stock market can overwhelm and cause a money imbalance when the amount of debt taken on to purchase stocks or land grows beyond the productivity of the economic system to pay for those purchases and debt displaces capital investments in productive opportunities that create jobs. The imbalance can cause a financial collapse like the ones listed in chapter one. Speculation in the stock market caused the financial collapse of 1929 because so much money was being bet on stocks and so little was being circulated in financial exchange for other economic purposes. This caused a bubble where stocks were overvalued relative to other parts of the economy. President Hoover saw economic losses mount despite the relatively few number of people trading in the stock market as compared to the total population: only 10 million of 120 million persons were in the stock market.[176]

The correction in stock values, their devaluation, removed money from circulation in other parts of the economy. A fall in stock values translated to financial losses in production firms. Many went out of business. These asset devaluations and losses in the stock market led to unemployment, which caused families to suffer deprivation. Banks failed in the hundreds and people lost their savings because the banks were uninsured. That meant that money was sucked out of groceries, housing, transportation and manufacturing when banks went out of business and refused to honor people's deposits. Even prudent people who had saved money in the bank for a rainy day lost their back-up cash. And many people's retirement savings disappeared. Hoover tried to bolster the economy hoping for a turn back towards prosperity. He authorized seven hundred million dollars for public works projects and two billion dollars for agriculture and industry but the amount was dwarfed by other billions of dollars in economic losses.[177] In 1933, Franklin Delano Roosevelt was elected, well after the financial crisis had bloomed into some kind of problem or worry for almost everyone.

The idea of a bank holiday wasn't Roosevelt's alone. Hoover and various state governors had already considered or implemented a bank holiday in various places around the nation.[178] But FDR's four days long National Bank Holiday started on March 6th, 1933. It was a sign to Americans of sweeping bank reform. It scared people who couldn't access any bank services while banks were closed down. But Congress acted quickly. Stricter bank regulation came out of the Bank Holiday that consisted of new governmental oversight and new organizational structure. The Bank Act of 1933, passed on March 9th, 1933, introduced regulations that separated commercial and investment banking, instituted the Securities and Exchange Commission (SEC) to monitor stock trading, and introduced the federally sponsored FDIC (Federal Deposit Insurance Corporation) to insure commercial bank deposits and restore ordinary people's confidence that banks wouldn't steal their money in a subsequent bank failure.[179]

Congressional legislation and FDR's policies changed American banking for the long term. The separation of commercial and investment banking took savings deposits out of stock market gambles and this part of the Bank Act of 1933 has been called the Glass Steagall Act. Inside the Banking Act of 1933, Glass Steagall referred to Sections 16, 20, 21 and 32 which regulated securities trading.[180] It regulated banks and reduced financial risks in commercial banking until its gradual repeal during bank deregulation of the 1980's and 1990's. The repealing legislation was in part, the Depository Institutions Deregulation and Monetary Control Act of 1980 and the 1999 Gramm-Leach-Bliley Act.[181]

It was repeal of Glass Steagall that permitted the banking imbalances that caused the 2008 collapse and subsequent losses. Congress decided that those losses should be covered by the U.S. Treasury in 2008. But investment banking was never meant to be insured by the government under the Banking Act of 1933. The deregulation of banking allowed mixing of commercial and investment banks and put everyone's assets in investment risk and commercial savings together. Removing the dike that separated kinds of bank interests endangered everyone's interests together when risk exceeded prudence under the exchange of toxic mortgage securities and the derivative bets that were made against or in favor of those assets. The American economy has yet to recover vitality several years after the collapse, as seen in employment figures, economic growth, real estate and economic well-being. Americans live on, day after day, in a sick economy. Life in America is the economic doldrums.

Federal Reserve policies haven't been consistent and haven't prevented financial collapse.

Some would expect Federal Reserve policy to follow a stable and prudent pathway to keep the economy healthy by supporting employment and avoiding inflation. That is what the Humphrey Hawkins Act of 1978 (also known as the Full Employment and Balanced Growth Act)[182] called for in the Carter Administration. But Federal Reserve policy has changed and behaved inconsistently over its short one hundred year lifespan. Centralized regulation of money value, inflation, employment and money supply have all been emphasized to varying degrees over history. Keynesian policies after WWII were adopted and utilized as part of Federal Reserve policy to manage inflation and employment. Under Keynesianism, sovereign debt was counted as an aid to productivity and federal debt grew. Later, neoliberal monetarist policies were utilized that came from Milton Friedman to increase the supply of money and to multiply its varieties in order to increase bank and corporate capitalization. This also helped to increase the number of transactions that banks could exploit to make money. It helped the government also to monetize its debt. In all cases, policies to centralize and regulate money have led to economic inefficiencies that subtract from wider economic growth.[183]

Describing the economy and money making activities of the modern liberal period brings a number of flashy historical elements into view such as The Great Depression (1929-1941), The Gilded Age (1878-1889), growth of the Military Industrial Complex, and Keynesianism.[184] Another feature has been increased taxation and the growing influence of the Federal Reserve. An emphasis on narrow specialization in academia and the predominance of experts in clarifying and describing economic policy and even politics *changed the kinds people who influence policy decisions.* Nowadays, they are people vetted in universities under specific theoretical models. And experts have closed off most people's exposure to the ideas that define the politic and economy. Illiteracy during classical liberalism closed some opportunities for people of that era, but the language used to describe the politic and economy was available to all literate people who had access to books. Economic jargon and policy based models have made economics too hard for many to understand in the modern liberal and the neoliberal eras.[185] Information inaccessibility has provided neoliberals with a political advantage as they make decisions that harm the economic public but that have served neoliberal objectives.

It wasn't academic titles that provided access to information and ideas during classical liberalism but rather the opportunity to become educated and to converse with others who were likewise part of the elite or the educated class of people. During twentieth century modern liberalism, opportunity costs went up in terms of the time it took to become educated and the money paid out to acquire specialized educational certification, not to mention the need to become accepted by a school that would provide higher education. But public education to provide a general education was more widespread during modern liberalism than during classical liberalism. Nevertheless, the discipline of economics shut people out who didn't have economics degrees and developed a niche language, using unfamiliar terminology and mathematical modeling for interpreting empirical observations. Specialists inculcated in specific economic schools of thought wrote about economics to please their economic cohorts often within the same economic school and in order to satisfy the government's need to use economics to justify a huge growth in sovereign debt.

Ricardo can help us to understand economic inefficiency.

The neo-classical model of economics (part of economic liberalism) was described in part by David Ricardo's (1772-1823) idea of comparative advantage. Under comparative advantage, markets were considered efficient under a number of requirements. Markets must have free trade between nations, no monopoly, also no government oligopoly, moderate transportation costs that don't eat too much profit when goods move across borders, and information that all potential buyers can access to learn accurately about goods for sale.[186] When these requirements were met, open trade could benefit all participants because it would be efficient in producing the most for everyone of everything that could be made anywhere and transported to where it would be needed according to what customers wanted. Stock market investments were important in Ricardo's time as they had been in Adam Smith's time and the stock market made the economy more dynamic by bringing money from diverse sources to invest in new ventures. To expand the reach of stock market investments, specialized labor and comparative advantage in free markets was desired.

What Ricardo's comparative advantage now helps people recognize is the kinds of market interferences that cause market inefficiency. Taxation, for example, in a regulated economy pulls money out of economic markets for use in political projects. The growth of very large industries can lead to cartels and monopolies that can deform the price structure by elevating prices higher than real demand would bring them to. Both taxation that diverts economic profits into politics and monopolies that raise prices in the market lead to market inefficiencies. They waste money that could have supported a healthier economy. What that means is that virtuous cycling of profits back into market growth is interrupted. This has created market shortfalls in production, in profit and in employment.

And the modern liberal period under a mixed economy structure had large monopolies that distorted prices, government taxes and regulations that distorted prices and pulled money out of economic circulation within the domestic markets where the goods were produced, advertising that distorted product information, and trade protectionism until after WWII. All of these caused market distortions that precipitated inefficiencies like unemployment and fluctuations in prices causing both inflation and deflation. Expansion of the supply of money in the form of real estate speculation loans and stock speculation outpaced true market productivity in the twenties and caused a bubble to form in finance.[187] This speculative mal-investment caused the Great Depression.

The limited value of economic models is because the economy is so complex.

One way to describe economic models used by modern liberal economists is to say that they measure a few specific economic indicators under an assumption of other factors being stable and predictable. This can create the appearance of false relationships that don't exist in the real market. Economic models can distort real markets by making them seem closed when they are open, for example, or by making certain factors such as inflation and unemployment have a strict relationship that might not be true if other elements were also considered. And models can make a policy regulated system seem like the only possible economic prerogative when other policy options are present. Models can create a simulacra of specified relationships in a system that is of limited predictive value because it measures certain market characteristics while ignoring others. Economic markets are an example of a complex adaptive system; they aren't static even when they are in equilibrium and appear momentarily stable.

Keynesian models analyze limited kinds of data while they pretend to predict outcomes for a regulated economy which has built-in inefficiencies. According to Roger Ransom, war, depression, inflation and unemployment show us that economists have been unable to create a stable economic environment in the United States.[188] Keynesian models specifically have required certain features to be present such as disposable income in people's everyday money handling and a stable economy in a state of balanced equilibrium.[189] Keynesian models don't work when there is a lack of disposable income, there is less asset ownership by everyday persons, or when the economic market is made unstable because of imbalances caused by bubbles fueled by mal-investment. These factors may explain why New Deal Programs and Keynesian deficit spending had limited success in ending the economic malaise of the Great Depression.

Summary considerations for modern liberalism.

Big winners of the modern liberal period included the Robber Barons of the Gilded Age when railroads improved national transportation and created new wealth for those who could take advantage of the market economy. Labor won some battles and lost some battles to get a safer, more reasonable and better paying workplace. But Unions moved from illegal strikes to legal ones back to mostly no more labor strikes. Today, with outsourcing and robotics, unemployment has increased as wages fall in the developed economies of the world, including the U.S. economy. Without many unions to negotiate, with Congress in support of outsourcing, labor is losing power under global pressures. This has happened because of politics where corporate interests were put first. Less pay and benefits for U.S. labor was a political choice and wasn't due simply to global competition. Also, military contractors won large sums during the Civil War, WWI and WWII as well as the Cold War. They have continued to spend in Middle East conflicts. The military became an ally of development in science technologies, during modern liberalism to advance new inventions into the political future. And the CIA grew to participate actively in global politics.

But many people died in destructive wars and they and their families lost out in terms of lives that might have happened without the war contests between nation states. Native Americans didn't get much political power with respect to their treaty rights (see *Lone Wolf v. Hitchcock (1903)*), but they fought in battles by joining U.S. military forces. Their willingness to fight for the U.S. gained them greater political recognition after the wars. The grant of a wider voter franchise helped people who had been excluded from participation in politics during the classical liberal period. Nowadays, the current rate of voter nonparticipation shows that the U.S. has a group of disgruntled Americans who may not know how to get political access or who don't want to participate in the U.S. politic.

The politic, like law, now charges an influence-fee among corporate competitors that most Americans can't afford to pay. Ordinary Americans are feeling vulnerable in the political and economic U.S. environment of the twenty-first century. Our system of government isn't working to prevent harms and more problems have surfaced in the U.S., such as difficulty in balancing the government's budget, or even creating a national budget, the controversies over Presidential actions that operate outside guidelines set by the Constitution such as having a Presidential "kill list" and failures to prosecute people who have committed fraud in the financial industry.

Modern liberalism lost momentum as a U.S. political ideology after WWII. To understand how far America has departed from the vision of hope in the hearts of modern liberals, it helps to remember a speech by FDR. On January 11, 1944, Franklin Delano Roosevelt gave a State of the Union address[190] in which he presented a Second Bill of Rights for the U.S.: "In our day these economic truths have become accepted as self-evident. We have accepted, so to speak, a second Bill of Rights under which a new basis of security and prosperity can be established for all regardless of station, race, or creed. Among these are: The right to a useful and remunerative job in the industries or shops or farms or mines of the Nation; The right to earn enough to provide adequate food and clothing and recreation; The right of every farmer to raise and sell his products at a return which will give him and his family a decent living; The right of every businessman, large and small, to trade in an atmosphere of freedom from unfair competition and domination by monopolies at home or abroad; The right of every family to a decent home; The right to adequate medical care and the opportunity to achieve and enjoy good health; The right to protection from the economic fears of old age, sickness, accident, and unemployment; The right to a good education. All of these rights spell security. And after this war is won we must be prepared to move forward, in the implementation of these rights, to new goals of human happiness and well-being. America's own rightful place in the world depends in large part upon how fully these and similar rights have been carried into practice for our citizens. For unless there is security here at home there cannot be lasting peace in the world."

This FDR quote already envisioned a global role for the U.S. in politics as seen by his use of the phrase, "rightful place in the world" and the idea of the U.S as a peace keeper. He also indirectly described the historical exchange of economic freedom under classical liberalism for economic security under modern liberalism. After looking at economic taxation and regulation, it's clear in the present that liberty has been sidelined under the promise of greater economic security. But current circumstances show a failure of American government to deliver FDR's promises under his second Bill of Rights.

Several problems are easy to recognize in the twenty first century: high unemployment and labor non-participation show the consequences of neoliberal job outsourcing, investment in robotics displacing workers, worker alienation because of management inflexibility, "low road policies" and profit maximizing policies that hurt workers, growth of minimum wage jobs under the poverty line, misrepresentation of GDP to pretend that neoliberalism works economically and misrepresentation of inflation to avoid paying higher amounts legally mandated for social security, curtailment of social welfare programs accompanied by an expansion of the prison system, corporate welfare for large multinationals and high tax rates for small domestic businesses which has led to failing small domestic business because of a competitive disadvantage sponsored by Congress, and high rates of global military actions and costs, enormous regulatory costs under a plethora of regulations, a huge tax increase to fund Obamacare but with evidence of declining quality and value in healthcare. FDR's plan to regulate the economy eventually failed to create the lasting economic security that he'd hoped for. Learning about neoliberalism answers the question of what happened to FDR's plan for greater economic security.

Fast Car Analysis for Modern Liberalism

People have rights and governments have powers.
The U.S. Constitution limits the power of the federal government.
Natural rights are rights that people are born with; they aren't granted by government.
Political factions are organized groups that seek the political grant of a favorable outcome to their interests.

Several events enlarged the federal government's power:
The Civil War, and the erosion of state's right to secede. Income tax.
"Presumption of constitutionality" adopted by the Supreme Court after the standard of "necessary and proper" was discarded.
Growth of the regulatory state; multiplication of laws without limitation.
No limitation of government debt and deficit.
The Supreme Court's acceptance of the military draft.

Several cultural influences led many during modern liberalism to revere power in the politic:
The Romantic Period: admiration of the sublime.
The economic power of the Second Wave of the Industrial Revolution.
The German Historical School of Economics' third wave, expressed by the ideas of Max Weber and Werner Sombart.
German Idealism and the embrace of limitlessness.
American Pragmatism.

The Civil War was both an economic and a political transition.
During the modern liberal period, federal government power grew; political factions sought to gratify their own particular interests through the power of the federal government; **income taxes increased both the propensity for war and the propensity to engage in political conflict at home**.
Expansion of the regulatory state **has exceeded the bounds of good government** designed into the U.S. Constitution by the Founders.

The unintended consequences of the regulatory state are many:
Increased economic factions vying for political advantage.
Growth of lobbies.
Increased incentives motivating political corruption.
Regulatory capture.
Fewer individual freedoms.
Expensive rent-seeking behaviors.
PACs and think tanks influencing policy makers.
A less capable Congress.
High costs of regulating.
Greater militarization of executive forces that enforce regulations.

Economic inefficiencies under the modern liberal regulatory state:
Growth of monopolies.
Growth of taxes on individuals and families.
Propaganda to promote specific ideas or industries; censorship.
Growth of government; growth of bureaucracy.
Bigger and more expensive wars.
Government expenditures from taxes displacing other investment opportunities by individuals and groups.
An erosion of society's wealth.

The **most virtuous cycling of money** involves the greatest number of exchanges inside a productive economy that has stable prices and values.

Capital in large quantities can affect prices both when it comes into and when it goes out of a market. This can affect the value of foreign exchange currency, the value of stocks, the value of traded derivatives and the value of assets.

Modern Liberalism Appendix

Chart of essential modern liberal characteristics.

1. Modern liberals departed from classical liberal political norms. They also acquired an interest in hidden processes. Society pondered topics such as the unconscious, evolution, genetics, spiritual experiences and supernatural insights. Theories came into being that conceptualized social processes as a hierarchy of phases in transition. For example societies were imagined as having different stages toward maturity. Skepticism grew regarding how well the human consciousness could manage human affairs; confidence in humanism diminished. Many lost faith in the idea that individuals thinking and acting alone or in social groups could adapt and change in positive ways when faced with modern liberal challenges or that man existed as the measure of all things. Politicians became fascinated with power.

2. Dramatic economic and political changes were experienced during modern liberalism because of expansion of the market economy under the influence of novel technologies. Pragmatists thought that society needed a strong government to solve big social problems erupting out of economic change. Optimism overruled caution among modern liberals who thought of government as a public servant that would serve the needs of people under the expanded voting franchise. Many modern liberals had optimism about technological change and the need to make way for novelty. Powerful economic growth stimulated the growth of government as expressed by Wagner's Law.

3. New public health initiatives, public services, and urban planning led to a population explosion in the U.S. and Europe. Amid prosperity, and fast changes, modern liberals lost any interest in natural rights and liberty. Security instead of freedom became the highest economic and political ideal. Some Progressives sought to enforce social conformity among diverse people who were part of the hugely increased urban populations due to immigration from Europe.

4. Modern liberal citizens had less political freedom, less economic freedom and paid higher taxes. The Supreme Court ruled that the draft was constitutional in *Arver v. United States (1918)*, along with similar rulings called the *Selective Draft Law Cases*.

5. Congress legislated positive laws to regulate the economy beginning with transportation. Modern liberalism saw expansion of the regulatory state. The cost of regulatory expansion was camouflaged by economic expansion that happened concurrently. Modern liberals chose prohibition for thirteen years, but they saw a huge increase in organized crime and corruption among local police forces and federal agencies charged with enforcing the ban of alcohol. There were also important improvements in

communication that connected nation states so that ideas could circle the globe more quickly.

6. Jim Crow violence and racial discrimination diminished the political rights of African Americans under the universal voting franchise. The Fifteenth Amendment that recognized African American voting rights was ratified in 1870; the Nineteenth Amendment that recognized women's right to vote was ratified in 1920. Remaining Native Americans were relocated to Indian Reservations.

7. Transportation and media grew and changed American society, connecting it in new ways. Rail expansion happened under generous land grants to railroad companies from the federal government but regulation eventually poached rail profits by interfering with train fares and routes. Political concerns became influenced by information in newspapers. Political lecture tours began to affect the politic.

8. The Supreme Court changed course during FDR's presidency to allow expansion of the regulatory state. The "presumption of constitutionality" replaced the liberty era's "necessary and proper" standards.

9. Participation replaced isolationism during WWI and WWII. Military technologies proved that war had become more destructive. There would be no way to externalize war costs to the loser. European war politics influenced the U.S. to adopt features of socialism in modern liberalism: income tax, welfare and warfare. But most industries weren't nationalized. The Sixteenth Amendment, mandating a permanent federal income tax, passed just before WWI, in 1913, but well after income taxes had been used by the Union side to win the Civil War. The U.S. became a world power through military strength and economic productivity.

10. The Federal Reserve failed to prevent the Great Depression. After the Great Depression, U.S. banks became strictly regulated under the Banking Act of 1933. Glass Steagall separated commercial and investment banking until neoliberal regulatory reform. Bretton Woods agreements, after WWII, introduced neoliberal globalization policies based on open trade in exchange for easy credit and debt and a temporary managed gold monetary system with the dollar as the international currency.

Modern liberal timeline

1857 Frederick Law Olmstead and Calvert Vaux design Central Park in Manhattan, 1600 New Yorkers were evicted from shantytowns by eminent domain to make room for it. *Dred Scott v. Sandford (1857).*

1859 John Brown acted against slavery in the Harper's Ferry raid.

1861-1865 Abraham Lincoln was elected to the Presidency; The Civil War; Matthew Brady's corps of photography assistants and Matthew Brady photographed the war dead; in 1865 the Thirteenth Amendment was ratified.

1862 The Merrill Act provided land grants for colleges.

1864 The New York Council on Hygiene raised sanitation standards.

1865-1877 Reconstruction showed that political influence backed by force has limited effect in changing society quickly.

1867 Dynamite was invented by Alfred Nobel.

1868 The Fourteenth Amendment was ratified.

1869 The Suez Canal opened; Union Pacific joined with the Central Pacific Railway at Promontory Point, Utah, to become the first transcontinental railway.

1870's-1890 The Gilded Age; in 1870 the Fifteenth Amendment was ratified.

1873 French Impressionism art debut.

1874-1890 Impressionism era in painting.

1876 Alexander Graham Bell invented the telephone. Pierre Auguste Renoir, *Moulin de la Galette*, impressionist painting.

1878 Major John Wesley Powell's report on the Lands of the Arid Region of the United States stated that surveyed lands were too dry for sustainable agricultural development.

1879 Thomas Edison invented the electric light bulb.

1884 Georges Seurat, *A Sunday Afternoon on the Island of La Grande Jatte*, pointillist painting.

1886 Dr. John Pendleton invented Coca Cola.

1890 Jacob Riis, wrote *How the Other Half Lives.*

1890-1915 Art Nouveau period. Avant Garde art and Modernism later became art movements that were international.

1892 Rudolf Diesel invented the diesel motor engine.

1893 Chicago World's Fair was full of novelty. Depression of 1893. Alfred Stieglitz, *Winter on Fifth Avenue,* photogravure.

1895 Lumiere brothers introduced the world to cinema.

1897 Henri Rousseau, *The Sleeping Gypsy*, painting.

1898-1899 Spanish American War occurred in the Philippines. Treaty of Paris 1898, Spain ceded the Philippines to the U.S. for 20 million dollars.

1899 Revolutionary Philippine forces fought for independence. Gugliemo Marconi's radio, also known as "the wireless" was invented.

1900 President McKinley established the Second Philippine Commission after too many political factions in the Philippines failed to organize a credible independence government.

1901-1909 Vice President Theodore Roosevelt took over after President McKinley was assassinated by an anarchist; Progressive political era began.

1907 Gustav Klimt, *The Kiss* painting; 1906-1909, Frank Lloyd Wright, *Frederick C. Robie House.*

1908 The first commercial radio transmission created a new kind of advertising.

1903 Wright brothers flew their airplane.

1904-1914 The construction of the Panama Canal enhanced global trade.

1906 The San Francisco earthquake destroyed much of the city.

1909-1913 Howard Taft became President; Progressive era continued.

1913 Income tax passed under the Sixteenth Amendment (or did it?).

1913-1921 Woodrow Wilson as President; Progressivism ended but influenced the New Deal era to come.

1914-1918 The Great War, WWI; tragic losses, damaged lives.

1917 The Russian Revolution began a practical communistic legacy that included mass murder and starvation.

1919 The first Trans-Atlantic flight linked people in far-away nations.

1920 Prohibition took effect under the Eighteenth Amendment; the Nineteenth Amendment for women's voting was ratified after a seventy two year struggle.

1924 The Indian Citizenship Act, also known as the Snyder Act granted citizenship to most Native Americans, but some state laws resisted citizenship until 1948.

1923 The "Red Wing Project" conducted by The University of Minnesota Department of Biosystems and Agricultural Engineering in partnership with Northern States Power Company proved that rural electrification could be economically feasible.

1928 Penicillin was discovered by Alexander Fleming.

1929 The Great Depression, a harsh economic correction that hurt many families began and its effects were long-lasting.

1933-1945 The New Deal era began under Franklin Delano Roosevelt as President.

1933 The Twenty-first Amendment repealed Prohibition; also the Industrial Recovery Act of 1933 reduced the work week to forty hours.

1935 The Rural Electrification Act and the Rural Electrification Administration provided "self-liquidating loans" to small communities in support of electrical power. The first analog and digital computers were designed.

1936 Dorthea Lange, *Migrant Mother, Nipomo, California,* Depression Era photograph.

1937 Pablo Picasso painted *Guernica*, his response to the Spanish Civil War of 1937, which was the first instance of an air bombing attack against civilians.

1938 Henry Moore, *Recumbent Figure*, sculpture.

1941-1945 WWII; the Atomic Bomb was used.

1944 The U.N. Conference at Bretton Woods redesigned the global monetary system.

1946-1989 Cold War.

1947 Marshall Plan; GATT treaties began to reshape global trade.

(Appendix sources listed after Modern Liberalism Endnotes)

The difference between money and wealth

The twenty first century global economy has mobile international capital, several economic schools of thought that don't agree, constant arguments about economic theories and economic jargon that confuses people regarding basic concepts. It would be helpful if every person understood at least the difference between their own money and wealth. In your everyday life, if you earn wages or a salary, the money you get as a paycheck comes from work that you do that is sold to make a profit. When your production makes a profit you get a portion of it. Profit from your work pays for your salary. If you work in government, your salary is paid for with taxes that are pulled from businesses that make a profit or from individuals' wages in the economy. And people who work in the government do work that benefits the politic instead of the economy.

The wealth that you accumulate is what's left over after the salary or wage is spent and the debt for ownership has been paid off. It's important to get wealth because few people can earn money throughout their lifespan. If you bought a house or an education, a car, or invested in a productive gold mine, that's wealth. It represents a surplus that purchased something of lasting value. Under current policies of easy credit, a person can't readily know another's wealth because a person with many fine possessions may be making payments for what they don't yet own. In any case, money is paid equal to a negotiated value. This includes work in a labor marketplace where work leads to a product or service sold to make a profit. Or an investment in a company's stock can lead to a dividend when the company does well or if the owner of the stock sells a stock that has gained value. A legitimate market reflects values based on real supply and demand.

Money is a useful thing in society and not just because you can use it to buy something. Money, according to Fitch's *Dictionary of Banking Terms*, serves at least three basic purposes. First, money is a tool of exchange between people in finance, business, and labor. This role of money, its buying power, allows it to transform into anything that money can buy, whether food, or healthcare or travel or a business asset like a machine that makes mufflers. Exchange of goods and services for money makes buying from sellers easier.

Second, money is a value holder that preserves the value of a traded good or service, potentially well beyond the time of its production and use. For example, without money, surplus agriculture couldn't be easily traded and would have to be entirely consumed at once by the producer or quickly bartered for something not perishable or transformed into a nonperishable product. In the absence of money, large farms wouldn't make sense because agricultural trading markets wouldn't exist. In the case of agriculture, money transforms a perishable thing into an almost imperishable thing. Money extends the timeline of value. Money facilitates exchange between producers and customers and its existence becomes a reason to develop exchange markets and transportation networks that bring agricultural goods, for example, to the customer.

Third, money can be a "unit of account for purchasing power". It measures the worth of a company that makes mufflers or a house that you bought twenty five years ago in a wholly different economy; did the value go up or down? Money is "legal tender for the payment of debts."[1] That's where the government comes in. The government prints money and collects taxes in money but it doesn't create the value represented by money.[2] Money's value rests upon productive work that produces products or services usefully exchanged between people in a marketplace. Wealthy nations stimulate productive processes by the way they formulate their economic policies and also by avoiding debt.

Virtuous cycling of money happens when money is exchanged between a buyer and seller for a valuable product. The producer who sold the product then uses money to buy another useful product or service. Money in a virtuous cycle can change hands many times and incentivize brainy labor and brawny labor to produce what society needs. In a healthy economy, prices and values reflect what supply and demand in an exchange marketplace show people are willing to pay in an exchange system that benefits both parties. The economy is made up of the many markets where people meet to agree upon price and value for goods and services. When an economy becomes centralized through government or monopolies, the marketplace's influence on price and value through supply and demand declines. Price negotiation declines and the market can fail to work properly to tell producers what to produce. That can encourage mal-investments. To be virtuous, money used in exchanges must retain its value. Inflation undermines the value of money. The most virtuous cycling of money involves the greatest number of exchanges inside a productive community that has stable values and prices.

Debt is the promise to pay and banks make debt more manageable by extending the time to pay with interest, which usually becomes a small profit for a bank. But debt obligations can discourage future economic liberty until a debt is paid off. Debt can also motivate people who need a job to keep a bad one in order to meet their payment schedule. Debt can limit people's political choices when they can't afford to advocate for changing what isn't working in the economy with new policies in the politic because they have to remain with the status quo in order to make their debt payments. And debt interest payments can drain profits out of otherwise successful and productive ventures. Debt can overwhelm a person's financial soundness and limit their ability to manoeuver beyond debt. Financialization happened after regulatory reform and it led to overgrowth of the financial industry as compared with other businesses. Financialization has led to massive debt, as will be considered in the next chapter.

Sixteen basic definitions from finance.

Capitalism- an economy where people enter into trade contracts by selling their work, their products or their know-how freely and without obstruction by the state. According to Thomas Sowell, in *Basic Economics*, "monopoly is the enemy of efficiency under capitalism or socialism. The difference between the two systems is that monopoly is the norm under socialism.[1]

Corporation- a business entity that has been granted a charter that allows incorporation such that the corporation has limited liability, ownership that can be transferred, and the ability to enter into contracts. In the U.S., corporate personhood under the Fourteenth Amendment has been granted based on a court reporter's notes on the Supreme Court case of *Santa Clara County v. Southern Pacific Railroad (1886)*. The notes created the idea of corporate personhood outside of actual judicial events or justice's opinions and solely because of the court reporter's summary. J.C. Bancroft Davis, was the court reporter, and he had previously been the president of the Newburgh and New York Railway Company.[2] Of course, justices could have ignored the court reporter's notes.

Deflation- when asset prices fall either in part as a single asset class or as a whole affecting an entire economy. Also a value correction in a free market that is based on falling demand or currency collapse. It can affect services in terms of availability, or factor costs (for example, the cost of labor) or commodity products (food or energy, for example).

Economics- "Economics is the study of the use of scarce resources which have alternative uses."[3] *The American Heritage Dictionary*, definition, "the science that deals with the production, distribution and consumption of goods and services.[4]

Federal Reserve System- President Woodrow Wilson's administration established the Federal Reserve System with the 1913 Federal Reserve Act. Twelve district Federal Reserve banks under a Board of Governors and twelve regional banks share responsibility for the Federal Reserve's operating policies. Its shares are privately owned and Congress and the President have some oversight of its operations.[5]

Fiscal policy- government debt; how the government handles taxing and spending.

Holding company- a company that owns greater than 50% of the shares of a corporation; often it is called a subsidiary. It is a company that can control one or several corporations by holding a majority of their stock. The Banking Act of 1933 first authorized Commercial Bank holding companies. The Federal Reserve has had oversight of them under the Bank Holding Company Act of 1956.[6]

Inflation- according to David Hackett Fischer, in *The Great Wave*: "at least seven kinds of inflation can be distinguished by cause...[1] expansion of the money supply, [2] increases in aggregate demand, [3] contraction in supply, [4] cost-push inflation, when wages and prices begin to spiral upward, [5] collusive price-fixing in oligopolistic industries (monopoly/guild/cartel), [6] bubble inflation, caused by a surge of speculative activity, [7] inflationary expectations."[7]

GDP- Gross Domestic Product- the value of a nation's productivity measured in terms of goods and services produced domestically by either a foreign or a domestic firm for the span of one year.[8] Currently reported U.S. GDP numbers are adjusted in ways that differ from earlier methods. Europe, the U.S. and other nations calculate GDP by different methods.

GNP- Gross National Product- the value of production by a nation's citizens produced at home or on foreign soil for the span of one year.[9]

Gresham's Law- bad money drives out good money; Gresham's law is how speculation in a manipulated marketplace can replace production investment in a real marketplace; this process has also been observed by others such as Nicholas Copernicus.

Monetary policy- how much money circulates in the economy, what the rate of interest is for borrowing, ease or difficulty of borrowing. Most of these policies are managed by the Federal Reserve.

Multinational company- a national company with foreign subsidiaries.

Principal agent problem- when a responsible party such as a manager chooses to seek his or her own advantage even when it conflicts with the company's advantage, often for a short term gain followed eventually by a loss. The manager will have collected his or her gain before the company's loss is realized.[10] Also known as control fraud.

Public private partnerships- PPP, business collaboration involving the use of public money often in the form of future taxes that are given to a private entity to achieve a public end. But project bids are sometimes restricted to insider investors instead of open bid, which raises costs. And the risk is borne by the public when problems arise such as a project failure or cost overrun. Insider investors can deliberately scuttle the project while gaining access to money taken from the public's treasury, which they keep even though the project failed. Sometimes public officials provide access for personal gain.

Trans-national company- a firm that operates on a global basis instead of a national one, seeking talented people, factories, raw materials or markets around the world.

Modern Liberalism Endnotes

1. Peter Kalm, *Travels into North America, (1749)*, and *Selections from the Economic History of the United States, 1765-1860*, "The Trade of the Middle Colonies, www.sjsu.edu/faculty/middle colonies04.htm, accessed Dec 2013.

2. David Hackett-Fischer, *Albion's Seed: Four British Folkways in America*, (New York: Oxford University Press, 1989).

3. David Galenson, "The Rise and Fall of Indentured Servitude in the Americas: An Economic Analysis", *The Journal of Economic History*, Vol. 44, No. 1 (Mar, 1984) 1-26, www.colorado.edu/ ibs/eblalston/ econ8534/ SectionIII/ Galenson_The_Rise_and_Fall_ of_Indentured_Servitude_ in_the_Americas.pdf, 1984.

4. Wikipedia, "United States Military Academy", enwikipedia.org/wiki/United States Military Academy, accessed 2013.

5. Wikipedia, "History of Rail Transport," wikipedia.org/wiki/History-of-rail-transport, accessed 2013.

6. Wikipedia, "Erie Canal," enwikipedia.org/wiki/Erie-Canal, accessed 2013.

7. Stephen Salsbury, "Twentieth Century Railroad Managerial Practices: The Case of the Pennsylvania Railroad," in *Research in Economic History*, Robert Gallman, ed., (Greenwich, CT: Jai Press, 1977), 43-47.

8. Wikipedia, "Erie Canal", enwikipedia.org/wiki/Erie_Canal, accessed 2013.

9. Matt Rosenberg, About.com Geography, "Erie Canal: The Building of the Great Western Canal," geography.about.com/od/urbaneconomic geography/a/eriecanal.htm, accessed 2013.

10. Matt Rosenberg, About.com Geography, "Erie Canal: The Building of the Great Western Canal," geography.about.com/od/urbaneconomic geography/a/eriecanal.htm, accessed 2013.

11. Roger Ransom, "The Economics of the Civil War," last updated 2010, eh.net/encyclopedia/article/ransom.civil war.us, accessed 2013.

12. Toke Aidt, Peter Jensen, "The taxman tools up: An event history of the introduction of the personal income tax, Journal of Public Economics, www.econ. cour.ac.ak/faculty/aidt/papers/web/taxman.pdf, accessed 2013.

13. Toke Aidt, Peter Jensen, "The taxman tools up: An event history of the introduction of the personal income tax, Journal of Public Economics, www.econ.cour.ac.ak/faculty/aidt/papers/web/taxman.pdf, accessed 2013.

14. Rise of Industrial America, 1876-1900: Railroads in the Late 19th Century, Library of Congress: Teachers, "Railroad Land Grants," www.loc.gov/teachers/classroommaterials/presentationsandactivities/presentations/timeline/riseand/railroad/grants.html, accessed 2014.

15. Wikipedia, "History of Rail Transport," enwikipedia.org/wiki/ History_of_Rail_Transport, accessed 2013.

16. Roger Ransom, "The Economics of the Civil War," last updated 2010, eh.net/encyclopedia/article/ransom.civil war.us, accessed 2013.

17. Reconstruction, "Reconstruction People," www.shmoop.com/reconstruction/people.html, accessed 2013.

18. Francis K. Pohl, *Framing America: A Social History of American Art*, (New York: Thames & Hudson, 2002), 61.

19. Wilhelm Ropke, *The Social Crisis of Our Time*, (New Brunswick, NJ: Transaction Publishers, 1992) 57-71.

20. Franklin Roosevelt, Franklin D. Roosevelt, XXXII President of the United States, 1933-1945, "Message to Congress on Curbing Monopolies, April 29, 1938," www.presidency.uscb.edu/ws/index.php?pid=15637, accessed May 2013.

21. Franklin Roosevelt, Franklin D. Roosevelt, XXXII President of the United States, 1933-1945, "Message to Congress on Curbing Monopolies, April 29, 1938," www.presidency.uscb.edu/ws/index.php?pid=15637, accessed May 2013.

22. Brian O'Connor, Georg Mohr, eds., *German Idealism: An Anthology and Guide*, (Edinburgh, UK: Edinburgh University Press, University of Chicago Press, 2006), 1.

23. Brian O'Connor, Georg Mohr, eds., *German Idealism: An Anthology and Guide*, (Edinburgh, UK: Edinburgh University Press, University of Chicago Press, 2006), 1.

24. Paul Sann, *The Lawless Decade: Bullets, Broads & Bathtub Gin*, (Mineola, NY: Dover Publications, Inc., 2010).

25. Edward Behr, *Prohibition: Thirteen Years That Changed America*, (New York: Arcade Publishing, 2011), 161-173.

26. Booker T. Washington, *Up From Slavery*, in Anthony Appiah, ed,. *Early American African Classics*, (New York: Bantam Classics, 2008).

27. Booker T. Washington, *Up From Slavery*, in Anthony Appiah, ed,. *Early American African Classics*, (New York: Bantam Classics, 2008), 376-377.

28. Booker T. Washington, *Up From Slavery*, in Anthony Appiah, ed,. *Early American African Classics*, (New York: Bantam Classics, 2008), 418-419.

29. Booker T. Washington, *Up From Slavery*, in Anthony Appiah, ed,. *Early American African Classics*, (New York: Bantam Classics, 2008), 437-438.

30. Booker T. Washington, *Up From Slavery*, in Anthony Appiah, ed,. *Early American African Classics*, (New York: Bantam Classics, 2008), 452-453.

31. Booker T. Washington, *Up From Slavery*, in Anthony Appiah, ed,. *Early American African Classics*, (New York: Bantam Classics, 2008), 475, 476, 478, 479.

32. Immanuel Kant, *Critique of Pure Reason*, J.M.D. Meiklejohn, trans., (New York: Prometheus Books, 1990).

33. Jeremy Stangroom, James Garvey, *The Great Philosophers from Socrates to Foucault*), (New York: Barnes and Noble, Arcturus Publishing, 2006), 90.

34. Hannah Arendt, "The Concept of History", Peter Baehr, ed., *The Portable Hannah Arendt*, (New York: Penguin Books, 2003), 278-284.

35. Peter Angelis, *Philosophy: In-depth Explanations and Examples Covering Over 3000 Entries,* (New York: Harper Collins Publishers, 1992, 132-134.

36. Robert Tucker, *The Marx Engels Reader, Second Edition*, (New York: W.W. Norton and Company, 1978).

37. Molly McGarry, *Ghosts of Futures Past: Spiritualism and the Cultural Politics of Nineteenth-Century America*, (CA: University of California Press, 2008).

38. Immanuel Kant, *Critique of Pure Reason*, J.M.D. Meiklejohn, trans., (New York: Prometheus Books, 1990), 68-69.

39. Georg Hegel, *Introduction to the Philosophy of Nature*, A.V. Miller, trans., in Brian Conner, Georg Mohr, eds., *German Idealism: An Anthology and Guide*, 405-406.

40. Wikiquotes, "Charles Darwin," wikiquotes.org/wiki/Charles Darwin, from *The Origin of the Species*, Chapter III, p61.

41. Karl Marx, preface to *A Contribution to the Critique of Political Economy*, in Robert Tucker, ed, *The Marx Engels Reader, Second Edition*, (New York: WW Norton and Company, 1978), 4-5.

42. Friedrich Nietzsche, "The Gay Science," in Jeffrey Walker, Glen McCann, eds., *Investigating Arguments: Readings for College Writings*, (Boston: Houghton Mifflin, 1991), 324-325.

43. Sigmund Freud, *Civilization and Its Discontents*, in Jeffrey Walker, Glen McCann, eds., *Investigating Arguments: Readings for College Writings*, (Boston: Houghton Mifflin, 1991), 330-331.

44. Geoffrey Ward, Ken Burns, *Not For Ourselves Alone: The Story of Elizabeth Cady Stanton and Susan B. Anthony*, (New York: Alfred A. Knopf, 1999).

45. Geoffrey Ward, Ken Burns, *Not For Ourselves Alone: The Story of Elizabeth Cady Stanton and Susan B. Anthony*, (New York: Alfred A. Knopf, 1999).

46. Elizabeth Cady Stanton, speech regarding the Declaration of Sentiments, in Geoffrey Ward, Ken Burns, *Not For Ourselves Alone: The Story of Elizabeth Cady Stanton and Susan B. Anthony*, (New York: Alfred A. Knopf, 1999), 41.

47. Frederick Douglas, the *North Star*, in Geoffrey Ward, Ken Burns, *Not For Ourselves Alone: The Story of Elizabeth Cady Stanton and Susan B. Anthony*, (New York: Alfred A. Knopf, 1999), 41.

48. Elizabeth Cady Stanton, *The Revolution*, in Geoffrey Ward, Ken Burns, *Not For Ourselves Alone: The Story of Elizabeth Cady Stanton and Susan B. Anthony*, (New York: Alfred A. Knopf, 1999), 112.

49. Susan B. Anthony, 1876, Independence Square recitation of the Woman's Declaration of Rights, in Geoffrey Ward, Ken Burns, *Not For Ourselves Alone: The Story of Elizabeth Cady Stanton and Susan B. Anthony*, (New York: Alfred A. Knopf, 1999), 153.

50. Jacob Riis, *How the Other Half Lives*, (USA: Digireads.com, 2009), appendix.

51. Jacob Riis, *How the Other Half Lives*, (USA: Digireads.com, 2009), commentary back cover.

52. Jacob Riis, *How the Other Half Lives*, (USA: Digireads.com, 2009), 8-9.

53. Jacob Riis, *How the Other Half Lives*, (USA: Digireads.com, 2009), 123.

54. Wikipedia, "University of Chicago," enwikipedia.org/wiki/ University_of_Chicago, accessed Sept 2013.

55. John Dewey, *The Public and Its Problems*, (USA: Ohio University Press, Swallow Press, 1954).

56. John Dewey, *The Public and Its Problems*, (USA: Ohio University Press, Swallow Press, 1954), 74.

57. John Dewey, *The Public and Its Problems*, (USA: Ohio University Press, Swallow Press, 1954), 182.

58. John Dewey, *The Public and Its Problems*, (USA: Ohio University Press, Swallow Press, 1954), 118.

59. John Dewey, *The Public and Its Problems*, (USA: Ohio University Press, Swallow Press, 1954), 174-175.

60. Jane Addams, *On Education*, Ellen Condliffe Langemann, ed., (New Brunswick, NJ: Transaction Publishing, 2009), pvii.

61. Jane Addams, *On Education*, Ellen Condliffe Langemann, ed., (New Brunswick, NJ: Transaction Publishing, 2009).

62. Jane Addams, *On Education*, Ellen Condliffe Langemann, ed., (New Brunswick, NJ: Transaction Publishing, 2009), 114.

63. Jane Addams, *On Education*, Ellen Condliffe Langemann, ed., (New Brunswick, NJ: Transaction Publishing, 2009), 152-153.

64. Jane Addams, *On Education*, Ellen Condliffe Langemann, ed., (New Brunswick, NJ: Transaction Publishing, 2009), 191.

65. Jane Addams, *On Education*, Ellen Condliffe Langemann, ed., (New Brunswick, NJ: Transaction Publishing, 2009), 217.

66. Brigadier General Smedley Butler, *War Is a Racket*, (Port Townsend, WA: Feral Publishing, 2003.

67. Brigadier General Smedley Butler, *War Is a Racket*, (Port Townsend, WA: Feral Publishing, 2003, 23.

68. Brigadier General Smedley Butler, *War Is a Racket*, (Port Townsend, WA: Feral Publishing, 2003, 36.

69. Walter Lippmann, *The Good Society*, (New Brunswick, NJ: Transaction Publishers, 2005).

70. Walter Lippmann, *The Good Society*, (New Brunswick, NJ: Transaction Publishers, 2005), 48, 49.

71. Walter Lippmann, *The Good Society*, (New Brunswick, NJ: Transaction Publishers, 2005), 7 and 9.

72. Walter Lippmann, *The Good Society*, (New Brunswick, NJ: Transaction Publishers, 2005), 40-41.

73. Walter Lippmann, *The Good Society*, (New Brunswick, NJ: Transaction Publishers, 2005), 65 and 67.

74. Walter Lippmann, *The Good Society*, (New Brunswick, NJ: Transaction Publishers, 2005), 78.

75. Walter Lippmann, *The Good Society*, (New Brunswick, NJ: Transaction Publishers, 2005), 216-217.

76. Walter Lippmann, *The Good Society*, (New Brunswick, NJ: Transaction Publishers, 2005), 273-275.

77. Walter Lippmann, *The Good Society*, (New Brunswick, NJ: Transaction Publishers, 2005), 289-290.

78. Walter Lippmann, *The Good Society*, (New Brunswick, NJ: Transaction Publishers, 2005), 319.

79. Walter Lippmann, *The Good Society*, (New Brunswick, NJ: Transaction Publishers, 2005), 307-308.

80. Walter Lippmann, *The Good Society*, (New Brunswick, NJ: Transaction Publishers, 2005), 320-321.

81. Jeffrey Walker, Glen McClish, eds., *Investigating Arguments: Readings for College Writing*, (Boston: Houghton Mifflin, 1991), 334.

82. Jeffrey Walker, Glen McClish, eds., *Investigating Arguments: Readings for College Writing*, (Boston: Houghton Mifflin, 1991), 333-335.

83. W.E.B. DuBois, "The White World", in Jeffrey Walker, Glen McClish, eds., *Investigating Arguments: Readings for College Writing*, (Boston: Houghton Mifflin, 1991), 337.

84. W.E.B. DuBois, "The White World", in Jeffrey Walker, Glen McClish, eds., *Investigating Arguments: Readings for College Writing*, (Boston: Houghton Mifflin, 1991), 356-357.

85. Jacob S. Hacker, Paul Pierson, *Winner Take All Politics: How Washington Made the Rich Richer—And Turned Its Back on the Middle Class*, (New York: Simon and Schuster Paperbacks, 2010).

86. Charles H. Ferguson, *Predator Nation: Corporate Criminals, Political Corruption, and the Hijacking of America*, (New York: Random House, Crown Business, 2012), 23.

87. Don Keko, "Credit Mobilier: America's Greatest Nineteenth Century Scandal," www.examiner.com/article/credit-mobilier-america-s-greatest-19ᵗʰ-century-scandal, accessed 2013.

88. Wikipedia, "Credit Mobilier of America Scandal," enwikipedia.org/wiki/ Credit_Mobilier_of_America_Scandal, accessed 2013.

89. American Experience: TV's Most Watched History Series, "General Article: The Credit Mobilier Scandal, www.pbs.org/wgbh/american experience/features/general article/tcrr-scandal, accessed, 2013.

90. Zerohedge, "The Magic of 100%+ Deflation In One Chart," www.zerohedge.com/news/2014-05-02/magic_100_hedonic_deflation_one_chart, accessed 2014.

91. Zerohedge, "US GDP Will Be Revised Higher By $500 Billion Following addition of "Intangibles" To Economy," www.zerohedge.com/news/2013-04-21/us-gdp-will-be-revised-higher-500-billion-following-addition-intangibles-economy, accessed Nov 2014.

92. C.H. Sterling, The Museum of Broadcast Communications, Deregulation, http://www.museu,.tv/eotvsection.php?entrycode=fairnessdoct, accessed 2013.

93. John Perkins, *Confessions of an Economic Hitman*, (New York: Plume Book, Penguin Group, 2004).

94. William Breit, Roger Ransom, *The Academic Scribblers, Third Edition*, (Princeton, NJ: Princeton University Press, 1998), 53-63.

95. Craig Green, "An Intellectual History of Judicial Activism," www.law.emory.edu/ fileadmin/ journals/elj/58/58.5/Green.pdf, accessed Oct 2013.

96. Primary Documents in American History, "Judiciary Act of 1789,: www.loc.gov/rr/program/bib/ourdocs/judiciary.html, accessed 2013.

97. Craig Green, "An Intellectual History of Judicial Activism," www.law.emory.edu/fileadmin/ journals/elj/58/58.5/Green.pdf, accessed Oct 2013.

98. Craig Green, "An Intellectual History of Judicial Activism," www.law.emory.edu/fileadmin/ journals/elj/58/58.5/Green.pdf, accessed Oct 2013.

99. Oliver Wendell Holmes, Jr., "Memorial Day Address, 1884," Wikiquote, "Oliver Wendell Holmes Jr.," enwikiquote/wiki/Oliver_Wendell_Holmes_Jr., accessed 2014.

100. Oliver Wendell Holmes Jr., "Learning and Science," Wikiquote, "Oliver Wendell Holmes Jr.," enwikiquote.org/wiki/Oliver Wendell Holmes Jr., accessed 2013.

101. Oliver Wendell Holmes, Jr., *Towne vs. Eisner*, 245 U.S. 418, 425, 7 January, 1918, Wikiquote, "Oliver Wendell Holmes Jr.", enwikiquote.org/wiki/Oliver Wendell Holmes Jr., accessed 2013.

102. Oliver Wendell Holmes, Jr., *The Common Law*, 1881, 1, Wikiquote, "Oliver Wendell Holmes Jr.," enwikiquote/wiki/Oliver Wendell Holmes Jr., accessed 2013.

103. Robert Danisch, *Pragmatism, Democracy and the Necessity of Rhetoric*, Columbia, SC: South Carolina Press, 2007), 96.

104. Craig Green, "An Intellectual History of Judicial Activism," www.law.emory.edu/fileadmin/ journals/elj/58/58.5/Green.pdf, accessed Oct 2013.

105. T. H. Watkins, *The Great Depression: America in the 1930's*, (New York: Little Brown and Co., 1993), 240-241, 307-308.

106. United States Senate Committee on the Judiciary, "Recess Reading: An Occasional Feature From the Judiciary Committee," "Franklin Delano Roosevelt's "Court Packing" Plan," www.judiciary.senate.gov/about/history/CourtPacking.cfm, accessed 2013.

107. Gallmann, ed., *Research in Economic History*, Salsbury, "Twentieth Century Railroad Managerial Practices: The Case of the Pennsylvania Railroad," (Greenwich, CT: JAI Press, 1977).

108. Wikipedia, "Interstate Commerce Commission," enwikipedia.org/wiki/Interstate Commerce Commission, accessed 2013.

109. "*Wickard v. Filburn* –Case Brief Summary," *Wickard v. Filburn (1942)*, www.lawnix.com/ cases/wickard-filburn.html, accessed 2013.

110. Timothy Egan, *The Worst Hard Time: The Untold Story of Those Who Survived the Great American Dustbowl*, (New York: Houghton Mifflin, 2006), 43.

111. Timothy Egan, *The Worst Hard Time: The Untold Story of Those Who Survived the Great American Dustbowl*, (New York: Houghton Mifflin, 2006), 59.

112. Wikipedia, "Wickard v. Filburn," enwikipedia.org/wiki/Wickard_v._Filburn, accessed 2013.

113. "*Wickard v. Filburn* –Case Brief Summary," *Wickard v. Filburn (1942)*, www.lawnix.com/ cases/wickard-filburn.html, accessed 2013.

114. The Bubble Bubble, "The U.S. Healthcare Bubble," www.thebubblebubble.com/ healthcare-bubble, accessed 2014.

115. Bill Ganzel, Wessels Living History Farm, "AAA, Agricultural Adjustment Act", www.living-historyfarm.org/farminginthe30s/water_11.html, accessed 2015.

116. T. H. Watkins, *The Great Depression: America in the 1930's*, (New York: Little Brown and Co., 1993), 309.

117. Wikipedia, "Commerce Clause," enwikipedia.org/wiki/ Commerce_Clause, accessed 2013.

118. US Supreme Court Media IIT Chicago-Kent College of Law, *Houston, east and West Texas Railway Co. v. United States*, www.oyez.org/cases/1901-1939/1913/1913_567, accessed 2014.

119. US Supreme Court Media IIT Chicago-Kent College of Law, *United States v. Lopez (1994)*, www.oyez.org/cases/1990-1999/1994/1994_93_1260, accessed Oct 2014.

120. US Supreme Court Media IIT Chicago-Kent College of Law, "*Heart of Atlanta Motel v. U.S. (1964)*", www.oyez.org/cases/1960-1969/1964/1964_515), accessed Oct 2014.

121. Randy Barnett, *Restoring the Lost Constitution*, (Princeton, NJ: Princeton University Press, 2004), 278-283.

122. Ibrahim Ola Balogun, "Theories of Public Expenditures," strategistng. blogspot. com/2013/02/theories-of-public-expenditures.html, accessed 2013.

123. The People's Vote: 100 Documents That Shaped America, "Interstate Commerce Act," www. our documents.gov/doc.php?flash= true&doc-49, accessed 2013.

124. Wikipedia, "Wabash St. Louis Pacific Railway Company v. Illinois," enwikipedia.org/wiki/ Wabash St. Louis %26 Pacific Railway Company v. Illinois, accessed 2013.

125. The People's Vote: 100 Documents That Shaped America, "Keating-Owen Child Labor Act of 1916 (1916)," www.our documents. gov/doc.php? doc=59, accessed 2013.

126. T.H.Watkins, *The Great Depression: America in the 1930's*, (New York: Little, Brown and Company, 1993,) 266-267.

127. Howard Zinn, *A People's History of the United States: 1492-Present*, (New York: Harper Collins Publishers, 2003), 400-401.

128. Howard Zinn, *A People's History of the United States: 1492-Present*, (New York: Harper Collins Publishers, 2003), 401-403.

129. Wikipedia, "The Wagner Act," enwikipedia.org/wiki/The_Wagner_Act, accessed 2013.

130. T.H.Watkins, *The Great Depression: America in the 1930's*, (New York: Little, Brown and Company, 1993,) 263-267.

131. Steve Hargreaves, *Money*, "Labor Participation Lowest Since 1978," Sept 6, 2013, money. cnn.com/2013/09/06/news/economy/labor-force-participation, accessed 2013.

132. OpenSecrets.org: Center for Responsible Politics, based on data from the Senate Office of Public Records, 2012, http://www.open secrets.org/ lobby, accessed 2012.

133. Jennifer Manning, "Membership of the 112th Congress: A Profile," Mar 2011, www.senate. gov/reference/resources/pdf/R41647.pdf, accessed 2012.

134. Wayne Crews, Ryan Young, The Public Policy, "Twenty Years of Non-Stop Regulation: Ten Thousand Commandments Have Given Way to More Than a Million," spectator.org/ articles/55475/twenty-years-non-stop-regulations, accessed Nov 2013.

135. Wayne Crews, Ryan Young, The Public Policy, "Twenty Years of Non-Stop Regulation: Ten Thousand Commandments Have Given Way to More Than a Million," spectator.org/ articles/55475/twenty-years-non-stop-regulations, accessed Nov 2013.

136. Maeve Carey, "Counting Regulations: An Overview of Rulemaking, Types of Federal Regulations, and Pages in the Federal Register," May 2013, www.fas.org/ sgo/ers/misc/R43056. pdf, accessed 2013.

137. Wikipedia, "Corporate personhood," wikipedia.org/wiki/Corporate-personhood, accessed 2013.

138. Wikipedia, "Corporate personhood," enwikipedia.org/wiki/Corporate-personhood, accessed 2013.

139. Jacob Hacker, Paul Pierson, *Winner Take All Politics: How Washington Made the Rich Richer—And Turned Its Back On the Middle Class*, (New York: Simon and Schuster Paperbacks, 2010).

140. Phillip Katcher, *The Civil War: Day by Day*, (New York: Chartwell Books, 2011), 125, 143.

141. Phillip Katcher, *The Civil War: Day by Day*, (New York: Chartwell Books, 2011), 83.

142. Modris Ersteins, *Rites of Spring: The Great War and the Birth of the Modern Age*, (New York: Houghton Mifflin, 1989), 139-140.

143. Roger Ransom in *Coping with Capitalism: The Economic Transformation of the United States from 1776-1980*, (Englewood Cliffs, NJ: Prentice Hall, Inc., 1981).

144. Roger Ransom, *Coping With Capitalism: The Economic Transformation of the United States 1776-1980*, (Englewood Cliffs, NJ: Prentice Hall, Inc., 1981), 129.

145. Filippo Cesarano, *Monetary Theory and Bretton Woods: The Construction of an International Monetary Order*, (New York: Cambridge University Press, 2006), 1.

146. Filippo Cesarano, *Monetary Theory and Bretton Woods: The Construction of an International Monetary Order*, (New York: Cambridge University Press, 2006), 22.

147. Filippo Cesarano, *Monetary Theory and Bretton Woods: The Construction of an International Monetary Order*, (New York: Cambridge University Press, 2006), chapter 3 and chapter 4.

148. Wikipedia, "World War I casualties, enwikipedia/wiki/World War I casualties, accessed 2013.

149. Thomas Greer, Gavin Lewis, *A Brief History of the Western World, Eighth Edition*, (Orlando: Harcourt College Publishers, 2001), 623.

150. Wikipedia, "World War II casualties," enwikipedia/wiki/World War II casualties, accessed 2013.

151. Thomas Greer, Gavin Lewis, *A Brief History of the Western World, Eighth Edition*, (Orlando: Harcourt College Publishers, 2001), p658.

152. Mark Harrison, "The Economics of World War II: An Overview," taken from *The Economics of World War II: Six Great Powers in International Comparison, 1-42*, www.2warwick.ac.uk/fac/soc/economics/staff/academic/harrison/public/ ww2overview1998.pdf, accessed 2013.

153. Mark Harrison, "The Economics of World War II: An Overview," taken from *The Economics of World War II: Six Great Powers in International Comparison, 1-42*, www.2warwick.ac.uk/fac/soc/economics/ staff/academic/harrison/public/ ww2overview1998.pdf, accessed 2013.

154. Neil Postman, "Five Things We Need to Know About Technological Change," in Paul DePalma, ed., *Technologies, Social Media, and Society, Annual Editions, Seventeenth Edition*, (New York: McGraw Hill, 2012), 3-6.

155. Adam Lebor, *Tower of Basel: The Shadowy History of the Secret Bank that Runs the World*, (New York: Public Affairs, 2013).

156. Wikipedia, "Rationing," enwikipedia.org/wiki/rationing, accessed 2013.

157. Modris Eksteins, *Rites of Spring: The Great War and the Birth of the Modern Age*, (New York: Houghton Mifflin, 1989), 139-140, 233-237.

158. C.L.Sultzberger, *American Heritage New History of World War II*, (New York: Penguin Group, 1997), 276 and 563.

159. Edward Herman, Norman Chomsky, *Manufacturing Consent: The Political Economy of the Mass Media*, (New York: Pantheon Books, Random House Publishers Inc., 2002).

160. Edward Herman, Norman Chomsky, *Manufacturing Consent: The Political Economy of the Mass Media*, (New York: Pantheon Books, Random House Publishers Inc., 2002).

161. Wikipedia, "Powers of the President of the United States," enwikipedia .org/wiki/Powers of the President of the United States, accessed 2013.

162. The Regents of the University of California, Slaying the Dragon of Debt, "1974 Congressional Budget and Impoundment Control Act," bancroft.Berkeley.edu/ROHO/projects/debt/budgetcontrolact .html, last updated 2011, accessed 2013.

163. Maisie Allison, The American Conservative, "Clarifying the War Powers Resolution," theamericanconservative.com/clarifying the war powers resolution, Sept 2013, accessed 2013.

164. Library of Congress, Law Library of Congress, "War Powers," www.loc.gov/law/help/war-powers.php, accessed 2013.

165. Phillip Katcher, *The Civil War: Day by Day*, (New York: Chartwell Books, 2010).

166. Wikipedia, "Executive order," enwikipedia.org/wiki/Executive order, accessed 2013.

167. Wikipedia, "Executive order," enwikipedia.org/wiki/Executive order, accessed 2013.

168. Wikipedia, "Executive order," enwikipedia.org/wiki/Executive order, accessed 2013.

169. Wikipedia, "Powers of the President of the United States," enwikipedia.org/wiki/Powers of the President of the United States, accessed 2014.

170. Wikipedia, "Greenback (money)," enwikipedia.org/wiki/Greenback.(money), accessed Dec 2013.

171. Wikipedia, "Greenback (money)," enwikipedia.org/wiki/Greenback.(money), accessed Dec 2013.

172. Wikipedia, "The Law that Never Was," enwikipedia.org/wiki/the Law that Never Was, accessed Dec 2013.

173. Wikipedia, "The Law that Never Was," enwikipedia.org/wiki/the Law that Never Was, accessed Dec 2013.

174. Ransom, *Coping with Capitalism: The Economic Transformation of the United States 1776-1980*, (Englewood Cliffs, NJ: Prentice Hall International, Inc., 1981), 169.

175. Wikipedia, "Federal Reserve Act," enwikipedia.org/wiki/Federal Reserve Act, accessed Dec 2013.

176. T.H. Watkins, *The Great Depression: America in the 1930's*, (New York: Little Brown and Company, 1993) 54.

177. T.H. Watkins, *The Great Depression: America in the 1930's*, (New York: Little Brown and Company, 1993), 55 and 62.

178. T.H. Watkins, *The Great Depression: America in the 1930's*, (New York: Little Brown and Company, 1993), 122-123.

179. T.H. Watkins, *The Great Depression: America in the 1930's*, (New York: Little Brown and Company, 1993), 122-123.

180. Thomas Fitch; Irwin Kellner, Donald Simonson, Ben Weberman, eds., *Dictionary of Banking Terms*, (New York: Barrons Educational Series, Inc., 1990), 282-283.

181. Wikipedia, "Glass Steagall Act," enwikipedia/wiki/Glass Steagall Act, accessed 2012.

182. Wikipedia, "Humphrey Hawkins Full Employment Act," enwikipedia/ wiki/ Humphrey Hawkins Full Employment Act, accessed Dec 2013.

183. John Tamny, *Forbes*, "Monetarism and Keynesianism: Identical Sides of the the Same Adolescent Coin," www.forbes.com/sites/johntamny/ 2013/04/07/monetarism-and-Keynesianism-identical-adolescent-sides-of-the-same-coin-print, accessed 2013.

184. A notation for the reader: John Maynard Keynes, *The General Theory of Employment Interest and Money*, was published 1936; but Keynesianism was developed only in part by John Maynard Keynes (1883-1946), a British economist, because others contributed as well.

185. Roger L. Ransom, *Coping With Capitalism: The Economic Transformation of the United States 1776-1980*, (Englewood Cliffs, NJ: Prentice Hall, Inc., 1981), 3.

186. Theodore Couloumbis, James Wolfe, *Introduction to International Relations: Power and Justice, Third Edition*, (Englewood Cliffs, NJ: Prentice Hall, Inc., 1986), 331-332.

187. T.H. Watkins, *The Great Depression: America in the 1930's*, (New York: Little Brown and Company, 1993).

188. Roger Ransom, *Coping With Capitalism: The Economic Transformation of the United States 1776-1980*, (Englewood Cliffs, NJ: Prentice Hall, Inc., 1981), 146.

189. William Breit, Roger Ransom, *The Academic Scribblers: Third Edition*, (Princeton: Princeton University Press, 1998), 65 and 76.

190. Franklin D. Roosevelt, XXXII President of the United States: 1933-1945, "State of the Union Speech to Congress, January 11, 1944," www.presidency.ucsb.edu/us/index.php?pid=16518, accessed 2013.

Endnotes for the Appendix

Timeline for modern liberal period

1. Eric Foner, "Reconstruction," www.nps.gov/resources/story.htm?id=233, accessed Aug 2013.

2. Timeline of American Planning History, "1785-1899," www.txplanning.org/media/files/page/Planning-History_1785?to_2000.pdf, accessed 2014.

3. Wikipedia, "Central Park," enwikipedia.org/wiki/Central_Park, accessed 2014.

4. Laughing Lemon, www.thinkglobally.co.uk/index2.php? option+ context&do_pdf= 1&id=9, last updated 2012, accessed 2013.

5. Wikipedia, "Timeline of Modern History," enwikipedia.org/wiki/ Timeline_of_modern_history, accessed 2013.

6. David Koeller, "The Industrial Revolution," www.thenagain.info/webchron/westeurope/indrev.html, accessed 2012.

7. Fritz Brundage, North Carolina State University, "Connections New Deal and Progressive Reforms," www.dlt.ncssm.edu/lmtm/docs/prog_newdeal/script.pdf, accessed 2014.

8. Marilyn Stokstad, *Art History Second Edition, Volume Two*, (Upper Saddle River, NJ: Prentice Hall, Inc., 1995).

9. Modern American Poetry, "About John Wesley Powell—Background to "The Gardens of Zuni," www.english. illinois.edu/maps/poets/m_r/merwin/jwpowell.htm, accessed 2014.

10. Wikipedia, "Rural Electrification," enwikipedia.org/wiki/Rural_Electrification, accessed 2014.

11. Wikipedia, "History of the Philippines," enwikipedia.org/wiki/History_of_the_Philippines_(1898-1946), accessed 2014.

12. Wikipedia, "Indian Citizenship Act," enwikipedia.org/wiki/Indian Citizenship Act, accessed Jan 2015.

The Difference Between Money and Wealth

1. Thomas Fitch, Kellner, Simonson, Weberman, eds., *Dictionary of Banking Terms*, "holding company," (New York: Barrons Educational Series, 1990), 299.

2. Bettina Bien Greaves, Percy L. Greaves, letter to Wall Street Journal, Aug 23, 1977; in Ludwig von Mises, *On The Manipulation of Money and Credit*, (New York: Free Market Books, 1978), 275-279.

3. David Korten, Living Economies Forum, As published in Business Ethics, 1999, "The Difference Between Money and Wealth: How Out of Control Speculation Is Destroying Real Wealth," http://livingeconomiesforum.org/the-difference-between-money-and-wealth, accessed 2012.

4. Pat S., Money Crashers personal blog, "Income vs. Wealth—What's the Difference? http://www.moneycrashers.com/wealth-and-income-difference, accessed 2012.

5. Kinesian Economics, "Wealth vs. Money: There's a Big Difference," http://midmagic. sgc_osting.com/withmony.htm, accessed Jun 2012.

6. Daniel Greenfield, "The Economics of Planned Global Failure," canadafreepress.com/ index.php/articles-infrastructure/56123, accessed 2012.

Sixteen basic definitions from finance:

1. Thomas Sowell, *Basic* Economics: *A Common Sense Guide to the Economy, Third Edition*, (New York: The Perseus Book Group, 2007), 173.

2. Wikipedia, "Santa Clara County V. Southern Pacific Railroad," http://enwikipedia.org/ wiki/Santa-Clara-County-vs-Union-Pacific-Railway, accessed 2012.

3. Thomas Sowell, *Basic* Economics: *A Common Sense Guide to the Economy, Third Edition*, (New York: The Perseus Book Group, 2007), quoting Lionel Robbins, 2.

4. *American Heritage Dictionary: Fourth Edition*, "economics," (New York: Bantam Dell, with permission from Houghton Mifflin, 2007), 272.

5. Kenneth Morris, Alan Siegel, *Guide to Understanding Money and Investing*, (New York: Simon and Schuster, Lightbulb Press, 1993).

6. Thomas Fitch; Irwin Kellner, Donald Simonson, Ben Weberman, eds., *Dictionary of Banking Terms*, "holding company," (New York: Barrons Educational Series, 1990), 299.

7. David Hackett Fischer, *The Great Wave: Price Revolutions and the Rhythm of History*, (New York: Oxford University Press, 1996), 278-281.

8. Diffen Economics, "GDP vs. GNP," http://www.diffen.com/difference/GDP vs GNP, accessed 2012.

9. Diffen Economics, "GDP vs. GNP," http://www.diffen.com/difference/GDP vs GNP, accessed 2012.

10. William Black, *The Best Way to Rob a Bank Is to Own One: How Corporate Executives and Politicians Looted the S&L Industry*, (Austin, TX: University of Texas Press, 2005).

Neoliberalism, since Bretton Woods in 1944 until the present-day.

History of neoliberalism: the earliest discussions were among Europeans.

The earliest discussions about "neoliberalism" began among Europeans between WWI and WWII. One of these Europeans was Luigi Einaudi (1874-1961). He was born before most other neoliberals and before neoliberalism itself had been imagined in the context of market economies. He was an Italian economist.[1] As mentioned in Modern Liberalism, market economies brought changes that modern liberals sometimes blamed on classical liberalism: increased populations, immigration, slums, growth of cities, economic churn and social suffering. Not a sign of failure, these changes were a byproduct of economic expansion because of improvements in transportation and communication. Growing populations and growing economies changed the politic and brought modern liberalism in the U.S. into being as a way to address greater economic complexity.

Market economies had increased demand for production factors like raw materials and labor used in manufacturing during the Industrial Revolution. This higher demand put nations into greater competition for production factors with each other.[2] Competition for production factors happened as nations were investing in factories and technologies. Economic competition led nations to raise tariff barriers to products from outside, closing their borders to production from other countries. A greater need for factors of production made nation states more competitive for materials, technology, and labor. Some nations wanted to expand their borders to get more natural resources. Nationalism, and the idea of economic autarky began to undermine European neighborliness. In 1916, Einaudi advocated for a unified Europe inside a federation of nations under a common customs union. Advocating for a European customs union revealed Einaudi's desire to put economic interests in common in order to reduce economic competition and unify Europe in a concerted strategy toward shared prosperity.[3]

History of neoliberalism: after WWII, Luigi Einaudi served in the Italian politic.

After WWII, Luigi Einaudi served Italy as the second President of the Italian Republic from 1948-1955. He also served as the Minister of Finances Treasury and Balance and as the Vice Premier from 1947-1948 and helped to form the new Italian Parliament.[4] He was a key political player in Italy after WWII and utilized his economics education in the politic. That was rare among neoliberal economists who rarely held political office. He hoped a customs union would unify Europe economically by providing common economic protections inside a cooperative organizational structure that would be more important than nation state sovereignty or nationalism. He wanted to nurture cooperative European economic interests.[5]

He imagined a Customs Union for all of Europe, not unlike the one in the United States that under the U.S. Constitution forbids tariffs to be charged by states for interstate goods that cross their borders. In the U.S. Constitution, Article One, Section Nine, it states, "No Tax or Duty shall be laid on Articles exported from any State." Economic cooperation among states in the U.S. was admired in Europe. But it was harder to achieve in Europe because of established interests that opposed changes because they might encourage greater competition. But if Europe could unify as a trading bloc it could gain two long-term advantages. The first advantage would be more European trade under more equal trading agreements inside the bloc, and the second would be global trading advantages in negotiating for the price of commodities and materials abroad under the principle of reciprocal demand.[6]

Later, after WWII, aspiration for trade in a global common market was an alternative to colonial expropriation of trade goods. But it fell short of a global customs union because the global system would be competitive instead of cooperative. Nevertheless, global open trade agreements were seen as an economic and political goal that would stop economic nationalism, reduce political nationalism and encourage the development of economic interests in common between nation states. It was a goal that many war weary people could agree upon. Global open trade would grow gradually, it would encourage more trading and it would help end colonial empire-making.

Well before WWII but after WWI, Einaudi joined the IUHEI (Institut Universitaire des Hautes Etudes Internationales) in Geneva, Switzerland. He was there with other eventual neoliberals such as Ludwig von Mises, and Wilhelm Ropke. In Paris, in 1938, Ropke, and von Mises, joined with others at the Colloque Walter Lippmann, a conference to discuss liberal topics after the publication of *Inquiry into the Principles of the Good Society*, written by Walter Lippmann in 1937.[7] Lippmann (see Modern Liberalism) was an American journalist and propagandist for modern liberalism. Fifteen of the conference attendees would eventually join together as neoliberals, though not Lippmann, who remained loyal to modern liberalism.[8, 9]

After WWII, Einaudi joined the Mont Pelerin Society (MPS). Albert Hunolt (who, with Wilhelm Ropke, later left the MPS) and Friedrich Hayek provided leadership in founding the Mont Pelerin Society in 1947, and it still exists today. It brought together mostly economists but also journalists, businessmen and politicians as advocates of prerogatives to save liberalism from socialism. The first meeting of the Mont Pelerin Society was sponsored by the Volker Fund of Kansas and the Foundation for Economic Education (FEE) of New York.[10]

History of neoliberalism: the Mont Pelerin Society.

After 1947, The Mont Pelerin Society began to build networks of organizations to promote neoliberal ideas. They would influence other groups that would carry neoliberalism around the world.[11] MPS neoliberals decided to portray neoliberalism as a continuation of classical liberalism, starting in the 1950's—to provide a sense of continuity with the past.[12] But this portrayal ignored MPS discussions that approached neoliberalism as an alternative to the perceived failure of classical liberalism and modern liberalism. Lumping neoliberalism with classical liberalism has been inaccurate also because they differ in political thinking and economic policies. The differences between classical liberalism and neoliberalism are obvious when their policies and ideas are compared.

Neoliberals eventually developed think tanks as policy influencing bodies acting at the center of politics. Think tanks have revolutionized American politics by concentrating experts together that advocate for a specific policy. The experts publish advocacy presentations and sometimes drafts of potential legislation that support a specific political goal. They can be useful to Congress because they outline controversies in a way that saves legislators' time and they select a position that their argument justifies to aid the legislator if the legislator chooses to promote their policy. This provides legislators easier access to policy proposals and ammunition for arguments whenever they arise.[13] Some examples of neoliberal think tanks include names that are probably familiar: the Institute of Economic Affairs, the American Enterprise Institute, and the Heritage Foundation.[14] Neoliberal economists also became part of academia. They taught in U.S. universities like Harvard, University of Chicago, Princeton University, Johns Hopkins University, University of Rochester, and Columbia University, for example, and spread neoliberal economics ideas among the educated elite.

Reconsidering the American politic up until neoliberalism.

During classical liberalism, the rhetorical arguments of English law had curtailed the power of the English monarch as mentioned in Classical Liberalism. Politically-transforming documents, The Magna Carta of 1215, the Petition of Right of 1628, and the 1689 Declaration of Rights diminished the power of the English monarchy and established a trend to limit power in the politic which Americans enlarged upon, as mentioned earlier. The Declaration of Independence and the principle of personal sovereignty as well as natural rights only partially listed in the Bill of Rights of the U.S. Constitution both limited the power of government in order to stop tyranny.

Limited government was a novel way of thinking about government at the time it came about. It broke with the traditions of divine right to rule that had allowed tyrants to oppress people. The partnership between capitalism and liberalism may have led to this logical limitation of power. Capitalism had empowered a new set of political players, the bourgeois, and encouraged economic innovation. In the context of capitalism, limiting power became a necessity because the power of government grew under a more prosperous economy. Under the fruitful partnership of finance for investments and liberal confidence in humankind to discover a rational better life, a limited government became an essential ingredient that prolonged further economic innovation. Unlimited monarchs could utilize ever greater political and economic resources to oppress people if they weren't restrained by a constitution that limited their power usefully.

As considered in the last chapter, modern liberalism enlarged the power of the government to regulate the economy. Enlarging the power of government was in opposition to stricter limitations on government power that were established under classical liberalism. This change happened because the economy had become larger and more complex with more specialized labor in large cities. The new economy threatened traditions. It was dangerous. Local economies during classical liberalism had been smaller and mostly self-sufficient. New urban lifestyles put workers into a position without self-sustaining agricultural products as a resource during lapses of employment. People could be brought quickly to desperation when they couldn't trade labor for money to buy what they needed in food or heat. Labor unrest had led to bloodshed and death in unregulated nineteenth century labor markets.

Enlarging the power of Congress to regulate labor seemed essential to some, but Congress didn't always choose wisely. During the early twentieth century, Congress increased grain production by subsidizing wheat farming, increasing the amount of wheat under cultivation. European nations did the same. They all sought food security in specialized market economies, but they caused a wheat glut that undermined the wheat market everywhere in the world.[15] This policy ended up being an economic bomb, exploding agricultural markets, and also causing terrible soil erosion in the U.S that led to the dust bowl.

After the policy mistake, Congress curtailed wheat production through further regulation. But livelihoods had already been damaged and that contributed to other hardships during the Great Depression. Growth in the complexity of the global economy indicated to some business people a need to limit governmental power over the economy. That's part of what neoliberals sought when they started deregulation but that's not what has happened. Instead there's been growth in the size of multinationals and finance organizations until they have come to dominate and harm the system of markets. Opportunity to be employed has declined in the U.S. and American families have lost economic advantages that they once had gained during the labor movement.

Neoliberal economists have worked at prestigious universities around the world and they have garnered academic awards and political commendations. Here's a description of some neoliberal economist's viewpoints.

The number of distinguished economists that can be considered under the neoliberal umbrella is large. Eight Nobel Prize recipients have come from the Mont Pelerin Society[16] and three economic schools of thought. One is the Ludwig von Mises branch of Austrian Economics that saw the market as a natural-world complex phenomenon that was too complicated and large to be successfully understood or manipulated.[17] His neoliberal arguments warned about the bad economic results of socialism and any other centrally managed economy. He opposed economic interventionism by the federal government.

Another branch of Austrian Economics, under Friedrick von Hayek, saw the market as being like a giant brain that organized and processed market exchanges[18] adjusting to demand automatically through market production and competition. He wanted a strong government under the rule of law that would defend opportunities for businesses and business wealth. He imagined that neoliberal governmental empire-keeping could defend market opportunities for all.

The third neoliberal economic school has been the Chicago School, under Milton Friedman. It has favored economism: market ideology applied in the politic. Chicago School economics structures an economy into certain statistical relationships between specific elements. To Chicago School advocates, these statistical relationships signal market improvements. But insistence upon these economic relationships has caused enormous social suffering that has destabilized the regimes that undergo Chicago School prescriptions. The University of Chicago has played a role in training neoliberal economists that have been active globally to institute Chicago School neoliberal changes in Latin America, and in Eastern Europe. The Chicago School has received the greatest amount of public criticism as compared to the other two neoliberal economic schools of thought. Naomi Klein, for example, complained about the Chicago School in her book, *The Shock Doctrine*.[19]

An overview of what neoliberal economists discussed together, based mostly on neoliberal economist's writings would include a variety of topics. Fiscal policy and monetary policy, global trade, issues in labor and the power of government were all topics of interest to neoliberals. As you read these few summaries and quotes it becomes obvious that neoliberal economists disagreed with each other on some topics. They mostly agreed that labor unions have been bad. This was true for Fredrick Hayek, Gottlieb Haberler, and Milton Friedman, although not for Fritz Machlup. He was a Jewish Austrian who immigrated and became an American, and was a union leader in the American Association of University Professors.[20] Some neoliberal economists have said that social welfare should be minimal, for example Friedrich Hayek.[21] Others, such as Ropke cared about social justice pursued through equal opportunity but not in pursuit of equal outcomes.[22] Corporate welfare has increased under the politics of neoliberalism and support for corporate welfare has been part of the neoliberal ideology. According to Forbes Magazine, "The Fortune 500 corporations alone accounted for more than 16,000 subsidy awards worth $63 billion, mostly in the form of tax breaks" since 1976.[23]

Political reductions in social welfare funding have included President Clinton's reduction of social welfare housing and introduction of time limits for public assistance, for instance, while President Reagan closed down housing facilities for the mentally ill. Neoliberal politicians have said that high taxes are bad but they reduced taxes more for corporations than for individuals. Under neoliberalism, real corporate tax rates have fallen and real individual tax rates have increased.[24] Besides globalization, one of the big political changes sponsored by neoliberals was deregulation, as mentioned earlier. It has had undesired consequences which will be discussed in a later section. Also, a strong government under neoliberalism has used the military to expand economic global enterprise and increased access to global markets.[25] Neoliberal politicians used law to grant advantages to corporations under the premise that law should protect businesses. Big government enforcement and big business opportunities have gone together.

Neoliberal politicians don't seem to have worried when multinationals are out-competing domestic industries. They haven't become concerned that a multinational corporate only marketplace could be a smaller overall market. And neoliberal taxation policies have harmed domestic businesses and small business. A shrinking economy should matter more to neoliberals than it has. Technology has been an important part of Digital Age markets, and a smaller economy can afford less technological investment. The size of an economy mattered in the context of classical liberal markets because specialization couldn't improve productive efficiency as much in a smaller as compared with a bigger market. The neoliberal unconcern about shrinking markets has shown one of their points of difference with classical liberals like Ricardo and Smith.

Neoliberal experts on international development have agreed that development is complicated by nation state heterogeneity. Some have noted that money aid hasn't always gotten to its intended target to improve the life of poor people and that it should therefore not be automatically advanced. Neoliberals fought hard to stop the United Nation's push for a New International Economic Order (NIEO).[26] The NIEO would have advanced greater cash aid to the third world in the 1970's.

The efficient market hypothesis probably influenced neoliberal politics.

Neoliberals have had faith that the politic could work like a market if corporations were regulating their own industries. They wanted to put corporate interests in the economic driver's seat. Neoliberals have seen markets as a self-organizing substitute for legitimate and representational politics. They have imagined that self-interest would always promote better policies that would aid the market and society. This attitude probably came from the efficient market hypothesis which envisioned an idealized marketplace on Wall Street with perfect efficiency and accurate information. The efficient market hypothesis has, however, proven inadequate to describe the presence of market mal-investments like the subprime real estate marketplace and the subsequent financial collapse.[27] It also failed to predict information asymmetries that have led to profits in high frequency trading (HFT).

In practice, neoliberal businessmen have been willing to pay cash incentives during elections to get their political pies baked to their own advantage in Washington. They have motivated legislators to favor large multinational corporations and big finance. But providing a cash incentive to policy makers is not an example of "self-assembly". Even if neoliberals were motivated by self-interest, their policies have been focused on the short term gain and reek of ethical conflict and bribery. Neoliberal influence shows political favoritism for the highest bidding political factions. Opportunistic neoliberals have made politics more transactional and even hurt legal disinterest under the rule of law. And while the neoliberal politic has suffered from public alienation and withdrawal, the economy hasn't been healthier under neoliberalism.

Unlike classical liberalism and modern liberalism, neoliberalism was assembled without grassroots involvement.

Neoliberalism hasn't been a representative ideology that relied on grassroots origins. It has been manufactured instead of organic.[28] American businessmen sponsored the immigration of European economic experts and gave large endowments to university economics departments. The history of the Mont Pelerin Society and the history of the University of Chicago show businessmen shaping public opinions by sponsoring think tanks and academia. Personal histories of Ludwig von Mises and Friedrich von Hayek, for example, both involve business patronage to bring them to the United States and sponsor them to teach in academia. Businessmen were hoping that neoliberal economists assembled mostly from Europe could provide state of the art economics advice. As a business investment for future prosperity, the importation of many neoliberal economists from Europe and their influence upon American students in economics has led towards other changes in the American economy and politic.

Neoliberal belief structures had positivist and constructivist shadings. They were meant to be universalized by governmental power prerogatives and justified by economic theories. Neoliberals have had faith that neoliberalism could self-assemble a politic through market forces and behavioral motivations based on self-interest rather than by organic grassroots support centered in cultural or social norms or mores. Neoliberals have made assumptions about economic and biological self-interest as a political and economic motivator.[29] But neoliberals have lacked respect for society's non-neoliberal inclinations and beliefs. And neoliberals have ignored natural rights in the context of American political foundations, as can be read in numerous examples where neoliberals say, like modern liberals, that the power prerogatives of the politic, "the sovereign state," eclipse everything else. And neoliberals don't respect the idea of natural rights despite founding documents such as the Declaration of Independence or the U.S. Constitution. Also of importance, neoliberalism has failed to be a rational system that can change its policies when they don't work.

Neoliberal acolytes have been from different nations, different disciplines and have worked in social institutions that spread neoliberal political changes into global controversy. U.S. foreign policy after WWII set up a new global economic system under Bretton Woods agreements and spread neoliberalism around the world (more on this later). Some European nations were eager to embrace neoliberal policies as an alternative to modern liberal or socialist policies which were economically costly. Recent public opposition to neoliberalism has included political opposition to intervention in Syria, public opposition to TARP, public opposition to the WTO, and opposition to Obamacare.

Neoliberal advocates have influenced every part of American society without being rooted in American traditions. That gives neoliberalism a subversive quality. And there hasn't been a neoliberal champion that tried to win over public opinion in favor of neoliberal policies. Avoiding policy discussions has been commonplace instead. Most politicians that follow neoliberal principles don't self- identify as neoliberal. And part of the chaos in U.S. politics is due to neoliberal organizations that have become influential in policy making without any public accountability. Discord in American politics has been stimulated by policy and issue avoidance in public while people loyal to neoliberal ideas have worked in think tanks to influence public policy from behind a neutral public façade.

Oppositional politics where different political parties face off on trivial matters or on political non-issues has become familiar to Americans as a characteristic of our dysfunctional Congress. Argument and non-issues strategically help to undermine political accountability while narrowing political choices. Even after the 2008 financial collapse, Congress has continued to favor an agenda that pays more attention to corporate welfare than public welfare. Some Congress members have called for a reduction in corporate taxes at the same time that the Affordable Care Act is charging individuals a new tax-on-life for a government health insurance program that has failed to provide health security.

This tax increase will be implemented after many Americans lost and never regained employment after the Great Recession. It puts many people into a new underclass.

According to Mirowski and Plehwe, in *The Road from Mont Pelerin: The Making of the Neoliberal Thought Collective*, neoliberals have been observed to take opposing sides of an argument as equally valid which can create rhetorical chaos. Mirowski and Plehwe see this as mixing utilitarian and libertarian value sets without creating sense out of them.[30] It has been an obstructionist technique that blocks meaningful political discussions. Except for Ronald Reagan in the U.S. and Margaret Thatcher in the UK, how few neoliberal politicians since Bretton Woods openly declared any political ideology in U.S. media and how few have admitted to neoliberalism as their own political philosophy.

But if you look for neoliberalism in the American politic it's easy to find it in foreign policy (open trade for trade partners, empire-keeping), militarization policies (numerous military bases abroad, and military tactical training and weaponization of local police forces), trade policy (blocking tariffs, blocking public resistance to corporate opportunism), tax policy (fewer corporate taxes, more grassroots taxation), regulatory reform (changing laws to favor corporations), changes in media coverage (infotainment, propaganda, advertising, and issue and policy censorship), fiscal policy (more debt, and reticence concerning a more than a 17 trillion dollar fiscal debt), monetary policy (fiat and more private debt through easy credit), deregulated finance (riskiness with a public subsidy), and Too Big To Fail banking (where the threat of insolvency can be used to extort subsidies). Yet the income disparities and poverty that now plague our U.S. economy are because of neoliberal policies that have been pursued for seventy years with little public recognition.

Even though neoliberal economists have been used by neoliberal politicians to justify neoliberal economic policies, quotes from neoliberal economists show that they didn't support the neoliberal policy package.

Ludwig von Mises lived from 1881 to 1973. He wrote a number of books and gave seminars in Austria and as a visiting professor at New York University (his salary was paid by Louis Fertig, a businessman).[31] Although he didn't receive the Nobel Prize in Economics, he was recognized for excellence when he received the Austrian Decoration for Science and Art. The Mises Institute lives on after him and continues to teach his principles of economy with regard to fiscal and monetary policy. He opposed socialism, communism and fascism. He believed that they were inevitably inclined to violence and self-extermination but only after leaving a trail of tragedy and destruction in society as collectivist political policies consumed their economies and culminated in totalitarianism. In his book, *Interventionism*, written in 1940, before the U.S. was in WWII, von Mises wrote criticisms of socialism and collectivism.

In the introduction, he recognized that mixed economy and socialism differed because a mixed economy only hampered markets but socialism would destroy them entirely.[32] In chapter seven, he wrote that a government's intervention in the economy makes people poorer without providing any improvement in real markets which are harmed.[33] In his concluding chapter, he wrote that mixed economy would never endure and that people could only realistically choose either a market economy under a democratic government or socialism and dictatorship.[34]

He noticed the rise of interventionism in the economy had coincided with the universal voting franchise. Newly empowered voters chose to believe that their government would serve their needs best with greater power. Mises saw this as a foolhardy choice.[35, 36] He thought that a more powerful government would grow in power enough to oppress rather than serve people. During his lifetime, he lived in Vienna, Geneva, and New York. However adept at surviving the cataclysms of the twentieth century, he was a resolute scholar who was not inclined to change his mind or change his opinions once he formed them. Many of his earliest comments can be found repeated in later publications of his work.

"In the capitalistic economy the means of production are owned by individuals or associations of individuals, such as corporations."[37]

"The fact that the smooth functioning and the development and steady progress of the economy is over and over again disturbed by artificial booms and ensuing depressions is not a necessary characteristic of the market economy. It is rather the inevitable consequence of repeated interventions which intend to create easy money by credit expansion."[38]

"It is obvious that a mere banking process like credit expansion cannot create more goods and wealth. What the credit expansion actually accomplishes is to introduce a source of error in the calculations of the entrepreneurs and thus causes them to misjudge business and investment projects....The boom is not *over*-investment, it is misdirected investment."[39]

"Interventionism has transformed parliamentary government into a government of lobbies. It is not parliamentarianism and democracy that have failed. Interventionism has paralyzed parliamentarianism as well as the market economy."[40]

Understanding Ludwig von Mises as a promoter of neoliberal ideas has made comparing his ideas with classical liberal founders a potentially helpful exercise. Especially because he was the founder of one of three neoliberal economic schools. Mises thought that the economy was a complex phenomenon that could never be either predicted or controlled. In his book, *Interventionism*, in chapter seven he wrote that "freedom is a sociological concept" alien to the natural world. This showed that he viewed natural rights differently than classical liberals such as Locke. He thought that governments granted liberty whereas Locke saw a person's natural rights as innate to them.[41] In the introduction to *Interventionism*, Mises expressed the idea that the government's "coercive power" protected against fraud and force. Once again this idea is not from American classical liberalism where law wasn't viewed as the arm of the state but rather under common law principles, the law was supposed to reflect people's cultural beliefs.[42]

In the *Selective Writings of Ludwig von Mises, Vol I*, there was a passage Mises wrote that linked democracy and markets. Here, Mises wrote that "each penny represents a ballot". He believed that private ownership of production paired with democratic government and made markets the foundation of democracy. Mises thought that in a marketplace consumers would control what was sold and that their power to choose market offerings increased with their wealth. But this statement confused the economy and the politic as though purchasing power and money should control the politic. Although the richest land owning Americans were the most politically influential during classical liberalism, this idea of consumer-voters by means of purchasing choices was different from the concept that political freedom required economic freedom.[43] The entanglement that Mises envisioned for the politic and economy was unlike what was believed under the concept of *laissez faire*, and political liberty where the state was limited and not coercive.

Note the difference here between Mises and Hobbes and Locke. Under Hobbes: liberty was defined as freedom from coercion and not a society's grant of opportunity. Or under Locke: the idea was that people are in possession from birth of the natural right to liberty and personal sovereignty, the power to choose the political form of their government including, through a constitution, a limited and not an all-powerful state. According to the principles of classical liberalism, the state did not grant and couldn't grant natural rights because people have been born with them. Mises instead was convinced of the power of state coercion and that the state granted or withheld a person's freedom. This view had roots in German Idealism and in a belief that power was the only political trait of importance. It wasn't a classical liberal viewpoint. This belief was also more German or European than American. It overlooked the English common law traditions that used rhetoric in law and legal documents to limit the power of monarchs. Limited government was seen as granting citizens freedom from political coercion and has remained a powerful part of the American political heritage.

A belief in the organic state, in the power of state coercion was a European idea that rested partly on their Imperial Roman Codex of laws that were written under the Roman Empire then copied in France and eventually circulated in Europe, under the direction of Napoleon Bonaparte. Mises assumed that state power could direct society by violence. Mises, having a Jewish heritage, fled his homeland during the rise of fascism and persecution of Jews during the Nazi storm before the U.S. was in WWII. Mises experienced political catastrophe and economic loss. Though he possessed the intelligence and flexibility to escape from persecution he couldn't stop the political power of the Nazis from hurting fellow Austrians. He believed that people had to choose either to be a participant in a market economy and democracy or to become a totalitarian subject of political control. He saw interventionism as a move toward socialism and he tried to warn people that interventionism would never be a stable system.

But even when Ludwig von Mises didn't believe in natural rights, he was helpful in explaining the consequences of expanding the capital stream using easy credit.[44] Expanding the money supply through government debt has been the kernel of Keynesianism and expanding it through private debt and new money forms has been characteristic of monetarism. Mises tried to warn people that monetarism could never work to create more wealth—it could only move capital from one place to another. As a point of difference between them, monetarism was advocated by Milton Friedman, another neoliberal, even though Ludwig von Mises opposed it.

One of Ludwig von Mises' most famous neoliberal associates was Friedrich von Hayek—another Austrian economist. He was the founder of the second of three neoliberal economic schools. He saw the economy as acting like a giant brain that used markets as way to establish economic homeostasis. In addition to the Nobel Prize in Economics in 1974, and The Presidential Medal of Freedom in 1991, Hayek was also awarded the Member of the Order of the Companions of Honor in 1984, granted by Queen Elizabeth II on the advice of Margaret Thatcher.[45] His most famous book was probably *The Road to Serfdom*, 1944.[46] It was written to argue against socialism. Hayek's *The Constitution of Liberty*, (1960),[47] was an effort to bring neoliberal ideas and Hayek's own political ideas into consideration. But it revealed that Hayek had a European legal mindset that differed from American legal traditions. Hayek has been better known as an opponent of socialism than he has been recognized as a champion of neoliberalism. But he was one of the chief Mont Pelerin instigators of neoliberalism's global spread. Unlike other neoliberal economists, Hayek was a specialist in two academic fields.

Hayek achieved recognition not just in economics but also in a second discipline, neurobiology.[48] He studied the brain and nervous system and published within that discipline as well as in economics. Thematic ties between the market and the brain, both complex adaptive systems, probably came more naturally for him than for many other economists. According to Norman L. Roth's book, *Telos and Technos: The Teleology of Economic Activity and the Origins of Markets* (2008), Hayek understood that as systems increase in complexity, any effort to control a single aspect of the system results in outcomes that become increasingly unexpected and unpredictable. Hayek understood that the economy isn't any kind of predictable and controllable machine.[49]

Friedrich von Hayek was interested in both the politic and economy and his books discussed a variety of topics. In *The Road to Serfdom*, and *The Constitution of Liberty*, Hayek wrote about the role of the government, of law, fiscal policy, monetary policy, socialism, mixed economy, how monopolies form under government favoritism and how inflation harms the middle class. In chapter six of *The Road to Serfdom*, Hayek saw law according to European models seemingly as Mises did, as can be discerned by his use of the phrase "coercive power" when he wrote about government. He wrote that the rule of law was the declaration of legal rules so that people could stay within the law before they transgressed the law. He stated that a social welfare system of redistribution would necessarily destroy legal fairness. He believed that there should be little discretion regarding legal enforcement in order to preserve justice.[50]

Hayek, in chapter three, was concerned that the legal profession and legislators barely understood the positive role that law could play in regulating the marketplace. He saw law as the protector of market structures such as information access and money flows. He was worried that current patent law and corporate law left markets vulnerable to destruction. He wanted the law to protect market competition. Hayek mentioned that the "precise definition of property" could influence a marketplace. This idea was similar to observations made by Walter Lippmann in *The Good Society*. But Lippmann had argued that having different legal definitions for different kinds of property could help the regulatory government to control corporations. But Hayek was on the side of corporations rather than on the side of the government. He wanted property definitions to strengthen market mechanisms that allow corporations to respond to business circumstances.

Regarding the topic of monopoly, in chapter four of *The Road to Serfdom*, Hayek wrote that public policy, rather than simply the economy of scale, might encourage monopolies to form in an atmosphere of political corruption.[51] He wrote, in chapter thirteen, that government sponsored monopolies would be protected against both "competition" and "criticism."[52] Monopolies, he thought distorted the market's adjustment to supply and demand and distorted pricing in favor of the largest market interests and with government collusion, the largest political interests as well.

Although modern liberal and neoliberal governments have often resorted to fiscal debt and inflationary policies, Hayek wrote in opposition to inflation. Hayek, in chapter fourteen, disliked the Keynesian policies that modern liberals had followed, supposedly to enhance employment, by adjusting inflation upward. He wrote that such inflation represented an injustice and that monetary policy to inflate couldn't really remedy underlying market tendencies such as unemployment. He saw monetary policy to remedy unemployment as an unproductive squandering of resources.[53]

In *The Constitution of Liberty*, in his essay on "The Monetary Framework", Hayek wrote that a fiscal policy to increase governmental debt would affect monetary policy by stimulating inflation.[54] In *The Constitution of Liberty*, Hayek wrote about historical inflation from 1913-1958. He noticed that it destroyed people's savings. He noted that inflation left only 11% and 12% of their savings to the people of France and Italy and 37% of savings to Germans, 50% to the U.K. people, 58% of savings value to the people of Canada and the U.S. and 70% to the people of Switzerland. What a swindle. These forty five years undermined people's ability to save money under monetary policies followed in these nations.[55] In terms of monetary policy, Hayek noted that Britain's strict gold standard maintained stable prices and values. That circumstance according to Hayek, stood as a stark contrast to the unstable prices and values of the mid twentieth century.[56]

In terms of the global market, Hayek wrote that nation states in pursuit of their own short term interests would inevitably experience conflicts.[57] But Hayek didn't trust a global economic authority to behave responsibly regarding diverse national interests.[58] Hayek expressed his wish for a "superior political power". Here, he probably meant the power and force of an empire-class nation that would restrain nations from causing economic harms to other nations.[59] His desire for the U.S. to play the role of empire keeping was implied in this section by what Hayek didn't say. Hayek never said that he hoped for a representational international ruling body or an elected international body. This desire for an American Empire reflected Hayek's Austrian heritage. Here are some quotes from Hayek.

"It is entirely fallacious when it is sometimes argued that the great power exercised by a central planning board would be "no greater than the power collectively exercised by private boards of directors....To split or decentralize power is necessarily to reduce the absolute amount of power, and the competitive system is the only system designed to minimize by decentralization the power exercised by man over man...We have seen before how the separation of economic and political aims is an essential guaranty of individual freedom and how it is consequently attacked by all collectivists."[60]

"Thus, the more we try to provide full security by interfering with the market system, the greater the insecurity becomes; and, what is worse, the greater becomes the contrast between the security of those to whom it is granted as a privilege, and the ever increasing insecurity of the underprivileged."[61]

"A state which is entangled in all directions in the running of monopolistic enterprise, while it would possess crushing power over the individual, would yet be a weak state in so far as its freedom in formulating policy is concerned."[62]

"For the moment the important fact is that, as long as government expenditure constitutes as large a part of the national income as it now does everywhere, we must accept the fact that government will necessarily dominate monetary policy and that the only way in which we could alter this would be to reduce government expenditure greatly.....Governments everywhere and at all times have been the chief cause of the depreciation of the currency. Though there have been occasional prolonged falls in the value of a metallic money, the major inflations of the past have been the result of governments' either diminishing the coin or issuing excessive quantities of paper money."[63]

"The inflationary bias of our day is largely the result of the prevalence of the short-term view, which in turn stems from the great difficulty of recognizing the more remote consequences of current measures, and from the inevitable preoccupation of practical men, and particularly politicians, with the immediate problems and the achievement of near goals."[64]

"Let us simply note, then, that inflation makes it more and more impossible for people of moderate means to provide for their old age themselves; that it discourages saving and encourages running into debt and that, by destroying the middle class it creates that dangerous gap between the completely propertyless and the wealthy that is so characteristic of societies which have gone through prolonged inflations and which is the source of so much tension in those societies."[65]

Of the three neoliberal economic schools of thought, the Chicago School, founded by Milton Friedman, was the only one founded by an American. Friedman's school used the manipulation of economic measures to create relationships between economic variables that were considered to advance a kind of economic control. Friedman's parents were born in what is now the Ukraine. So, even though he was an American, European ideas and culture were part of his life. Milton Friedman was a popular and well known economic personality who famously had a PBS program in 1980, and an accompanying book, both called *Free to Choose*. His neoliberal prescriptions were marketed by him as a return to classical liberalism. But they were really a radical substitution of market rationalisms for political regulation. The idea that the Chicago School was founded on classical liberalism has always been a misrepresentation. But Friedman, unlike most neoliberal economists was willing to address a general audience. His book, *Capitalism and Freedom*, published in 1962, sold half a million copies.[66, 67]

Friedman, in chapter one of *Capitalism and Freedom*, seemed to agree with Ludwig von Mises when he wrote that the act of purchasing was a kind of ballot. He wrote that consumerism was free of "coercive power" and therefore an exercise of liberty. Then he also wrote that economic power could vie for power with the politic.[68] This viewpoint seemed to see the politic and the economy in a competitive relationship, not a symbiotic one. But that idea differed from the classical liberal concept of commonwealth. In chapter one this idea resurfaced when Friedman wrote that only some political and economic pairings would produce stability and the separation of the politic and economy could allow for two arenas of power to co-exist, and "enables one to offset the other."[69] Was this a balance of power argument or did it express Friedman's view that the economy and politic would compete for political and economic power? The classical liberal view was that dual freedoms in the politic and economy provided greater liberty, but not necessarily greater political or economic power. Like Hayek, Friedman saw the fiscal policy of high debt as destabilizing and Friedman wanted the government to pay down its debt.[70] But unlike the Austrian economists, Friedman advocated for monetarism, or a steady expansion of the money supply to create 5% inflation in order to offset government debt.[71]

Groups in the politic and economy interested Friedman and he commented on monopolies, unions, and government industries. But Friedman wasn't always fair in his discussions because he would sometimes contextualize his descriptions in economic models that had no real-world counterpart. For example, in his discussion regarding unions, in chapter eight, he expressed the idea that when unions organize for higher wages they necessarily lower other worker's wages.[72] But this would incorrectly suppose that all labor is the same and all labor markets connected. The complex economy has been full of independent professions that don't affect other professions. If gardeners got a wage increase, physicians wouldn't suffer a pay cut. Complex market economies have been full of separate niches. The nation's economy by way of GDP or industry profits may be affected as a whole when unions negotiate, but other individual laborers in the U.S. probably wouldn't suffer a wage cut. Although Friedman didn't contextualize his comments to global markets, he may have been thinking about them when he made comments against higher wages. He may have noticed that outsourcing labor to cheaper markets abroad could put downward pressure on domestic labor in the U.S. by reducing wages and benefits in the U.S. labor marketplace. Certainly that trend has become obvious today.

In his discussion of monopolies, Friedman acknowledged on the one hand that monopolies could "limit voluntary exchange" by reducing product choices. On the other hand, Friedman resented the idea of "social responsibility" and thought that this idea endangered the goal of having a free society. He thought that corporations had a responsibility only to follow laws and to pursue their own interests. He didn't think that a corporation should consider the public's wellbeing or how business practices could cause harm except in the context of legal statutes.[73]

In his conclusion, Friedman saw graduated income tax legislation as causing the increasing size of corporations because he thought that high taxes caused corporations to reinvest in themselves rather than take a profit. A modern day example of this idea may be stock buy-backs that have become common among American corporations. But these buy backs may also be happening because corporations are trying to prevent a decrease in the value of their stocks as the public's demand to purchase stocks has declined. Friedman noticed that there were a number of loopholes that allowed corporations to escape a tax on their profits. And there remain many loopholes in the U.S. tax code today. He saw graduated income taxes as a failed effort to redistribute wealth but Friedman believed that instead of redistributing wealth, the graduated income tax harmed capital markets.[74]

Friedman resented "fair employment practice commissions" oversight of unfair hiring practices that demonstrated race discrimination. He wrote that these commissions interfered with the freedom to make contracts. But in his discussion, he ignored the "equal protection" clause of Section One of the Fourteenth Amendment. Instead, he discussed the limitations of majority voting in arriving at a just outcome.[75] This was a misstep in analysis since the Fourteenth Amendment would be more relevant. Constitutional protections put people's interests in common regarding innate human rights as compared with majority voting which pertains more to elections. In his conclusion, Friedman saw the military industrial complex as dangerous to the maintenance of free markets because it concentrated too much economic power in the purchase of defense products. He saw this government money as competing with private enterprise. The nuclear age, in Friedman's opinion, had led to the growth of the MIC (military industrial complex). And he resented "new government programs" as a further challenge to private businesses.[76]

Friedman's effort to reach the general public with his opinions was a departure from an academic focus that characterized most other neoliberal economists. Many of Friedman's ideas have motivated people to try new options in society such as school vouchers, ending the military draft, and floating foreign exchange international markets. He also worked in the government as a bureaucrat during the Depression Era, and devised the automatic payroll deductions that have been used to collect wage taxes in the United States. He taught at the University of Chicago for thirty years, retired and then made appearances to speak at neoliberal think tanks such as the Institute of Economic Affairs, in the UK. He also spoke at the Hoover Institute at Stanford.[77, 78]

In addition to the Nobel Prize in Economics from 1976, and the Reagan Administration's award of the Presidential Medal of Freedom in 1988, he also received the National Medal of Science, again under the Reagan administration.[79] Friedman's view of the economy and politic as competitive with each other differed from either classical liberal or modern liberal viewpoints. This idea may arise out of deference for power in the politic which developed in Germany under the German Idealists and that influenced the modern liberals, as already mentioned. This view of power also influenced the neoliberals as has seemed obvious from their comments.

If power had been the most important characteristic of the politic, then it would also be important in the economy. And if the economy and the politic were both measured by their power rather than by people's experience of opportunity, then a person could imagine a contest between them. And the power of market economies during the Industrial Revolution was larger than any other economic power had ever been. It seemed in Friedman's view that economic power could compete with political power for domination of society.

The idea of power competition between the politic and economy may have occurred to Friedman because global trade, global banking and mobile capital push investments beyond national borders. Some neoliberals may imagine that globalization makes investors more powerful than politicians (even though government subsidies prove that investors can't fly by their own power to generate their own success). But this view would reflect too much power adulation. It would be a radical departure from the tolerance views imbedded in classical liberalism, and from the classical liberal view that the best measure of the politic is people's happiness. Classical liberals worried about political tyranny not competition between politicians and business people. And power adulation would depart from respecting people's liberty to seek happiness and to be free of political coercion. Here's a few quotes from *Capitalism and Freedom*. The first one expressed the idea that the economy and politic could balance each other's power instead of working synergistically. In the second quote, Friedman disparaged the modern liberal belief that the government could use Keynesian public debt to better balance the public's interests.

> "…that there is an intimate connection between economies and politics, that only certain combinations of political and economic arrangements are possible, and that in particular, a society which is socialist cannot also be democratic, in the sense of guaranteeing individual freedom… Economic arrangements play a dual role in the promotions of a free society. On the one hand, freedom in economic arrangements is itself a component of freedom broadly understood, so economic freedom is an end in itself. In the second place economic freedom is also an indispensable means toward the achievement of political freedom…The kind of economic organization that provides economic freedom directly, namely, competitive capitalism, also promotes political freedom because it

separates economic power from political power and in this way enables the one to offset the other."[80]

"Whether the views so widely accepted about the effects of fiscal policy be right or wrong, they are contradicted by at least one extensive body of evidence. I know of no other coherent or organized body of evidence justifying them. They are part of economic mythology, not the demonstrated conclusions of economic analysis or quantitative studies. Yet they have wielded immense influence in securing widespread public backing for far-reaching governmental interference in economic life."[81]

Gottfried Haberler (1900-1995), a native Austrian, immigrated to the U.S. in 1936. He taught at Harvard and also worked as a policy expert at the American Enterprise Institute, a neoliberal think tank[82] starting in 1971. His expertise in international trade was extremely important for his era because the objective of U.S. foreign policy was to open global trade between nations. It was important to understand some of the consequences to mixing the economies of very different nations and Gottfried Haberler tried to understand and explain what would happen as world trade increased. He also wanted to examine what the effects of floating foreign exchange and increasing capital flows might be. Haberler was a careful academic narrator and he provided generous explanations in his essays. Unlike some other economists, he often considered history.

In the *Selected Essays of Gottfried Haberler*, edited by Anthony Y.C. Koo, various economic topics were included. Regarding the topic of fiscal policy, economic policy and inflation, Haberler agreed with the other Austrian economists, but he thought that the causes of inflation had grown more complex. He wrote that instead of having a single cause in government policies, inflation had new roots in the amalgam of governmental fiscal debt policy, monetary policies and exchange rate policy.[83] He wrote that any monetary policy to correct inflation would lead inevitably to unemployment and recession and he believed that global wages would eventually become reduced in all developed economies in order to improve the investment environment.[84]

Haberler wanted nations to have a combination of both tighter fiscal policy and tighter monetary policy. He wanted to reduce government spending instead of raise taxes in order to pay down the government's debt. And he saw the developed economies as being impaired by high taxes, monopolies and political factions. Haberler wanted widespread "structural reforms" and the cessation of monetarism (or expansion of the money supply, which Friedman had advocated). Haberler saw labor union's demands for higher wages as hurting the global competitiveness of developed economies and as a motivator of government inflation-producing monetary policies which would increase wages[85] without increasing real earnings.[86]

But Haberler's perspective that wage reductions could provide greater profitability would make greater sense in an economy that has stable prices and values, like an economy under a strict gold standard. In today's fiat economies, under artificial prices and unstable values that aren't set by market supply and demand, this idea that reduced wages could produce a higher profit is no longer true for the economy when it is considered in total. Lower wages in developed economies produced a demand gap that has shrunk markets, hurting profits. And fewer people participate in labor markets under reduced labor incentives. But shaving a dime in competitive conditions has led American employers not only to outsource jobs but also to import already trained workers from foreign countries. American companies have been motivated to hire more foreigners in technical positions in science and engineering.

According to one source, foreign workers made up 11% in 1990, 17% in 2000 and 21% of scientists and engineers in the U.S. in 2010. According to another source, Congress has been pressured by U.S. employers in technical fields to import foreign labor under H-1B visas, TN and L-1 programs. Employers can get a larger pool of potential workers and they pay lower wages for scientists by hiring from outside of the United States.[87, 88] The debates to change immigration policy are motivated in part to import cheaper technical labor from abroad even though this increases domestic unemployment for the American technical worker.

Regarding issues of global trade, Haberler thought the IMF should act to prevent "exchange rate manipulations" by parties seeking an undeserved "competitive advantage". Haberler opposed "split exchange markets, multiple exchange rates, import deposit schemes" all of which could choke off "current transactions". By this it has seemed that Haberler wanted less volatility in international markets to grow international capital flows.[89]

In his essay, "A Survey of International Trade Theory, Haberler noted that Lerner and Samuelson thought that "under certain assumptions", global free commodity trade would equalize the prices of production factors, but Haberler didn't comment on the kind of monetary system that would make that likely.[90] Haberler wrote that government policy should avoid changing income distribution, and that some trade protectionism might aid nations to maintain their economic strength in a global system of free trade.[91] This viewpoint differed from American trade policy that called for a widespread end to protectionism.

Haberler recognized that a "deviation from ideal conditions" can result from price and wage rigidity and that involuntary unemployment can be the outcome. People he believed couldn't be completely flexible regarding what would constitute a sufficient wage. In order to protect people's employment, Haberler advocated strategies such as "import restrictions, stimulation of exports…currency devaluation."[92] This view was an alternative to present-day U.S. free trade policy.

Haberler acknowledged that the Great Depression had caused a drop in prices that was most harmful to the developing nation's terms of trade with developed nations. He noted that floating fiat monetary systems don't protect national economies from deteriorating terms of trade that happen during international depressions.[93] Here are a few quotes from *Selected Essays of Gottfried Haberler*.

"both Lerner and Samuelson came to the conclusion, to their own surprise that under certain assumptions free trade in commodities will result in *complete* equalization of the prices, both absolute and relative, of all factors of production as between trading countries. This proposition was further developed by Tinbergen, Meade, and Laursen. It would thus seem that free trade may be a complete and not merely a partial substitute for free international mobility of labor and other factors of production."[94]

"Static theory tells us that under "ideal conditions"—free competition and the absence of "external economies"—free trade will maximize world income. It does not follow, however, that free trade would also necessarily be the best possible policy from the point of view of each individual country. On the contrary, it can be shown that even under these "ideal conditions" it would be in the interests of any country to restrict imports or exports to some extent (a) if the elasticity of foreign demand is not infinitely great, and (b) if no retaliatory measures need be feared."[95]

"In pure theory, economic processes are assumed to be reversible...All of this is, of course, only approximately true and is correct at best with considerable qualification. Even a demand curve is not always reversible."[96]

"...inflation is in my opinion a major world problem. But world inflation has no longer anything to do with a lack of control over global reserves; it has roots in *national* monetary, fiscal, and exchange rate policies primarily in the major countries.[97]

Karl Brunner (1916-1989) was a Swiss neoliberal economist and well known scholar of monetarism. According to the *Dictionary of Banking Terms*, a monetarist is a person who wants to control economic cycles through adjustments upward of the money supply.[98] Austrian School neoliberals didn't agree that monetarism would be a good policy prescription. The disagreement between monetarists and non-monetarists has been a topic that has caused disagreement between neoliberal economic schools of thought.

Brunner helped to found the Shadow Open Market Committee, with Allan H. Meltzer. He doubted that the Federal Reserve's policies were stabilizing of the American economy—instead, he believed that their policies of interest rate adjustments were destabilizing. He was a member of the faculty of the University of California at Los Angeles, and became the Gowen Professor at the University of Rochester after teaching there for eight years. He became a U.S. citizen and contributed to founding two academic Journals, *The Journal of Money, Credit and Banking*, and the *Journal of Monetary Economics*. He collaborated to write several books, coauthored with other distinguished economists.[99] Brunner edited and contributed to the book, *The First World and The Third World: Essays On The New International Economic Order*, 1978. Karl Brunner's essays in, "The First World, The Third World, and the Survival of Free Societies, 1977-1978," were neoliberal propaganda that opposed the New International Economic Order that was being suggested by the United Nations.

Debate over the New International Economic Order (NIEO) was inspired within the developing world by OPEC's success at dramatically raising the price of oil and by a theory that was eventually called "dependency theory". This was a belief that large wealthier countries manipulated commodity prices to permanently disadvantage developing nations and to keep them in a lower economic strata. According to some, dependency theory is less popular now, after the rise of "Asian Tigers" which have utilized exports to improve their economies.[100] An alternative view regarding the issue of who benefits most from global trade may be found in a different theory from the classical liberal period, as already mentioned.

The principle of reciprocal demand deals with the issue of how total trading profits are shared in a market. As far back as John Stuart Mill (1806-1873), it was thought that the division of trade profits would be decided by the terms of trade as determined by reciprocal demand of each country for the other's products.[101] The principal of reciprocal demand proposed that powerful economies have greater influence over price determination because of their larger demand power in a global system. In the wrestling competition of different sized economic partners inside a competitive system, a larger size has a favorable effect on the profitability of trade.

During the later twentieth century, there was a growing difference in political ideology and approach to politics between neoliberals and people working in the United Nations. The NIEO debates separated groups of people into opposing camps. The neoliberals wanted globalization to continue as sponsored by an authoritative United States making way for markets. Others, those who were inspired by Woodrow Wilson's Progressive policies, wanted trade to be based on an international cooperation between equally sovereign states.[102] Neoliberal discontent with U.N. policies were partly based on U.N. policy origins in collectivist approaches from the modern liberal period that neoliberals have consistently opposed as part of their political mission.

The First World and the Third World: Essays on the New International Economic Order, provided the neoliberal side of the argument for global trade that favored policies as described by the Washington Consensus. Neoliberals wanted the U.S. government to reject the U.N.'s NIEO policy suggestions. They saw the UN as a political predator that would "exploit all possible avenues and institutional opportunities" in order to take money from developed nations and give it to developing nations.[103] Neoliberals saw the NIEO as a "New Marxian-Leninist Manifesto" that would fail economically and that would "encourage a *private* use of *public* resources."[104]

Neoliberals wanted the U.S. government to overtly promote "a free society" but saw "individual human rights" as an unimportant measure of freedom. They wanted organizational freedom. This viewpoint expressed how important organizational politics was to the neoliberal political ethos. Neoliberals wanted the government to stay out of the economy and allow corporations to dominate in markets under private property protections, limited government regulation and "market mechanisms."[105] Neoliberals wanted the U.S. government to stabilize capital markets, "lower barriers to international trade", and put an end to foreign obstacles that inhibited private investors. Neoliberals claimed that their investors would increase jobs in foreign nations and they wanted the U.S. government to pressure developing nations to pursue neoliberal economic policies. Neoliberals wanted a new set of "rules of the game" in developing nation economies that would promote foreign direct investment.[106] Here's a quote from Brunner's essay, "the First World, and the Third World, and the Survival of Free Societies," from *The First World and the Third World: Essays on the New International Economic Order*. Brunner thought that developing nation's demands for a higher standard of living represented an expectation that corporations pay for their higher living standard with a profit curtailment. He didn't want to pay what he may have perceived as a kind of extortion. But this view overlooked problems that can be created by mobile capital investments that remove most profits out of the communities that produce them and break the virtuous cycle of profit circulation at the profit source.

> "Recent trends in political language have sharply separated human rights from property rights....But in its modified meaning, "rights" have come to represent an allocative claim to specific resources: "the right" to housing, to food, to a job, to medical care, etc. Such "rights" also imply, however, detailed claims on society's members. Such claims are imposed by coercive political institutions with the role of determining and supervising the details of resource allocations between individuals or between production units and industry."[107]

In her book, published in 2006, *Multinationals and Corporate Social Responsibility*, Jennifer A. Zerk [108] touched briefly on the NIEO and brought the issue up to the present day. She wrote that the NIEO was the forerunner of other organized efforts to define the relationships between multinational corporations and the countries where they have operated. Nations with less development were worried about neo-colonialism. After the NIEO failed, subsequent documents were written that articulated expectations for transnational corporations. These included the UN Code of Conduct on Transnational Corporations drafted in 1975, and the OECD Guidelines in 1976, followed by the ILO's Tripartite Declaration of Principles concerning Multinational Enterprises and Social Policy, in 1977.[109] Zerk listed numerous concerns among different stakeholders, including the desire of multinationals to avoid the nationalization of their factories. In addition she mentioned the interests of labor unions regarding their loss of power in view of multinational corporate mobility in a more diverse labor market, consumer's concern about "quality and choice", the concerns of foreign nations that they would lose power over segments of their economies or that multinational corporations wouldn't show respect for the cultures inside foreign nations.[110]

A long lasting debate about how to think of corporations has been ongoing during neoliberal globalization. Globalization, open markets, multinational investment in the third world has changed the way corporations affect communities where corporate owners don't reside. Those corporate owners can be disconnected from the consequences of their operations inside a local community. Because foreign investors live somewhere else, they may be ambivalent about harms that their industry could cause. Externalizing harms has been a strategy in the pursuit of profits. Community activism has sometimes been needed to protect the community's interests. And the need to protect the community's resources has stimulated the drafting of new international laws that take into consideration the way corporations can affect the localities of their operations. For example, large foreign corporations may easily outcompete small domestic companies which can hurt future local business development. And environmental resources also need protection. There has been a debate regarding what constitutes fair dealings between people who want greater independence for corporations that are overseen by stockholders and corporate boards and those who want to protect sometimes impoverished communities that may lack protective political structures to guard the interests of local stakeholders.

Karl Brunner (1916-1989) collaborated with Allan H. Meltzer (born 1928), when they wrote a book together called: *Money and the Economy: Issues in Monetary Analysis*, published in 1993. Essays in this book were lectures on topics of monetary policy. Keynesianism, rational analysis and monetarism were discussed and compared and the predictive powers of economic models were considered. The book brought together Meltzer and Brunner to explain topics in pure economics.

Allan Meltzer was a foremost scholar on the Federal Reserve, and as mentioned above helped to found the Shadow Open Market Committee. He was also the President of the Mont Pelerin Society from 2012-2014. He has been a visiting scholar at the American Enterprise Institute, a neoliberal think tank, and received their Irving Kristol Award in 2003. He also was the Chairman of the International Financial Institution Advisory Commission, a congressionally sponsored group also known as the Meltzer Commission.[111]

Money and the Economy: Issues in Monetary Analysis, by Brunner and Meltzer, showed three things. First it showed that economic models sometimes have served specific policy interests. Second it showed that there has been disagreement between groups over what policies should be followed. Third, it showed that the focus of these models has been on short-term time intervals in the operations of markets. Neoliberal economic models have lacked consideration for long term outcomes which has hurt non-investors. Communities are the most vulnerable to economic depression because most people lack large capital reserves. When long-term outcomes aren't considered, negative economic outcomes often hurt people in the community most of all. Balancing the interests of different financial groups and considering more vulnerable non-investors who also participate in and contribute to the money stream should be a consideration of regulations that protect vulnerable people from harm.

In Brunner and Meltzer's *Money and the Economy: Issues in Monetary Analysis*, the authors expressed some dismay at the experimental nature of governmental economic planning. They said that "there's little agreement on the structural model" of how government policy should be chosen and applied, or what the foundation of sound money would be.[112] When considering Keynesianism, they expressed little confidence in the idea that government bureaucrats act in the public's best interests, or that information relied upon by Keynesians would be free of political bias. They observed the advance of a permanent debt economy.[113] They noted that the Federal Reserve failed to predict GDP accurately and that the Federal Reserve has a record of underestimating inflation rates. This led them to doubt the Federal Reserve's ability to coordinate monetary policy actions with what was needed by the U.S. economy to promote stability in "output and prices."[114] Here are some quotes.

> "Economists have not produced a reliable, fully identified model relating policy variables to outcomes. There are large uncertainties about the size and timing of responses. Forecasts of the future are conditional on a number of variables, but there is uncertainty reflecting unresolved analytic differences about the elements of the set of conditioning variables. In addition, shocks to output prices, employment and other variables are partly permanent and partly transitory."[115]

> "The thesis we present is that forecasts of main economic aggregates on which discretionary policies depend are so inaccurate on average that discretionary policies based on forecasts are unlikely to minimize variability....The record of more than twenty years of economic forecasting

in the United States is summarized by the finding that, on average, the most accurate forecasters cannot predict reliably at the beginning of the quarter whether the economy will be in a boom or a recession during that quarter….One plausible explanation of the size of forecast errors is that for the best forecasts, the average errors that remain mainly reflect unpredictable, random shocks that hit the economy. The shocks may result from real events—changes in productivity, weather, and the like —or they may result from unanticipated or misperceived policy action."[116]

Peter Thomas Bauer (1915-2002) was born in Budapest and died in London. He began as an Austrian when Budapest was part of the Austrian empire, studied law first and then economics and when his life ended, he was a member of the British Peerage, nominated to become Lord Peter Thomas Bauer (Baron Bauer of Market Ward in the City of Cambridge) by Margaret Thatcher.[117] He joined the Mont Pelerin Society, a prominent neoliberal group, and was a member of the British Academy. He was Professor Emeritus at the London School of Economics.[118] He visited the third world, Asia and Africa, and he appreciated direct observation as the best foundation for opinions regarding the economics of the Third World. The way that Bauer valued direct experience has been rare among some neoliberal economists, like those of the Chicago School, who have relied heavily on theories and math models based on assumptions that ignored observations of the real world.

Peter Bauer wrote about global development in his book, *The Development Frontier: Essays in Applied Economics,* which was published in 1991. In his essay, "The Third World Debt Crisis: Can't Pay or Won't Pay", Bauer made several points. According to Bauer, when he examined 17 developing nations in 1986, the debt ratio to GNP (gross national product) was about 5% of total GNP. Bauer believed that payment of this debt wouldn't have harmed these country's living standards. He also thought these nations had other funds that could have been used in debt payment that weren't part of GNP.[119] Bauer thought that the developing nations were unwilling to pay their debts but not because they couldn't afford to pay. Bauer thought that developed nations, the U.S., Britain and Europe, put pressure on banks to lend to developing nations, and because of that developing nations expected easy credit even in the case of loan default. If they couldn't get more private bank loans then they could get aid or more loans from international organizations such as the World Bank and the IMF.[120]

In the essay, "Industrialization and Development: Nigeria," Bauer bemoaned the pittance left to farmers and other agricultural workers when government regulatory boards taxed their profits to establish government oversight of agriculture. He saw this regulatory oversight as impeding development rather than helping it. Going further, Bauer thought that politicization of the economy harmed it by diverting resources from economic production to the politic.[121] In his essay,

"Import Capacity and Economic Development: India", Bauer wrote, "It is the value productivity of the resource that matters, regardless of whether the output is sold at home or abroad". Bauer believed that getting the most productivity mattered more than which market bought the product for whatever price. He esteemed productivity more than profits. But Bauer may not have realized that if goods produced in a developing nation went to a foreign buyer and paid a sum owed to a foreign bank, and if the producer made a very small wage, little benefit would accrue to the community. The transfer of cash to foreign investors might be problematic because capital couldn't circulate virtuously in the local community. Sending capital away from its source would break the virtuous cycle.

But Bauer thought that local communities benefitted from engaging in economic production. In his essay, "Development Economics: A Retrospective View," Bauer wrote that most goods weren't produced by Western foreigners in developing nations. Instead, local owners, and local labor produced goods, traded goods and transported goods. Bauer thought that the lives of people engaged in economic production were improved through their work, and their ownership.[122]

Bauer wrote in "Development Economics: A Retrospective View", that Westerners failed to appreciate the value of local traders. Traders substituted their activity and the convenience of local small scale trading for capital that they didn't have to buy inventory and set up a permanent store. These itinerant traders would sell a small quantity of an item in demand, like matches, for a small amount of money and this slowly improved the selection of goods that a small amount of money could buy. Westerners criticized the number of middlemen in layers of trading and imagined that middlemen increased costs. And Westerners restricted the number of traders or interfered with the chain of trade. But Bauer recognized that this restriction only created hardships and reduced the useful availability of goods until subsistence was the only alternative.[123] Here's a quote from Peter Bauer that explained how foreign aid created a politicized economy in LDC's (least developed countries) that did more for the political influence between nations than it did to help the poor.

"On foreign aid I wrote little, beyond saying that it was not indispensable for the progress of poor countries and that it often served to underwrite and prolong extremely damaging policies commonly pursued in the name of comprehensive planning...I must acknowledge a serious misjudgment. I failed then to appreciate the pervasive significance of the politicization of economic life in LDC's....By the late 1950's the principle measures included state monopoly of major branches of industry and trade, including agricultural exports; official restrictive licensing of industrial and other activities; controls over imports, exports, and foreign exchange; and the establishment of many state-owned and state-operated so-called cooperatives. Several of these individual measures gave governments close control over the livelihood of their subjects. When applied simultaneously, these measures conferred even greater power on the rulers…In these conditions the acquisition and exercise of political power became all-important. The stakes, both gains and losses, in the struggle for political power increased. These developments enhanced uncertainty, anxiety, and political tension, especially in the many LDC's that comprised distinct ethnic, religious, or linguistic groups. They thereby diverted people's energies and resources from economic activity to the political arena."[124]

Wilhelm Ropke (1899-1966) was a German who won a distinguished award, the Willibald Pirkheirmer Medal in 1962, in Nuremberg, Germany and also the Swiss Hugo Grotius Medal in Munich in 1960. He fled Germany when Nazis began to threaten him because his opinions were contrary to theirs. During his life, he lived in Germany, Turkey, and Switzerland. He was viewed as an economist who cared about people and their vulnerability to economic and political outcomes.[125] He hoped that government involvement in the economy could be undertaken independently of political factions and their demands in favor of special interests. He hoped that government could own natural monopoly industries such as utility companies and operate them in the public interest without interfering with the larger economy. He also wanted government to provide tax subsidies to aid in job retraining when economic change increased unemployment because of industrial change.

In Wilhelm Ropke's book, *The Social Crisis of Our Time*, Ropke wrote about problems by first taking a wide view and then considering more narrow issues. In part one, chapter one, he wrote that economic competition should be kept within bounds to prevent political harms. He saw "giant cities" and monstrous industrial areas" as problems brought on by economic competition. He worried about the transformation of German and English peasants into proletariats during the Industrial Revolution when their economic well-being was slowed by the growth of their populations. Large groups of working people were brought into a marginal economic existence until prosperity could increase beyond upward shifts in population numbers. Instead of planning a way past the problems of working class people, liberals, according Ropke, just took an optimistic wait-and-see attitude. But this delay led to political and economic changes outside the purview of politics.[126] Ropke also wrote that as the populations of cities grew, the appeal of greatness through size also grew. After the Napoleonic era, people thought bigger, that is they appreciated "the cult of power and unity". Living large began to eclipse smaller cultural contexts where meaningfulness had once been centered in a human sized life. Ropke saw this as change toward a kind of "dehumanized" existence.[127]

Like Milton Friedman, Ropke, recognized that not every combination of economy and politic would survive. He thought that any politic and economy would undergo a test of viability.[128] He saw collectivism as a nonviable combination of the politic and economy that could never succeed. And Ropke thought that individuals needed legal protection from the government and from other individuals. Ropke wrote that market economies relied on the individual's willingness to employ their "enterprise and risk" in markets and therefore, people needed a legal system that protected their efforts and gave them a chance to succeed. And Ropke believed that the greatest accomplishment of liberalism was "the conquest of arbitrary might through right."[129]

Like Haberler, Ropke wrote that boom/bust economies were caused by "imperfections of the money and credit system" and "of the allocation of capital" and therefore rested with financial industries.[130] Like other neoliberal economists, Ropke recognized that using monetary policy to "prolong the boom" antagonized corrective economic policies that would have been better employed to fix economic imbalances. Ropke thought that "boom and bust" economies were dangerous economies that were propelled by financial and political interests.[131]

Ropke objected to giving governments control of economic enterprises because he recognized that more power granted to a government could lead to evil outcomes.[132] Ropke hoped that moral standards could stop political factions from disrupting the economic interests of larger society. He spoke against monopolies, against socialism and collectivism, in favor of government manipulations of the economy but only if government policy didn't interfere with the market's price mechanism and market competition. At the same time he didn't believe in "economism," because he didn't see value in judging all social ends by an economic ruler.[133] Here are a few quotes from Ropke's, *The Social Crisis of Our Time*, (1941). Ropke's statements highlight a conceptual cultural shift that promoted limitlessness and the predominance of organizational politics after WWII.

"Since the cult of the colossal reduces qualitative greatness to mere quantity, to nothing but numbers, and since quantity can only be topped by ever greater quantity, the intoxication with size will in the end exceed all bounds and will finally lead to absurdities which have to be stopped…. By abandoning humanism one lost the capacity for making man the measure of things and thus finally lost every kind of orientation. Life becomes dehumanized and man becomes the plaything of unhuman, pitiless forces."[134]

"By organizing themselves into powerful associations, the various groups divide political life up in terms of specific economic interests, and political power becomes the price which incites everyone to take part in the struggle. The extent of this alarming development is as clear to us as is the hardly comprehensible error of those who believe in all seriousness that they will be able to base a new and better state, i.e., the corporate state on these group interests. We also have to add that the unification of the various interests in well organized groups makes matters even worse by producing a "pluralism of the second degree," namely, the creation of an "associational" bureaucracy which, pursuing its special tasks, does not only lend extra momentum to the conflict among the interests but also fight for the interests of its particular group with an intransigence which many of those whom it represents would rather see modified."[135]

Fritz Machlup (1902-1983), another Austrian economist, immigrated to the United States to escape the Nazis in 1933. He had been educated in Vienna, and he educated many American economists through several university postings including: the University of Buffalo, Johns Hopkins University, Princeton University and New York University, over a span of forty-eight years. He became an American citizen in 1940.[136] A group of his students assembled a book of his essays to honor him in 1962, *Economic Semantics*, and presented it to him on his sixtieth birthday. This gesture may show how well his students respected Machlup's careful attention to foundational teachings in economics.

In Machlup's, *Economic Semantics*, the author wrote that political policies based on economic theories became problematic as "ends in themselves" instead of devices by which economists might address an economic problem. Regarding economic policies deployed in developing nations, Machlup believed that combined "monetary expansion" and "unadjusted exchange rates" and "direct controls on imports and payments" were bad for long term "economic development" even though these economic strategies were applied under the belief that they would increase economic growth. Even though these theories were confidently implemented, Machlup wrote that they fell apart in real world applications.[137]

In his book, *A History of Thought on Economic Integration*, Machlup wrote that income distribution could be affected by how goods were assembled. And already in 1977, Machlup recognized that outsourcing might cause income disparities. He listed five methods of manufacture. Each was an option that would occur under different political and technological circumstances. The first method was complete assembly by a team working at one location. The second was workers in tandem on an assembly line, each worker doing a different job. The third method was an "intraplant division of labor" at the same factory but on different assembly lines. The fourth method was "intrafirm division of labour" in different factories but under one management plan. The fifth method was labor outsourcing to different plants under different management systems producing some part of a final product where final assembly occurred later under another team.[138]

Machlup also recognized that capital risk for investments in foreign nations could be affected by a number of elements beyond the control of an investor. Risk would vary depending on what kind of investment occurred in what country. He thought that loan maturity (short term or long term), investment "liquidity" (how fast an investment could be changed back into cash), the "credit worthiness" of the investor, and the investor's confidence could all affect real risk, perceived risk and also profits. Capital markets could change quickly. Doing business in a foreign nation would have inevitable perils, such as "differences in legal institutions", changeability of exchange rates between nations, and differences in monetary inflation between nations. Investors wanted free capital movements between nations but even if they had this essential element, their likely returns could diminish quickly inside foreign markets that were vulnerable to adverse outcomes because of changes in the value of money.[139] Machlup saw foreign investors as an essential component of global capital circulation in a global system. Higher risk in foreign markets may be what encouraged congressional tax subsidies in support of foreign direct investments (FDIs). Congress decided that the public should defray some risk encountered by investors. Taxes should support FDI as part of U.S. foreign policy. Tax policy has been used to soften negative potential consequences that could impact American FDI.

Machlup believed that modern industrial processes required expertise in terms of experience and know how. He imagined that Industrial Revolution technologies required ever greater levels of training. He thought that international cooperation among like industries and multinational corporate development would happen because "hands on" training would be essential to passing on specific technology "know how."[140] Thinking like Machlup in modern-day factories, if you wanted a computer chip factory in a developing nation, the employees at that factory might need "hands on" training or job experience at a factory where computer chip "know how" was available. Or an expert familiar in computer chip "know how" might need to train new technologists. The requirement of "know how" training has meant that capital alone can't develop an experience-based resource.

Machlup recognized that the need for "transportation and communication" has "been one of the oldest insights" about how to integrate economies. He saw that a further requirement for any trading group has been the need for a multination "monetary system" that facilitates foreign exchange payments of "principle and interest" between parties engaged in trade. But "controversy", wrote Machlup has often erupted out of disagreements on the policies and methods of capital exchanges, even though a capital union would be advantageous to many. Tense negotiations have included "monetary policy", and how to accomplish "capital transfers", and what "government regulations" to employ, and finally the potential of replacing each nation's currency with a uniform currency in common for the trading union. Negotiations to determine international monetary system policies have sometimes failed to establish a stable agreement.[141] Money and monetary policy would involve various parties with disparate interests even in the same nation and designing a monetary system in common between nations could be easily imagined as interfering with already vested national interests. And Machlup's discussion rested partly on the way that governments have used their monetary policy to make adjustments to their fiscal debt. Organizing a uniform trading currency would remove that advantage from indebted nations.

Of the neoliberal economists considered here, Machlup offered the most valuable basic information. He provided clarity about origins of economic terms and about why economists would differ in their conclusions. Machlup provided the keys to basic economic ideas that he unlocked for his students and readers. Examples included, for instance, the difference between static and dynamic equilibrium, the meaning of "marginal analysis", the early and subsequent uses for the term "integration" as international trade grew after WWII and his differentiation of microeconomics and macroeconomics. It is by reading Machlup that the reader can come to realize how much short-term concerns have eclipsed long-term considerations in economics during the twentieth century and even now. And how this is different from past economic scholarship. He showed his readers that the discipline of economics has had room for the study of both long-term and short-term outcomes.

Here are a few quotes from Machlup's *A History of Thought on Economic Integration*. They show that economics doesn't have a sure policy recommendation for many problems because economies are so complex. Machlup pointed out the limitation of economic theory.

"The trouble with most economists is that they try so hard to answer questions for which neither a theoretical model nor historical experience nor observation of present conditions can furnish any reliable clues, at least not at the present state of knowledge. The question about foreign and domestic investment, as it was formulated above, offered nine possible combinations to choose from, but we could easily have added more possibilities."[142]

"In statistical descriptions of developments in international trade certain ratios of trade to other magnitudes have been assigned significant roles, particularly with regard to what is purported to indicate 'progress' in economic integration. The ratio of a country's trade with other *members* of its trading bloc, customs union, or free trade area to its total international trade, and the changes in that ratio over the years, have been regarded as highly significant. Other widely advertised ratios have been those of interregional, intraregional, and world trade, to the gross national product of the country or group of countries concerned. Unfortunately, the theoretical support for the inferences drawn from the statistical observations was often lacking; and if the ratios, and any trends shown by their changes, were said to be significant, one can hardly help asking: 'significant for what?' "[143]

Deepak Lal, another neoliberal economist, was born in 1940 in India before the British partition of it. Two nations were born out of that partition including the Dominion of Pakistan and the Union of India. A further separation later created the Islamic Republic of Pakistan and in 1971, and the People's Republic of

Bangladesh, separate from Pakistan. Deepak Lal, was the James S. Coleman Professor Emeritus of International Development Studies at UCLA and has worked as a member of the Indian Foreign Service, as a consultant for the Indian Planning Commission, and as a researcher for the World Bank. He also has worked as a neoliberal senior fellow at the Cato Institute and has been a longtime member of the Mount Pelerin Society.[144, 145, 146]

Lal viewed empire keeping as a role that destiny required of the United States.[147] "Indirect imperialism" through economic policy and military operations abroad supported neoliberal economic policies to invest in foreign firms and enterprise. He viewed the Vietnam War and the Cold War as "consolidation of this indirect imperial rule." But Lal noticed that most Americans didn't see the U.S. as an imperial power. Instead, they supported Wilsonian doctrines from the modern liberal era.[148] During the modern liberal period, Woodrow Wilson had set up the League of Nations in the hope of creating a "new world order" where strong and weak powers would have the right to equal political and economic self-determination.[149] Lal differed with Wilsonianism. He wanted the U.S. to have a military enforced global hegemony. The CIA played a covert military role in empire keeping that helped advance U.S. hegemony under the public's radar detector because of political secrecy and false statements in the press (see CIA timeline in the appendix).

Lal saw Africa and the Middle East as places where the region's politics had failed to assemble stable nation states. And these regions possessed rich energy resources or other natural resources that according to Lal, were misappropriated as rent by a ruling overclass. Lal rationalized that "depoliticization" of these resources would be "required to restore order". By this comment, Lal might have rationalized the West's appetite for these raw materials. Lal seemed to believe that these resources were wasted by the ruling groups in Africa and the Middle East. He thought that restricted foreign aid and expanded foreign trade would be a prescription for better neoliberal outcomes. He thought that "direct imperialism" would fail in the Middle East and in Africa because the states there needed to find their own political order. His comment to "depoliticize" the resources seemed to imply a future struggle over natural resources in those regions.[150]

Lal wrote about post WWII global political and economic planning. He described the managed gold standard, Bretton Woods agreements, the IMF and World Bank as "transnational institutions", and GATT treaties that eventually paved the way to assemble the WTO. As the Bretton Woods system matured, Lal said that it fell apart because of short-term capital speculation.[151] These topics will be developed soon. Lal said that after the strict gold standard was abandoned by the UK, global capital flows declined. Lal wrote that this global capital flow reduction helped Keynesianism to work better. Probably, this was by way of reducing the flow of foreign investment so that domestic investment was concentrated in developed economies. And reduced global capital flows also diminished speculation in capital markets which could have otherwise competed with investments in production.[152]

Lal also wrote about the United Nations' opposition to globalization. He saw the UN as having its own agenda that differed from the "imperial Pax" goal of creating "peace and prosperity." But it may well be that both the neoliberal and UN groups have had a political agenda that strives to acquire funding and empowerment to influence the world according to opposing plans to benefit different groups. While the UN has some representational structure in terms of the participation of many nations, UN programs aren't self-funded and they have always relied on the U.S. government for a large part of their funding. Lal complained about the UN being "staffed by rent-seeking international bureaucracies." Lal viewed agencies of the UN such as the ILO (International Labor Organization), the UNIDO (United Nations Industrial Development Organization), UNCTAD (United Nations Conference on Trade and Development), and UNESCO (United Nations Economic and Social Council) and FAO (Food and Agriculture Organization) as having outlived their usefulness. But this view may be based on these organization's opposition to neoliberal development strategies in foreign places.[153]

One of the points raised by this book was the different opinions that Americans have about the U.S. acting as an empire in foreign policy. Lal stated that except for an elite military faction, most Americans have opposed this approach. As tension in possible uses for economic resources has increased since 2008's financial problems surfaced, many Americans have wanted to reduce political investments in military objectives abroad. What this may show is a political consequence of neoliberalism's fractured birth outside of the mainstream of American political norms, adapted for power in nation state competition but not for power from the people. This is another weakness in neoliberalism. Lal agreed with other neoliberal economists that have favored unregulated capital flows.[154, 155] Here's a quote from Lal, *In Praise of Empires, Globalization and Order.*

"…since the Second World War the imperial mission has been pursued surreptitiously by a foreign policy elite which has shown a remarkable consensus about the aims of U.S. foreign policy. These aims are not only to maintain U.S. military superiority for purposes of national security, but also "to maintain international order, thereby enabling the process of globalization to continue and the American people to reap its rewards. As Secretary of Defense William Cohen [in the Clinton administration] explained 'economists and soldiers share the same interests in stability.' By tapping American military power, 'we are able to shape the environment in ways that are advantageous to us and that are stabilizing to the areas where we are forward deployed, thereby helping to promote investment and prosperity…business follows the flag."[156]

Understanding neoliberal ideas through economic policies has revealed market faith and political expediency instead of market expertise.

Neoliberalism formed to serve political interests sponsored by political organizations with political agendas. In his book *Financialization*, Thomas Palley said that economists provided a kind of justification for neoliberal politicians' economic policies through their economic theories.[157] But many neoliberal economists didn't support the fiscal and monetary policies of neoliberal politicians. This shows that neoliberal politicians have cared more about political goals than economic ones. Economic advice was ignored whenever political expediency overruled economic rationales. Neoliberal politicians supported policies that enhanced their own momentary political power, even when growing economic malaise would hurt the nation later.

Many neoliberal economists approached both the politic and the economy from a European perspective. In the group of ten impeccable neoliberal economists we have considered, there were five Austrians, Hayek, Mises, Machlup, Haberler and Bauer, two Americans, Meltzer and Friedman (though his family came from the Ukraine, a former Austrian territory), one German, Ropke, one Swiss, Brunner, and one Indian, Lal. All were members of the neoliberal Mont Pelerin Society. According the *The Road from Mont Pelerin*, by Philip Mirowski and Dieter Plehwe, the Mont Pelerin Society and neoliberalism was a conjoint collaboration of Europeans and Americans, with Europeans predominating. "Contrary to the conviction of many on the left that neoliberalism is an ideology "made in USA," fifteen of twenty-four MPS presidents have been European, and six have come from the United States…Twenty-seven general meetings between 1947 and 2004 took place in Europe compared to just four in the United States and one each in Canada, Chile, Hong Kong and Japan."[158]

The predominance of Europeans among neoliberals probably contributed to the neoliberal choice of deregulation through statute law instead of by a constitutional amendment process. A constitutional remodeling probably couldn't have happened anyway, even if it had been attempted in order to move neoliberalism forward, because there was no grassroots support for it. Many Americans still wanted the nanny state at the end of WWII. Although constitutional amendments were added that changed the American polity under modern liberalism, neoliberals haven't pursued as many of their political reforms through constitutional amendments as they have through congressional legislation.

According to Mirowski and Plehwe, in *The Road From Mont Pelerin*, the Mont Pelerin Society was a "thought collective"; people gathered together imagining a new ideology that would be an improvement over liberalism. They wanted it to preserve markets while improving their efficiency under the power of government. But they never published a formal definition of neoliberalism.[159] The economy was too complicated all across the world even for skilled economists to understand it in its entirety and few of them knew much about the politic. They produced instead, a list of topics to discuss in what was to them a topsy-turvy world right after WWII. They didn't know what kind of "legal and institutional framework" to build,[160] but they hated arbitrary power and they wanted to control government through the law. Being mostly European, they thought of statute law instead of constitutional law. Ideas they approached included "creation of an international order."[161]

As neoliberals, some of them differed from each other regarding topics in monetary policy, for example, where Friedman was in favor of monetary expansion and constant low level inflation but Austrians opposed it. Brunner and Meltzer studied monetarism and criticized the Federal Reserve. From the quotes it seems that neoliberal monetarists favored monetarism not as a panacea to solve problems in a nimble economy but as a palliative in an economy harmed by enormous fiscal debt. The Austrians all agreed that monopolies were bad for markets as did Wilhelm Ropke. Even Friedman mentioned monopolies as bad for markets and more so when entrenched by government sponsorship. Few political or economic suggestions were made by them to curb the development of monopoly because they left political policy formation to politicians.

The neoliberal economists were just expert advisors. Many of them opposed monopolies in their rhetoric. But they didn't become politically active against monopolies because as economists, they worked mostly in academia, teaching students or giving speeches rather than acting directly in a political or a market context. The political inactivity of neoliberal economists except in the context of giving advice and teaching, distinguished them from classical liberals like John Locke or Thomas Paine who risked their livelihoods and sometimes their lives to write and talk about classical liberal politics. And neoliberalism has transformed the politic and economy gradually. Neoliberalism, though it may be a revolution, has been a slow one that started in the United States in the 1940's.

To be fair about neoliberal economists, many of them had already taken a political stand against the Nazis and had left their native countries and lost their homes. Their intention to begin constructing the neoliberal ideology was a political act of resistance to collectivism but one without direct activism except in terms of contributing their ideas toward the genesis of neoliberalism and the subsequent years they gave in terms of economic advice. Instead of acting politically at the individual level they acted through organizations like the Mont Pelerin Society, think tanks and universities. Their advocacy of a partnership between government and corporations provided them a place in America. The new political partnership between neoliberalism and corporations sought to strengthen both the politic and economy in order to aid American competition with other nation states. But partnership between the government and corporations also increased moral jeopardy.

The European focus on statute law, and positive law differed from the early American traditions that depended on limited law that wasn't positive law.

Americans would tend to think more of community derived common law and constitutional law. Deregulation and reregulation began even before the Reagan Administration made political factions more powerful and strengthened the partnership between Congress and corporate and financial giants with big purses. Constitutional law could have bypassed this relationship by reinforcing interests in common between political factions. Also the outcome of deregulation hasn't reduced the number of regulations or the size of the regulatory apparatus. The combination of deregulation and reregulation has multiplied statutes and made it too easy to break the law, too hard to understand the law. Selective enforcement now can further the predominance of factional politics by sparing some and prosecuting others.

Changes in economic school approaches were motivated by changing political policies.

When the U.S. economy changed from a land based economy to a market economy, its complexity increased. Complexity also increased because of a population explosion in Europe and the U.S. after improvements in public sanitation. Americans living in a market economy believed that under the general voting franchise that included people who didn't own property, government would look out for average Americans. And they were optimists in thinking that the government would work to support common interests. When Congress began to tax incomes during the Civil War, and expanded its power of economic oversight through legislation that created regulatory agencies, most Americans didn't realize that having more powerful legislators with more money at their disposal would encourage greater numbers of factions in politics. Factions that wanted an economic advantage could get new opportunities through congressional favoritism. Signs of corruption began appearing from the moment that income taxes were levied to support the Union cause—the Credit Mobilier Scandal was one of the early signs of below board financial dealings between corporations and legislators in 1872.[162] Another scandal, The Teapot Dome scandal, involved the Secretary of the Interior and petroleum reserve leases diverted from the U.S. Navy to two oil companies that got non-competitive bids between 1920 and 1923.[163]

By the early twentieth century, everyone knew that lobbies were powerful in Washington.[164] Lobbies fought on behalf of political factions. But Americans ignored increasing factionalization and focused instead on their hopes for government action to take care of problems. Government was seen as a powerful force multiplier that could get things done quickly that would benefit everyone at once. It was thought that government policies could correct undesirable trends in the economy and produce full employment and no inflation. Many economists disagreed with this optimistic belief.[165, 166] But while the political promise of full employment and low inflation pleased the common man it also justified a higher tax levy. During the early expansion of regulatory government, income taxes were still not nearly as high as they would become after WWII and the burden of the regulatory state's bureaucracy hadn't become as large as it eventually would. People didn't realize the political threat or expense of the federal government growing ever larger. Besides, the whole market economy was still growing larger, so growth of the bureaucracy seemed to make sense. Remember Wagner's Law, the idea that a larger economy would require a larger bureaucracy.

According to Fritz Machlup, a politicization of economic terms happened during the modern liberal period when government was trying to manipulate the economy to provide useful economic outcomes to working people. Some economic terms, like the term "equilibrium", for example, underwent a political transformation of meaning and of usage.[167] According to Machlup, economic "equilibrium" began as a term that described part of an economist's mental exercise where certain sets of economic relationships in a stable economy would be related to each other according to math equations. Such equations described how a limited set of economic factors affected each other, often in sets of two or three market elements, like inflation, employment and discretionary income.

Economists wanted to provide policy makers with specific tools for adjusting an economy to get a desired result. It was hoped that policy manipulation of some factors would favorably influence others. Differential calculus provided economists with a novel approach to examine small temporal slices of continuous processes. But this new approach was opposite to the economic approach used up until that time by the German Historical School of Economics. The German Historical School of Economics had been active during the nineteenth century and into the twentieth century. In the United States, the economics profession was dominated by German economists from the Historical School[168] during the nineteenth century. It had empirically examined longer periods of economy-in-history in order to make observations in the real world. The Historical School used real world economic outcomes as an "economic laboratory."[169] But history didn't matter to modern liberals because they wanted to command the future instead of study the past. They wanted to move the levers of economic control through the regulatory state.

While it was never meant by economists to describe all of the elements in a system of dynamic economics, an analysis at equilibrium that referenced a slice of time, could make certain kinds of guesses for a limited number of elements. Later, "equilibrium" was transformed into a term that described a system of economic manipulations to achieve specific political ends such as full employment and no inflation. This new idea of "equilibrium" began to mean the broad set of desired outcomes favored in government policies—the economic goal set. And this was a change of meaning.[170]

The politicization of the term "equilibrium" made it less useful as an economist's tool because it was then suited for use only in limited contexts set out in government policy instead of in broader situations of the real economy or in the context of a real market.[171] The politicization of economics led economists to serve the government goal set. Their economic models described the economy inside the context of political policies. New economic models were drawn up by economists without acknowledging economic inefficiencies brought about by government policies. Government policy was treated as unchangeable. A broader view would not be presented, just a short term picture of current economic relationships inside a bureaucratic goal set. This new approach eventually multiplied the number of economic schools of thinking to accommodate different political circumstances.

The multiplication of economic schools of thought happened because each school worked within the context of a specific policy approach to economic manipulation by government. But the politic and economy are both complex adaptive systems and they are changing instead of stable. So schools of thought in economics have had to change too. According to Roger L. Ransom in his book, *Coping With Capitalism: The Economic Transformation of the United States 1776-1980*, "Virtually all the models built since Adam Smith started all this in 1776 have been formulated with a fixed set of postulates which define the institutional setting and the way people behave. And once this institutional setting is fixed, it is not allowed to change substantially as the story unfolds."[172] Instead of formulating and changing policy for a changeable economy, economists were supposed to meet policy goals by manipulating the economy to get a politically desirable outcome.

People outside of economics can't understand an economic model unless they also understand the political contexts that formulated the model. Under the growth of bureaucracy during late modern liberalism, Keynesian principles dominated that promoted fiscal debt as an economic stimulus. Modern liberal economists, well steeped in Keynesian principles, also described other schools of economic thought. Looking back in time, the classical school of economics was identified with free trade in a system of nation states that traded raw materials and finished products by ship all around the world under colonialism, where keeping a positive trade balance and low fiscal debt mattered because of economic competition with other states. Neo-classical economics was associated with free trade and greater specialization utilizing specific nation state advantages under the law of comparative advantage, under maritime shipping but emphasizing less self-sufficiency and narrower product specialization.

Keynesians planned economic policies to focus on outcomes in the short term.[173] Keynesians wanted to increase fiscal spending, or government debt to stimulate a lagging economy. The federal government would continue to use the printing press to stimulate the economy, under the pretext that government could be a productive part of the economy when really it was using taxes or borrowing capital but never making a profit or preserving capital. Instead, capital expenditures fueled political influence instead of contributing to greater economic health.

Like Keynesians, monetarists also focused on the short-term gain. They wanted to increase private debt among individuals, corporations and governments. They multiplied kinds of money to increase capital flows in every class of money in order to prevent an economic slowdown. Monetarists began to think of money as a tradable commodity in an international market where values could be manipulated through capital flows to create arbitrage that would multiply capital for those with more capital resources and increased liquidity. Although some of these economic schools came about before differential calculus was used in economics and before the bloom of twentieth century policy-serving economics, the schools were discussed in the context of differentiating them from more recent schools of economic thought that existed under policies of economic intervention.

Neoliberal reach for global economic resources.

Neoliberal multinational companies under government sponsored globalism have wanted to harvest the world's resources in a global manufacturing system. They have wanted to benefit by getting cheaper labor and raw materials. Under piecemeal manufacturing, multinationals could make the most of the cheapest factors of production all around the world. Never-you-mind domestic unemployment inside developed economies or falling wages. In contrast to modern liberal goals of minimizing unemployment and eliminating inflation for the working many, domestic decline under neoliberalism was viewed as an advantage to corporations by lowering the price of wages. They call this an enhancement to global competitiveness.

Neoliberal bankers wanted to increase capital flows and financial arbitrage in a global international financial system, using government deregulation to secure trading and investment rights in a mostly unregulated global system. Economic schools have served a different economic policy set initiated by different administrations. Policies were also designed to provide opportunities for economic factions. Policies were supposed to accomplish political goals for government and economic goals for economic factions. Economists acted as economic facilitators to accomplish policy objectives. These approaches were complex, interactive and profit seeking but only in the short-term.

Neoliberals sought economic development in a changed contextual relationship between government and corporations. Government and corporations would collaborate, government negotiating for development opportunities abroad, multinational corporations developing new markets. Politicians were trying to capture the same kind of power that Hitler had used to develop his military strength through combining the power of the politic with the power of the economy. But this time, corporations would direct all of that power to achieve market based goals. It was hoped that the government could use military force abroad to enhance market opportunities in far-away places and also control employment, inflation, and prices.

Since the new global context became more complex as trade increased and became more open, the advice of economic experts was needed. Unfortunately, it is obvious from numerous comments by neoliberal economists that expert economists were never able to predict economic policy outcomes or produce successful economic forecasts, or even develop a set of reliable measures for economic growth in different economies.[174] Their failure to produce a successful forecast or reliable policy set was because of the complexity of market economies. And market economies became even more complex when they became more global.

The narrow approach of policy-suited economics failed the science of economics.

In the Afterward of William Briet and Roger Ransom's Book, *The Academic Scribblers, Third Edition,*[175] the authors described economics as having become narrowly focused and math based to its detriment. While Briet and Ransom perceived that economics hadn't progressed beyond the broad schools of thought and basic theories of the past, which they had described in their book, it seemed to them that the economics discipline had become less useful even to economists. Politicization of economics has led to abstractions of the real world into equations that narrow problems to the point that wider issues can't be addressed. Economic health as a whole has been ignored. This has served the politic without succeeding for economics. By the twenty-first century, economics had become almost imponderable to outsiders. It became shaped by economic school approaches that ignored real-world based explorations of economic situations in favor of math models within a policy set of considerations.[176]

Economics in the hands of politicians has been utilized for political ends and this has reduced the usefulness of economics to society as a discipline that can be used to analyze economic happenings. Economics has become limited by political interests to serve only some political ends instead of the wider goal of understanding a multitude of possible economic options and consequences. An example of political influence in economics is the focus on short term time periods. A politician would be most concerned with the next election instead of the dynamic long term changes that the economy will take over time. This short-termism also has undermined the usefulness of economics, which in previous historical periods paid a lot of attention to the long term. The discipline of economics lost its ability to innovate when it became politicized.[177]

Neoliberal experts have focused on problems pertinent to their expertise. Politicians have utilized neoliberal economic theories to justify bringing market approaches to politics. But they also used economists as experts that took some political heat off politicians when economic theories that have been used to justify political practices haven't worked out. Instead of considering past strengths and weaknesses in American political approaches of history, politicians bring out economic theories and produce mathematical and statistical constructs through experts that appear to justify their political choices within neoliberalism. Or neoliberal politicians say "most economists agree" even when many don't agree. Besides making economics less capable of analysis, this puts the politic into a realm that is hard to understand both for politicians and for the public.

These politicized economic constructs, for instance, models that justify Keynesian policies or monetarism, ignore the real world and make the long-standing program of neoliberal modifications in the politic and economy seem like the only choice available. Yet neoliberal economic theory has failed to predict market failures or ensure market successes. Americans face growing economic and political insecurity. Economists as proprietors of new policy based economic schools have failed to create an approach that delivers success, as can be seen by twenty first century market weakness and political instability.[178] Their failure is nested in complexity and economic change in a context of economic politicization that blocks adaptation to new circumstances. American politicians have used the expertise of economics to evade political accountability and avoid policy changes that are needed.

American neoliberal politicians often talk about the market as though it is a measuring tool for political progress. Yet they now refuse to measure the economy accurately. Hedonic adjustments have been used to inflate GDP estimates. The methods used for calculating GDP, or unemployment or inflation have changed in order to deceive the public and minimize political consequences for a shrinking economy and fewer jobs under higher inflation. New measuring methods change the way that employment or GDP is described in order to make unemployment less obvious or declining GDP less obvious. Inflation has been understated in the categories that matter, food and energy and that helps to keep cost of living payment increases lower for government checks given to social security recipients. Also the new measuring methods that provide economic statistics haven't adapted to piecemeal manufacturing among multinationals.

Measuring GDP hasn't adapted to multination ownership of a factory or partial value-added production methods. Nor have tax methods changed to accommodate intra-firm transfers of goods between subsidiaries. The tactic of offering misleading or incomplete information obscures the political consequences of neoliberalism. Changing economic realities that have come about as populations have grown, resources have become dearer and the Industrial Revolution has ended have also been ignored. Politics is deciding "who gets what". Neoliberals pretend that the market determines who gets what instead of political policy. But if you look for it, you will find that political deal making underlies the neoliberal market. Neoliberals have sometimes taken the position that the market can be the politic or that it can eclipse or compete for power with the politic.[179] And the functional distinction between the politic and economy seems to escape many neoliberals. The strange mixture of economic excuses for political choices has become a way to avoid political accountability.

By allowing their profession to become politicized, economists have failed greater society. Economists have allowed political bias to narrow their academic research. They have failed to show inefficiencies caused by government intervention that have harmed the economy. And financialization's reliance on debt interest payments has diminished production and technical innovation. A less vibrant economy has been what we live with after following the political-servant-elite economists. Although neoliberalism has further increased economic interventionism by political policy, it wasn't that way during classical liberalism. In the American classical liberal system the federal government's economic policy was limited by limiting overall government power. The economy was decentralized by keeping the federal government out of it. Modern liberalism reduced state and individual economic independence from federal interference and neoliberalism has made the economy even less free.

When legislators and judges during modern liberalism removed power limitations through expansion of the regulatory state—when they removed the limitation of "necessary and proper"—they created two problems. One has been more economic centralization. The other has been neoliberal political opportunism that externalizes negative economic consequences to the public. Now the partnership between liberalism and finance that dates back to the twelfth century has degraded from liberalism and capitalism into neoliberalism and financialization. High debt and high risk undermine the strength of the U.S. both politically and economically.

What a monetary system does and how many kinds there are.

Lionel Robbins said that "Economics is the study of the use of scarce resources which have alternative uses."[180] This idea isn't trivial. It accounts for the understanding that an ill used resource can be wasted, the idea that resources have many possible uses, and the idea that a resource might be used up. Robbins' statement also has provided another insight: that whatever size the economy, waste is harmful to the whole and enough waste may undermine economic well-being. This means that externalizing financial harms outside the financial industry doesn't prevent them from having an overall economic impact that's harmful. If you study economics, if you study the political policies that affect the economy, it becomes an unavoidable truth that everyone can't have everything in an unlimited quantity. And in any monetary system the principle of scarcity is important to remember. The discipline of economics can't magically overcome the principle of scarcity. Monetary systems don't decrease scarcity. They only can provide a means to effect market exchanges that use money.

According to Filippo Cesarano in his book, *Monetary Theory and Bretton Woods: The Construction of an International Monetary Order*, there have historically been three proper monetary systems, which he called "monetary orders": "the Roman Byzantine, the gold standard and Bretton Woods."[181] Cesarano wrote: "The first, which spanned an immense period, originated with the exercise of imperial power. The second was the result of a historical process, whose development generated and consolidated a set of institutions. The Bretton Woods monetary order differs radically from its predecessors, being the product of a formal agreement, the fruit of discussion of reform schemes that established a framework of rules for the operation of the system." Since Cesarano's book was about the Bretton Woods system and he stated that it made way for our current fiat system, fiat should also be considered. It's helpful to recognize this set of monetary systems so that the concepts of monetary policy happen within a context that is limited. When modern governments determine monetary policy, it can help to know that they have been constrained to a set of monetary choices. Governments can't choose from an infinity of possibilities when it comes to monetary policy.

Monetary systems help people to move money around. How much money is produced and made available may affect the value of money with respect to the goods it can be used to purchase. But it has no immediate effect on real productivity, or the amount of real goods that are available in the system of market exchange. A shortage of circulating money can reduce people's ability to purchase or invest. Banks can overprint money and create inflation, or hoard money and reduce the number of exchanges that are possible. Bank policy can create harms to people outside the financial industry and therefore bank regulations are important to reduce the frequency and severity of harms.[182]

Also, money isn't a creation of governments or of law.[183] Instead, money reflects people's exchanges according to their negotiated values for goods and services. Society's markets create the demand for money used in exchange and only people's negotiations ensure that money retains its value holding ability. Confidence in money's ability to represent authentic value underlies its use in exchanges.

Monetary systems have features that make them attractive to money users. Money users can be classified into three groups. First are individuals and single owner businesses. Second are corporations and banks. And third are governments. Differences between one monetary system and another can make the utility of money differ in different groups of money users. Bankers are among the most skilled money users. But according to Anat Amadhi and Martin Hellwig, who wrote in the context of our fiat money system under current government policy, "the incentives of banks with respect to the risks they take and to their borrowing are perversely conflicted with those of society."[184] Adam Smith said something similar about other business interests back during classical liberalism.[185] Considering monetary systems since the birth of the U.S., has already led to discussions about the First and Second Bank of the United States. After the Napoleonic Wars, and after the Louisiana Purchase, we now consider the UK's sponsorship of the strict gold standard.

The strict gold standard existed under UK sponsorship for about a hundred years and it supported global trade by creating a useful set of advantages.

The strict gold standard was instituted by Britain after the Napoleonic Wars until it was damaged by WWI. It had desirable features that today's fiat monetary system lacks. For example, the strict gold standard provided stable values and prices across the globe. And, it made gold *the global currency* with a value basis in real markets. Gold was less vulnerable to value manipulation by banks or governments. Also it brought governments more quickly back into equilibrium with market values when they overprinted their currencies which were exchangeable for gold. This provided a brake on government spending. The value of gold was set by its quantity and its exchange value in a gold trading market. The gold-trading market-determined value-of-gold acted as a stabilizer. Commodity trading of gold in markets combined usefully with a policy of gold held as money by governments. This combination of market price determination and gold as money in limited actual quantities stabilized the values of all other commodities.

That gave the strict gold standard market based system three important traits: "stability, credibility and symmetry."[186] Commodity based money, when it existed as a uniform standard like the strict gold standard did, was like a "monetary union", similar to a customs union.[187] Under this monetary union, people could utilize a consistent set of money rules, "the rules of the game". Many nations participated in and upheld the "rules of the game." Part of the "rules of the game" was that an economic stressor, war, for example could trigger a temporary escape from the strict gold standard.

After the stressor had been survived the strict gold standard could be readopted under the "restoration rule", when parity, or the original value ratio of gold to currency unit, would be restored. For about one hundred years, from after the Napoleonic War until WWI, the UK was the center of the strict gold monetary system, and its currency, exchangeable for gold, made the system reliable for everyone else. Even people in nations that were too small economically to hold significant gold reserves, were benefitted by the stability of prices that were maintained by such a system. The strict gold standard helped the market to stay at "equilibrium", meaning in this case, to have price and value stability. The market price of commodities rarely crashed or inflated. Long term investments were supported in the environment of stable commodity and currency values.

The "rules of the game" and the market based values inherent in the strict gold standard meant that a nation that overprinted its currency would be brought back to equilibrium through their trading with other nations. If a nation did print more currency than could be supported by their national productivity, their exports numerically increased because they declined in price relative to the products of other nations, while their imports from other nations became more expensive and declined in quantity. This situation of trade increased the nation's gold reserves through export trading to match the higher amount of circulating currency and that restored equilibrium. Sovereign powers weren't as likely to spend without discipline during the strict gold standard because everyone would recognize the overspending and that could be economically and politically damaging.[188]

People travelled under fewer passport restrictions under the strict gold standard before WWI. And they had a good idea of what commodities and services would cost during their travels to other countries under the strict gold standard. Passports were utilized only after the Great War which undermined the strict gold standard. Globalization under the UK at the time of the strict gold standard happened under a uniform currency—gold. With so much talk about globalization in the twenty first century, it is remarkable that there isn't a global currency now. Although numerous currencies exist and currency values are set in an open currency trading market, there's no market based commodity "anchor" to stabilize currency values and ratios of prices between nations the way that gold accomplished.[189] The monetary union achieved through the strict gold standard brought nations into price accord and that increased trust between them. The market set values of gold meant that no nation could dominate values of goods in other nations because there was already a fair market price; values were uniform and set in line with traded values of gold based on the quantity of gold throughout the world.

There were some disadvantages of the strict gold standard. One of the disadvantages could be gold hoarding. If nation states or banks hoarded gold and printed less money, that action restricted gold's availability for currency redemption. That could restrict an individual or small business person's opportunity to purchase. American farmers complained about such gold hoarding in the Crime of 1873, after Congress enacted the 1872 Coinage Act that got rid of silver and ended American bimetallism. Wages fell from 1873 to 1876, employment fell, and many railroads went bankrupt.[190]

Another disadvantage is that a commodity based monetary system that sets value based upon a market traded commodity is vulnerable to decreased value if more of that commodity is discovered. This affected European gold values during gold strikes in California and Australia. It also affected gold values during the days of Spanish Conquistadors that brought back gold from the Americas and even the price of gold during Alexander's ancient world conquests. Technologies that could improve processes of gold extraction could also increase the quantity of gold and reduce the value represented by each ounce of gold. A change in the quantity of gold that affected its value was important but usually only for the short term while the market adjusted.

Many factors made gold a good commodity choice to back currencies. For example, the quantity of gold was stable compared to many other commodities. And gold itself remained a physically stable element. A market set price of gold was another advantage; people preferred a market set value instead of some kind of arbitrary governmentally assigned value. The usually limited quantity of gold made gold an attractive commodity to back currencies. And the universal acceptance of gold that had become commonplace made it a good global currency backing when compared to other potential choices.

The greatest disadvantage that bankers experienced from the strict gold standard was its restriction of the amount of money in circulation. Bankers profit from money in use and the more kinds of money forms and uses that there are, the more that bankers can profit. Restriction on the quantity of money was severe under the strict gold standard, and that restricted the opportunity of bankers to make money when money circulated. The amount of money represented by gold deposits was supposed to cover the amount of money that was circulating. Bank runs could happen under a loss of confidence in the bank's ability to exchange gold for dollars. After the Civil War there was an expansion of fiduciary money that circulated more bills of exchange and checks. These monies increased the money quantity but bankers wanted still more money in circulation and for loans. Bankers would benefit to the extent that they could increase the circulation of money for more transactions in greater quantities of dollars. The strict gold standard put a damper on monetary expansion. The "rules of the game", corrected monetary expansion, reestablished equilibrium at the prior money quantity (based on the amount of gold) and foiled strategies of money expansion.[191] While this created stable prices and values it kept banks smaller than they wanted to become.

A final disadvantage of the strict gold standard was a disadvantage to governments. They had a restricted spending account. Politics is about who gets what and having more money by printing more money allows politicians to spread their influence to more people and nations. The strict gold standard didn't allow governments to affect values and prices by their currency quantities because under a gold standard of global money, values and prices were connected to gold values and overprinting currency had a bad effect on the relative values of commodities. This kept nation states on a strict ration of limited currency release.

But it is important to notice that gold had advantages and disadvantages for every group. Stable values and prices made markets less volatile which was good for everyone. And although individuals, bankers and governments couldn't control money values to manipulate a short term advantage for themselves, the strict gold standard had both good and bad to offer every interested party. That came to be recognized as a kind of fairness. Whether gold supply could keep up with the expanding world economy eventually came to be a doubt that gave people misgivings about the permanence of the strict gold standard. The peak years of the strict gold standard for the historical period in the U.S. under discussion was from the middle of the classical liberal period into the modern liberal period. The UK maintained the strict gold standard from the end of the Napoleonic Age in

1819[192] until 1914. The American free banking era under Greenbacks during the Civil War benefitted from stable values and prices under the anchor of the strict gold standard even though Greenbacks were unbacked by gold. After WWI, there was a strict gold standard reinstatement by the UK briefly from April 1925-Sept 1931. But it was destabilized by currency flows and the hardships left over from WWI, so it didn't last long.[193]

After WWI, prices for commodities had diverged in many nations and they couldn't apply the "restoration rule" to link their currency with gold values because there was no room after war's destruction for economic austerity. Spending was needed in order to rebuild. Depreciation of currencies was non-uniform and even the UK couldn't restore the pound's parity with gold.[194]

The managed gold system had different traits and advantages than the strict gold standard had.

Conversion to the managed gold standard after WWII had been necessitated by financial shocks that were so costly that the strict gold standard couldn't be reimplemented. WWI had expanded capital in the world past the quantity of gold in existence for convenient circulation under devalued currencies where capital expansion was relied upon to devalue government debt by creating inflation. This monetary overexpansion was triggered by war spending, war production, war destruction and the abandonment of the strict gold standard. The "rules of the game" couldn't be restored by using the "restoration rule". The Bretton Woods agreements which will be described shortly, organized the abandonment of the strict gold standard as a policy standard and instituted the managed gold system as an alternative to take its place. The managed gold system was founded on "bank theory" instead of upon proven performance. So, the Bretton Woods monetary system was experimental. It involved uncertainty.

The managed gold system was a totally different monetary system as compared with the strict gold system. The only thing it shared was that gold played a role, but gold's value was no longer set in the open market of metal trading. And its effects differed as well. For example, the managed gold standard couldn't hold the world economy at equilibrium. But just the idea of gold being part of the managed gold system disguised differences between the strict gold standard and the managed gold standard for many ordinary people outside finance. For them "good as gold" would still apply, somehow. But the managed gold system didn't have either fiscal discipline or monetary discipline as part of its money management.

Instead of market based gold values, the government at the center of the managed gold system, the U.S., assigned a value to gold that it would defend with its currency. This made gold into a "price supported commodity."[195] This value was arbitrary and not market based but it held from 1944 until the time of JFK (1960-1961).[196] Under the managed gold system, fiscal discipline deteriorated in most nations, monetary discipline deteriorated and speculation increased. This made financial markets more volatile. At the time the Bretton Woods System failed, the dollar went from $35/troy oz. gold to $44/troy oz. gold. The dollar peg to gold failed.

Before the collapse of the Bretton Woods System which occurred in 1971, central banks did what they could to support it. In response to the depreciation of dollars relative to gold, a collaboration of central banks formed to intervene in gold markets involving central bankers from the U.S and seven European nations. By putting together some of their gold reserves, they formed the **London Gold Pool**. The price of gold was then regulated by central bank gold sales and purchases to keep the price of gold pegged to the $35/ troy oz. value. People working in the London Gold Fix communicated the price of gold to the central bankers so they could act in support of gold values relative to dollars. This rescued the dollar and reestablished the dollar's value relative to gold. The London Gold Pool was abandoned in 1968; Bretton Woods ended at the time of the Nixon Shock in 1971. At that time, President Nixon ended the exchange of dollars for gold, that is, he closed the gold window. That action brought in the third monetary system, fiat.

The advantage of the Bretton Woods Agreement to establish the managed gold system was that it reestablished a monetary policy system after nations failed to restore the strict gold standard. This new system didn't universalize commodity prices or currency values with respect to gold but instead, the United States acted at the center of a system of exchange that offered increased stability by subsidizing gold's value and offering exchange with dollars at a stable rate. This was better than a twilight of money management in the absence of a strict gold standard. After WWII, trade was needed to restore the world's economic prosperity and to rebuild it after desolation had raked across most of Europe. WWII had proved that autarky wouldn't work in a market economy. But the market economies of the world needed trade to restore food imports/exports and product and materials imports/exports. Without such trade, shortages were severe. But Bretton Woods was more than just a monetary system for money exchange. It also established transnational regulatory agencies that pushed to open global trade and established neoliberal policy as an approach in foreign economies (more on Bretton Woods after the section on fiat money).

Fiat money systems have a limited lifespan and the greatest financial system volatility.

Filippo Cesarano, in his book, *Monetary Theory and Bretton Woods: The Construction of an International Monetary Order*, wrote that there were only three successful monetary systems in history.[197] In this discussion we included fiat in addition because it's the system under use currently. But probably, Cesarano didn't include fiat in his classification of monetary systems because fiat systems don't endure for long periods of time. And if a fiat system does endure, its currency depreciates in value. Today's fiat is a system of floating currency values exchanged on the global exchange market where valuations are determined by international currency trading demand.[198, 199] Under the managed gold system, the price of gold couldn't anchor other commodity prices. The value of gold set outside of the gold market, invalidated the "rules of the game" that had been integral to the strict gold standard. The stable thread of gold values that ran through commodity markets no longer could homogenize pricing or currency values. The end of the strict gold standard and transition to a managed gold standard had meant that the global commodity system of uniform and stable pricing was over. Later distrust reflected in NIEO battles was based in part on distrust because of non-uniform prices and values in trade. After prices around the world for factors diverged people began to believe that values and prices were being manipulated to benefit some more than others. The Nixon Shock along with OPEC agreements to raise the price of oil, created more price and value volatility. But volatility has been a hallmark of fiat currency money systems in history.

Fiat money has no commodity backing. It has been money that can't be redeemed for gold or any other metal. Instead it has been exchanged in transactions where it represented a value-holder based on the government's assurance that it would be acceptable as currency-of-the-realm and the public's confidence that it could be used for economic exchanges. Just like commodity based money, counterfeiting would be illegal. That's an important point because fiat money has involved a lot of money printing by governments. In the U.S. the Treasury has printed money at the behest of the Federal Reserve's Open Market Committee, out of nothing but paper with the loose idea that the amount printed should be based not on gold reserves but on the size of the economy and economic policy. The Federal Reserve has bought treasury bonds and issued an equivalent amount of currency. Old currency has been replaced by the Treasury when bills get worn out but the amount of money in circulation has been up to the Federal Reserve's discretion. The Federal Reserve can reduce the circulation of money by deciding to do so in order to slow down economic activity[200] or it can increase circulated money to speed up the economy.

The Chairman of the Federal Reserve sometimes has made controversial decisions because not everyone benefits from Federal Reserve policies. Chairman Volker restricted money in circulation in the 1970's to stop inflation which raised mortgage interest rates and Chairman Greenspan increased the circulation of money in the early 2000's to speed up the economy and lower interest rates. The Greenspan easy money stimulus encouraged the housing bubble. The Great Recession has pushed the Federal Reserve's monetary policies to their limit under quantitative easing (QE). Huge amounts of toxic assets were purchased and the treasury recapitalized banks with treasury money printed out of thin air. The government has been charged interest payments on the creation of every dollar. Those interest rates were lowered in order to reduce interest charges on government debt, but low interest rates have also hurt savers.

The Federal Reserve has raised interest rates or lowered them to adjust economic activity down or up, respectively, in commercial banking or in the discount rate of short term loans to other banks. It has also raised or lowered reserve requirements for commercial loans to increase or decrease circulating capital. A loose monetary policy with easy credit has sometimes speeded up the economy. To see if the system of values among foreign currencies has been stable, a comparison can be made of trading values between currencies over time. A nation's currency can lose value if it has been overprinted and over-circulated or if the government has risked default on its balance of payments or if the political regime has become unstable, for example. And fiat money has been thought to have a limited lifespan. Some claim the average lifespan for fiat money is only 34 years. Since there's no gold brake on government spending or on capital flows because of gold, fiat currencies tend to lose value over time because of currency overprinting.[201, 202, 203]

Understanding the advantages of each monetary system can clarify today's money problems.

Understanding neoliberal money depends on understanding the different advantages of each monetary system. Under the strict gold standard, bankers and politicians were forced into greater spending and capital restrictions. Those capital restrictions created more stability in both the politic and economy. The gateway from the strict gold standard to the managed gold system was the ravages of WWII, after other previous shocks, WWI and the Great Depression. When the restoration rule couldn't be implemented after world wars people needed a workable alternative. The managed gold system went into effect with less discipline over spending in the politic, looser monetary policy and expansion of capital flows at the financial industry's level. This led to economic inefficiencies. Built-in economic inefficiencies led to more inflation in the U.S. and fewer jobs, or stagflation. The eruption of fiat money after the Nixon Shock led to the loosest monetary policy of all three systems.

After the 2008 global financial collapse, fiat money has shown the limits of its flexibility. Four problems have surfaced. First has been fiscal debt, and the limit of fiat to address problems caused by fiscal debt. Second has been negative consequences of easy credit monetary policy and QE such as mal-investment (bubble economies). Third has been currency devaluation where a dollar can't buy as much as it once did even when other currencies have also lost value on the international foreign exchange. Fourth has been financialization, where the debt economy has grown but the means to lower debt by stimulating productive work has declined. No monetary system is infinitely flexible and a sound monetary system is necessary to create stable nation state politics. Nation states have experienced greater unrest since 2008. Next, consider the Bretton Woods Agreements. They were the historical moment of inauguration for the managed gold system which would eventually lead to fiat money.

Bretton Woods negotiations happened between the U.S. government and the British government before the other attendees arrived.

The Bretton Woods System was a UN meeting in New Hampshire that happened in 1944. Before the first official Mont Pelerin meeting, near the end of WWII, a United Nations Conference was held in the United States, called the Bretton Woods Conference. The UN was just forming at this time. The United Nations Bretton Woods conference in 1944 brought 44 Allied nations together to renew their alliances with each other. But the re-alliance would be under a new economic disciplinary structure that had been negotiated before the meeting by the declining and ascending Allied economic powers of that time— the UK and the USA. This new structure was the Bretton Woods Monetary System.[204] After the U.S. and UK had finished their negotiations, they assembled the group of 44 Allied nations to draw up the final treaty.

The policy-birth of neoliberalism and its planned global expansion dates from the incarnation of Bretton Woods disciplinary organizations, the IMF and the World Bank (the World Bank was once the IBRD, or the International Bank for Reconstruction and Development). These international organizations enforced neoliberal policies which were imposed upon the world's economies dating from the conference in 1944. The World Trade Organization was established only in 1995. Its incarnation was delayed by political resistance. After WWII people could only agree to GATT treaties and an effort to establish the ITO, International Trade Organization, failed to generate international support. Nations agreed to remove tariff barriers and barriers to foreign investments through a treaty process. The IMF was to provide loans to nations that had a shortage of funds to meet their sovereign debt obligations, or to help them restructure their debt by changing currency exchange values. The IBRD/later World Bank was intended to loan money for infrastructure in Europe and the underdeveloped areas of the world.[205, 206]

The political goal of globalizing trade by removing tariffs and the existence of transnational globalization organizations have outlasted the Bretton Woods monetary system (the managed gold system). The Bretton Woods System survived only until the Nixon Shock in 1971 when the partial gold backed money system ended.[207] Much of the Bretton Woods strategy was based on a theory of what was needed after WWII to restore prosperity and stave off further global warfare. It was hoped that freer international trade would allow countries to obtain goods through trade to prevent shortages and stop tensions that can lead to war. The Bretton Woods monetary strategy that treaty signees imagined into existence worked well to restore Europe's prosperity, to enhance American power and it prevented new global-theatre warfare in the short term.

Problems with Bretton Woods and the later fiat monetary system have been global.

Without a stable global currency, globalization under the Bretton Woods organizations failed to establish economic trust between nations. Values and prices have been unstable and inconsistent between nations and trading has happened in a context that lacks international legal oversight that might otherwise have protected social and financial interests. Bilateral agreements have begun to replace more pluralistic agreements. Also, trade agreements have become progressively focused on greater corporate welfare instead of community well-being. This shows neoliberalism's true benefactors to be corporate interests.

According to Elaine Bernard, in her essay, "What's the Matter with NAFTA?"[208] the purpose of NAFTA was to protect corporate interests by regulatory reforms that helped corporations. New protections of corporate profits and lower tariffs have been integral. NAFTA required some social services to become privatized. And according to this source, NAFTA made it harder for communities to regulate corporations to prevent them from harming community interests. When GATT treaties were blocked by public demonstrations, NAFTA was implemented to get around the public. Treaties such as NAFTA have blocked the government's ability to respond to public needs whenever meeting those needs could harm corporate profits.[209] Here again community interests haven't been supported while corporate interests have been.

Corporate interests have also been the point of the TPP negotiations. According to Joseph Stiglitz, the TPP, or Trans Pacific Partnership that is being negotiated behind closed doors, may be removing consumer protections or labor regulations.[210] Public opposition to and controversy about WTO meetings are a sign of worry about policy favoritism being enacted for corporations under government sponsorship. Therefore TPP negotiations have been happening behind closed doors in order to prevent public resistance to the parceling out of global opportunities between large corporations. These private negotiations may be externalizing harms to communities who lack any influence in the content of negotiations. This exclusion of public input and the extension of corporate advantages has led to social unrest.

Describing the Washington Consensus.

Considering the neoliberal emphasis on corporate welfare, leads to "The Washington Consensus". "The Washington Consensus" was an economist's description of neoliberal economic policies under the transnational organizations set up at Bretton Woods: the IMF, and World Bank. It has been the description that many have come to accept as providing a clearer picture of neoliberal economic policies. John Williamson was describing the minimum policy prescriptions recommended by neoliberal think tanks and Bretton Woods transnational organizations within the aegis of neoliberal economic theories according to the Chicago School.[211, 212] The Washington Consensus had ten policy goals that were designed to aid corporate transnational investments and to advance neoliberal policies. Goals included policies like reducing government overspending, tax reform to improve tax collections and penalties for tax non-payment, and tax reform to reduce progressive taxation and increase the tax base (taxing the bottom income brackets more), the utilization of market determined interest rates for loans, increasing foreign direct investment opportunities for multinationals, privatization of government services, and removal of tariffs.[213] These economic policies have been disruptive to previously accepted political policies. Revolutions have followed on the heels of these policy enactments in Latin America.

The possibility of positive economic outcomes for many stakeholders has been undermined by political instability when the Washington Consensus ten point program brought Chicago School ideas to nations abroad. Naomi Klein described economic problems following Chicago School prescriptions in Brazil, Chile and Argentina.[214] Neoliberal programs in Latin America have mostly come and gone, leaving a legacy of retarded development and a record of arrests and indictments issued against neoliberal instigators for crimes against persons or against society.[215]

Neoliberal global policies have been touted as a way to increase the world's productivity, favorably increase its political ties, diminish economic nationalism, and increase wealth. So many promises but they haven't become realized. Multinationals have grown in terms of access to capital, but people trapped in export economies face challenges that are hard to overcome in terms of their nation's economic development because they become trapped by debt and low wages instead of attaining economic independence. Economic stability has remained elusive throughout the global economic system. Neoliberal outsourcing because of mobile capital has created economic imbalances in both developed and developing nations (addressed soon during the discussion of financialization).

Law; deregulation and regulatory reform; dominance of the economist's cost benefit analysis; consequences of allowing corporations to regulate themselves.

In 1513, Niccolo Machiavelli captured the spirit of his political times in his book, *The Prince*. It was the first-text-ever of political realism. In chapter eighteen, Machiavelli wrote, "You must know, then, that there are two methods of fighting, the one by law and the other by force: the first method is that of men, the second of beasts; but as the first method is often insufficient, one must have recourse to the second." This section outlines how neoliberals have used law to change the politic and how applying the law has changed under neoliberalism. But keep in mind the quote from Machiavelli, because the next section will address how neoliberals have used war. Both, according to Machiavelli have been tools of the politic.[216]

In consideration of America's politic, legal actions have a different personality under each American political ideology. This has been because legal actions have been taken on behalf of different competing interests in a changed historical context under a different policy regime during each period. During classical liberalism, positive law, or law that would require certain actions, was rare; instead law protected liberty by limiting government. The "necessary and proper" clause and the concept of federalism were interpreted to protect individuals and states from unnecessary federal government power over liberties. During modern liberalism, positive law increased under the regulatory state when legislators passed laws that expanded their role. Increased political power because of bigger spending budgets under income taxes and other taxes increased the government's reach into everyday life. Even the size of government increased. The courts eventually supported the government's new regulatory role. Social optimism about the state acting in the interests of society led to the court reinterpretation of "necessary and proper" clause and a change towards "assumption of constitutionality" in legislation. This removed some of the protections of liberty law.

Modern liberal socialism began to gather political power inward toward the federal government. Progressivism and New Deal politics reshaped the role of the federal government. Also, the fourteenth amendment was interpreted to include personhood rights for corporations. This gave corporations a new kind of political power. Under neoliberalism, positive law has extended itself to the protection of corporate profit-making opportunities which have come to be in partnership with state authority. Public private partnerships are one manifestation of this relationship. Corporate welfare, deregulation and regulatory reform have revised Progressive and New Deal laws and changed them. No longer do old laws grant political advantages to labor or to the poor. At first, neoliberalism seemed to attack the regulatory state under regulatory reform and deregulation. But since the number of laws has only increased, it would seem that the regulatory state has been modified under deregulation/regulatory-reform to serve the interests of multinationals in finance and business.

The regulatory state, during modern liberalism, grew in response to market economy changes that caused society-wide disruptions in housing and employment. Modern liberal regulation was meant to correct problems. Regulators were trying to reduce public harms and thereby improve their political image as being helpful to the public welfare. The modern liberal regulatory state had regulated mostly to correct problems that threatened people's security for instance in labor, or transportation. New inventions in agriculture increased competition. Competition in agriculture reorganized farms which bought tractors and mechanical harvesters. New capital investments in modern equipment pushed sharecroppers out of making a living by farming. Agencies at that time came into being in order to correct harms to people displaced in the new economy, like sharecroppers. But later the neoliberal regulatory state gained a further ambition.

It began regulating to prevent harm. Starting in the 1960's and 1970's the regulatory goals of Congress began to extend to comprehensive oversight of every part of American life, from safety to quality in labor, energy, and the environment. Sub-agencies began to form inside other agencies like the Department of Education inside the Department of the Interior.[217] Continued regulatory expansion offended business interests. The business faction wanted to stop or change the regulatory state. According to the Office of Management and Budget, economists, during the Ford Administration began to change the way regulations were evaluated. The multiplication of regulations was a left-over from the Progressive era. Neoliberals supported a different kind of regulatory state: one that respected the needs of businesses to make a profit.

Every American president since President Ford has issued executive orders to modify how regulations are written and to try to reduce the number of existing and new regulations. When the economy slowed during the 1970's President Ford became worried that regulations were hurting business profits and causing unemployment. He asked the Office of Management and Budget (OMB) to do inflation impact studies for regulations under Executive Order #1182. The OMB became affiliated with another U.S. agency, the Council on Wage and Price Stability (CWPS), which was supposed to check the effect of regulations on labor and market prices. Economists in the CWPS introduced the **cost benefit analysis** to replace the inflation impact study. At first, this was controversial but this method was introduced at universities and used in college textbooks and it eventually took over the estimation of regulatory effects.[218] Under neoliberalism, deregulation and regulatory reform have proceeded on a cost benefit basis. And economists have influenced how cost benefit analysis studies are performed and interpreted.

President Reagan, in his "Address Before a Joint Session of the Congress on the Program for Economic Recovery," February 18, 1981, said "Adding to our troubles is a mass of regulations imposed on the shopkeeper, the farmer, the craftsman, professionals and major industry that is estimated to add $100 billion to the price of the things we buy, and it reduced our ability to produce... This plan is aimed at reducing the growth in government spending and taxing, reforming and eliminating regulations which are unnecessary and unproductive or counterproductive...American society experienced a virtual explosion in government regulation during the past decade. Between 1970 and 1979, expenditures for the major regulatory agencies quadrupled. The number of pages in the code of Federal Regulations increased by nearly two-thirds. The result has been higher prices, higher unemployment, and lower productivity growth."[219]

The nanny state made so many regulations that a person had to specialize in their scrutiny in order to understand what a regulation did.

After the nanny state grew larger in the 1960's and 1970's, regulations became so comprehensive that people had to split their discussion of regulations into specific categories. Regulation-piecemeal instead of regulation-in-total created a mosaic of new oversights and concerns. The economy had already become complex and its regulations became even more so. Along with transportation regulation, agricultural regulation and labor regulation, came environmental regulation, energy regulation, and many more kinds. To address anything about how regulations were formulated and enacted required in depth specificity. For instance, consider environmental regulation. Consider more specifically, how cost benefit analysis has served the process of evaluating environmental regulations.

According to Frank Ackerman and Lisa Heinzerling, cost benefit analysis has distorted people's evaluation of environmental regulatory costs and benefits. But to discover this requires careful scrutiny. That's because bogus numerical conclusions based primarily on imagined estimates of costs for imaginary circumstances have been used by experts as though they describe real world regulatory situations. A variety of distortions have been used as a rhetorical tool in order to make arguments against environmental regulation. Costs of regulations have been inflated, potential lives saved have been deflated, and some regulatory studies have claimed that regulations will be costly enough to diminish the life expectancies of the poor. This has been to argue in favor of less regulation. Less regulation would advantage corporations. These distortions were introduced into academia and have been cited from several authors many times until the distortion has eclipsed sight of the real.[220]

According to the Office of Management and Budget (OMB), there are three kinds of regulatory studies, a "monetized estimate" which counts dollars, a "quantitative estimate" that estimates non-dollar quantity parameters and a "qualitative estimate" which includes a verbal description. Economists put a premium on numerical estimates, but the OMB says that some parameters of regulatory concern can't be quantified because differences in kind are hard to tabulate into the same units for comparison purposes.[221] The translation of analysis into a numerical assessment of costs is another example of economism. And rhetorical deceits by statistical misinterpretation are an example of the politicization of economics.

Economists working to quantify outcomes often imagine possible outcomes and in accord with the principle of scarcity, they try to determine how much it will cost in terms of lost profits or lost life-years, etc. But these imaginary outcomes have been calculated estimates rather than real world measurements. They have exaggerated the costs and reduced the benefits imagined for regulation in examples cited by the authors.[222, 223]

Regulatory reform narratives have changed over the period of re-regulation because of harmful consequences.

Descriptions from the 1990's explaining motivations for regulatory reform sounded more optimistic than descriptions of reforms after consequences developed. Publications from the 1990's are rife with economic "efficiencies" to be acquired by shrinking the regulatory state. But later unforeseen costs have undermined other expected gains. And those costs have been paid by the public. From 1990's enthusiasm to 2008 dismay, optimistic claims about regulatory reform didn't prove true when they were compared to what people said in the twenty-first century. Early optimism of the 1990's has been replaced in the twenty-first century by pessimism based on bad experiences.

A publication from 1999, titled "The Effects of Deregulation on Competition: the Experience of the United States," sounded celebratory. Richard A. Posner, in 1999 wrote about deregulation of the financial industry: "Most economists agree that the net effect of the deregulation movement in the United States has been to increase efficiency, with resulting increases in consumer welfare... Banks are [were] limited in the number of offices they can [could] have and in their geographical scope, and are [were] blocked from entering complementary activities such as securities underwriting and mortgage financing, while other financial institutions are [were] barred from accepting demand deposits. Many of these restrictions have now been eliminated or relaxed, to the point where the financial-services industry can be regarded as largely though not completely deregulated."[224] This viewpoint contrasted sharply with later statements for instance about the financial problems in 2008. And consumer welfare has been shown since 1999 to have decreased in several financial scandals.

The next quote is from Bethany McLean and Joe Nocera's book, *All the Devils Are Here: The Hidden History of the Financial Crisis.* "A year earlier the president had signed a law that repealed Glass-Steagall, which had split commercial from investment banking so many years before. Gramm Leach Bliley, as the new law was called, also had Summer's strong support....the core problem was that even as the old regulatory firmament was disappearing, nothing was being created to replace it...There was nothing the government, or anyone else, could do to hold it back any longer. Some thirty years in the making, the financial crisis had finally arrived. The volcano had erupted."[225] The quote referred to Gramm Leach Bliley which was the last deregulation step to end Glass Steagall, and showed that regulations were needed (but lacking) to prevent the 2008 collapse. Their book demonstrated how deregulation caused a tsunami of banking problems from imbalances that occurred after deregulation that no one had any power to prevent. Many consequences of deregulation have led to long term losses after what at first appeared as short term gain.

These two sources show a cultural shift in how deregulation has been perceived. The financial market's complexity caused unpredicted changes after deregulation which caused unexpected harms. This has been true through-out neoliberal remodeling of the regulatory state. What has been troubling about neoliberalism has been the way that harms have been externalized to the public which grew accustomed to regulatory protections under modern liberalism. This change was politically possible after expansion and redirection of government power. Neoliberal opportunists took advantage to rearrange regulations to serve their interests. Public protections have been lost. And economic harms have been accumulating that weaken the overall economy even though some groups carry more economic burdens than others.

Other changes caused by regulatory reform.

According to Posner, who wanted regulatory reform, deregulation can cause change to erupt in markets. Deregulation can cause changes in the organizations that make up an industry, how much innovation happens in the industry's market, changes in costs and prices, and adjustments in the thinking of managers. Furthermore, the costs of deregulation can fall onto people who don't benefit in any way from the new regulatory structure, and people in different groups might be affected differently. Deregulation can change wealth distribution in society because it gives corporations broad new powers to shape their markets. It reduced wages by getting rid of government sponsorship for organized bargaining among groups that lobbied for higher wages during the New Deal period of modern liberalism. The unpredictability of these outcomes can be attributed in part to the complexity of large economies.

Despite Posner's comments about economist's optimistic assessments, the neoliberal goal of reaching greater "efficiency" isn't regarding how to use resources less wastefully or how to preserve free choice among consumers or how to reduce government regulatory expenses. Instead greater efficiency has been a goal to give corporations the kind of power that governments have had in the past to determine how they will develop market opportunities. Deregulation and regulatory reform have been efforts to take government out of the economic driver's seat and put corporations into it. A quote from neoliberal economist Wilhelm Ropke's *The Social Crisis of Our Time* ties in with this idea of corporate control, "Instead of transferring the direction of the economy to the state, could one not confidently entrust it to the professional and business associations, made up of non-political experts, the trusts, co-operatives, labor unions and production groups, in short is it not possible to make use of the magic formula of "corporativism"?"[226] Unfortunately, in the U.S. since the Ropke quote was written just after WWII, competition, accelerationist policy (explained shortly) and regulatory reform have enhanced the power of the largest corporations and eclipsed the power of small businesses and unions. In the political determination of who gets what, it has been obvious that corporations wanted political advantages as much as politicians did. Reasonable legal oversight to prevent fraud and theft are important whether politicians or corporations organize the economy. But partnerships between the government and the corporation increase moral hazard which has led to failures of prosecution for social harms.

Neoliberals have taken it on faith that corporations would follow sensible market plans which would not endanger or destroy their markets. This attitude came from the efficient market hypothesis. But ongoing problems stemming from 2008 financial collapse have shown that the finance industry can be motivated by short term gains, just as was seen of politicians organizing the economy during modern liberalism. That has meant that economic interests have been no better at organizing markets than political interests have been. Factions have had an impact on information and have possessed political influence that can distort policy planning away from society's best outcome and toward outcomes maximized to benefit corporations. Organizing for the short term has caused harms in the long term. In addition, externalizing risks and consequences to larger society causes social harms. And the financial markets continue to resist regulation that would stop them from endangering social assets and wealth. This has created widespread social, political and economic insecurity. Corporatists have been oblivious to the connected nature of the whole economy where economic losses externalized to the public can't really be escaped. The unhealthy economy is the outcome.

Posner's four areas of regulatory reform had effects that have damaged consumer choice.

Posner identified four areas of deregulation: energy, communications, finance and transportation. One of the consequences of regulatory reform in communications has been mergers of media companies that have destroyed American access to source variety among information resources in the United States.[227] Five or six media giants control most media in the United States.[228] This endangers freedom of the press in terms of content. Quality news access hasn't been available in terms of issues that were once part of coverage under earlier regulatory requirements in broadcasting for fair and accurate content.[229] Media ownership among a few companies has expanded media opportunities to limit and control content.

But the move to deregulate was originally anticipated as a way to expand media and provide opportunities for expanding new technologies. Instead it has increased mergers and information monopoly. According to neoliberals, this may be more efficient because it consolidated corporate media power. But it has failed to serve Americans in their need for understanding issues that affect government and industry in the politic and economy. Also, America has gotten behind many other nations in broadband opportunities both in terms of access and pricing. Allowing corporations to control their markets has seemed like a mistake in the communications industry from society's perspective.[230]

Deregulation's consequences mean that Congress failed to write good policies for society.

In terms of the four areas of deregulation named by Posner there have been a number of problems that have hurt larger society. To discover what the problems were and how regulatory reform contributed to the problems requires research into laws and specific industries, as mentioned earlier. If you actually investigate specific laws that regulate specific industries you will inevitably have to examine the actions of your nation's Congress. Congress oversees the nation's legislation. Most people don't take much time to appreciate legislation but under the regulatory state, legislation affects most every aspect of American life. Congress's loyalty to corporations under neoliberalism has been obvious if you look at legislation since Truman, after Bretton Woods was organized by FDR and Truman empowered the CIA to begin its covert operations. Lately, the expansion of government into healthcare has further enlarged the federal government's power over individuals.

The 2008 financial recession was the consequence of legislative remodeling in response to financial industry lobbying. Corporate money dominance further shaped legislation in post-2008-crash lobbying. Failures to prosecute financial frauds that caused significant social harms, and the continuation of too-weak financial corporate regulation have shown that legislation continues to fall short of protecting the public. Here's a quick recap. It will show how Congressional legislation over several administrations altered the opportunity set relied upon by the financial industry to make a profit and reduced public protections against financial fraud. From the public's point of view, these deregulatory reforms have been policy failures.

The Great Recession shows a pattern of policy failure. The public wasn't protected from financial harm either before or after the 2008 collapse. Prioritizing the public's well-being has continued to be absent in policy design.

Securitization was invented by the government to organize FHA and VA loans in 1970 in Fanny Mae and Freddy Mac.[231] Securitization turns a loan into a commodity that subsequently gets a risk label and becomes marketed on Wall Street as a tradable asset. There were also a number of legislative changes Congress initiated that caused the buildup of market toxicity. The 1980 Depository Institutions Deregulation and Monetary Control Act "abolished state usury caps," and got rid of the legal distinction between a loan to buy a house and a loan for house improvement. The 1982 Alternative Mortgage Transaction Parity Act (also known as the Garn-St. Germain Depository Institutions Act) allowed the marketing of ARM's (adjustable rate mortgages; they caused many defaults when the housing market collapsed).[232] The 1986 Tax Reform Act (also known as REMIC, Real Estate Mortgage Investment Conduit), allowed mortgage securities to be pieced into tranches of securities at different levels of perceived risk.[233] The REMIC law redirected the consequences of mortgage payment from loan issuers, so that bad loans weren't the issuer's problem.

Congress also passed the 1999 Graham Leach Bliley Act to repeal the last of Glass Steagall bank solvency protecting regulations under the Banking Act of 1933 that had separated commercial and investment banks. This crucial separation under Glass Steagall had kept FDIC insurance exclusive for commercial banking only and not for investment bank gambling on Wall Street. The 2000 Futures Commodity Trading Act also allowed market toxicity to grow under unaddressed financial imbalances because it kept the derivatives market largely unregulated. The derivative market has become more than ten times larger than the real market of services and goods trading. That has encouraged speculation to replace production in the U.S. economy. These laws removed protections to society and made the mortgage business heat up. That heating up was really just the buildup of toxicity. Failures to prosecute financial frauds that happened in the toxic mortgage security crisis in 2008 have been characteristic of government and corporate collusion to exploit financial opportunities for finance insiders at the public's expense.

Deregulation caused money from other potential economic investments to course into mortgages, ratings agencies, mortgage appraisal groups, and mortgage securities, including collateralized debt obligations. Money moving through the mortgage industry motivated fraud. Rating agencies overrated financial securities as AAA safe without fully understanding mortgage securities risk.[234] Mortgage companies made mortgage contracts with unqualified buyers using unverified information. These earned the nickname of "liar loans" in the financial world.[235] Property appraisers inflated values of properties for sale. Mortgage title filing procedures were neglected. Goldman Sachs bet against the same securities that it recommended as a good investment to its clients. Insurance carriers insured coverage on securities products that weren't studied or understood. Illegal short-cuts led to subsequent disaster.[236] All of this became an economic tornado that **destroyed 47 trillion dollars**, according to one source.[237] But no significant criminal prosecutions of bankers, mortgage lenders, rating agencies, appraisers, or brokers has happened.[238]

Without meaningful prosecution, people who lost their investments due to fraudulent product misrepresentation have never been compensated. According to Charles H. Ferguson writing in *Predator Nation: Corporate Criminals, Political Corruption, and the Hijacking of America*, there has been widespread evidence of fraud and criminal behavior that happened to cause the financial problems of 2008.[239] Legislators in Congress claimed the excuse that the financial system had to be saved. But the idea that further financial sacrifices were needed from American bystanders in place of criminals who should have been prosecuted in court, has demonstrated a lack of resolve to implement the rule of law under existing statutes. Further it has shown a permissive Congress, enabling deregulated finance to be rewarded by receiving Treasury money to replace bad subprime loans.

If legal processes had been followed instead of obstructed by the Attorney General and others, legal satisfaction that protected individual investors from losses might have compensated individuals for the problems that deregulation had caused. Fraud would have received the penalty it deserved instead of financial bonuses. According to Ferguson, deregulation of finance has been criminogenic; the financial industry has become a parasite that drains vitality out of the rest of the economy. To learn more about the 2008 financial collapse, read *All the Devils Are Here: the Hidden History of the Financial Crisis,* by Bethany McLean and Joe Nocera. To learn more about the larger financial industry, read Charles H. Ferguson's *Predator Nation: Corporate Criminals, Political Corruption, and the Hijacking of America* or view his DVD, *Inside Job.* To learn about the history of bubbles in financial investment markets, read *Panic: the Story of Modern Financial Insanity,* edited by Michael Lewis.[240]

Neoliberal policies to deregulate the financial industry have caused harms that have already been long lasting and which still persist.

Every day, the financial industry affects both the economy and the politic in America. Conflicting interests between investors and savers, between banks that want to embrace risk and ordinary workers who depend on solvency and use money in their everyday life are in play all the time. High levels of sovereign debt among nations puts governments in the position of borrowing money and brings them into the financial play by play as non-neutral participants. Proper regulation could balance all of these interests while deregulation has increased imbalances. The gradual repeal of the Banking Act of 1933 caused financial catastrophe in 2007. But after the securities market blew up, Congress stepped in to limit harms to the financial industry and brought consequences onto American society instead. And Congress failed to reinstate the regulatory precautions that had safeguarded the American banking system in the public's interest in the Banking Act of 1933.

Congress's desire to protect bankers shows its commitment to corporations ahead of society. Members of Congress have argued that they had to save banking by providing it with American tax dollars in order to save the economy. This argument ignored many other viewpoints. It ignored the misplaced faith that neoliberals had in corporate self-regulation that began regulatory reform. It ignored the regulatory role of Congress that caused new problems. Congress also has failed to meaningfully change regulation in finance to protect society from insolvency since the collapse in 2008. According to the *New York Times,* the House of Representatives passed eight bills in 2013 softening and repealing parts of the already too mild Dodd Frank regulations in response to lobbies working for the financial industry.[241]

Congress's actions since the 2008 financial collapse have accomplished the opposite of the goal of the Banking Act of 1933. It was written to safeguard savers but under the Congress in session in 2008, long after the repeal of the Banking Act of 1933, bankers have been protected and society has been harmed. Congress' decision to implement TARP and QE after the 2008 collapse was a subsidy for the financial industry instead of a penalty. And it was a subsidy not only to commercial interests but also to speculative investors at the periphery of risky finance. Americans outside of finance were harmed when they were stuck with an expense that they didn't owe. The expense of the 2007-2008 financial collapse has had both political and economic ramifications for the future of America.

Congress allowed the Federal Reserve and Treasury to take dramatic steps to "save the financial industry", but Congress had caused financial problems to erupt in the first place, because it removed the protections that once had safeguarded banking solvency. Problems from 2008 have been ongoing. The 2008 collapse increased debt for most Americans. Many lost their homes and looked financially better on paper after they were divested of the balance left on their mortgage but all home owners experienced a significant loss of property value.

The 2000 Commodities Futures Modernization Act also contributed to the 2008 collapse. It left derivatives such as the toxic mortgage securities unregulated by the CFTC or any alternate regulator.[242] Regulators weren't allowed to voice concerns about the securities market which had divorced loan making from loan paying. Without the potential of money losses for lenders because securitization prevented losses at the lender level, loan makers were less concerned about mortgage qualification. After mortgage securities began to flood investment markets, the rating system falsely rated them as AAA. No regulatory system inquired about the basis of those ratings because Congress reduced or stopped regulatory oversight. The negative outcome of the Great Recession that reeks of policy failure hasn't been acknowledged as a failure that would require redress with a different set of policies. Banks have continued to hold everyone's money at risk.

According to Charles Ferguson, part of the trouble with the financial industry is that it has become cartelized by too few very large banks. These are the Too Big to Fail Banks. This has been a consequence of regulatory reform. According to him, five banks control all but 5% of global derivatives trading. Only about twelve banks control the LIBOR. IPO's (initial public offerings) are divvied up between about five large banks, setting uniform fees. Risk indexes have become influenced by these same big banks.[243] Deregulation has allowed banks to control their markets, and to grow ever larger but not in society's best interests.

It's important to notice that after being granted expansive powers by Congress to shape their market, banks haven't become stronger, or more secure. And the financial world has expanded to poach opportunities for production investment by substituting speculation instead. Banks risk more than they should and externalize losses. Externalizing loss jeopardizes and harms economies around the world. The size of derivatives markets and HFT has expanded well beyond the confines of real production markets because innumerable bets can be made on a single outcome. This also increases risk. And the American housing market hasn't recovered. There have been fewer jobs, a depressed economy, and too many empty overpriced houses.

The economy has been less active and more insecure. The Federal Reserve failed to prevent the Great Recession and it issued a lot of dollars to be held in central banks in Europe and the U.S. This was an experiment to see if monetary policy could reduce severity of the oncoming economic downturn by recapitalizing large banks and taking the smaller failed banks out of operation. All that money has trapped and immobilized American prosperity. Despite labor non-participation at record levels, fewer available jobs, and low velocity of the dollar, stock market highs remain because of a combination of corporate stock buy-backs, HFT and Federal Reserve QE. Nevertheless, the economy's real production, sales and performance have continued declining. And the idea that high stock market valuations represent economic recovery is wrong. Stocks require a buyer for the stockholder to realize money from an investment in the stock market. But the values of stocks have been artificially inflated not by robust individual investors like the ones that bought stocks in the past, but by corporate buy backs financed by debt and by Treasury purchases financed by debt.

The Federal Reserve has set up its policies to avoid deflation but avoiding deflation by pumping money into the stock market and central banks hasn't helped economic growth. It created the illusion that demand exists when demand has declined. It prevented prices from falling when they should fall to reflect true value losses. Americans feel economically insecure because they are economically insecure. Corporatists have re-legislated to their advantage, and now the rest of America can't renegotiate for broader prosperity because prices and values aren't tied to markets. Instead the Federal Reserve has propped them up. Everyone's treading water in a huge and seemingly bottomless pool. But swimming in debt will never restore American prosperity. Regulating the financial industry to rebalance social interests has been strongly resisted by bankers. The financial doldrums have continued in the meantime.

Grain markets show that neither the federal government nor financial interests have regulated grain as successfully as a market can.

Recall the tragic imbalances in agricultural markets caused by nation state subsidies for grain that happened in the U.S. and Europe in the early twentieth century. Politicians thought they were enhancing food security. They brought tax subsidies to bear in supporting more grain agriculture and caused a market glut that exploded like a bomb in agricultural markets and that caused the Dust Bowl in the United States.[244, 245] That event was a historical example of how governments don't succeed when they try to affect or control an agricultural market. As a reaction that offered an alternative to government controlling markets, neoliberals put corporatists into the driver's seat of the economy. They did this by accomplishing regulatory reform through Congress that gave corporations more control over their markets. How has this affected grain markets in the twenty-first century?

According to one source, neoliberals have increased the price of grain after the 2008 financial collapse by large percentages that have hurt the poor. They did this by exploiting arbitrage opportunities in high frequency trading for grain commodity futures. The traders have affected markets by buying grain options in large quantities in order to bid up the price of grain. After the price increases, they can cancel most of their order but also benefit from the price gain that they caused. Under the Commodities Futures Trading Act, which President G. W. Bush signed into law, "financial players" can "profit from changes in food prices."[246] Neoliberals have caused price increases which have caused social unrest in the Middle East, Africa and Latin America.

These price shifts have happened independently of supply and demand. According to this source, 61% of wheat futures market is investment opportunity for financial speculators such as Goldman Sachs.[247] It seems clear from this example that corporations don't belong in the economy's driver's seat any more than government bureaucrats did. They aren't managing market opportunities but are instead manipulating markets to their own short-term advantage after regulatory reform removed consumer protections. Notice that government bureaucrats caused an accidental grain market glut in the early twentieth century, while grain speculators in commodity markets now, are acting as middle men to raise prices and make money for themselves while cheating poor people of what would have been a cheaper price if prices were based on real demand within the production market. They are toll gathering insiders of trading circuits at society's expense. They will only stop when laws are enforced that prohibit this rip off.

Examples of landmark cases in the neoliberal justice system and what they show about neoliberal courts.

There are more neoliberal landmark court cases by far than the number of them during the modern liberal or classical liberal period. After the expansion of the regulatory state into most aspects of people's lives during the early neoliberal period, numerous conflicts arose. Out of the list of landmark cases provided by Wikipedia[248] some broad generalizations can be made. And further research into case briefs or more detailed sources can provide more extensive case information. One observation about neoliberal landmark cases is regarding the number of cases brought to court in specific categories of actions during the neoliberal period. The category where most cases were addressed was regarding the behavior of police considered in the context of a person's constitutional rights. It's unsurprising that this would be the largest category since a multiplication of laws and regulations would naturally cause complications for law enforcement.

Rulings on topics from searches and seizures, to warrants for electronic surveillance, to issues of capital punishment, to the right to have an attorney and the right of the executive branch to seize corporate property were made during this period. There were more than forty cases on these kinds of issues involving police arrests, terrorist detainments and executive power. Regarding property nationalization, for example, the Supreme Court ruled against President Truman in *Youngstown Sheet & Tube Co. v. Sawyer, (1951).*[249] The next busiest category was free speech under the First Amendment. There were more than twenty rulings on topics related to free speech, including draft card burning and flag burning, issues to do with pornography, and issues of free expression.

More than twenty rulings were also made to resolve conflicts between church and state in the public schools, in public office and regarding federal funding. Other important areas of landmark legislation included issues related to civil rights and desegregation of public facilities (seventeen rulings), women's rights (fourteen), and issues regarding elections (eight). Controversy also erupted out of The PATRIOT Act and issues of both interracial marriage and same sex marriage, issues of contraception, corporate influence on elections and gun rights under the Second Amendment. Some issues had few court case rulings but outcomes that caused concern among specific groups included property owners, Native Americans (treaty rights), Supreme Court rulings that affected environmental regulations regarding carbon dioxide, genetics patents and healthcare under the Affordable Care Act. Legal oversight of every aspect of people's lives can hardly become more extensive. But this has created too many laws for most people to really keep track of. And government regulatory power has invaded private life.

Controversies have been common in the neoliberal period. One early example was FDR's executive order #9066, which authorized the removal of Japanese Americans to internment camps during WWII. The Supreme Court ruled in 1944, in *Korematsu v. United States,* that Japanese Americans could be deported to holding reservations and they lost their property and liberty. The Supreme Court also ruled that this action was constitutional at the time, even though a number of the Japanese people were American citizens. Many Americans now regret that this happened. The Civil Liberties Act of 1988, under the Reagan administration, granted limited reparations of $20,000, to surviving Japanese Americans who had been interned.[250] This historical sequence shows that political actions can take a long time to play out in the executive, judiciary and legislature. Justice can be slow, inconvenient and incomplete.

The PATRIOT Act of 2001, has also caused controversy. It has provisions that were used by the NSA and FBI to justify internet data mining, which has been an ongoing controversy that has become familiar to people who care about privacy. Breaches of *habeus corpus*, the use of rendition, the use of torture, the existence of a Presidential kill list are all actions by the executive branch that have alarmed people. Rulings have happened in response to a few issues related to these controversies and some of them happened simply to clarify the court's authority to rule on them. But many of these issues are still playing out in the legislature, executive and courts. Justice remains in motion and many issues await a court hearing, or a series of court appeals. Of course, the Supreme Court can choose not to hear some issues. And political interests can sometimes prevent the appearance of malfeasance or controversy by discouraging litigation in the first place.

Also, pardons can stop a penalty that could be determined by the judicial system. For example, President Obama pardoned Bush administration officials for any wrongdoings that offended constitutional law in their handling of terrorism issues. Eric Holder reviewed instances of torture in the U.S. service corps and failed to prosecute members of military leadership even for fatal acts of torture. Also interesting, have been breaches of privacy for data mining by the FBI or NSA that were undertaken under the PATRIOT Act, and FISA (Foreign Intelligence Surveillance Act), sometimes under gag orders written into National Security Letters. Congress wrote amnesty clauses into spy legislation that immunized internet companies for breaches of privacy whenever they provided access for spy agencies. These clauses inoculated internet companies from litigation for privacy invasion by offended internet customers. Spy agencies such as the NSA also paid $3,500 per internet tap that rewarded internet providers for giving access to federal agents.[251, 252] This amnesty ahead of time or after the fact for breaches of constitutional rights and natural rights has seemed incongruous in a Constitutional Republic that is a rule of law nation. These examples also show that neoliberal justice has become transactional instead of penalty based.

Describing twenty one neoliberal landmark cases that demonstrate a change in how the court views four groups of issues.

Here is a brief description of a few landmark Neoliberal cases. There has been a lot of Supreme Court activity since 1944. Selecting only some cases from the Wikipedia landmark cases listing,[253] here are only twenty one cases out of 177 that will be briefly described. They have been selected to show changes in how the neoliberal court views four groups of issues.

The first group of issues concerned natural rights including property ownership, and constitutional rights (mostly the First, Second, Fourth, Fifth, Sixth and Fourteenth Amendments); these issues affect individuals during interactions with police or a government bureaucrat. The second group involved election issues. The third group included landmark cases that dealt with executive power to extinguish a person's ability to resist the government's direct power to issue a directive or to incarcerate without recourse to court oversight under *habeas corpus*. The final group of landmark cases dealt with science according to a Supreme Court declaration. A Supreme Court declaration clarified regulatory oversight in one case, and in another case provided a ruling on whether a company could obtain a genetic patent.

The landmark cases can show you how legislation or executive action or a lower court ruling eventually led to Supreme Court decisions. Landmark cases also show how the neoliberal court interprets the U.S. Constitution. Court scrutiny over issues brought about by the multiplication of Congressional legislation has gone further toward increasing government influence over people's lives and the multiplication of laws continues to complicate and diminish American freedoms to conduct domestic business, utilize health resources, and enjoy liberty. And it seems that court rulings get increasingly narrower.

The first group of landmark court cases included the greatest number of any group considered. Here are eleven cases involving the police. Mostly these involved individual interactions with police or a government bureaucrat. In 1966, in *Afroyim v. Rusk*, Beys Afroyim, a naturalized American citizen voted in the 1951 Israeli government election and was denied American citizenship under Section 401e of the 1940 Nationality Act by the U.S. State Department. The Nationality Act stated that an American citizen voting in the elections of another nation would lose their right to citizenship. The issue was whether a law passed by Congress could revoke a person's citizenship. The issue went through the District Court and the Second Court of Appeals until it was taken up by the Supreme Court which overruled the lower court's rulings. The Supreme Court ruled that a person could give up their citizenship voluntarily but the Congress could not revoke it through legislation.[254] This decision was a five to four decision.

Another case showed an individual's struggle for civil rights after he was committed to an insane asylum. This case was, *O'Conner v. Donaldson (1975)*. The case was an early effort to reform protections for the rights of persons confined under a mental illness diagnosis. The Supreme Court took up Kenneth Donaldson's case after he had struggled to get out of an asylum for years and had finally been released. The Supreme Court ruled that prolonged confinement against a patient's will couldn't be automatically acceptable after a mental illness diagnosis unless the patient was likely to harm himself or others. The Supreme Court also ruled that a mental health hospital could be required to award damages if the facility violated the patient's constitutional rights.[255] This decision was a unanimous Court decision.

The next landmark case in this group, *Bivens v. Six Unknown Named Agents of Federal Bureau of Narcotics (1971)*, pertained to a person's right to sue for damages from harm caused by federal agents acting under the color of the law but outside legal guidelines such that they trespassed against a person's constitutional rights. Webster Bivens was at his apartment with his family when six federal agents entered, handcuffed him and searched his apartment. The search happened without a warrant or probable cause. Bivens was arrested, brought to the

Federal Courthouse, visually strip searched, interrogated and booked for arrest but the drug charges were dropped after the U.S. Commissioner dismissed them.

Bivens sought damages in the amount of $15,000 per agent. After both the District Court and Court of Appeals dismissed Biven's complaint on the grounds that it was not an actionable claim, the Supreme Court took it up, and found in favor of Bivens based on Fourth Amendment Protections. The Fourth Amendment states, "The right of the people to be secure in their persons, houses, papers, and effects, against unreasonable searches and seizures, shall not be violated, and no Warrants shall issue, but upon probable cause, supported by Oath or affirmation, and particularly describing the place to be searched, and the persons or things to be seized."[256] This decision was six to three.

The next case showed a Supreme Court ruling to balance moral concerns about abortion that arose years after *Roe v. Wade (1973)* with a woman's right to terminate her pregnancy. This case was *Planned Parenthood of Southeastern Pennsylvania v. Casey (1992)*. This Supreme Court ruling upheld *Roe v. Wade (1973)*, but added some new requirements claiming that states had an appropriate interest in the life of the unborn and therefore the Supreme Court added new "undue burden" standards to replace the trimester schedule under *Roe v. Wade (1973)*. Clinics that provided abortion services would have higher reporting standards, and women would be provided with "informed consent" papers regarding their abortion procedure.[257] This was a five to four decision. Public controversy regarding abortion has continued to the present-day.

The next case regards artificial life support for patients who have become physically unable to maintain their own life. It addressed the state's prerogative to extend life when the patient's family would choose to end life support. The case, *Cruzan v. Director, Missouri Department of Health (1990)*, involved Nancy Cruzan, a twenty five year old who had been injured in a car accident, and placed on artificial life support. After five years without improvement, the family wanted to terminate life support feeding so that their daughter could die.

The state was already paying for her care after the family could no longer afford to pay. The issue was whether the state of Missouri or the Cruzan family should decide to continue or terminate her care; the state's Department of Health wanted to continue giving life support and the family wanted to end it. The Supreme Court ruled that the state of Missouri should decide her life support status unless the family possessed a document that could prove that Nancy Cruzan would choose death. Today people call these kinds of documents "living wills". After the Supreme Court ruled that the state possessed the power to determine Nancy Cruzan's life support status, the state of Missouri ruled in a separate proceeding that care could be terminated; Nancy Cruzan died several days later.[258] This decision was a five to four decision.

The kinds of crimes that can justify a death penalty were determined in, *Kennedy v. Louisiana (2007)*. The case involved an African American man who was found guilty of child rape but in a state that would send black child rapists to death more often than white child rapists. The Supreme Court, in a 5/4 decision found that according to the Eighth Amendment, the death penalty for rape would be inappropriate.[259] The Eighth Amendment reads, "Excessive bail shall not be required, nor excessive fines imposed, nor cruel and unusual punishments inflicted." Today, the death penalty can be applied only for murder or treason.[260] This decision was a five to four decision.

The next court case was mentioned earlier. It involved property rights of homeowners in the City of New London in Connecticut. In *Kelo v. City of New London, (2004),* the city used eminent domain to take homeowner's houses (with compensation) in order to redevelop the land in a scheme that was expected to bring money into the community. Many of the residents didn't want to sell their houses. But the City of New London was offering the corporate pharmaceutical firm Pfizer tax incentives to relocate to the residential area and the planning group wanted to bring in other businesses as well to stimulate the local economy and raise tax revenues. The Supreme Court referred to the Fifth Amendment in their ruling.

The Fifth Amendment reads, "No person shall be held to answer for a capital, or otherwise infamous crime, unless on a presentment or indictment of a Grand Jury, except in cases arising in the land or naval forces, or in the Militia, when in actual service in time of War or public danger; nor shall any person be subject for the same offence to be twice put in jeopardy of life or limb, nor shall be compelled in any criminal case to be a witness against himself, nor be deprived of life, liberty or property, without due process of law; nor shall private property be taken for public use without just compensation."

Residents of New London said that the city couldn't take their land if it wasn't for a public purpose. The Supreme Court ruled in New London's favor in a five to four opinion that "pubic use" wasn't a literal term that required a "public purpose" or community wide benefit. Previously, the idea of public use in cases of eminent domain had excluded economic development.[261] The ruling has remained controversial. Afterwards, forty state legislatures wrote laws to make eminent domain for economic development purposes illegal at the state level of eminent domain.[262]

Another landmark case is *Riley v. California (2013).* David Leon Riley was a gang member. His cell phone was examined by police at the time he was arrested after he was apprehended driving a car with expired registration stickers. His driver's license was also suspended at the time which led police to impound it. At the time of the arrest, his cell phone, which was in his pocket, was taken by police. Two guns were also found in the impounded car. Those guns were tested and linked through ballistics to a drive-by shooting of a car filled with a rival gang. The cell phone contained photos that caused police to link him with the Lincoln Park gang of San Diego and because it provided these clues, it led police to do the ballistic testing that linked him with the drive-by shooting.

Riley was convicted on three counts: "shooting at an occupied vehicle", "attempted murder", and a firearm assault. The police believed that they were acting within the law when they examined Riley's cell phone; Riley's attorney appealed his conviction based on police cell phone examination being classified as a warrantless search. The appeal would be under the Fourth Amendment, which reads, "The right of the people to be secure in their persons, houses, papers, and effects, against unreasonable searches and seizures, shall not be violated, and no Warrants shall issue, but upon probable cause, supported by Oath or affirmation, and particularly describing the place to searched, and the persons or things to be seized". In a unanimous decision, the Supreme Court ruled in Riley's favor. They said that a cell phone is a data filled computer and it doesn't fall into the same category as a threat object like a gun, or a personal belonging such as a wallet. The court ruled that a warrant is necessary to search a cell phone unless a police emergency indicates the need for instant access.[263]

The next landmark case is *Montejo v. Louisiana, (2008)*. This case involved the Fifth and Sixth Amendments. The Sixth Amendment reads: "In all criminal prosecutions, the accused shall enjoy the right to a speedy and public trial, by an impartial jury of the State and district wherein the crime shall have been committed; which district shall have been previously ascertained by law, and to be informed of the nature and cause of the accusation; to be confronted with the witnesses against him; to have compulsory process for obtaining witnesses in his favor, and to have the assistance of council for his defence."

Jesse Montejo was convicted of murdering Lewis Ferrari during a burglary. At the time of his arrest he had waived his Miranda rights (based on *Miranda v. Arizona, (1966)*). The state of Louisiana had automatically assigned him an attorney. But before Montejo spoke with his attorney, he was interviewed by police. During the police interview, Montejo agreed to help the police find the hidden murder weapon and he agreed to write a letter of apology for the murder to the victim's wife. When the attorney met with his client, the attorney said that the cooperation of his client prior to talking with council produced evidence for Montejo's trial which was inadmissible.

Montejo's conviction had resulted in a death penalty. Mr. Montejo's attorney appealed the conviction. The Supreme Court decision was five to four and it found for the state of Louisiana. To find for the state of Louisiana, the Court overruled an earlier case, *Michigan v. Jackson (1986)*. This case had determined that a person's waiving of their Miranda rights was overruled when they requested an attorney at the time of arraignment and this meant that police couldn't interrogate without the lawyer's presence at the time of questioning. But in Louisiana, the defendant was automatically assigned an attorney and had no opportunity to declare for one. The Supreme Court ruled that *Michigan v. Jackson (1986)*, was unworkable in jurisdictions that assigned council automatically. It ruled that Montejo's self-incriminating evidence which was obtained before he spoke with council was admissible and that the conviction would stand.[264, 265]

The next landmark case involved firearms and the Second Amendment. The Second Amendment reads, "A well regulated Militia, being necessary to the security of a free State, the right of the people to keep and bear Arms, shall not be infringed." The case, *McDonald v. Chicago (2009)*, was brought to the Supreme Court in response to Chicago's gun bans. This case and others like it had already been dismissed by the Federal District Court and by the U.S. Court of Appeals. But another Supreme Court case, *District of Columbia v. Heller (2008)*, had already decided that a gun ban in Washington D.C. was unconstitutional. The Supreme Court chose to hear *McDonald v. Chicago (2009)*. It was found by the Supreme Court in a five to four decision that the right to self-defense is protected under the Second Amendment and also this right carries into the states by the Fourteenth Amendment, Section One, which reads, "All persons born or naturalized in the United States and subject to the jurisdiction thereof, are citizens of the United States and of the State wherein they reside. No State shall make or enforce any law which shall abridge the privileges or immunities of citizens of the United States; nor shall any State deprive any person of life, liberty, or property, without due process of law; nor deny to any person within its jurisdiction the equal protection of the laws."[266]

The final landmark case in the first group of eleven is *Salinas v. Texas (2012)*. In a double homicide case, a man agreed to come to the precinct to be questioned by the police. When the officer asked him if his gun would match the murder weapon, the man didn't answer, even though he had answered other police questions. When his gun was tested, ballistics testing showed that it was the murder weapon. The man went on the run and evaded the police for fifteen years. But later when he was located, he was convicted on the evidence obtained in part from his interview and then from the ballistics test.

The man's attorney said that Salinas was protected by the Fifth Amendment against self-incrimination during the police interview. The Supreme Court found that a person's immunity from self-incrimination must be specifically invoked and that a person's silence isn't enough to protect them under the Fifth Amendment. If a person invokes Fifth Amendment protections, the police can offer immunity or argue that the question would not be incriminating. The Supreme Court also said that if evidence were obtained under coercion, it would not be admissible, and that a person doesn't have to attend a court proceeding in order to claim Fifth Amendment protections.[267] This case, like the previous one, was important in revealing a trend of less protection during police questioning.

The next four landmark cases involved elections. One case demonstrated that the federal constitutional framework for congressional terms can't be changed or usurped by the states and the other cases showed the growing power of corporations to influence elections. According to Justice Stevens, Americans have always fought to keep corporations out of election politics. And opposition to corporate influence in the elective process has a basis in common sense observations about the "for profit" nature of corporations, their "limited liability" immunities and the "transactional nature" of politics in the corporate sphere, as well as the quid pro quo potential of election funding.[268]

The first landmark case concerning elections, *U.S. Term Limits v. Thornton, (1994)*, involved laws that states passed to limit the terms of their own Congress members. Arkansas passed laws limiting House of Representative terms to three elected terms and Senate terms to two election cycles. In a five to four ruling, The Supreme Court ruled that states can't limit the terms of their Congress members because to allow such a limitation would undermine the Constitution's rules. What this case showed was the frustration of states that view longer terms of Congressional service to be against their state interests. Federal politics in Washington D.C. can be far removed from the ordinary concerns of states like Arkansas. The decision invalidated twenty three state's laws limiting Congressional service.[269, 270]

The next three cases have contributed to an avalanche of laws where the Supreme Court has tolerated greater influence of money in elections and in opposition to recent legislation already in force that sought to reform elections. The rulings overall make arguments that say that money can be a kind of speech. It can create election influence from information offered in broadcasting or money advantages channeled into politics by supporters. The court has shown support for the idea that money should influence the politic. If money can bolster political influence, the court's ruling reinforces the idea that a purchase is like a ballot. Recall that Friedman and von Mises envisioned that a purchase could be like a ballot. But preventing corruption by bribery has been a concern of the court in the past.

During the period of time for *Buckley v. Valeo (1975)*, The Federal Election Commission (FECA) was set up to oversee elections and prevent corruption. The link between money and favors was obvious to people in politics at this time, just after Watergate, when public cynicism was on the rise. Preventing governmental corruption was a topic of consideration in the context of election reform. The FECA set limits on electoral expenditures. The Supreme Court in a seven to one decision overruled limitations on overall campaign expenditures but allowed restrictions on each person's contribution to an election candidate.[271]

In 2008, the most controversial election landmark case of *Citizens United v. Federal Election Commission* was ruled on by the Supreme Court in a five to four decision. The ruling happened in the context of another election reform effort, The Bipartisan Campaign Reform Act (BCRA). The BCRA restricted "soft money" donations to political parties, banned the solicitation of such donations by candidates, put limits on ads sponsored by unions, corporations and not-for-profit organizations for sixty days before an election and limited the amount of political party funds that could be used on advertising.[272]

The Federal District Court had ruled to prohibit the showing of a film, "Hillary: the Movie" that was to be shown close to an election, in an injunction that considered a preceding case, *McConnell v. Federal Election Commission (2003)*. The Supreme Court threw out the injunction, overruled *McConnell v. FEC (2003)* and partially overruled *Austin v. Michigan Chamber of Commerce, (1989)*. The Supreme Court ruled that funds from corporations could not be limited in election broadcasting under the First Amendment. The First Amendment reads, "Congress shall make no law respecting an establishment of religion, or prohibiting the free exercise thereof; or abridging the freedom of speech, or of the press, or the right of the people peaceably to assemble, and to petition the Government for a redress of grievances."

The Supreme Court ruling considered money spent for advertising as speech freedom for corporations. It viewed corporations as having the right to express political positions in broadcasting. The Supreme Court ruling supported the ban on direct corporate and union donations to candidates.[273, 274] This ruling has encouraged a blooming controversy which continued under the next landmark case, *McCutcheon v. Federal Election Commission (2013)*.

McCutcheon v. Federal Election Commission (2013), was another five to four ruling that happened in the context of the Bipartisan Campaign Reform Act (BCRA). The case was brought by Shawn McCutcheon who wanted to donate more money to the Republican National Committee but was prevented by the BCRA's aggregate amount limit. The Supreme Court found that the aggregate limit interfered with McCutcheon's free speech expression through money donation. Henceforth, according to Justice Clarence Thomas, the BCRA should undergo strict scrutiny to determine whether its provisions would stand under tests of First Amendment protections.[275]

But this ruling with the others, shows the Supreme Court's determination to erode the Congress's efforts to limit organizational influence upon elections in favor of individual influence. They showed the Supreme Court on the side of corporations and big money. These rulings have provided greater opportunities for organized groups to influence elections. Preventing corruption of elective offices by money donations, preventing corporate influence over elections through broadcasting, incentives by elected officials to pay back major contributors by tailoring their legislation to corporate interests, the overwhelming money power of corporations as compared to persons, has been ignored by the Supreme Court even though these topics were of greater concern in the past. These narrow rulings regarding free speech issues attached to campaign reform ignored the characteristics of corporations and organizational politics and put the political realm into the hands organizations that often have no personal interest in politics at all. Their interests are profits not principles. These rulings show the Supreme Court's failure to defend public interests at the level of individuals. These rulings also reflect the importance of organized politics in the neoliberal period.

The next four cases involve the executive branch of government and its power to oppress individuals and groups and also its power to resist oversight. The first case is *New York Times v. United States (1970)*, a case that was similar to *United States v. Washington Post Co. (1970)*. These cases were decided together in a six to three ruling by the Supreme Court. The issue was whether the Defense Department could withhold the Pentagon Papers from being published. These documents were regarding U.S. actions during the Vietnam conflict. President Nixon argued that national security was threatened by information in the Pentagon Papers. The Supreme Court ruled that this "classified information" should be made publicly available for First Amendment reasons under freedom of the press.[276]

The next landmark case wasn't a Supreme Court Ruling. Instead it was a ruling under the Foreign Intelligence Surveillance Court (FISC). The FISC was set up by Congress under the Foreign Intelligence Surveillance Act of 1978 to oversee intelligence activities in a secure and classified environment. The Chief Justice of the Supreme Court appoints federal judges to the FISC. FISC rulings can be reviewed and changed by the Foreign Intelligence Surveillance Court of Review and by the Supreme Court. Published opinions of the FISC are sometimes released with large redactions.[277] The large, sometimes almost complete redactions have been criticized by the ACLU. The ACLU has suggested that redactions should only "protect information" that is "properly classified" for a specific reason[278] and not wipe out the entirety of content.

Materials have been classified not only by the nature of the information itself but also by what the information reveals about methods of collection. Some of these collection methods have recently been found to be unconstitutional. In FISC cases, judges have been unable to forbid data collections by government agencies that went beyond legal avenues of access. For this reason, NSA and FBI actions have come under criticism while the FISC has been embarrassed by its lack of power to prevent actions that breach Fourth and Fifth Amendment privacy protections under the Constitution.[279] Fear of terrorists and fear of terrorism has led to justice department inertia with regard to protecting constitutional rights. Judges didn't want terrorists to gain an advantage that would allow them to harm Americans. The Judges and FBI and NSA employees may have imagined that harm at the hands of terrorists would be worse than the momentary loss of constitutional protections.

The landmark case of interest, *re Directives (2008), pursuant to Section 105B of the FISA Act,* determined that the Fourth Amendment's warrant requirement could be ignored in the case of specific kinds of surveillance. Surveillance for national security purposes conducted to intercept information from foreign powers or agents of foreign powers that were located outside of the U.S. could be legally conducted in the United States. This directive recognized the intelligence advantage of internet development in the United States. Internet transmissions along fiber optic cable or phone lines would travel by the least expensive route and much internet traffic from foreign locations went through the United States. The directive sought to take advantage of internet routing to spy on terror networks. But according to The New York Times, July 6th, 2013 article written by Eric Lictblau, "In Secret, Court Vastly Broadens Powers of N.S.A.", an intelligence source told Lictblau that "The definition of 'foreign intelligence' has been very broad", and a variety of threats have qualified under the umbrella. According to Lictblau, the FISC court has never refused any requests from intelligence agencies, though it has modified them.[280]

Controversy erupted after the NSA and FBI used the PATRIOT Act (2001) to conduct electronic data mining of U.S. internet accounts and phone accounts. There was controversy for at least four reasons. One reason for controversy was because of National Security Agency letters (NSL's) that were issued that forbade American internet executive operators to talk to anyone about the government's demand of customer account access. These letters alone were a cause of controversy. They forbade all speech about the NSL's specifically and also about the government's access.[281, 282]

According to the ACLU, "In 2008, a federal appeals court ruled that an analogous gag order provision relating to "national security letters" was unconstitutional."[283] But additional controversy came out of improper access to communications that offended Fourth Amendment privacy protections.[284] Also, payment to internet providers at $3,500 per information tap, utilized tax monies to pay for breach of rights protected under the Constitution.[285] And Congress provided amnesty for the breaches in its spy legislation so that internet providers were exempted from civil lawsuits.[286] A fourth reason for controversy was the fact that the intelligence services improperly shared their unconstitutional access to internet and phone accounts with other crime fighting government organizations in a further breach of Fourth Amendment protections not permitted under FISC guidelines.[287] These issues were brought to people's awareness by Edward Snowden,[288] the ACLU, Nicholas Merrill (an internet site provider) and other worried Americans.

Two other landmark cases originated from controversies about executive power during conflicts involving the Middle East. They are *Hamdan v. Rumsfeld (2005)*, and *Boumediene v. Bush (2007)*. In the first case, *Hamdan v. Rumsfeld (2005)*, Salim Ahmed Hamdan who was imprisoned in Guantanamo Bay, petitioned for a writ of *habeas corpus* in order to challenge his imprisonment. He was afterward classified by a military court to be an "enemy combatant." But the district court ruled that he would be given a hearing to determine if, under the Geneva Convention, he should be tried by a military court. The DC Court of Appeals reversed the decision. This led to a Supreme Court proceeding where the court found for Hamdan in a five to three decision. The Supreme Court ruled that a military court wasn't authorized under the Constitution to rule in

Hamdan's trial and neither was the Presidential or Congressional power capable of assigning Salim Ahmed Hamdan's case to a military court.[289]

After *Hamdan v. Rumsfeld (2005)*, Congress legislated to get around *habeus corpus* rights affirmed by that decision. It passed the Military Commissions Act of 2006 (MCA). This act tried to change federal court jurisdiction so that detainees couldn't challenge their imprisonment by using *habeas corpus*. The case *Boumediene v. Bush (2007)*, went through the D.C. Circuit Court twice; on the second appeal, the prisoners said that the Suspension Clause in the Constitution's Article One, Section Nine made the MCA unconstitutional. The Suspension Clause reads: "The Privilege of the Writ of Habeas Corpus shall not be suspended, unless when in Cases of Rebellion or Invasion the public Safety may require it." The D.C. District Court had found that the detainees couldn't use *habeas corpus* to challenge their detention because of the Military Commissions Act and because Guantanamo was outside the United States. But in a five to four decision, the Supreme Court reversed the D.C. District Court ruling. The Supreme Court ruled that the MCA was unconstitutional and the Guantanamo detainees could challenge their imprisonment under *habeus corpus* even though the Cuban base was outside of the United States.[290]

The next landmark cases are examples of the Supreme Court making a fact determination that influenced the granting of a patent or the extent of regulatory reach. The first case is *Massachusetts v. Environmental Protection Agency (2006)*. Controversy about science topics occasionally enters the public's awareness and the controversy over greenhouse gases and their effects on temperature or climate has been longstanding. In this case the state of Massachusetts wanted the Environmental Protection Agency (EPA) to regulate car emissions for carbon dioxide under the Clean Air Act of 1963. The EPA was reluctant to do so because the extent of carbon dioxide's effects in the environment has remained controversial. The D.C. Court of Appeals ruled in favor the EPA's reticence and their decision not to regulate. But the Supreme Court, in a five to four decision overruled and decided that Massachusetts could sue the EPA for potential damages if it failed to act. The issue of how to prove causality between carbon dioxide levels and global warming was the basis of the EPA's reticence, so the Supreme Court ruling was a politicized determination that didn't stand on an uncontroversial and clear scientific basis. Nevertheless, Justice John Paul Stevens saw global warming as a threat to Massachusetts "quasi-sovereign interests" as a state.[291]

The last landmark neoliberal case to be considered here is *Association for Molecular Pathology v. Myriad Genetics (2012)*. This case concerned the patent for genes BRCA-1 and BRCA-2. These are genes where inherited genetic mutations cause breast cancer. Myriad Genetics which held the patent, was challenged by the Association for Molecular Pathology. The challenge was based on the recognition that genes are found in nature. And according to patent law, a product of nature can't be patented. But Myriad claimed that by isolating and discovering the genes it had removed them from a natural context as part of an undistinguished massive number of genes in the human genome. The District Court had ruled that genes were a product of nature and that they couldn't be patented. The Court of Appeals for the Federal Circuit overruled, saying that isolated genes have been removed from the context of nature and are therefore patentable.

The Supreme Court overruled. It ruled that discovery in a laboratory and isolation of a gene sequence doesn't remove it from the context of nature. According to the Supreme Court, a genetic sequence found in nature isn't patentable. This ruling was a unanimous nine to zero ruling. The Supreme Court also ruled that the synthetic creation of a new sequence of genes or proteins that are unique and unlike a natural product is patentable.[292] This idea may protect the patent rights to genetically altered slower acting and faster acting insulins, for example. These genetically altered insulins have been produced by *E. coli* bacteria genetically enhanced for that purpose in a laboratory.

Legal controversies aren't always brought to court, but legal arguments can still be made to clarify issues at stake.

Controversial legal issues have also arisen regarding the partial privatization of the U.S. military. But the Bush Administration kept this issue out of the courts in the case of missing money and equipment as shown in a Vanity Fair article that will be quoted shortly. Military action in concert with private military corporations operating as assets for the U.S. military in the Middle East has led to worries among people living abroad who are subject to violence at the hands of private security companies. Civilians have been killed and harmed. Excessive corporate violence outside of military guidelines has resulted in death, and torture but potential litigants have been blocked from obtaining legal remedy by at least five legal obstacles.

These legal obstacles arise in part because of jurisdictional confusions as to available legal remedies outside of the U.S. physical territory. But also, legal obstacles can be a convenient political dodge for the U.S. government's actions abroad. According to Jenny S. Lam, writing in the *California Law Review,* "Accountability for Private Military Contractors Under the Alien Statute," the five legal obstacles include: (1) *"forum non conveniens"* (2) the requirement that local legal remedies should first be exhausted (3) "the political question doctrine" (4) "the government contractor defense" and (5) "the state secrets privilege."[293] More discussion on U.S. militarization will be considered in the section dealing with neoliberal war.

One of the few potential avenues for legal redress in the U.S. court system for crimes that private security companies commit against foreign nationals may be by tort litigation under the Alien Tort Statute which was passed during the classical liberal period, in 1789. Under this statute a private military corporation may be prosecuted if either (1) the litigant is a foreign national (2) the offense is a tort offense or (3) the violation of tort is either against the law of nations or against U.S. treaty.[294]

The Alien Tort Statute (ATS) was applied only once in its first 172 years of existence. It was used in *Filartiga v. Pena-Irala*, in 1980 for the torture and subsequent death of a Paraguayan man by a Paraguayan police officer after both sides in the lawsuit, the deceased person's family and the accused had immigrated to the United States.[295] Since that case, the ATS has been applied in a series of court cases involving private security companies, some of which are discussed in the article mentioned above by Jenny S. Lam. She provided information helpful to understanding the judicial issues that individuals face in trying to get justice for government actions and private military corporation actions that have caused them harm. She showed the hurdles and failures of justice and gave the legal reasons for this failure. She also argued for a more just outcome and described the benefits that society would gain from legal penalties applied to individuals that harm others outside the rules of war under the color of law in places such as Iraq.

One of Walter Lippmann's observations during modern liberalism (in 1936) about legal oversight was the advantage of money in civil lawsuits that provided non-criminal court remedy for tort offenses. He also wrote in *The Good Society*, "The business corporation, as we know it, is founded on the fact that legislatures and courts gradually invested incorporated associations with new rights, rights which did not exist a hundred years ago, rights which can, therefore, by no stretch of the imagination be regarded as anything but conditional and subject to alteration."[296] Little did he imagine that those corporate rights would be extended further. He didn't foresee the advantage that corporate money provides in politics that has allowed even more legislative changes to further advantage corporations. This can be observed in regulations that affect finance, for example.

He further didn't realize that global multinationals would operate in a global legal vacuum because of jurisdictional confusions when several partial owners residing in different nations operate companies abroad. Money has provided corporations huge advantages that has given them dominance in court contests where individuals can't bring the same capital advantages. Individuals also can't compete with corporate immortality. Corporations can appeal court findings and endlessly litigate whereas an individual can't. Private military corporations can be perceived in the nations where they operate as both powerful and unaccountable to ordinary military standards for operations in a military theater.

Neoliberal legal controversy shows regulatory expansion's negative consequences.

Neoliberal law as understood through these examples shows consequences that have arisen in a complex legal environment under a host of regulations that constantly increase. Ever more narrow rulings show two things. First, narrow rulings show that courts have already produced rulings that cover many details of social interactions in a legal environment that grows ever more complicated. Second, narrow rulings show that the U.S. courts have penetrated into life's minutiae and they don't recoil from regulating most details of people's life. Courts show that they approve of political oversight in what was once considered private life; issues of terminating life support, abortion, and marriage. The growth of the surveillance state, spying on people's e-mails, and phone conversations show a further invasion of privacy. National Security letters trespass against First Amendment, Fourth Amendment, Fifth Amendment, and Sixth Amendment rights. The neoliberal Supreme Court also has helped corporations and organizations to be more influential in elections. Political money used in elections makes ordinary Americans worry about corruption permitted by the neoliberal courts. And legislation that has provided tax loopholes to multinational corporations has given the largest corporations advantages not shared by businesses that operate in a domestic context without foreign subsidiaries. Examples of regulatory reform showed how corporations have used representative government to get the legal system that they want. Their super-human corporate power gives them advantages that individuals lack. A legal vacuum in which private security companies operating in the Middle East committed crimes shows what happens on a global stage without global legal oversight.

Failures to prosecute the financial industry after the 2008 financial collapse have highlighted the size advantage of corporations and their entanglement with government. The proliferation of regulatory oversight and comprehensive legislation has led to an overly complex legal environment that still has failed to regulate American companies operating abroad. Neoliberal regulations have stimulated domestic litigiousness and opposed earlier American traditions in classical liberalism's protections for liberty under a prosperous commonwealth practicing economic liberalism and commercial freedom. They also have behaved contrarily to modern liberalism's optimism regarding the government's positive role in regulating a prosperous society where individuals would experience economic security. Neoliberal law has failed to properly administer justice within the context of political policies that affect economic outcomes. Ever more powerful corporations in the economic driver's seat have failed to produce political or economic security.

As the next section on war comes into focus there's something new to consider about war making. It begins with global trade's consequences to war making. As Richard Cobden argued back in the classical liberal period, one of the goals of open trade has been to reduce hostilities between nation states by using trade to give nation states more interests in common. During the history of war's destruction of property and human lives, harms were externalized to the losers. But externalizing harms didn't work after the industrial revolution improved the tools of war. Destruction was too widespread and too expensive in an economically connected world of nation states. War reparations payments after WWII were required of Japan and Germany, but they didn't pay for the full cost and consequences of the war.[297]

After WWI, bankers in Europe and America invested in the rebuilding. Their investments were shared among both winners and losers. Losses from WWI couldn't be externalized to the losers, though Europe tried to do so by forcing Germany to pay extensive reparations. But Germany got loans from the Dawes and Young plans under the ruse of paying reparations and then used the money to build the German war machine.[298] Germany chose war instead of repayment. The bankers and industrialists that had made investments in Germany didn't want to lose their money which they'd sunk into Germany's factories. Instead of stopping the growth of Hitler's war machine, they watched it grow in hopes that it would secure their investments in German industrial companies.[299]

When the Allies tried to externalize costs to the loser of WWI, Germany, they motivated Germany to manufacture war materials for WWII. Germany couldn't make good on the debt and it needed to get out of making payments. Renewed war was seen as a way out of debt. The winner of the next war wouldn't pay for the last war. But then Germany lost WWII and it still couldn't pay. That shows how externalizing losses couldn't work in the global market economy; investments were scattered across the developed world and economic outcomes would affect the entire globe. After WWII reignited fighting in Europe, the damages of that war cost even more. Previous wars had made money for munitions and war supply companies, construction companies and also increased banking transactions as rebuilding proceeded. But costs and consequences negatively affected everyone, even in financial and political groups. The rebuild was costlier and everyone had to pay for it.

Globalization has brought an important question to consider. That is whether war costs can be externalized or whether economic interests in common have made that now impossible to achieve. A related question regards the legitimacy of war among trading partners. Can violence be meted out on moral grounds against people who no longer seem so foreign, since their nation supplies goods in the pool of international trading? Have nation states come to inhabit this one world as a shared space where war or economic prosperity are shared more equally? Is war winnable economically? And if it isn't winnable economically, how can it be winnable politically? Can the nation state system resist warfare as a prerogative of power?

War in the neoliberal era.

War and finance are connected by money. War uses money and creates debt. Here's a historical overview of the war/finance symbiosis since the Revolutionary War until now. It recapitulates some economic and political lessons from chapters one and two. The overview shows how society's political and economic choices can be shaped by public and private organizations that exist as part of government and business. Because war causes the most harm to those of lesser political power and economic means, the history of war also shows how power in banking and the military requires restraint in the interests of broader society. The American Revolution disrupted the monarchic system and facilitated a transition to classical liberalism. Similarly, the American Civil War disrupted states' rights in the classical liberal system and facilitated a transition to modern liberalism. World War II, likewise played a role in the transition from modern liberalism to neoliberalism. But it's important to remember that war accomplished disruption and offered little more. War alone couldn't accomplish a stable transition. Organized interests in the politic and economy prepared for these changes and made way for them.

The American Revolutionary War and the War of 1812 of the classical liberal period were expensive conflicts with financial obligations which necessitated the creation of the First and Second Bank of the United States (BUS) to help organize debt payments. Controversy about money's role from economic factions outside of financial interests in the U.S. interrupted BUS operations both times and they closed down. The Civil War incented the Union side to begin taxing income which ended economic liberalism in the North when the Union side began its income tax program and in the South when the South lost the war. The Sixteenth Amendment made income taxes permanent and served the political purpose of increasing the power of the government by increasing the size of its purse.

Under modern liberalism, the federal regulatory state grew inside the mixed economy. WWI ended the global system of commerce that used the strict gold standard sponsored by the UK. WWI was an expensive conflict which left a residue of lasting economic problems that led eventually to WWII. The U.S. had been under an independent free-banking system after the end of the second BUS, but nevertheless had benefitted from global economic stability under the influence of the UK's strict gold standard. Global markets that had traded under the authority of market based gold values lost their anchor after WWI. Prices and values became unstable. The Federal Reserve was created by Wilson in 1913 under the Federal Reserve Act. It organized central banking for the U.S. which has been with us for about a hundred years. Central bankers in Europe and America have combined their money power in order to influence the world's economy and politics.

After the Great Depression and WWII, U.S. taxes were higher, the government bigger and the world got by under Bretton Woods on the managed gold system. The managed gold system was a monetary policy that expanded sovereign debt and capital flows. The London Gold Pool, during the Kennedy Administration and outside of the public's awareness, was an example of central bank cooperation between European banks and the Federal Reserve to buy and sell gold in order to affect its price relative to the dollar. That stabilized the gold peg at 35 dollars per gold troy ounce for about ten years. After the Nixon Shock, people around the world have experienced increasing volatility under the fiat money system that came after Bretton Woods ended.

Public and private debt in the U.S. have increased under financialization. The federal government's debt is over 17 trillion dollars in 2014. Now, economic freedom has been replaced by financial obligations under the debt economy. The IMF and World Bank have used debt as a tool of political manipulation in foreign nations during the twentieth century to encourage the spread of neoliberalism and for this reason large pools of debt in the U.S. are especially worrisome as a source of political vulnerability. The UK has dipped into IMF funds and it's easy to wonder if the U.S. may be moving toward its own IMF loan. Such loans hamper political freedoms. Opening up trade for globalization was a political obligation enforced by the IMF on other nations by debt obligation. And debt economies have grown in most nations. Financialization has eclipsed many other economic opportunities in non-financial sectors of the economy. It shows us, as seen earlier in the BUS periods, the conflicts that arise between economic interests inside and outside the financial industry when banks gain too much power.

War and debt have changed the politic and economy underway in the United States in each historical period. In the present time, increased speculation has replaced investment in production and the market economy has begun shrinking. The market economy may come to an end under unstable values and prices and risky finance. War played an important role in these transformations. It has acted as a tool of destruction that has brought political chaos. Debt has also been a tool that has established both political and financial obligations. Wars in the Middle East have cost U.S. taxpayers at least four trillion dollars with projections of further expenses going to six trillion dollars.[300] Considering this war debt next to the cost of the 2008 financial collapse should convince you that war and finance are combining to change America's political and economic options. The CIA's history shows change in the nation's war objectives during neoliberalism.

The CIA has been more than most people thought that it was.

The National Security Act of 1947 created the Air Force as a separate military service category, the National Security Council, the Office of the Secretary of Defense, and the CIA, or Central Intelligence Agency.[301] In 2007, *Legacy of Ashes: The History of the CIA*, was published by Doubleday. Tim Wiener wrote it and got a Pulitzer Prize for his measured prose retelling of the CIA's actions during and after the Cold War. He researched carefully and revealed detailed happenings that differed from earlier press statements that had been released in the United States. Those earlier press statements had hidden real events of the moment. For example, CIA records and "sworn testimony" from CIA officers that was declassified between 1998 and 2004, gave a different account of the Kennedy assassination than press reports had given.[302] Weiner wrote that Lee Harvey Oswald, an American Marine married to a Russian woman had defected to the Soviet Union in 1959.[303] Wiener wrote about Harvey Oswald's meeting with an agent from the KGB Department of Assassination prior to the Kennedy assassination.[304] This report puts the Soviets and Cubans on one side and two of the Kennedy brothers on the other as counterparties in the Cold War attempting assassination as a political expediency.[305]

Wiener also revealed CIA covert actions conducted in at least eleven countries during the Kennedy administration.[306] He told the story of the CIA operations on a timeline to make sense of seemingly senseless acts that began when Truman gave symbolic "black cloaks, black hats" and "wooden daggers" to the Director of the CIA and one of his CIA associates.[307] The cloak and dagger symbolized nefarious operations that were to remain secret and for that reason almost politically unstoppable. Confusing military actions such as invading Vietnam when the Gulf of Tonkin attack was a fabrication[308] didn't really make sense to many Americans even in the context of the Domino Theory of the Cold War. Weiner's book cleared up some confusions that were allowed to persist from the earliest to more recent CIA history.

CIA actions have been publicly denied by Presidents but supported by them behind the scenes from Truman to Eisenhower to Kennedy in the early years. In later years, Reagan was connected to the Iran/Contra scandal, Carter to arms/hostage trading, Clinton removed Cedras from Haiti's government and put in Aristide, the Bush Administration has been connected with extraordinary rendition and scattered international torture facilities, Obama has been connected with the drone kill list. Secrecy has obstructed CIA accountability in various instances to the President, to other agencies and to ordinary American citizens. But secret aggression supported by U.S. taxes has occasionally become publicly known. And CIA scandals have breached outward political decorum again and again.

First term Presidents who brought in a new administration, but who didn't get elected after serving as Vice President, have come into office uninformed about ongoing CIA operations. They have inherited the CIA's set of current operations when they take the office of President. These operations have been outside constitutional boundaries. The CIA's secrecy keeps its missions from being stopped by constitutional power limitations. Some CIA records that would provoke controversy are still being withheld from the public[309] while other CIA records have been deliberately and illegally destroyed.

To explain the expansion of covert CIA actions after WWII, you should go back to the context of the World Wars. Recall that WWI and WWII showed the futility of Germany's autarky and America's isolationism. Germany's bid to expand by invading other nations failed when Allied powers of Europe and the U.S. united to defeat her military. Germany's bid toward empire also failed in part because Germany couldn't be self-sufficient and because the Allies cut off Germany's access to raw materials supplying her war machine. Germany was dependent on imports.[310] After WWII, the U.S. instituted the Marshal Plan which provided aid and began to assemble global trade connections.[311] Treaties such as the Paris accord, and Agreement for Intra-European Payments and Compensation, allowed the U.S to proceed, according to Adam Lebor in *The Tower of Basel: The Shadowy History of the Secret Bank that Runs the World,* with "imposition of a new transnational financial, economic and political structure, whether the people of Europe wanted it or not."[312]

Although colonialism ended when the U.K. and other European nations pulled back their naval authority and let their colonies self-assemble into more independent states, the temptation of access to raw materials, and cheap labor in less developed regions remained irresistible to neoliberal politicians and corporations. Neoliberals used the CIA's hidden money resources to shape nation-state economic options over time under the neoliberal world plan, now called the International New World Order. Wiener showed in his book that the CIA was not very successful at knowing what would happen ahead of time in the world events that it monitored—that it failed at spying.[313] Wiener wrote that the CIA's deceptions to the President, to Congress and to the public made it less effective by hiding its failures. With failure hidden, the CIA couldn't improve by addressing its own shortcomings. And these hidden shortcomings became missed opportunities to improve, Wiener believed. The CIA failed to know or report secrets before everyone else knew them.

But despite Wiener's able timeline, and detailed descriptions there's another important point that can be made from the information in Wiener's book. Spying out intelligence and finding out secrets may not have been the CIA's most important mission. Instead, it may have been more important that it guard American economic interests. Access to trade for European and the U.S. multinationals was a prize that the CIA arranged covertly by driving other competitors from the economic field. The CIA denied market access to communists. This was achieved by CIA's sponsorship for insider political competitors in foreign nations who would overthrow politicians who might ally with a communist country. These political competitors were often found in the military and they would set up a dictatorship. The U.S. would recognize their power as long as they supported open markets and agreed to spurn communistic advances. For the U.S., imbrication into global trading networks that it dominated, was a strategy to achieve economic dominance and to win political contests. It was a strategy to resist the advance of communism on the world stage.

Neoliberals fought communists in the Cold War to deny them access to the global trade network. Toppling governments and inserting U.S. approved heads of state, covert acts of espionage, support of insurgencies, sabotage, assassination and organizing criminal elements to fight for the CIA[314]—-all these tactics kept capital assets in the trading network out of the reach of communists and other non-neoliberal political competitors. Even foreign national leaders, such as Indonesia's President Sukarno, who said they wanted neutrality during the Cold War were targeted for removal.[315]

Anytime communist governments began to form, and especially when they were negotiating ties with other communist governments, the CIA caused an insurgency by providing money or military training or military supplies to their opposition. The CIA agents and foreign persons who died in those insurgencies and covert operations made way for neoliberal trading and development deals. More importantly, such actions blocked communists from making deals that would form a competing trading network. Wars between nations during classical liberalism were often over territory. But wars among nations in already formed market economies during modern liberalism and neoliberalism were about market and trade access. During the neoliberal period, the clandestine service of the CIA did a good job at ruining market opportunities for anyone not a neoliberal.

American neoliberal military goals have been more aggressive in terms of their global reach than at other periods in American history. According the Deepak Lal, as mentioned earlier, U.S. military objectives have been organized by the idea of empire keeping.[316] Empire keeping has been helped by new technologies in the Digital Age. Digital Age investments have been concentrated in three areas. These three areas have provided a measure of greater social control which has been an alluring political goal. They are the military, media entertainment and finance. Unfortunately, these areas have relied on superior access to data speed and capability that is exclusive. What that has meant is that larger society can't use IT advances to create economic growth as well as sponsored industries, the military, finance and media that can provide political advantages. Some have seen IT as the silver lining of military investment but its tendency to remain exclusive has kept it from benefitting most of society. Because it has been predominantly in industries that siphon money out of the economy for political gains instead of aiding production, IT has made people poorer.

Preemptive war under the George W. Bush presidency was a new American war strategy based largely on technology superiority but it has been a policy that many have opposed.[317] It has been called the Bush Doctrine. U.S. investments into 700 military bases scattered in 130 foreign nations[318] show military support for a neoliberal trading empire based on open trade among neoliberal nations. Significantly, the neoliberal empire still lacks a global currency. And defending "American interests," has come to mean aggressively pursuing U.S. economic interests for multinational corporations through political alliances including alliances that rely on America as the world's military force by proxy. This saves other allied nations from funding their own militaries. But it offends American traditions that respect nation state autonomy and the preservation of liberty at home under classical liberalism and abroad under modern liberalism.

American citizens don't support this empire role, nor does the American economy have the power now to pay for this goal. According to Lal, the Wilson Doctrine of sovereign state self-determination dominates most of America's thinking.[319] As empire policies marched forward under neoliberalism, Americans have protested. The Vietnam protests were an important example. That was the moment when Americans said no to the military draft. People supported their children's evasion of the draft for operations that didn't make military sense because they were happening for the sake of corporate market access. The National Guard took over military operations requiring soldiers on the ground after Vietnam. This was a volunteer force taken from the economically most disadvantaged Americans. They would seek military service as a form of employment and training.

According to Andrew Bacevich in his book, *The New American Militarism: How Americans Are Seduced By War*,[320] failures can already be recognized in the Bush Doctrine. Bacevich identified four failures. First, in Iraq, preemptive war failed because it took ten years when it should have been quick to finish. Second, it showed a lack of depth and staying power in the small military force even when PMC's (private military companies) were utilized. Third, it revealed a failure of strategy among commanding generals when they failed to recognize that greater aggression would increase resistance, and fourth, it revealed a failure of military discipline when torture was employed in Abu Ghraib.

The use of torture, according to Bacevich, invalidated the possibility of a moral justification for military actions taken in Iraq. For all these reasons, the Bush Doctrine of preemptive war failed.[321] And despite significant military investments, the world isn't more peaceful or more economically productive. An effective war machine can't also erect markets where social unrest prevails. Private contractors in charge of rebuilding after military bombing haven't executed design-build contracts successfully to repair significant damage. Wars take time to repair and the neoliberal economy lacks long term goals. In Iraq, a new war strategy was tried which failed according to Bacevich. But it brought forward a host of questions. In Iraq, the presence of private military companies meant that privatized war destruction had become linked up with war reconstruction performed by multinationals as an economic opportunity.[322]

This combination of destruction and reconstruction may be an outgrowth of earlier-period infrastructure-building in developing nations that was described by John Perkins in his 2004 book, *Confessions of An Economic Hitman*.[323] Perkins' book described how he was hired to oversee development projects in underdeveloped regions so that foreign construction companies from the U.S. and Europe could make money during the time period 1963-1981. He would get paperwork in order for an underdeveloped nation to acquire loans from the World Bank.

These loans would create debt that relied on local taxes to pay it off. The people being taxed would be the mostly impoverished nationals of the developing nation and they sometimes experienced cuts in social programs as described under the Washington Consensus. The debt was approved by elites in the underdeveloped nations who would then get plumbing or electrical infrastructure built for them by foreigners. This made factories possible because factories require exactly such basic infrastructure. The second wave of development would then be factory construction or purchase by multinationals who could exploit the region's cheaper raw materials and cheaper labor. That's how out-sourcing of American industry got a foothold in faraway locations. The new privatized war package is similar but instead of construction to address underdevelopment, it's destruction followed by reconstruction. The immorality of this scenario can be easily recognized by everyone.

Privatized war, destruction first, rebuilding second, accomplished by corporations paid for with public money has appalling social toxicity that should be recognized and stopped. Profiteering has been questioned during earlier wars, for instance Brigadier General Smedley Butler's book, *War Is A Racket*, mentioned earlier. But war profiteering has been accepted when it helps the military achieve its objective. The amount of waste in Iraq rises to levels not seen in the past and the Iraqi conflict was not successful. In Iraq, destruction happened but not rebuilding and this has harmed and destabilized the entire region. Profiteering as the primary objective is fraud. It's also true that the Iraqi strategy was improperly planned, lacked proper oversight and has escaped public accountability.

How well has the goal of empire worked out? The Middle East has suffered without achieving stability. And war for empire using American forces and American funding has been ruining the American economy because there's little political restraint on government debt. Additionally, rules prohibiting torture under the Geneva Convention have been ignored in the recent wars in the Middle East and that has bad international political consequences. Private military companies involved in Middle East war have operated under the color of the flag but acted outside military operations protocols. War seems to have become an avenue to raid public treasury money under no standard of legitimacy for bad outcomes. Post war financial oppression has become another parcel in the financialization mixture (discussed soon, in the banking section).

Private military companies and the malfeasance associated with their deployment in Iraq.

The idea for privatizing government has been ongoing under neoliberalism since at least the Clinton Administration. Privatizing government evolved from the Clinton administration's "reinventing government". Reinventing government later led to privatization of military operations during the G.W. Bush administration. There was a story circulated that private industry would be more efficient. But reinventing government to reduce regulatory oversight had already proven criminogenic in the savings and loan financial industry.[324] Just as the S&L Crisis cost taxpayers, privatizing government has also led to treasury theft.

Private military companies (PMC's) have been hired to do what soldiers normally do and that has gained them access to treasury money but outside defense budget spending limitations. This makes funding them outside of congressional oversight. Little or no oversight of how money was spent and where exactly it went to in Iraq was part of the package that PMC's operated under. Furthermore, corporations operated independently of political pressures to spend money in the public's interest. The Iraq war wasn't even fought on legitimate information, but like the Vietnam War, a threat was fabricated.

Many Iraqis have subsequently died and many soldiers. PMC's have sometimes spent public money as though Americans never had to work in order to earn it, as though the money exists independently of economic health and balance. But American taxpayers have a reasonable expectation that public money should be spent in the public's interest. U.S. operations in Iraq carried forward destruction without rebuilding that has made Iraqi lives unhappy and unsafe. Operations in Iraq weren't legitimate on moral grounds or successful operationally. Tax money has become the spoils to which the MIC and now private security corporations are entitled to as arguably the most successful lobbying faction. And war has been a way to obtain treasury money in large quantities for over one hundred years in the United States.

The link between money and war is brought home powerfully in an article written for Vanity Fair, by Donald L. Barlett and James B. Steele, Oct 1st, 2007, titled "US: Billions over Baghdad; the Spoils of War."[325] The article had verbal imagery that showed how much money went to Baghdad and how much money remained unaccounted for. Here's a few excerpts: "Though accustomed to receiving and shipping large quantities of cash, the vault had never before processed a single order of this magnitude: $2.4 billion in $100 bills…Forty pallets of cash weighing 30 tons were loaded that day…That transfer of cash to Iraq was not, however, the first such shipment of cash to Iraq. Beginning soon after the invasion and continuing for more than a year, $12 billion in U.S. currency was airlifted to Baghdad".

Regarding fraud, an excerpt reads: "…Fraud" was simply another word for "business as usual." Of 8,206 "guards" drawing paychecks courtesy of the C.P.A., only 602 warm bodies could in fact be found; the other 7,604 were ghost employees. Halliburton, the government contractor once headed by Vice President Dick Cheney, charged the C.P.A. for 42,000 daily meals for soldiers while in fact serving only 14,000 of them." The C.P.A. was the Coalition Provisional Authority, run as an organization of the Pentagon under Paul Bremer. It was the pay master that passed out money in Iraq to coalition forces and other payees. The C.P.A. was a provisional organization, however so it wasn't subject to ordinary government oversight of its operations. Sixteen billion dollars has remained lost out of Baghdad, some of it Iraqi oil money and some of it American tax payer money. It hasn't been found and will never be found by the American government. According to the authors of this information rich article, the Bush administration avoided prosecutions for war profiteering under the False Claims Act and refused do a proper accounting for Iraqi expenditures and losses.

To conclude considerations of neoliberal war making, several points have been made. The first is that war remains a political tool that works in concert with debt to create financial and political obligations. It keeps taxes high, and war has been used by neoliberals opportunistically to open global markets to some while closing them to others. Under the goal of global economic empire, neoliberals have expanded the American military role to operations at 700 military bases around the world but in contradiction to American values that are in opposition to empire keeping. Political pressure to end American militarization has been mounting for both historical reasons and for practical ones. The principle of economic scarcity suggests that war destruction and investments in war-making wastes resources that could be used otherwise.

Economic globalization also may have undone the ability of nation states to externalize war costs. That may mean that war can no longer be justified on economic or on moral grounds. And the U.S. can't afford this extravagant expense. There's no money in the treasury—only IOU's. The U.S. debt has become enormous. Additionally the political choice to use military violence to enforce global economic dominance has not accomplished the homogenization of global politics. There are still many forms of government around the world that tend to disagree. Instead of creating a more uniform global politic, war has increased political resistance of outsider groups, for example in the Middle East. A reasonable question might be whether the goal of empire might be better served with a stable global currency than with a global military hegemony. A stable global currency and a global monetary system that conserves wealth instead of undermining it could help minimize global tensions and establish greater trust between nations. It could also help nation states to reestablish their fiscal sovereign discipline. Financialization, described in the next section, creates social harms and it shouldn't be dominant over other/better options in monetary policy.

An expert defines financialization and brings it into focus.

Greta R. Krippner has been a leader in helping to define financialization. She wrote a paper entitled "The Financialization of the American Economy," in 2005, published by the Oxford University Press and the Society for the Advancement of Socio-Economics.[326] Later analysts of financialization often cite Krippner. She put neoliberalism, globalization and financialization into a set of related happenings in our post-industrial economy. She cited G. Arrighi and Mark Suchman for helping her to define financialization. Krippner credited Arrighi with saying that finacialization is: "a pattern of accumulation in which profits accrue primarily through financial channels rather than through trade and commodity production. Suchman was credited by Krippner with this description: "…'Financial' here refers to activities relating to the provision (or transfer) of liquid capital in expectation of future interest, dividends, or capital gains."

According to Krippner, financialization's economic effects are seen in growth of banks, finance companies, brokerage houses, but, more surprisingly but of equal importance, an increase in non-financial corporate investing behaviors in financial markets instead of in productive markets. The trend of greater investments in finance instead of production by non-finance corporations, undermines the influence of labor by making labor less important to profit maximizing goals. In the context of off-shoring operations abroad, according to Krippner, financialization has been prevalent, though financialization has also been important in domestic investments by causing CEO's to emphasize profits in the short term. Bankers, according to Krippner, are the most powerful members of interlocking corporate directorates. Because financialization began with regulatory reform through changed government policies, Krippner points out that finacialization also has revealed change in the relationship between finance and government. Government has adapted its policies to better support Wall Street. Krippner made important points to consider as we read other descriptions about financialization. Most importantly, she demonstrated that **financialization has erupted out of governmental policy changes**. Those policy changes caused three subsequent organizational changes. There have been changes first in multinational corporations, second, in domestic businesses and third in domestic banks. These policy changes were neoliberal.

Neoliberal banking; fiscal debt and banking practices show how banks differ from other corporations.

As mentioned earlier, a lack of fiscal discipline led to greater government debt during modern liberalism. Keynes' theories supported government indebtedness to fund government projects inside the mixed economy. This notion of government debt being acceptable contrasted with traditional expectations for government fiscal discipline and limited government from classical liberalism. Later neoliberal economists, writing about economic health mentioned in several already outlined examples that government debt and deficit would undermine a healthy economy. As fiscal debt grew, interest charges would erode the government's tax base and its funding. Under modern liberalism, the government played a larger regulatory role and used tax money to fund government projects such as the interstate highway system and military expenditures for war. The labor and production associated with these domestic projects funded by taxes at least were virtuous. That is to say that they circulated benefits domestically in the form of social improvements and wages. But that can't happen if tax subsidies go abroad in the form of corporate welfare. Neoliberalism has thwarted the virtuous cycle.

Even though the government utilized taxes to pay for government projects, some people during modern liberalism, began to see the government as an active producer in the economy. Government jobs meant to some people that the government acted as an economic participant. For many, anyone with a job for them was a producer. Instead of acknowledging government work as a contribution to the politic, they imagined that government work was a necessary part of the productive economy. But the idea that government could be a wealth producer was wrong. Government redistributed money but never produced it. Whatever a bureaucrat does, it supports the politic not the economy. The higher taxes after WWII became part of the neoliberal purse.

Taxes aren't at all like a business profit. They diminish wages and business profits. And there could be alternative uses for that money. If the money was wasted, it would be lost to what might have been a better use. Under classical liberalism, it was thought that people could find the best uses for their own money. That changed under modern liberalism where big problems called out for big government solutions and people naively thought that the government would use income taxes only in the public's interests. Newspapers dramatized problems during the modern liberal period. The new media shaped public opinion and focused attention on featured issues.

But taxes subtracted incentives from the production stream. And they have provided incentives for special interests to grow more powerful inside the Washington D.C. money flow. Under neoliberalism, taxes have been used to promote the corporate good instead of the public good. Corporate lobbies gained power and further influenced the politic. Corporations have owned and controlled large media companies.[327] Neoliberals can influence public opinion and they have lobbies and money to influence the politic. Policies to benefit corporations can be harmful to the public's interests and offend the ethical goals of good governance, at least according to classical liberal political philosophers and according to the modern liberal goals of increasing government power to help the public's interests and not for advancing corporate interests.

Government spending beyond tax receipts led to expansionist monetarist policies during the neoliberal period. Monetarism as supported by neoliberal economist, Milton Friedman, rationalized the expansion of money's quantity in circulation. Multiplying the money stream, kinds of money and international circulation of money has continued into the present day. After the Bretton Woods system ended, regulatory reform and deregulation in finance remodeled the set of rules followed by finance. As already discussed, this rule revamp has caused problems. But it also enlarged the financial industry which has been a growth leader under the influence of policy changes and deregulation. Banks continue to be a part of the complex finance industry of the present day.

Why banks are both like and unlike other corporations.

According to Anat Admati and Martin Hellwig in *The Banker's New Clothes: What's Wrong with Banking and What to Do About it*, banks are and aren't like other corporations. Banks, like other corporations, serve their shareholders by making a profit, that can be applied into earnings equity also referred to somewhat confusingly as bank capital.[328] But banks, unlike other corporations, also act as a publicly essential conduit for pay activities associated with the production stream. People work to produce a valuable good or service, get paid and deposit money in the bank. Money can serve as a value holder in the production stream only under conditions of bank solvency. Production capital from work is only one part of the capital stream; there is also finance capital from investments. These two roles of banks as a profit maker and a money-production conduit can be seen as being synergistic but only as long as banks remain solvent. As soon as they become insolvent, people in different interest groups become competitors for what's left of bank assets. And the value holding job that money performs in solvent banks is essential to both the public's production stream and to bankers acting in commercial or investment banking. Another difference between some banks and other corporations is that central banks don't pay taxes. And other banks sometimes utilize tax loopholes to substantially reduce their taxes.

The 2008 financial problems have revealed how bank insolvency has become subsidized and how policies that reward insolvency put banks in opposition to their social responsibility to be solvent. Risk, of course is always part of banking because of uncertainty in the future after an investment is underway. But reckless risk pursuit in order to obtain government subsidy has been a policy failure and a bank offense against society. The capitalist innovation that liberalism and double entry bookkeeping got going in the fourteenth century depended on provident uses of lending to promote social productivity. The public good of enabling production was served under the pairing of liberalism and finance with rational and humanist methods and goals. But neoliberals have abandoned liberal methods and goals and pursued opportunism instead. Under neoliberalism, the banker's interests to embrace higher risk for greater potential profitability has become antagonistic to the public's need for bank solvency. Regulatory reform has unbalanced diverse interests and allowed bankers' desire for more risk to grow more important than the public's need for solvency under U.S. monetary policy over the period of regulatory reform since the 1970's. If risk caused widespread losses of savings held in reserve throughout the economy to pay for deficiencies, those losses would cause an economic collapse. But if widespread risk led to currency failure, for example failure of the dollar, it would cause global chaos. In the U.S. it would lead to a failure of the politic and a change of political regime.

The Great Depression of 1929 was an example of an economic collapse and the Great Recession of 2008, another. The Great Depression destroyed the savings accounts of many people who weren't even investors in the stock market, as mentioned earlier, and the savings losses that happened before the Bank Holiday that marked bank reorganization, were lost for good. The more recent losses in mortgage assets and valuations that happened during the wave of foreclosures after 2008 Financial Recession were another example. These events weren't fair. Mal-investment to overbuild the housing market caused deflation when the sub-prime boom ended. And non-risk takers who only bought a home but didn't invest in mortgage backed securities were imposed upon to make good on risk when their property values plummeted and when treasury money was used to re-capitalize TBTF banks. Risk takers profited for years before the collapse and they left with their money. But the short term tally when the market collapsed seemed to have been more losses than gains for many investors. Those losses were certainly painful. The entire economy suffered under recession or depression conditions as the consequences of failed ventures in finance spread out from banks and into employment, real estate, insurance and production.

What banks do in financial markets, and the Greenspan Put.

In considering the financial industry, awareness of the money stream brings attention to both banks and markets. Banks act as a bridge between entities with money to lend and entities with a need to borrow.[329] Banks also borrow from each other. And banks in the current policy regime often hold very little profits as equity in reserve to cushion against possible losses. Instead they rely on government subsidy to make up for losses that would threaten the economy if banks failed because of insolvency. In this way the government's policies support risk taking at the public's expense.[330] Industries outside finance rely less on government and more on their own equity.

A lender can be as simple anyone with a savings account. A borrower can be anyone that the bank is allowed to lend to according to bank regulations and who also meets the bank's lending qualifications. Loans carry both a risk of interest rate changes in the interest rate marketplace, as was seen for instance as a trigger during the Savings and Loan Crisis, and also a risk of default. The spread between what the bank pays in interest to its depositors and the amount the bank charges for a loan is the amount of money to be made by lending. The very low interest rates, since 2008, keep interest on the government's debt low but banks continue to make some money from loaning to private borrowers. Some think that the policy of low interest encourages risk taking in the speculative markets because the loan markets are weaker under low interest rates.

Government policy through the Federal Reserve, has focused on reducing interest on government debt. Government debt increased in order to support failing banks, all at the public's expense. The government's debt as of July 2014, has grown to $17,687,723,410.59.[331] Read it again, that's more than 17 trillion dollars. The government is still borrowing more. And increased fiscal debt continues to hurt the economy and offers a growing threat to prosperity and government solvency. The government and banks have a mutually supportive relationship by protecting each other's opportunity to increase their debt, and each other's risk in a continuous feedback loop which is harming the economy. According to Anat Admati and Martin Hellwig, "Banks and governments have always had a symbiotic relationship. Since the beginnings of modern banking in medieval Italy, lending to governments has been a key activity of banks. It is easy to make large loans to governments, and they can be very profitable—until the government defaults on them. Historically, governments failing to pay their debts have been the most important causes of banking crises."[332]

Banks also profit by service fees for bank services such as "making an electronic funds transfer", holding valuables in a safety deposit box, or by stocks or securities investing either for the bank directly or for a bank client. According to the *Dictionary of Banking Terms*, the Bank Act of 1933, segmented banks into categories based on whether the bank was a commercial bank that made loans from depositors, or an investment bank that invested in stock markets and made further investments from investment income.[333] FDIC insurance was intended only for commercial banks. Investment bank's risk wasn't insured against losses by the government. Insurance for only commercial banking expanded, however, under Alan Greenspan's Federal Reserve oversight during bank deregulation. Deregulation erased the separation between investment and commercial banks. Even though no laws were passed to change FDIC support and add investment banks into FDIC, Federal Reserve Chairman Alan Greenspan, who supported finance industry deregulation also promised central bank support for investment bankers in the **"Greenspan Put."**[334] He believed that bankers would invest prudently to prolong their profits. Evolution of new products in finance also has created new segments of finance that are riskier and less regulated. Neoliberalism's government support for financial corporations becomes clear when these policies are considered.

Kinds of financial markets.

Markets vary by what they trade. There are capital markets in stocks or bonds, commodity markets that trade physical goods like corn, money markets which circulate short term loan money that is very liquid and under a short-term contract, the derivative security market that can be used for purposes such as managing risk for unstable values in securities, the derivative futures market, another derivative market but based on speculation on future price outcomes for a given time span, the foreign exchange markets that bet on the carry trade difference between currency valuations and price movements among foreign currencies and even the insurance market which can be like a derivative market but only to provide a remedy for a loss not a profit on a gain in price.[335] The financial markets are all about price changes.

Changes happened in American businesses that were caused by financialization.

One way that financialization changed how Wall Street works was by making credit easy to obtain. This led to changes in the corporate world by two mechanisms: hostile takeovers and CEO stock options. The historical Wall Street was a place to promote the growth of new companies. An entrepreneur would start a company and offer shares of it when the company gained value and when more money was needed for growth. People could invest in companies by buying their stock. If the company did well, the stock did well. The company owners could sell their stocks and divest to get out of the company, or stock investors could sell shares to get money. Dividends were also available in good times when money would go to shareholders. Easy credit changed all that.

This virtuous cycle changed when CEO pay began to be valued partly in stock options, and those options weren't listed as a company expense (that is, until after Enron's expensive collapse).[336] CEO's were directed by their own stock ownership to maximize the short term profit in order to maximize their share price. CEO pay in stock options was partially a way to discourage a hostile takeover, "Managers of targeted firms often defended their turf by loading the firm with debt-financed stock buybacks or special cash dividends to deter potential raiders."[337] Hostile takeovers happened under huge loans to take over companies and their employees were often fired or their wages were reduced or their retirement system plundered or all of the capital goods might be sold off for a short-term liquidation profit. But this process deconstructed important productive enterprises in the economy and destroyed jobs. It also changed company planning.

If companies were to be strong enough to withstand a takeover, they had to emphasize the short term profit in order to keep their share price higher. When banks made so much money available to would-be takeovers they changed the game from production to liquidation. This has led to less production overall. In 1998, the hostile takeover of Nabisco cost twenty five billion dollars, and twenty three billion of that money was debt-financed.[338] It became difficult to withstand such attacks. They changed business in America.

The increased complexity of finance affected other corporations and businesses.

As economies have grown over the last several hundred years, complexity has increased and the complexity of banking and finance has also increased. Another way of seeing finance can be learned from an essay by Wallace C. Turbeville, "Derivatives: Innovation in the Era of Financial Regulation."[339] According to this author the public service that banks perform is called "capital intermediation," and it happens on at least three levels. Some levels have been part of finance since it began and some are newer. Primary finance is found in commercial banks.

Banks use their profits and deposits to "fund capital needs in the economy." The bank funds moderate "mismatches" between capital demand such as are found among customers between maturity rates, interest rate, and credit. This allows people to take out a loan for a mortgage, for example. Primary finance charges an interest fee for loan risk and uses a capital base to allow for slow maturity even though capital needs are generally for the immediate present. Primary finance loans let a buyer pay off a high dollar expense slowly. Trading markets are secondary finance capital intermediation. Stock securities are issued by a business owner in order to raise capital for capital improvements and securities can be sold at a later time in order to buy alternative securities or to raise capital by those who have purchased them. Trading markets have allowed firms to learn how the public values their stocks and it has provided them a way to sell out and seek other opportunities. Tertiary capital intermediation is derivatives trading. Derivative product innovation has produced the newest form of capital intermediation and it confuses people the most.

There's more than one way to make a derivative trade but what a derivative does according to Turbeville, instead of eliminating risk, is to change the consequence of risk for buyers and sellers of derivative swaps in terms of option to buy and forward price. Derivative options are the opportunity to buy at a future date if the price exceeds a set minimum figure. Forward price is the price increase or price decrease of a commodity at a specified time. Banks can make ten times more money from selling a similar level of riskiness in a derivative as compared to a loan. And banks have been the most common traders of derivatives, the four biggest banks sell more than 90% of this market. They sell to corporations, investment banks and commodity traders. To issue a derivative is to redirect the connection between an asset and a change in asset price. A person who owns a derivative can make or lose money depending on asset valuation without ever having bought the asset.[340]

Derivative markets have been hard to understand because people find understanding abstractions to be difficult. Most people buy, sell, and make their livings in the real world of buying food or selling labor. Few have an education in abstract sciences or information technologies and it was people in these fields that helped to construct derivative abstractions for the financial markets. The trouble with derivatives is that they are confusing to most buyers. Banks know how much money they are making from derivatives but they don't really explain it to buyers. Buyers are easily confused by having information on only their side of the derivative deal.[341]

According to Turbeville, "The marketplace is biased toward complexity because it favors market participants with "asymmetric information advantages" and "oligopolistic market power." Under these circumstances there is an inherent bias toward risk-taking by large financial institutions: the larger the risk, the larger the reward; and if the rewards are structurally higher, immediate profits (which translate in to shareholder value and executive compensation) can be seized. The periodic catastrophic failure is worth it for traders and executives who keep their earnings."

But derivatives have also been confusing in the ways that they introduce maladaptation into the real markets.[342] For example, if a business person hedges against loss of product value, they may delay changing their product lineup when they otherwise should change it in response to changing market demand. This topic of mal-adaptation can also be addressed by comparing the difference in risk preparedness between a cash reserve and a derivative. This comparison will be addressed in a future section when considering Anat Amadhi and Martin Hellwig's suggestion that banks keep greater equity in reserve as an alternative to betting in the derivatives markets.

Controversy erupted in HFT because of informational speed advantages that went against customers.

Another controversial segment of the financial market should at least be mentioned because it has been part of trading markets since just before the Great Recession of 2008. In the spring of 2014, Michael Lewis, through WW Norton & Company Ltd, published his book, *Flash Boys: A Wall Street Revolt*.[343] It was an interesting reference that helped to inform people about the practice of high frequency trading (HFT). It showed the evolution of finance to use IT technology in order to make more money inside the financial industry but not for the finance industry's clients. It revealed conflict of interest in financial markets between money maker brokers and those who participated in the market less aggressively as small-time investors, for example, in retirement plans.

In *Flash Boys*, Lewis chronicled the motivations of people who tried to discover what HFT was, and then tried to circumvent the middle men in high frequency trading. High frequency traders have used faster internet access to front-run orders made in trading markets. They bought access to dark pools, entered other trading networks and bid up orders to increase their own profits inside the order spread. These were middlemen who exacted a fee because of their superior trading speeds on faster routes of fiber optic cabling. People who have invested money in the faster cable routes have been able to make large sums of money by providing access to faster trading.

High frequency traders made profits by front running orders, bidding up the price of a large order by making a large coincident bid which was soon cancelled after the market moved. This added a few cents to large volume trades which high frequency traders kept as a profit. Estimators guess that these small gains made HFT middlemen from ten to twenty two billion dollars a year.[344] The profits were non-virtuous because they didn't stimulate production. They also gainsaid trust in the markets. Meaningful regulations to stop this practice have been lacking.[345] As mentioned in the chapter on Modern Liberalism, HFT also caused commodity inflation that has harmed the world's poor and has even inflated U.S. commodity prices in food and energy.

Our fiat monetary system has led to more arbitrage and that has meant more money making opportunities for banks in speculation.

Under fiat monetary policy, our current monetary system, as discussed earlier, prices are volatile and markets move quickly. This can lead to a gain/ loss binary. Gain for some who bet the way the market moves and a loss for others if their bet goes the wrong way. But betting on the market's changeableness by using derivatives is how bankers have adapted to the fiat monetary system. First, it gives them an additional profit stream where clients pay a premium for loan risk that the bank collects. Whereas the strict gold standard produced stable prices and values, the fiat system has produced instability which has been used by bankers for making money on loans against risk in speculative investments. Second, banks can also speculate directly themselves. HFT just takes the exploitation of trading to another level. Unfortunately, large capital gains in speculation create a feedback loop for even more non-virtuous speculation. It doesn't lead to greater amounts of goods or services or infrastructure like roads. So there's nothing to show in society for the capital that is created. And this speculation is one of the problems inherent in the fiat system. Now, speculation has become as much a dominant feature of financialization as debt.[346]

Regulatory reform erased regulatory restrictions on the kinds of financial risks that banks engage in. Banks now can mix commercial and investment banking. They can grow larger than before through hostile takeovers funded with debt until their insolvency would threaten the whole financial system. They can get loan fees from more clients engaged in speculative markets. They can borrow money with little bank equity to bet the bank in speculative derivatives markets, foreign exchange, stocks, commodities, under conditions of high capital leverage and government subsidy in the case of a loss. Deregulation and regulatory reform have made banks the kingpins of the corporate world and led to financialization. And finance speculation continues to be encouraged by low interest rates and few production investment opportunities. As long as the government can bail out failures, financialization will make the largest short-term returns possible through changes in prices and bets on those changes.

Familiar changes caused by financialization surround us all.

Neoliberal regulatory reform brought forward alterations outside banking that are also familiar. For example, deregulation invited new accounting tricks that avoided investment accountability and permitted spectacular financial recklessness that destroyed a number of once promising firms such as LTCM, Enron, and some Savings and Loan Banks. These enterprises failed because they couldn't pay their debts—- they became insolvent. This insolvency harmed their stock holders who lost their investment. The insolvency also harmed the public because the firm had become a conduit for mal-investing in failed ventures that didn't lead to profits. Investment profits that, for example, could have been put into better equipment, people's training to improve job performance, or stock holder dividends. Lots of retirees lost their savings in the Enron failure. And public money that was paid in order to fix the problems caused by failed companies through accounting fraud and riskiness, for instance in the S&L bank failures could never become available for better ends. According to William K. Black, in his book, *The Best Way to Rob a Bank Is to Own One*, the cost of the S&L crisis to the public was between $150 billion and $175 billion estimated in 1993 dollars.[347] The costs of regulatory reform have harmed the public by causing enormous treasury losses that have made the public poorer in terms of public services and infrastructure. This loss of public money has suited the neoliberal agenda, however, which has opposed expenditures supportive of the public.

Regulatory reform in finance has also changed the way that financial rewards circulate in the economy by changing the amount of capital that is required for certain financial gambles, such as hostile takeovers and derivative purchases. Finance has redistributed financial rewards to a smaller group of individuals in society and polarized wealth earnings. Part of the income differential between finance and other parts of the economy happened through large capital investments that most people in the public could never make because they lacked access to large amounts of capital.[348]

It has also put many businesses into a short term profit strategy that has kept stock valuations on paper higher even though real productive capacity may be in decline because of a failure to invest in employee training, or invest in better technology or purchase equipment or innovate new products. The need to maximize profits has narrowed choices in employment and reduced economic security throughout the world of work, increasing unemployment, and decreasing wages and benefits. It has emphasized liquid capital over equity capital. It has encouraged corporate finance speculation instead of investments in research and development or entrepreneurship.[349]

The unhappy neoliberal workplace has cheery branding.

Millions of people have lost positive work experiences under the pressure of short-termism inside companies. Short term profits can become the company's focus instead of customers or employees. In employee evaluation interviews, brand propaganda has been substituted for honest conversations with employees about the real market performance of companies. Employees are expected to know and validate brand propaganda and not to complain. In the article "Doing the Right Thing? HRM and the Angry Knowledge Worker,"[350] Jean Cushen and Paul Thompson wrote about human resource policies in technical work for a job where workers were promised that they controlled their own destiny by meeting training and other goals. But "structural constraints" on pay rate to market average rates weren't matched to employee performance, and employees were required to perform increased duties without rewards of promotion or pay increases.

Cushen and Thompson described how the employee's performance review would be based on an internal system of measures unrelated to the employee's real value according to their production contribution within the company. Instead the development plan would be used as a measure of the employee's value but this plan wouldn't be connected to work production. The authors also described how management decisions that negatively affected the work environment would be presented as events that should be welcomed by employees. "Outsourcing and centralization were claimed to offer opportunities for career and skills development."[351]

Employees were not given any opportunity to negotiate for a performance based wage increase. Wages were fixed at a given rate before management conversed with employees regarding employee pay. In this article, HR was presented as a marketer of company branding rather than as a negotiator between labor and management. Under this system where meaningful communication had broken down, an employee's only choice would be to stay or leave the company. In any case, employees acquired no sense of loyalty to a firm that failed to recognize employee work excellence in terms of production measures, in a company that failed to reward employees for producing value for the company. Employees would see that their work was difficult and necessary but their workplace contribution wouldn't be treated as valuable by the company. Corporate short-termism led the company according to Cushen and Thompson's description to adopt aggressive and changeable "low road" management programs demanding more production without greater compensation. And the company might downsize an employee's department at any time.

It seems plausible to imagine that this "low road" policy set has caused the increased levels of labor non-participation in the United States. Technical workers often invest in education and experience-based training in order to be eligible for technical work. If the jobsite were to become hostile, or unreasonably demanding without rewarding an employee's efforts, the employee who left to seek some other position would face a variety of challenges. He might have college loans to pay off and there might not be many jobs in his field in the city where he lives. He might have to relocate which could be expensive and inconvenient. And even with relocation, he could find another adverse work environment. If his profession had become less rewarding to employees everywhere, changing careers to try to get a more rewarding job would be a huge cost that might not improve his working environment. And most people probably would find it financially unaffordable to reestablish entirely new credentials in another field.

Corporate inattention to incentives that encourage employee performance can damage work outcomes, especially in a technical field where communication, training and proper equipment use are all essential aspects of the production plan. Workers need support to solve problems so that they can focus on technical details in order to maintain work quality. And a supportive workplace invests in training, communication and problem solving that extend beyond short term profitability in order to nurture a healthy long-term work environment. In technical work, if technical problem-solving and work incentives that support production aren't of interest to management or to the corporate leadership, problems can develop but remain unaddressed. HR issues are only one facet of the work environment that could impact production outcomes. And even though technical work has been seen as an important part of the future job market, "low road" policies and fewer incentives in technical work may lead to fewer people who are able and willing to invest in training for it.

When technical workers become unemployed because their job has been outsourced or their work environment offers few incentives while demanding improved productivity they may not find another job where they can contribute their technical talents. Losing the skills of technically competent workers because of an emphasis on short term profits is wasteful. It wastes education investments by public tax and private spending. It wastes on-the-job training where a person would gain appropriate and useful work experiences. It wastes the opportunity to pass "know-how" on to new employees. It's wasteful of a person's chance to succeed and invest her earnings in her community.

Company ownership has correlated with longer term growth strategies and better working environments.

Another view of workplace policies under financialization was written by Ulrich Jurgens, entitled, "Ownership Structures, Corporate Governance and Labor."[352] This author looked at the automotive service industry but his discussion may be pertinent to employment groups in other technical fields. In Jurgens's view, the way a company has been financed directly affected how it treated its employees. He differentiated three kinds of firms. The first group was those that were funded by private capital. The second group was those funded with shareholder investments or with a lot of institutional investors. The third group was in debt to and funded by financial investors or banks. Among these groups, private funding led to long term strategies that included better employee relations, and better employee training or "high road" strategies. The firms having more debt funding with financial investors had the worst employee relations that were bracketed by short term financial considerations that minimized the importance of employee contributions or that utilized "low road" work systems. The intermediate form was shareholder funded and it was somewhere in between the two extremes, "using strategies that included some off-shoring into low wage countries" and "financial indicators" to motivate business strategy but somewhat less short-termism. The author compared firms in Germany, Sweden and the

U.S. and found that funding source had a greater impact on the work environment than national location did.[353]

How neoliberal accelerationist policy has led to conflicts between what is good for society and what helps monopoly industries.

In his book, *The Politics of Industrial Change: Railway Policy in North America*, 1985, Kent Weaver, a research associate at the Brookings Institute, postulated that the best approach to industrial change would be more market intervention by the government. Remember that Ludwig von Mises specifically warned against economic interventionism. Weaver called his version of economic interventionism "accelerationist policy."[354] Under accelerationist policy, the tendency in business to emphasize short-term gain continued and it became associated with an imagined industrial life-cycle of "sunrise", "maturing", and "declining phases". These show a vision of industry that imagined an unsustainable horizon.

This notion resembled earlier theories about cultural evolution that put industrial nations at the top of a social developmental pyramid. Historical materialism imagined a similarly inevitable social cycle that would lead to strife between classes. A belief in irresistible processes such as these have be used to justify policy approaches that wouldn't make sense if they were considered for a sustainable system. An "industry lifecycle" also nests in ideas that are rooted in beneficial market competition. But expectations for beneficial market competition aren't in accord with current market failures which have happened because of bad economic policy design. And accelerationist policy and industrial policy has had shortcomings with regard to public welfare.

Weaver wrote that a successful industrial policy should end tariff protectionism and embrace accelerationist policy instead. That's because protectionism was believed by Weaver's neoliberal experts not to work. Under a "failing market," because of market overregulation and favors for political factions, neoliberals have imagined that only accelerationist policy would work as opposed to market oriented macroeconomic policies. The argument suggests that if policies had already changed the performance of the economy then a more activist policy approach would be needed because market mechanisms could no longer create a desired change. A failing market, according to Weaver, can be recognized by certain characteristics such as "monopoly power", "high transaction costs", "poorly developed capital markets", or when "political interests overwhelm economic interests."[355] But this line of argument began by blaming the modern liberal policy package. It missed the policy importance of neoliberal economic changes that were part of policy design after the modern liberal period. Neoliberal policy approaches caused additional factionalization of the politic. Complex economies are economies in motion. The dominance of political direction over market mechanisms through government regulation during modern liberalism intensified under neoliberalism when policies were redirected to help the largest corporations. Weaver pretended that neoliberals didn't interfere with economic policy when they did so through regulatory reforms. Neoliberal reforms interfered with market mechanisms much like modern liberal policies had.

Weaver recognized that "industrial adjustment" can conflict with "public needs goals". Public needs goals, he wrote, included: "maintaining employment levels, maintaining an adequate industrial base for defense, reducing environmental pollution, promoting industrialization under new corporations, and avoiding monopoly."[356] What has become obvious during neoliberal regulatory reform has been the growth of a few large monopolies in deregulated industries, declining employment, and fewer new firms (declining market competition). But unlike Weaver's anxiety, the neoliberal defense industry maintained its funding and technology for wars in the Middle East.

According to Weaver, accelerationist policies would determine winners and losers instead of allowing markets to winnow out firms that don't meet public demand for their products. That manipulation of markets through government subsidy has happened according to Weaver, because market discipline had already failed under market distortions caused by the regulatory state. The author did a cost/benefit analysis of how policies impacted different groups under three economic policy sets: macroeconomic policy, protectionist policy and accelerationist policy. But he advocated only for accelerationist policy, the most aggressive form of economic interventionism. Under Weaver's description, accelerationist policy provided corporate welfare to the strongest firms. The author imagined that consumers would get cheaper commodities from more efficient industries, though with insecure employment.

He ignored the known harms that monopolies can cause to market economies. However, he did acknowledge that weaker firms would be forced out and their workers would become unemployed. Finally he thought that taxpayers would pay for transitional assistance and corporate welfare to soften the adverse outcomes people would experience from accelerationist policies.[357] He seemed to imagine a large reservoir of public money to offset accelerationist harms despite lower wages, less employment and high government debt. This was of course a fantasy that anyone could indulge only temporarily through greater debt (financialization).

The author postulated conditions under which democratic governments could pursue accelerationist policies. First, he imagined that the government would be politically "united" in favor of accelerationist policy with few "veto points". Second, he imagined a cadre of bureaucrats in government that would possess "autonomy" and "expertise". Third, he imagined that the government could "compel compliance" through strong "government mechanisms". He lamented that the U.S. and Canada at the time of book's publication didn't possess these characteristics.

But after the PATRIOT Act of 2001, the U.S. has increased its strong arm political tactics, perhaps much in line with what Weaver imagined. And the growth of monopoly which Weaver mentioned several times has only continued into the present-day. Monopoly and government subsidy continue to distort economic markets. Healthcare, the automotive sales industry, and public education, are some examples where public subsidy has increased costs. Putting Weaver's analysis of accelerationist policy with what we can observe today, the partnership between government and industry under neoliberalism has harmed market demand based pricing mechanisms, increased the presence of monopolies, discouraged fiscal discipline, increased political intervention in the economy, increased the incentives toward empire keeping and harmed the public's welfare.

Mobile capital has been a feature of neoliberalism but hot money flows can create booms followed by busts. Asset depreciations have heavily discounted investments for neoliberal opportunists.

Financialization has increased speculation by banks and corporations and produced money in a highly mobile liquid form, also known as "hot money". Hot money has circulated the world stimulating boom and bust economies that made governments less stable in Argentina, Mexico, Turkey, Brazil and South Korea.[358] Destabilized foreign economies have become sites for fire-sale asset purchases by multinationals. Neoliberal policies along the Washington Consensus have led to booms followed by crashes and then foreign direct investments in devalued domestic firms. Another side of financialization is the affect that its growth has had on the Digital Age, as James Tobin discussed in a speech he gave.

Nobel Prize winner, James Tobin, spoke out about IT technological investments in finance.

In 1981, James Tobin won the Nobel Prize in Economics. Here's a quote from him: "I confess to an uneasy Physiocratic suspicion, perhaps unbecoming in an academic, that we are throwing more and more of our resources, including the cream of our youth, into financial activities remote from the production of goods and services, into activities that generate high private rewards disproportionate to their social productivity. I suspect that the immense power of the computer is being harnessed to this 'paper economy', not to do the same transactions more economically but to balloon the quantity and variety of financial exchanges. For this reason, perhaps, high technology has so far yielded disappointing results in economy-wide productivity."[359]

He attributed the decline of profit making associated with IT in the post-industrial era to the influence of finance which has diverted IT efforts into speculative enterprises inside finance and out of production. IT product production has also been outsourced to cheaper labor nations through international finance so that production of IT products can't contribute to increased labor opportunities in developed economies. This diversion of domestic labor out of IT has harmed U.S. labor's opportunity to be a productive beneficiary of the IT industry in the Digital Age. Disconnecting economic benefits of IT labor production from developed nations doesn't alter other effects of new technologies. IT has been disruptive. But the loss of production benefits in the post-industrial age has been a blow to the economic health and employment of developed nations.

The developed nations that had supported education and technology were shortchanged even though they most deserved to reap the benefits of IT. Having paid in taxes to enhance public education, developed economies nevertheless couldn't employ many of its educated people when IT production moved off-shore. Neoliberal investors have utilized globalization to interrupt virtuous cycles in labor that ordinarily would produce more wealth for everyday people. Piece-meal manufacture in far-away places has broken down what would have been virtuous money cycling.

Trading merchants who did business in the past brought trade goods from far away to exotic ports of call and took away trade goods to bring back home. They made money on both legs of their trip and brought trade goods into port that people wanted to buy. But financialization capitalists, take capital to foreign nations and invest it but carry away its profits and its goods to keep for themselves. Local communities don't have a bank that invested or a gainful wage that can migrate into in a local cycle of money circulation. Unlike the merchant trade where dislocated goods produced a profit for merchants and provided desirable products for local use, dislocated capital goes to no virtuous end. Neoliberal IT investments in the military and in media also have failed to produce a product that would circulate capital virtuously and broadly in society. Investment in finance, war and media has served a political end more than an economic one.

More experts comment on neoliberalism and warn against harms.

According to Gerard Dumenil and Dominique Levy, who wrote in the essay entitled, "Costs and Benefits of Neoliberalism: A Class Analysis,"[360] most, if not all, analysts on the Left now agree that neoliberalism is the ideological expression of the reasserted power of finance." The Great Depression put a temporary end to the expansion of financial power in 1929. Dumenil and Levy wrote that "The term 'finance' itself refers to a framework of institutions interlocked in a complex network; behind these institutions stand individuals."[361] Neoliberals supported and have used institutions to organize political and economic advantages for themselves or for their group. The authors also see neoliberal financialization as being a crisis instigator. Financialization processes motivated capital to remain liquid which has contradicted capital investment in long term processes. This short termism has created bubbles. The authors link bubble crises with recessions, unemployment and long term growth decline.[362] The importance of financial interests has been emphasized by these authors who say that financial interests have motived policy changes and see those changes serving banks most of all but in conflict with society's better interests.[363]

John Belamy Foster writing in his article, "The Financialization of Capital," observed that although financialization doesn't embody a new evolution of capitalism what is does represent is a hybrid between monopoly finance and capital. He saw capital as being "trapped in a seemingly endless cycle of stagnation and financial implosion."[364] Foster wrote about a build-up of excess capacity during the stagflation of the 1970's, the diminishing set of business investment opportunities in production and the subsequent concentration of speculative investing in finance. Money became less dependent on production and more dependent on gambles, loans, indebtedness. He made several useful points.

One of Belamy Foster's points was that malinvestment bubbles have been only part of financialization's outcomes. The process of rewarding debt under government tax breaks for debt encourages greater indebtedness and subsequent speculation. The price instabilities produced under the fiat monetary system have encouraged speculation and some investors have made money. But price and value instability also have harmed market economies by making real productivity more uncertain. And price and value instability can harm nation state relationships and undermine trust because only some people or some nations can benefit from the fluctuations. This multiplication of riskiness also diverts the ordinary productive investments of corporations and brings them into finance where they can get a bigger return on investment. He saw the Bretton Woods international institutions as serving the interests of developed economies and has recognized developing world vulnerability to hot money that has originated mostly from developed nations. He noted that many people have become aware of growing instability in financial markets and have experienced growing concerns over the risk being courted in derivative and hedge fund markets.

Why financialization has been a bad policy.

Some people, like neoliberal politician Margaret Thatcher, have said that "there is no alternative" to neoliberalism. And now people also say there's no alternative to globalization and financialization, even though neoliberal policies aren't like they were imagined by economic experts or explained by politicians. Thankfully, after so much financial upheaval, some people have other policy options in mind and can say that there are policy alternatives to neoliberalization, globalization and financialization.

Adam Smith cared about the difference between virtuous and non-virtuous economic processes.[365] He liked the idea of virtuous economies where more people could do well. That's what he hoped for when he advocated for more specialization in labor—that more specialized labor would increase productivity, increase employment, and help grow markets. After the Bretton Woods Monetary System broke down, fiat money caused stress in the market economy by creating less stable values and prices and more market volatility. Fiat money has followed the Bretton Woods experiment but fiat usually hasn't been a long lasting kind of monetary policy. Fiat in market trading for commodities and currencies has not maintained stable values or stable prices. And governments have abused their printing presses to overprint national currencies without discipline. This has been monetary policy abuse in Western economies. Fiat monetary policy has now led to speculation instead of productivity. And our fiat monetary system combined with mobile capital and monetarism has made money unsound.

A natural limitation exists in the size of an economy based on the amount of real production in that economy. Inflation happens whenever more money is printed than represents real value with respect to production. By increasing the number of financial products and securitizing them, finance has increased speculation but it has decreased productivity in the real economy. And a mostly speculative economy produces little other than gains on paper. Over time a speculative economy erodes the real economy.

It might have once been hoped that off-shoring would bring more developing nations into productive pursuits. But debt has politically hampered the evolution of export industries from foreign owned factories in developing economies. Developing economies with foreign owned factories don't produce products for local consumption to make people genuinely better off. If people were better off their economy could transition to become an importer as well as an exporter. But high debt has limited the growth of real productive capacity and economic evolution in developing nations. FDI broke the virtuous cycle of production by exporting most products, using foreign financiers and by paying low wages. Low wages were essential in FDI (foreign direct investment) negotiations. Instead of healthy and independent economies, financialization brokered by the international organizations of Bretton Woods, has created client states. They remain hampered in their development by debt.

Financialization has increased the capital stream because of gambles in the speculative markets.[366] It has helped to build infrastructure with debt obligation in the developing economies. It has maintained the higher standard of living in developed economies through credit. But it has left too much debt behind which now hampers growth in developed nations as in did in developing ones. Debt has continued to hamper further economic evolution that would tend to increase real wealth. Debt has been non-virtuous. Speculation has been non-virtuous. Export only economy has been non-virtuous. Outsourced labor at low wages has been non-virtuous. Debt has hampered growth, innovation, wage improvements, and new product development. Living in a debt economy has put a shadow on productive potential because it has tied up capital resources non-virtuously.

Increasing the capital stream hasn't helped society because it has produced a non-virtuous economic cycle that has undermined savings and productive investments that would ordinarily generate social wealth. And political and economic volatility will continue to increase until a virtuous economy can find its feet again. Several challenges face economies that want to improve and work towards de-financialization and toward genuine wealth building in virtuous productivity. Several writers have suggestions to improve the economy and to undo financialization in order to increase resources for a more productive wealth-building and less capital intensive economy.

Policy suggestions from experts to divert financial resources back into production and out of speculation.

To fix the economy, experts suggest policy reforms in finance. Policy reform would begin to rejuvenate the sick economy. In fact, individual problems in banking can't be addressed without policy changes. Anat Admati and Martin Hellwig in their book, *The Banker's New Clothes: What's Wrong with Banking and What to Do About It*, offered suggestions that were easy to understand. They also explained how banker's arguments to resist regulatory reform deserve to be ignored and reformed through new regulations for the public's good. Most importantly, they suggested that banks should hold more of their profits as equity to reduce their use of government subsidy in case of insolvency. Government policies that rescue banks from risky investments could then be curtailed or ended.

According to Admati and Hellwig, having greater equity would increase the exposure of earned bank monies to risk engagement and this would temper riskiness by causing the bank to experience a loss in case of default. The authors meaningfully addressed banker's protests regarding the provision of higher equity in banks and showed that this step would not reduce money available for loans. They also suggested that government policies that support debt instead of equity, should be changed both for banks and for corporations. Under Basel III, banks have been required to keep equity of only 3%. The authors wrote that 20-30% would be more appropriate. Increasing equity reserves would offer an incentive to avoid all-out risk taking at the public's expense.[367] Defaults would become less commonplace and would carry a sting of consequence instead of being rewarded with a subsidy that extirpates the consequences of bad investments.

According to Admati and Hellwig, "Bankers fight higher equity requirements, but the only way that having more equity might actually be costly to them is by preventing them from benefiting at the expense of taxpayers and creditors." Admati and Hellwig wrote that three problems have erupted in banking because of regulatory failures. Banks are first, "too big", second, "too interconnected" and third, "too political". Higher equity requirements would tend to reduce these bad qualities that make banking less safe. By allowing banks to approach insolvency, by failing to regulate banks to protect bank solvency in order to safeguard the public's interest, our policy makers in Washington have been failing the public in the U.S. and in other nations.[368]

International banking has global effects. And Admati and Hellwig clearly stated that banking regulations that happened after 2008, under Dodd Frank have failed to make banks safer.[369] Some of the regulations that were strengthened have already been repealed. According to Jennifer Taub writing in the *New York Times*, "The top six bank holding companies are 37 percent larger than they were before the 2008 crisis, and banks still borrow excessively in the short-term wholesale funding markets, leaving them vulnerable to Lehman-style runs."[370]

Wallace C. Turbeville, in his essay, "Derivatives: Innovation in the Era of Financial Regulation," also advocated for more equity to hedge against losses in a volatile marketplace instead of using derivatives as a hedge. Turbeville wrote that when a derivative swap is used to cushion against a declining price, the corporation can't benefit if the price increases. But by substituting equity, the upside can be profit generating. Also, when a derivative hedge is used, it locks a corporation into an inflexible position that prevents other ways of addressing a fall in price. If equity were used instead to hedge against a fall in price, it would allow the corporation to more nimbly change its business plan and shuttle resources away from falling-in-price product lines. The whole market can suffer when businesses become locked into derivative bets that preclude market flexibility. It can cause a corporation to stay with a bad business configuration for much longer than it should.

Yet another disadvantage of derivatives according to Turbeville is that they "allow total amount of exposure of asset price risk to multiply far beyond the actual assets that exist." This increased exposure is how the derivatives market has grown ten times larger than the real market and is also how it has endangered the real market. During the mortgage crisis in the run up to the Great Recession, derivatives were what unbalanced the banks. Toxic assets were derivatives like mortgage backed securities, and other more exotic synthetic tranches of debt risk that had been further abstracted and packaged for sale to the unwitting. After the housing market began to collapse, margin calls were made on derivative bets that unbalanced the whole financial marketplace.

Like Admati and Hellwig, Turbeville saw Dodd Frank as too weak to address the risk of further financial collapse brought to the financial markets by derivatives. But banks have liked derivatives because they have been their great money maker. Even more so because few customers understand what they buy. Bank lobbies have convinced legislators to water down regulations and bank investors have thereby evaded meaningful transparency that would require a full explanation of risk and cost to customers. Derivatives have continued to create "capital intermediation inefficiencies". That is to say that derivatives waste social resources, have caused a conflict of interest between banks and their customers and have threatened the health of the entire financial marketplace. More stringent derivatives regulations have been needed.[371]

The 2000 Commodity Futures Modernization Act prevented the CFTC from regulating derivatives and they remain opaque trading vehicles. They can be used for off-the-book hidden trading by using holding companies. Losses can be passed on to a parent company in the case of default. The Asian crisis happened partly due to a default in derivative payouts.[372] The LTCM (Long Term Capital

Management) crisis was caused by derivative trading that went wrong under capital leverage of 250 to 1. For every real dollar of derivative investment there were two hundred and fifty dollars in debt. Derivatives didn't have adequate capital requirements, and "the notional value of its derivative book was more than 1.25 trillion", in 1998.[373] Enron was also undermined by derivative trades that went bad. Derivatives were used by Enron to dodge taxes by hiding profits.[374]

Robert Pollin suggested in his essay, "Applying a Securities Transactions Tax to the US: Design Issues, Market Impact and the Revenue Estimates," that a STET, or security transaction excise tax could be used to provide two benefits: a reduction of short term speculation and a tax revenue. He mentioned that the U.S. already has a small STET that raises one billion dollars for the operations of the SEC. The Tobin Tax as suggested by James Tobin in 1978 was a STET on foreign currency markets. Resistance to such a tax has been based on perceived distortions that a STET might cause in financial markets, the perception that a STET could harm competitiveness between nations with different tax structures, or that it would increase the cost of capital, fail to slow volatility by stemming short term investing and also fail to raise revenue usefully. Japan had a STET which it repealed, in 1999.[375]

Pollin's essay was written sometime between 2001 and 2005. Fast and short term trading using computer algorithms has vastly increased the number of trades since then and also increased volatility of markets in present day trading. A STET might be used to create an equity reserve for potential failures in volatile markets. Pollin suggested in his essay that different rates of STET could be applied in different markets, "bonds, 0.01 percent per year until the bonds maturity, futures, 0.02 percent of the notional value of the underlying asset, options, 0.5 percent of the premium paid for the option, interest rate swaps, 0.02 percent per year until maturity of swap agreement."[376]

Others have suggested that HFT should be stopped to take out a middleman player in capital markets that inflates values non-virtuously at the public's expense. According to Michael Lewis in his book, *Flash Boys*, HFT brings Wall Street banks into conflict with their customer's better interests, HFT makes speed rather than stability the paramount trading hurdle, raises the cost of Wall Street trades and gives money to HFT middle men gained only through their hidden advantages over other market participants. HFT changes Wall Street for the worse by moving large sums of money gotten by new criteria into opportunistic influence. That influence has been felt in Washington D.C. and in financial markets.[377]

Economists who have focused on international finance, such as Ilene Grabel, have suggested that neoliberal financial imperatives have room for improvement. She wrote in her essay, "Averting Crisis? Assessing Measures to Manage Financial Integration in Emerging Economies," that there are five kinds of risk that developing countries face when they develop their economies under neoliberal guidelines. Those risks are "currency risk, flight risk, fragility risk, contagion risk, and sovereignty risk." She wrote that in order to lessen these threats, global markets should have restricted capital flows rather than totally free capital flows. This suggestion opposed the neoliberal insistence on free capital flows. She suggested that the number of domestic loans should more nearly match the number of foreign loans to reduce the risk of capital flight. She suggested that loan maturity agreements between lenders and borrowers should match the time of the loan duration so that loans don't require refinancing before the loan term is completed.

Grabel also asserted that hot money flows should be restricted and that full convertibility should be stopped to slow down money migrations in times of crisis. Crises sometimes have triggered money to exit from vulnerable economies. The exodus of money can leave these developing economies in bad capital shape and cause devaluations across the nation's vulnerable industries. She, like Admati and Hellwig, and others suggested that banks should be required to keep a greater reserve of equity to offset risk. Grabel also advocated for more transparent derivative markets to diminish "off balance market activities". Regarding derivatives, she suggested that "The only way to target the risks of off-balance sheet activities is to restrict them altogether or to mandate their transparency."[378]

Derivatives markets have acquired some strange descriptions.

Derivatives are so confusing that they have inspired a variety of strange descriptions. In 2012, Ron Rimkus, CFA, in his brief discussion, "Derivatives: The Anti-Money," suggested that derivatives eat up money, or that they are "anti-money."[379] This seemed fanciful and inaccurate since money tends to consistently belong to you or to someone else. Debt is just a promise to pay at a future date. When someone can't pay, they become insolvent. If derivatives create too much debt, that still isn't anti-money. Along the same vein of argument, an online article[380] suggested that when a person quantifies M, or the circulating money in the economy, they should subtract foreign direct investments that go outside the country of origin and also subtract derivatives. Derivatives, according to this author diminish circulating money. But the derivative bets from the subprime mortgage crisis stimulated Treasury money printing to recapitalize failing banks and that increased circulating money.

Derivatives have winners and losers. Some parties to derivative transactions are hidden in holding companies with unknown ties to other banks. Since banks trade 90% of derivatives, it seems likely that they are often on the winning side of derivative trading and not only in terms of fees. Most discussions regarding the 2008 collapse focused only on the losers. The question of who the winners were in the run up before the crisis and how much they made has been mostly ignored.[381] But it's obvious that since banks have lobbied to keep derivatives unregulated, they are defending their money-maker. Single winners who shorted the market and got financial gains in 2008 have been mentioned but little has been said of large banks that have traded heavily in derivatives for sometimes as long as decades and how their long term gains compare with losses they suffered at the 2008 collapse. How much money they made on their own positions and fees hasn't been tallied for the public.

Of course, with opacity in the derivatives market it may be that money's migration in derivative bets isn't knowable. Two internet sources speculated that derivative trades might involve deliberate defaults that could lead to cash payouts.[382, 383] Lucrative profits gained during catastrophic collapse would probably access public money as well as counterparty money. Recommendations regarding new regulations for the derivatives market have had a lot to do with these kinds of uncertainties and even suspicions regarding the derivative trade.

Randall Dodd, in his essay, "Derivatives Markets: Sources of Vulnerability in US Financial Markets", suggested some precautions in the form of regulatory change. He wanted more transparency in derivative trading so that market positions would become public knowledge. He also suggested more "capital and collateral requirements" (cash equity resources) to decrease loss exposure inside transactions. He worried about "daisy chain risk" in a rehypothecation chain where derivative risk would be reassigned to another party. He advocated an end to rehypothecation. He opposed allowing companies to become "super margined", where they would be expected to supply money when the market moved against their position. He opposed the use of "inferior assets" in derivatives trades, or assets that couldn't be converted to cash easily. He advocated for derivative traders to be reclassified as market makers, as treasury security dealers have been. He advocated for "know thy customer" provisions in derivative transactions.[384] Anat Admadi and Martin Hellwig also advocated for greater derivative trading transparency to provide more stockholder scrutiny of derivative risks.[385]

A question about derivatives to consider, especially after the Federal Reserve has increased the amount of money that is being held by banks in order to offset the losses caused by toxic mortgage securities is whether derivatives bets in 2008 accomplished money creation. Do derivatives create money? According to Paul Singer, a hedge trader who had 21.1 billion under management, derivatives have got at least a "similar power" to "money creation". He wrote: "In effect these transactions by investors and non-bank dealers represent many of the characteristics of the creation and dissipation of money, but they are outside the traditional and commonly understood mechanics of fractional reserve banking."[386] According to this hedge trader, the Federal Reserve's Keynesian policies are not able to cope with the power of derivatives; the Federal Reserve doesn't understand the new money supply and how derivatives affect it. And they haven't adapted their policies. According to Article 1 of the U.S. Constitution, Section 8, only Congress has the power "To coin Money, regulate the Value thereof". Congress has directed the Federal Reserve to regulate the dollar, but it certainly has not asked derivative traders to do that. It may be that derivative trading is unconstitutional for that reason.

"No matter how far you've gone down the wrong road, turn around."
——Turkish proverb

Reviewing fiscal policy and monetary policy shortfalls during neoliberalism and considering the opportunity for change.

Neoliberals have utilized political obstruction to block their own political accountability. But obstruction doesn't really stop political change because the politic is a complex adaptive system and change will inevitably come about. Neoliberals have had seventy years to proof out their theories and they have failed in their early goals. They haven't really ended collectivism. Instead, they have only changed to crony capitalism instead of social welfare. Their policies have harmed the economy by wasting economic resources, diminishing economic production and they have created a demand gap because of high debt, low wages and fewer jobs. Their system isn't as dominant and unchanging as they wished for. Political resistance has begun to form and political non-participation and labor non-participation both attest to people looking outside the current system for a meaningful alternative. A political coalition that would address the tension building up from unmet political and economic expectations might gather support from the grassroots. What a political competitor would need to offer is a better system than the one operating now.

Although some people would say that financialization began with regulatory reform and monetarism, the arguments for monetarism began because of excessive government debt. That's what encouraged monetarism to begin with. Regulatory reform gave banks free reign to circulate as much capital as they could generate through both private and government loans, and speculative risk. Clinton era "reinvention of government" discouraged regulation in finance and encouraged regulators to allow and even facilitate more financial risk. Generally accepted accounting principles were ignored during the S&L crisis and Enron's frauds. And financial frauds aren't the only way public money has been wasted. Military privatization has been another disappointing rip-off. And military privatization actualized political over-spending outside congressional oversight on neoliberal military projects over a decade span of making war in the Middle East that has led to many harms.

One of the reasons that financialization has continued has been to enable debt permissiveness and to cycle money into the economy by asset liquidation. A return to austerity has been tried in the UK. But austerity, whether in spending cuts or in tax increases or by a combination of both in order to reduce government deficit doesn't make sense in a fiat system where relative currency values can change quickly. The lack of a market anchor like gold under the strict gold standard makes austerity unable to progress against constantly increasing government debt. Unstable values and prices have led to malinvestments that have created more government debt and more public debt. Monetary policy that perpetuates monetarism and inflation devalues money so that it is less capable of paying off debt. So, in addition to fiscal indebtedness by the government and monetarism, the fiat monetary system is part of the debt economy problem, too. Monetary policy without a market based anchor can't stabilize values and prices. If stable values and prices could become re-established, a stable cooperative system could reduce global tensions, and austerity measures could begin to reestablish savings. Savings could fund loans instead of relying on debt capital creation in speculative markets. Only after monetary policy stabilized values and prices could sovereign debt be reduced by implementing government spending cuts or tax increases.

Corporations have taken over American politics but have practiced economic strategies that have relied on short term goals, mobile and liquid capital, speculation, tax breaks, favorable government policies, foreign direct investments and debt. Abstracting capital and using it like a commodity has stripped capital rewards from producers and caused the economy to shrink. Here's a list of some problems that have already been discussed earlier. A political plan to improve any of these problems could aid a political competitor in gaining public support for reorganizing the American politic mostly through legislative actions by using constitutional amendments or other legislation.

Thirteen neoliberal political and economic problems (problem in bold):

1. **There's more than 17 trillion dollars of government debt and an absence of political accountability to prevent further government debt.**
   This debt is the greatest obstacle preventing political change. Neoliberals have deliberately kept it growing through bad fiscal policy, bad monetary policy and war. It represents a financial claim against future earnings. It harms economic health and economic liberty. It's time to shrink it down through congressional reforms. Reforms should curtail overspending by requiring a balanced budget and a fiscal debt payment plan. Past attempts to achieve a balanced budget bill have failed. Maybe it's time for an amendment now. The global banking system will also require international cooperation to initiate reforms including default on unpayable loans.
2. **More than one million regulations exist that choke the justice system leading to selective enforcement. Transactional justice harms the poor.**
   This problem threatens civilization itself by undermining the rule of law. Legislators have a higher responsibility than putting pork into legislation that benefits a Congress member's state, or providing a corporate bonus to a campaign contributor. The proliferation of regulations can be stopped if Congress chooses to limit the number of laws. As long as harms to people and property are addressed through financial transactions, most harms won't be prevented and the poor will lose in judicial contests. Civilized society protects all people regardless of their power in the economy or the politic.

3. **Banking self-regulation has resulted in the end of Glass Steagall regulations and the continual risk of insolvency.** Now has come the time for banking reform to protect the production stream and bank solvency. The system of speculative financing should come to an end. Congress should ignore banker's profit motives and protect American solvency. Perhaps auditing the Federal Reserve or ending the Federal Reserve would begin to establish a new outlook on what a healthy solvent banking system could accomplish for a more productive America. Global economies have become linked through international banking but without international regulations to protect solvency. And Congressional thinking about the banking system has been muddled for too long. Banking isn't about political favors or economic advantages. Congress needs to protect the production stream of currency circulation that should be rewarding and protecting producers.

4. **Monetarism isn't any kind of sound money policy. The increased complexity of banking and larger bank size with fewer banks have been bad for society.** Monetarism should end and banks should be split into smaller units.

5. **The eclipse of productive pursuits by speculative pursuits has harmed the economy's vitality and consumed real wealth.** Derivatives should be regulated and transparent; eventually derivative gambles should become less common in favor of equity as a backstop to investment.

6. **Financialization has been a bad policy to support a failing neoliberal economic system. The debt economy has been replacing the production economy for a long time. A shrinking economy has been evident.** Easy money policy has harmed the American system of business enterprises. There should be an end to buyouts funded with 23 billion in debt like the Nabisco buyout. Such financing from banks has been destructive of production enterprises. If money retained its value, and if American enterprises could plan for the long term, CEO salaries would also come back into line with production metrics instead of being incented to support capital formation in speculative gambling.

7. **Unlimited corporate size: TBTF banks, giant media conglomerates, giant transnational and multinational corporations and the disappearance of many small businesses have hurt variety and competition. Increased corporate influence in the politic has hurt political interests that reside outside of subsidized monopolies.** This happened because of accelerationist policy, and deregulation in an atmosphere of corporate personhood. Corporations can be beneficial to communities but only when corporate interests are balanced with public interests and most profits are allowed to remain in the economy.

8. **Tax subsidy for corporate debt has been a political policy that has encouraged greater indebtedness.** This has been a bad tax policy.

9. **Revolving door connections between lobbies and members of Congress demonstrates corruption.** It has failed to serve the goal of having a moral government or the opportunity to participate in a marketplace without monopoly distortion.

10. **Outsourcing subsidy, and tax deferments for profits earned abroad has brought widespread domestic unemployment and is non-virtuous.** It should end.

11. **We have an ailing and broken economy because of too much centralization.** Value and price have been determined independently of supply and demand, there's been higher real inflation than reported inflation, lower real GDP than reported GDP, higher than reported unemployment, falling wages, declining labor benefits, and subsidized businesses that pass on inflated costs to their customers. Differential pricing has been rising in some markets under falling demand (see Neoliberalism Appendix). Insufficient political and economic opportunity for individuals has caused a demand gap. The government's sponsorship of corporations has not served American economic interests; it's time to decentralize.

12. **War that has served corporate interests and as an economic channel to treasury funding. Treasury funding has been the incentive for more war making. It should end.** Political and economic adaptation to the great wars led to permanent war making which shouldn't continue. Congress and the President share political oversight of war. Empire keeping wouldn't be essential under a sound global monetary system which would also stimulate global trade.

13. **The Affordable Care Act, a tax on life, a manifestation of biopolitics** (Fast Car Analysis) **and a governmental attempt to centralize another 18% of the economy has been a terrible neoliberal policy package. Passage of the ACA has been an act of political oppression.** The ACA has multiplied healthcare problems, worsened economic centralization and harmed people's right to privacy and information security. The ACA should be repealed. A constitutional Amendment might be drafted to protect people from laws that require the purchase of a mandated product.

Since WWII, Congress has protected and nourished an economy of titans through economic interventions such as accelerationist policy. This has harmed the domestic grassroots economy in the U.S. and caused a demand gap. Congress or the states have a constitutional amendment process and it can be used to change this broken neoliberal political system. Congress can stop subsidizing corporations, Congress can stop overspending, Congress can decentralize the American economy, Congress can reduce the number of regulations because a million of them is too many, and Congress can meaningfully regulate American banking to protect the circulation of money in a robust and solvent banking system. Systemic problems caused by bad fiscal policy, bad monetary policy, and economic centralization will require a wider and longer term vision than Congress has had. Ignoring this challenge jeopardizes the strength of the nation and its ability to support freedom and opportunity for all. People have rights and governments have powers. Congress has the power to fix these problems, if not with its current members, then with a newly elected Congress. Neoliberal obstructionism shouldn't deter Americans from finding their way to a healthier economy and politic.

Fixing the problem list can't be accomplished without a sound money system. A global monetary system is needed that offers stable values and prices. A new monetary system based on a market based commodity value such as gold, and greater fiscal discipline to change the debt economy into a wealth producing economy aren't simple changes. They aren't easy ones. Fixing the problem list and recreating a sound money system will fundamentally change the relationship between the politic and the economy. New amendments only come about in the context of urgency. But the experiment of Bretton Woods and our current fiat money system has failed to establish economic or political stability. Our fiat monetary system should end.

Change could begin with recognition that what is happening in finance hasn't been an efficient and effective use of society's productive capacity. And government participation in moral hazard, deficit funding in an unlimited budget, too many regulations, and unsound banking has harmed the public's prosperity and continues to put the public's prosperity further into jeopardy. Policies that have caused these problems shouldn't have to wait for a political and financial collapse to change. The Amendment process can be a way to change the politic and economy for the better as it has done in the past.

Concluding remarks.

Since the politic is where the nation decides "who gets what", economic policy has been a way of understanding political players and political stakes. Although neoliberalism began in Europe, it came to the U.S. when American businessmen imported European neoliberal economists. European economists from the Historical School of Economics had already been teaching in the U.S. since the 19th century. Neoliberal economists utilized differential calculus to offer a shorter-term and more policy activist approach. Neoliberalism now pervades the American politic and because of American free trade foreign policy, it has travelled all around the world. Both political parties have neoliberal attributes. Although neoliberal politicians, for example, the UK's Margaret Thatcher, declared that there wasn't an alternative to neoliberalism, she was wrong about that.

Neoliberalism became resistant to political accountability because of the public's acceptance of the nanny state which neoliberals opposed. When reviewing neoliberal economic texts, it has seemed that neoliberal economists opposed a lot of neoliberal economic policy that was applied by neoliberal politicians. For example, although Milton Friedman supported moderate inflation and monetarism, he did this only because of already high U.S. fiscal debt. He nevertheless wanted greater fiscal discipline. And all five of the Austrian neoliberal economists opposed both fiscal debt and monetarism. Ludwig von Mises opposed interventionism and he would likewise have opposed accelerationist policies. Although economics has been supposedly the bastion of ideas that defends neoliberal policy, foremost neoliberal economists haven't genuinely supported neoliberal economic and political policies.

Neoliberals wanted to defeat socialism, communism and fascism, but by coveting that kind of power, neoliberals only modified collectivism in support of corporate monopolists. The danger of totalitarianism has remained.[387] The goal of making way for corporate capitalism with CIA operations that undermined trade agreements among communists succeeded only halfway. While communism waned for both political and economic reasons, and less trade was among those reasons, neoliberal politicians have alienated political allies. And neoliberal policies have harmed the U.S. economy by redistributing wealth in an economically centralized collectivist system that uses economic opportunity as a political commodity.

In many nations, CIA political operations undermined a healthy politic. Neoliberals could use covert operations to encourage greater political disorder for a brief period, but they couldn't really control the political choices of people in faraway nations. After the Vietnam War came to an end, the Vietnamese adopted communism. Neoliberal economic experiments in Latin America failed too. And militarism in the Middle East has created a situation of ongoing violence and political strife. The model of private mercenary armies has now become established in Syria and Iraq but no political peace or economic prosperity resides there. Stabilizing world trade could be better accomplished through a global currency that offered stable prices and values. A political solution that strives to enforce economic and political reciprocity, arranged by diplomatic agreement and military strength, has already alienated potential political friends and harmed world prosperity.

Neoliberal propaganda has promoted corporatization abroad by transnationals under the idea that it would promote jobs and prosperity for developing nations. But economic opportunity has mostly been for corporatists, including bankers. Neoliberals seem to have thought that access to natural and capital resources in foreign trade would be a prize worth gaining. And this idea had its roots in territorial colonialism. But capitalism is better sustained by mutually rewarding exchanges. Also, neoliberal politicians overlooked negative long term political consequences at home when tax subsidies went into profits gained abroad that stayed abroad or went into speculative capital creation. The economies and economic markets of developed nations have been shrinking for decades. Using taxes for corporate purposes to develop global corporate opportunity has wasted alternative uses for taxes that benefit more Americans, like infrastructure investments. A hollowed out U.S. infrastructure bears witness to how damaging tax subsidies that go abroad have been when that tax was needed domestically to repair public infrastructure. And it is a ruinous idea that the U.S. can go more deeply in debt to fund infrastructure projects without changing unsound political and economic policies.

Regulatory reform realigned modern liberal political tools to corporate advantage. But neither modern liberalism nor neoliberalism have shown the radical promise of classical liberalism's liberty protections. Liberty promoted entrepreneurial investments and wealth building. Liberty also challenged Americans to finally end slavery and work toward greater social equity. Neither neoliberalism nor modern liberalism have succeeded economically to build wealth. They have parasitized economic successes that began under classical liberalism by either redirecting profits into politics or by liquidating American enterprises. Accelerationist policy has harmed technology development by channeling digital age investments into politically advantageous applications. And modern liberalism's and neoliberalism's disrespect for natural rights and the U.S. Constitution's restraints on government power have not made for a genuinely more powerful government economically or politically. Also, the non-virtuous redirection of capital from capital sources has been a failure for communities everywhere.

Political and economic stability rely on well regulated banking, just laws and restricted warfare. Right now in America, special interests have too much influence in the politic. Banking has been and continues to be poorly regulated. Banking self-regulation by self-interested parties in the financial industry has not protected the public's money. Failures in finance have been episodic and will continue until real reform takes place to balance a larger set of interests in the production stream. In terms of law, U.S. security organizations such as the CIA, NSA and FBI routinely have ignored natural rights in the U.S. Constitution, and they have done this for too long. Public servants in the executive department pretend that they have been above the law as they breached their oaths to the U.S. Constitution. But like neoliberal actors in Latin America were condemned after the Chicago School failed to establish a stable politic and economy, American society may eventually condemn American neoliberal actors for damage done to the American political and economic system and to Americans themselves.

Trespasses against constitutional guidelines have led to less privacy, and less security against state sponsored violence all across America, from militarized police to National Security Letters prohibiting speech, to wholesale information trolling of online and telephone sources. The boundary that prohibits overreaching governmental power is fundamental to the American political heritage. And although foolish neoliberal politicians have sometimes discounted the importance of sacred American political documents, the U.S. Constitution still matters to Americans all over the United States. Tragically, wars in the Middle East have continued. Money invested in military adventures overseas has been wasted and there's no end to the MIC's appetite for conflict. Most Americans want less militarism. Empire-keeping has been outside of American values and it goes far beyond what people in this country can fund. Raiding the U.S. treasury to pay for munitions and military operations has become the most important incentive for military actions. Few can find any other dividend for military operations in the Middle East. Whatever the grand visions may have been that motivated U.S. and Middle Eastern conflicts, these conflicts have hurt and not helped globalization goals.

This book has outlined three ideologies, classical liberalism, modern liberalism and neoliberalism. Classical liberalism ran out of new lands to expand into and the market economy motivated political changes. Modern liberalism ran into monstrous world wars that stripped wealth out of developed economies and changed global cultures. Politicians wasted a lot of the wealth that the Industrial Revolution produced. After the wars, corporations that resented a heavy tax burden and insisted on government support for their interests redirected politics in support of global trade but mostly to maximize corporate profits in high risk environments for short term gain. Neoliberals have redirected money away from production and community until the grassroots wealth that was built up in earlier periods has declined. This subtraction of wealth from community producers has denied them prosperity and undermined incentives to go on with neoliberal experiments. Neoliberalism has now run into financial difficulties that carried forward from the past and that have been compounded in the present. Austrian neoliberal economists warned about what Ludwig von Mises called "the crack up boom economy", that can happen when governments overprint their currency in order to escape debt obligations. Well past seventeen trillion dollars of debt is too much debt. A shrinking economy has little hope of paying this debt down and certainly not under the same bad neoliberal policy set.

Public support for a new politic will necessarily begin with an understanding of connections between the politic and economy and between our society's history and the present. Both the politic and economy are powerful but they work best when they work synergistically. Neoliberals tried to create their own rulebook for a whole new neoliberal world but they have failed to create a viable partnership between the neoliberal politic and economy. Power as a singular economic and political goal has again failed to balance interests in the economy, the politic and society. The Occupy Wall Street and Tea Party movements attempted to initiate political change away from neoliberalism, but they failed to capture enough public support. It has seemed obvious that the people in these movements needed more rhetorical tools to describe what's wrong, why it's wrong, and how change might go forward. It is to be hoped that the network of connections between the politic and economy described here can inform a program that would make sense and succeed for more of society.

Fast Car Analysis for Neoliberalism

Economism is the practice of measuring society and its motivations according to financial or material gain and expecting self-interest to be the only important social motivator.

Biopolitics uses the set of vulnerabilities people experience that come from being a living organism. The Ancients recognized necessity and reciprocity as being natural and shaping politics; neoliberal opportunists have thought that people's need for food, clean water, health and energy makes them politically vulnerable.

Neoliberalism began among European economists between WWI and WWII. **European neoliberal economists were imported** to teach at U.S. universities. During the Ford Administration, the "cost benefit analysis" spread economism among American academics. The politicization of economics that started under modern liberalism progressed under neoliberalism. Politicized economics embraced monetarism. **Think tanks** were politically innovative neoliberal organizations that have been adept at influencing legislators on specific policy issues.

Neoliberals have sometimes expected economic interests and political interests to compete for power. But **the politic and economy work better when they cooperate** to support society synergistically.

Regulatory reform has caused problems including:
The growth of monopolies which are fewer and larger enterprises has distorted the market price mechanism. Monopolies create economic inefficiency, less entrepreneurial development, less R & D, and a less nimble business community. Media monopoly shared among a few media corporations has led to less newsy news and more **censorship**. Too Big to Fail Banks each represent both enormous power and riskiness after finance deregulation. Bank profits have come at the public's expense because the Federal Reserve under Alan Greenspan provided a subsidy for bank failure in the **Greenspan Put**. Monopoly inefficiencies and outsourcing tax policies have gobbled up public money and now there's less money for American infrastructure.

Easy credit financialization has changed business practices, reduced the number of businesses and reduced the number of jobs.

Job destroying neoliberal policies are many: corporate welfare under tax subsidy that has supported outsourcing; financialization that encourages short term profits over long term investments; debt for hostile takeovers with subsequent enterprise liquidation; speculation that has displaced investing in production; government accelerationist policy to promote the spread of monopolies and the decline of small business; non-prosecution of criminal financial frauds.

Even though neoliberal economic theories have been used to justify neoliberal political policies, **neoliberal economists have often disagreed with neoliberal political policies.** Neoliberal politicians **have evaded any political accounting** of their policies and policy failures. They ignore problems that their policies are causing.

There are three successful monetary policy approaches in history. But not fiat. **Fiat isn't a sound money system.** Fiat monetary systems aren't long lasting and their currencies lose value. **Unsound money can cause nation state unrest, financial losses among groups and individuals and it can collapse political regimes.**

There are **three neoliberal economic schools** of thinking with three neoliberal founders: **Ludwig von Mises** saw the economy as a complex adaptive system. **Friedrich von Hayek** saw the economy as being similar to a giant brain that can adjust and adapt. **Milton Friedman** who founded the Chicago School, used what Williamson described as Washington Consensus policies to reorganize a nation's politic and economy.

Ludwig von Mises **opposed economic interventionism**, which would include accelerationist policy, or a policy where the federal government subsidizes corporate winners it chooses.

There have been more neoliberal landmark judicial cases than there were classical liberal or modern liberal ones. Laws have been remodeled to help corporations. **Neoliberals have also multiplied laws to create legal chaos. This technique undermines civilized society.** Policy alternatives to neoliberalism continue to be formulated. Many alternatives exist.

Neoliberal policies have advanced by rewarding opportunists at society's expense, but neoliberalism fails to succeed economically. It alienates Americans who care about the rule of law, political accountability and prosperity.

Neoliberalism Appendix

Essential characteristics of Neoliberalism:

1. Neoliberalism has been a positivist, constructivist, political-resistance response to the WWI collapse of the gold standard, the events of the Great Depression, the violence of WWI and WWII, and the destruction and displacements that these happenings caused. When fascists, communists and socialists utilized the complex power of nation states with complex market economies to form totalitarian states, people were frightened of that process. As they saw Hitler's ambitions destroy so much of Europe, Hitler's kind of power was both admired and feared. Neoliberalism was meant to prevent totalitarian destruction while preserving the market economy. And Hitler's kind of power would be harnessed by partnering government regulatory power and corporate economic development but with corporations in the economic driver's seat. Mobile capital has been an important part of neoliberal strategy.

2. The machinery of expanded government built by modern liberalism to serve public interests was diverted toward supporting global corporations in a bid to remake global economies under neoliberal modeling. These policies were described in part by John Williamson as the "Washington Consensus". The nation state system lacked international legal oversight of trans-national business operations and that gave corporatist developers greater independence. Natural rights were ignored by neoliberals, political accountability was avoided by them and debt-finance began to dominate markets for the benefit of money empowered economic elites. U.S. foreign policy has supported global corporate growth by defending it militarily. American corporations penetrated into every corner of the world through easy-credit financialization and mobile capital.

3. The highest neoliberal political ideal has been the quenching of political rivals while advancing neoliberalism through economic and financial mechanisms. The CIA's function may have been to prevent the formation of global economic networks among politically non-neoliberal groups. U.S. neoliberals have ignored the U.S. Constitution. And whenever legislation has impeded corporatist's interests, corporatist lobbies have gotten Congress to add a loophole that spared their interests.

4. Both economic and political power became more centralized in partnership networks between global corporations, Too-Big-To-Fail financial institutions, giant media, and interventionist government. Centralized-power limited novel approaches when problems developed within the domestic economy. Redesigning economic opportunities for a smaller number of Americans and eliminating economic opportunities for many people has caused class restructuring, an ominous political change. People who have

fallen out of prosperity have been blamed even when they were affected adversely by political policies that harmed their interests. Regulatory oversight also invaded private life and extravagant regulatory tendencies have reduced individual innovation and liberty. Neoliberal press substituted infotainment for information and has prevented policy reevaluation when neoliberal policies have harmed the public's interests.

5. Under neoliberalism, the government's job has been to defend opportunity for corporate clients. Under accelerationist policies, the government has picked economic winners and losers. Economic winners have influenced public policy more than any other political group because they have the most capital advantages. Big money sources contributed more than ever before to political campaigns. A feedback loop recycled power that has formed between corporate contributors and government. This power loop encouraged corporate monopoly-like power, governmental moral jeopardy and discouraged political interventions on behalf of larger society. Politics motivated by power instead of merit has destroyed the meritocracy that grew under modern liberalism.

6. Neoliberals externalized some groups from wealth. These political paupers have fewer productive options. Under the Affordable Care Act (ACA), neoliberals have created mandatory public welfare. Obamacare is a tax on life that has been implemented as the economy shrinks in order to liquidate people's financial resources. Declining employment, falling wages and lesser benefits are part of neoliberal global outsourcing policies supported by federal tax incentives that pay corporate welfare while trimming social welfare. Neoliberal programs for education don't empower American youth to become economically successful in the neoliberal landscape. There's been less economic opportunity in the U.S. and more poverty.

7. The market economy trading-web of developed nations has been supplanted by mobile capital. Mobile capital has led global monetary investments into nations with the cheapest factors. Fiat money's unstable prices and values has encouraged greater speculation in financial markets. And Wall Street investing has become more of a speculative game. Wall Street plays a lesser role in supporting investments in real productivity or for start-up companies. Digital computer technologies have been utilized for information mining and fastest-trading-advantage in finance. These computer moderated strategies have caused further distortions in price and value. Markets have become less influenced by real marketplace demand. Inflation and deflation have had a new cause in high frequency trading and derivative hedging.

8. International legal anarchy has existed in the space between nations where multinationals and transnationals have operated. Global trading without a stable international currency exacerbated distrust between nations under

the nation state system. The discipline of economics which was politicized during modern liberalism has continued to be politicized under neoliberalism. A politicized economics cadre has validated monetarism. But narrowly focused neoliberal economists have failed to address economic problems by offering alternative economic approaches. Policy changes could undermine the neoliberal policy agenda. Other branches of science such as climate science have also become politicized (references listed in source notes after Neoliberalism endnotes). Neoliberal think tanks and Ivy League economic programs have supported the neoliberal model.

9. Neoliberals were as fascinated as modern liberals were with the use of political force. But military violence has now failed to enforce neoliberal political and economic dominance in the Middle East. Militarization of U.S. urban police forces through transfers of military equipment to local law enforcement, training in the use of military force under lethal prerogatives, and the presence of increasing social disruptions caused by unemployment associated poverty has led to lethal clashes between the police and society. Computer surveillance technologies have become tools used by local police and they are on the rise. Neoliberals oppose public resistance through surveillance and police violence.

10. If military enforcement can't be the servant that neoliberals envisioned to keep neoliberal policies dominant, or if the nation state system rejects neoliberalism, or if local communities reject the neoliberal program, then it is likely that a new political and economic partnership will form. But social disruption and chaos have already become a part of a neoliberal political implosion through harms that neoliberal policies have caused to the public and to the economy and by neoliberal disruption of public policy reform.

(Appendix sources listed last in Neoliberalism Endnotes)

CIA timeline:

1947 President Truman signed the National Security Act of 1947, which created the CIA, the National Security Council, the Office of the Secretary of Defense and the Air Force. The National Security Council oversaw the CIA instead of Congress which meant that bureaucrats instead of elected officials were overseeing bureaucrats.

1948 CIA obstructed communists in Italian voting; the communists lost.

1949 CIA propaganda broadcasts began through Radio Free Europe.

1950 Senator McCarthy gave speeches to make people afraid of communism and to whip up fervor against individuals that were suspected of communist leanings; UN entered Korean conflict and U.S. soldiers were the most numerous of any national group; the Korean conflict lasted until 1953, U.S. opposed China along the 98th parallel.

1952 President Truman created the National Security Agency.

1953 Mohammed Mossadeq, the Iranian Premier was overthrown in a CIA assisted coup; The Shah of Iran replaced him; SAVAK police forces undergirded the Shah's power.

1954 Jacobo Arbenz, Guatemalan President was overthrown in a CIA assisted coup; he had suggested nationalization of the United Fruit Company. Forty years later, under various dictators, 200,000 Guatemalan civilian casualty deaths had occurred.

1956 Hungarians revolted against the Soviets in response to a Radio Free Europe broadcast of a speech by Kruschev. 30,000 dead Hungarians, 7,000 dead Soviets.

1957 U.S. began bombing Laos; CIA disrupted Laos elections that favored the Pathet Lao.

1958 CIA covert action in Indonesia was exposed after the rebellion collapsed and the American pilot Allen Pope was shot down.

1959 U.S. President authorized a coup to dislodge Duvalier in Haiti after military support had previously empowered the Haitian dictator. Francois "Papa Doc" Duvalier also stole U.S. economic aid to shore up his political influence. But CIA arming of dissidents failed to produce a coup. 100,000 Haitians died during Papa Doc's dictatorship.

1961 CIA sponsored force made up of Cuban exiles attacked Cuba and failed to overthrow the Fidel Castro regime; Bay of Pigs; President Kennedy fired Allen Dulles from the CIA. Secretary of Defense organized the DIA, or Defense Intelligence Agency. The CIA helped arrange the assassination of Rafael Trujillo of the Dominican Republic. The Dominican Republic's Juan Bosch, who replaced Rafael Trujillo was also displaced in a military coup in 1964. Under CIA intimidation, Vice President Carlos Aroseman of Ecuador displaced Ecuadorian President Jose Velasco but Aroseman himself was supplanted by another CIA coup two years later. Patrice Lumumba of Zaire (Congo) was killed by an uprising that was engineered by the CIA's replacement, Joseph Mobutu. But Mobutu was unable to consolidate a stable power base for five years of political chaos.

1962 CIA director John McCone handed President Kennedy a memo listing "covert operations in eleven nations, including Vietnam, Laos and Thailand, Iran and Pakistan, Bolivia, Columbia, Ecuador and the Dominican Republic, Guatemala and Venezuela" (1).

1963 Ngo Dinh Diem regime ended under CIA influence; U.S. President Kennedy was assassinated by Oswald, who had contacted a Soviet assassination expert.

1964 Gulf of Tonkin Resolution approved by Congress; U.S. Vietnamese involvement increased. The CIA backed a military coup to overthrow Brazil's Joao Goulart and CIA trained death squads enforced the junta's power.

1965 Indonesia's Sukarno was overthrown by a military group. His replacement, Suharto killed at least 500,000 in Indonesia.

1966 *Ramparts* magazine published a story stating that the National Student Association was a CIA recruiting organization.

1967 The Overseas Internal Security Program, set up originally by President Eisenhower trained secret police forces in "Cambodia, Columbia, Ecuador, El Salvador, Guatemala, Iran, Iraq, Laos, Peru, Philippines, South Korea, South Vietnam, and Thailand" (2), some became death squad leaders and massacred civilians" (3). The Arab-Israeli War (Six Day War) happened with Israel winning. A Greek military group overthrew the Greek government without first notifying its CIA connections; but U.S. government remained on friendly terms with the junta despite the junta's use of torture and jail to undergird its power.

1972 Congress voted to end funding for the CIA after Cambodian operations came to light. The Watergate operation that involved CIA trained agents put Congress further out of sorts with the Executive branch.

1973 The Paris Peace accords ended the Vietnam War. There was a CIA sponsored military coup in Chile that replaced Salvador Allende with Augusto Pinochet who murdered more than 3,200 Chileans.

1974 Hughes Ryan Act passed in Congress to help Congress monitor non-intelligence CIA activity.

1975 The Church Committee investigated the CIA; The Rockefeller Commission countered with "whitewash" campaign; of eight members on the Rockefeller Commission, five were from the Council on Foreign Relations.

1979 Shah of Iran deposed; Iran U.S. hostage crisis; Soviet invasion of Afghanistan; CIA gave arms to Afghan resistance; CIA backed Nicaraguan dictator Anastasios Samoza II, fell to Marxist Sandinistas, and remnants of Samoza's guard became the Contras.

1980 Civil War in El Salvador, 63,000 deaths.

1981 Polish Solidarity movement was suppressed by Polish Communist government. Iran/Contra, CIA arms selling to Iran raised funds for Contras, which Congress had defunded.

1984 Boland Amendments tried to cut off aid to Nicaraguan Contras forces; Iran/Contra scandal surfaced a few years later, in 1986.

1988 Libyan terrorists blew up Pan American Flight 103.

1989 Tiananmen Square protestors were killed by Chinese government forces. The Solidarity Movement in Poland was restored to legal status. The Berlin Wall was torn down which marked the end of the Cold War. The U.S. invasion of Panama and U.S. detainment of Manuel Noriega.

1990 Iraq invaded Kuwait. Germany's reunification in NATO happened. Operation Desert Storm began.

1991 USSR broken up into individual states.

1995 U.S. sent 20,000 American troops into Bosnia.

1996 Gary Webb investigated CIA ties with crack cocaine dealing in Los Angeles as a means of raising money to fund the Contras of Nicaragua. The "Dark Alliance" series later became a book. Mainstream press undermined Webb's story through personal attacks but his facts held up.

1999 NATO and Yugoslavia ended Serbian occupation of Kosovo.

2000 U.S. Cole terrorist attack.

2001 Terrorist attack destroyed the World Trade Center buildings; Operation Enduring Freedom began in Afghanistan.

2003 Operation Iraqi Freedom began.

2004 Intelligence Reform and Terrorism Prevention Act.

2005 London Subway bombing by an Islamic terrorist group.

2009 Establishment of the CIA Center of Climate Change and National Security.

2011 Special Forces killed Osama Bin Laden.

2013 Edward Snowden illegally provided information regarding NSA privacy breaches and that information also provided an estimate of the CIA's budget. Five hundred billion dollars were spent on U.S. intelligence after Sept 11, 2001 according to the Black Budget. The CIA budget, which was larger than the NSA budget, purchased "secret prisons," "interrogation," "drone assassins," and growth of "counterterrorism"

2014 Senate Torture Report summary was published.

Differential pricing to enhance selling within a market under conditions of falling demand.

In a healthy market economy, demand from customers, competition from other firms and what people can afford sets the price. Price reflects what it costs to make something and the minimum price is the cost of production which includes materials and expenses like labor. Less than the cost of production is a loss. But differential pricing happens when different prices for the same item are charged depending on who is buying. In 1996, Victoria's Secret used differential pricing in a "mail order campaign" where some customers were mailed lower and some were mailed higher priced catalogues. A consumer who received a higher price catalogue filed a lawsuit but a judge ruled against her in *Katzman v. Victoria's Secret Catalogue*.[1] The judge also penalized her for bringing a "frivolous lawsuit."[2] The judge thought that the corporation should be allowed to practice differential pricing.

Differential pricing in the Digital Age has presented at least two problems. One has been that companies can collect information on potential buyers which they can sell to others or utilize for their own purposes. If the information collected caused certain pricing strategies to be used by companies on a person it could be both beyond their knowledge and it could reduce their ability to get a good deal. If comparison shopping won't reveal a lower price because sellers use a similar algorithm that profiles a person to be in a higher price category, then the customer's ability to comparison shop could be damaged. That seems to represent both privacy violation and unfairness. It's an interruption of ordinary market economy supply and demand pricing but it also puts the consumer outside of the price setting dynamic. This information asymmetry is an example of a business activity that undermines consumer market confidence. Consumers have no control of how their electronic data is being used by marketers and often can't know how information about them could affect pricing.

According to one source, when there is falling demand, the downward sloping demand curve, which shows a reduced demand, can be shown mathematically to allow for a larger profit in the case of differential pricing as compared with universal pricing when everyone is charged the same price. More product would be sold and the seller would make more. As incomes become more divergent, product pricing can become class sensitive in order to sell the greater amount of merchandise by quantity. Besides falling demand, high fixed costs can encourage firms to charge some customers more for the same goods or to modify the goods slightly to create a justification for the price differential. This allows the seller to more quickly regain the money that was sunk into fixed costs. High regulatory fees can also add to fixed costs.[3, 4]

Today's markets exhibit a demand gap that has been growing and if the U.S. economy continues to shrink, price discrimination may become more commonplace as a remedy for sellers in a shrinking marketplace.[5] Arthur Cecil Pigou (1877-1959), a neoclassical economist,[6] examined price discrimination and he came up with three classes: first degree, second degree and third degree. First degree price discrimination is when the seller can perfectly profile the buyer and know what their maximum price is. Second degree price discrimination is when discounts are applied according to quantity, like a bulk discount for example. Third degree price discrimination happens according to customer profiling using information about where someone lives or what kind of purchases that the person made in the past.[7]

Some forms of price discrimination have been commonplace and fairly well accepted by consumers, like: senior or student discounts, discounts on prebooked airfares, grocery club discounts and coupon discounts. "Discounting" has been a form of differential pricing. More controversial price discrimination examples have included such things as higher medical charges for uninsured persons, higher drug prices in wealthy nations with prohibitions on importing cheaper drugs, and product price differences determined by algorithms employed by e-commerce companies based on buyer information. Some forms of price discrimination such as those done based on a person's race, culture or gender are supposed to be illegal. Many forms of price discrimination may be hidden from consumers who are unaware that the same product will be sold at a different price to another person. The informational asymmetry bothers people.

Comparing the attitude of twenty first century price discrimination with the ethical pricing methods of colonial Massachusetts reveals a stark contrast of attitude. Consider the following quote from John Winthrop (1587-1649):

"The rules for trading are these: 1. A man may not sell above the current price…2. When a man loseth in his commodity for want of skill, etc., he must look at it as his own fault or cross, and therefore must not lay it upon another. 3. Where a man loseth by casualty of sea, or, etc it is a loss cast upon himself by providence, but where there is a scarcity of the commodity, there men may raise their price; for now it is a hand of God upon the commodity and not the person. 4. A man may not ask any more for his commodity than his selling price, as Ephron to Abraham, the land is worth thus much."[8]

Winthrop lived during mercantilism and what a difference his ethical concerns show regarding price setting as compared to the neoliberal price discrimination where business persons should charge as much as they can and fairness is whatever you can get away with in a declining economy using government policy subsidies and information asymmetry.

Neoliberal timeline:
1937 Pablo Picasso's *Guernica* painting.
1939-1945 WWII, U.S. entered in 1941
1944 Bretton Woods Conference, where the U.S. and Britain engineered a new global monetary system, getting 44 Allied nations to agree.
1949 Mao Zedong defeated the Nationalists who retreated to Taiwan and he announced that China would be under the Communist Party.
1950 Jackson Pollack's *Autumn Rhythm (Number 30)*.
1950-1953 Korean Conflict.
1953 DNA was discovered by Johann Friedrich Meischer; he called it nuclein.
1954 USSR made electricity from a nuclear power plant for the first time.
1955 First Civil War in the Sudan. Physicists discovered how to make antimatter.
1956 Sudanese, Tunisian and Pakistani independence. The Suez crisis ensued when Gamel Abdel Nasser nationalized the Suez canal.
1957 Sputnik's successful launch inaugurated the Space Race. The birth control pill became available.
1958 The Great Chinese Famine began.
1959 The Cuban Revolution began. The first AIDS cases were identified. World population was at three billion. COINTELPRO (Counter Intelligence Program) was a series of FBI activities that tried to disrupt domestic political organizations; it continued until 1971.

1960 The Beatles formed in Liverpool, England. The first laser was invented by Theodore Maiman. Muhammed Ali won a gold medal in Rome Olympics. The first voyage was made to the Mariana Trench.

1961 The Berlin Wall was built.

1962 Kennedy's Cuban Missile Crisis unfolded. Algerians achieved their independence from France, the Yemen Arab Republic formed but the North Yemen Civil War began and the Sino-Indian War began. Andy Warhol's *Marilyn Diptych*.

1963 Kenya achieved independence. Malaysia formed. Martin Luther King's "I Have a Dream" speech was given. President Kennedy was assassinated. The first geostationary satellite was put into orbit.

1964 The Civil Rights Act went into effect.

1965 The Second Indo-Pakistani War.

1965-1975 The Vietnam War.

1966 Chinese Cultural Revolution began and it resulted in the deaths of one and one half million people.

1968 The Poor People's campaign ended with the assassination of both Martin Luther King Jr. and Robert F. Kennedy.

1969 NASA astronauts landed on the moon and Woodstock celebrated the Counter Culture Movement. The Libyan Arab Republic formed under Muammar Gaddafi's leadership.

1970 Ratification of the Nuclear Non-Proliferation Treaty. Containerization became widely accepted and it transformed global shipping.

1971 The Microchip was invented by Jack Kilby and Robert Noyce. The Nixon Shock closed the gold window for the convertibility of dollars to gold which meant that world currencies began to float on the foreign exchange market and the Bretton Woods managed gold system had come to an end.

1972 Ferdinand Marcos declared martial law in the Philippines.

1973 Skylab was launched. The first oil shock affected global economies as OPEC limited oil sales to drive up the price. During the 1970's global production chains were gradually relocated from the developed world to manufacturing centers with cheaper labor and fewer regulations.

1974 Turkey occupied Cyprus. Ethiopia's Haile Selassie I was overthrown. Judy Chicago's *The Dinner Party (1974-1979)*.

1975 The Khmer Rouge won the Cambodian Civil War and killed as many as three million people.

1976 The first documented Ebola outbreak. Steve Jobs and others invented the Apple I.

1977 Deng Xiaoping gained political power after Mao Zedong died. Personal computers became available.

1978 First laboratory-produced insulin not made from animals (it was made by bacteria).

1979 Soviet-Afghan war began. Margaret Thatcher became UK's Prime Minister. The Khmer Rouge was overthrown.

1980 President Reagan was elected; he broke the air controller's strike. John Lennon was killed.

1981 The Space Shuttle entered "orbital flight".

1982 The UK/Faulkland's War. Maya Lin's *Vietnam Veteran's Memorial* in Washington D.C., at the Mall.

1983 The U.S. Grenada invasion. Beirut bombing of U.S. Embassy.

1984-5 Famine in Ethiopia; Live Aid. Sino-British agreement stated that Hong Kong would belong to China after 1997.

1986 Chernobyl disaster. Challenger was lost. Space Station Mir went into orbit. The London "Big Bang" happened when London banks were deregulated and became internationalized. Global bank investors, many from the U.S., converged on London to take advantage of novel opportunities. But the Big Bang caused bank industry fragility because Too-Big-To-Fail-Banks interlinked banks across a global network that was interdependent and too risky.

1987 Stock market crash of '87. World population reached 5 billion. The "fairness doctrine" in broadcasting ended the model of broadcasting as a public service.

1988 The Channel Tunnel began construction.

1989 The fall of the Berlin Wall ended the Cold War; breakup of USSR. Tiananmen Square deaths in China. Soviet Afghan War ended. Exxon Valdez oil spill damaged pristine coastal waters in Alaska.

1990 Sir Tim Berners-Lee created the World Wide Web. Hubble telescope was launched. Intergovernmental Panel on Climate Change issued an Anthropomorphic Global Warming Assessment.

1990-1991 the Persian Gulf War.

1992 Maastricht Treaty formed the European Union. Bosnian War. NAFTA began.

1993 Frank Gehry's *Bilbao Guggenheim Museum*.

1994 Apartheid ended in South Africa; leadership of Nelson Mandela in elected office began after years spent in prison.

1995 The North Korean Famine eventually killed two and a half million people.

1996 The Telecommunications Act led to further media deregulation.

1997 1.5 trillion dollars of foreign exchange trading per day. The Asian Financial Crisis.

1998 Good Friday Agreement in Ireland to "end the troubles".

1999 World population reached 6 billion. WTO protests happened in Seattle. Enron scandal; WorldCom scandal. 1999 Gramm, Leach, Bliley Act, led to further financial deregulation.

2000 Commodities Futures Modernization Act, kept derivatives outside regulatory oversight.

2001 Terrorists attacked the World Trade Center Buildings. U.S. declared a War on Terror. Wikipedia was founded.

2001-2010 Afghanistan War.

2002 Guantanamo Bay was built.

2003 Completion of the Human Genome Project. The WTO meeting in Mexico was shut down by protestors. U.S. Iraq War led to global protests.

2003-2010 Iraq War.

2004 Terrorists bombed the train in Madrid, Spain. Tsunami fatalities of 230,000 occurred along the Indian Ocean.

2005 The Kyoto Protocol became active. The IRA ended its Irish military activities.

2006 Terrorists bombings happened in Mumbai. Sadaam Hussein was executed by the United States.

2007 Global Great Recession began after subprime mortgage securities lost value on the global market; real estate lost value across the globe. There was a spike in food and energy prices that occurred independently of real market use demand because of speculation in food and energy.

2008 President Obama was elected. He forgave Bush Administration officials for acts of rendition and torture and failed to prosecute Too-Big-To-Fail banks. He pushed through the ACA under Democratic support, with a mandatory tax penalty for not buying his lackluster health insurance product and he thereby expanded market subsidies to healthcare to keep the prices higher than demand would have them.

2009 The federal government declared an end to the Great Recession but global unemployment remained high and real estate failed to recover lost value. The injured real estate market was too weak to enhance economic recovery.

2010 The Fast and Furious Scandal came to light, where BATFE sold 1500 guns to Mexican criminals that were utilized in crimes including the murder of Brian Terry. Corruption in the BATFE was obvious when officials who acted improperly, outside the color of the law, and who caused the deaths of innocent people were promoted and whistle blowers were harassed and fired.

2012 Eric Holder dismissed the charges against the last two remaining U.S. torturers.

2013 Edward Snowden leaked NSA classified security information to the press and fled the United States. A Senate Intelligence Committee Report admitted that CIA torture included the torture of innocent people, was useless except for producing false information and was harmful to the United States. Also in 2013, 97% of criminal court cases that went to trial in the

U.S. were settled by a plea bargain which circumvented the jury trial and allowed prosecutors to dominate judicial outcomes.

2014 The Islamic State expanded out from the Civil War in Syria into Iraq by using U.S. made weapons. Also, *Ebola Marburg* flared into an epidemic in Western Africa. Several Freedom-of-Information requests for current ACA enrollment figures after April were still waiting for enrollment information. This represented censorship of government figures.

Neoliberalism Endnotes

1. Fabio Masini, "The Making of the Neoliberal Project: A Contribution from Italy," www.iernit-u-ac.jp/~nisizawa/masini.pdf, last updated 2010, accessed 2013.

2. Wilhelm Ropke, *The Social Crisis of Our Time*, (New Brunswick, NJ: Transaction Publishers, fourth printing 2009), 38-82.

3. Fabio Masini, "The Making of the Neoliberal Project: A Contribution from Italy," www.iernit-u-ac.jp/~nisizawa/masini.pdf, last updated 2010, accessed 2013.

4. Wikipedia, "Luigi Einaudi," wikipedia.org/wiki/Luigi Einaudi, accessed 2013.

5. Fabio Masini, "The Making of the Neoliberal Project: A Contribution from Italy," www.iernit-u-ac.jp/~nisizawa/masini.pdf, last updated 2010, accessed 2013.

6. Fritz Machlup, *A History of Thought on Economic Integration*, (UK: Columbia University Press, 1977), 219.

7. Notation for the reader: the book title was shortened in the 2004 reprint by Transaction Publishers.

8. Phillip Mirowski, Dieter Plehwe, eds., *The Road to Mt. Pelerin: The Making of the Neoliberal Thought Collective*, (Cambridge, MA: Harvard University Press, 2009), 13.

9. Walter Lippmann, *The Good Society*, Gary Dean Best's introduction, (New Brunswick, NJ: Transaction Publishing, 2005), xxiii-xl.

10. Phillip Mirowski, Dieter Plehwe, eds., *The Road to Mt. Pelerin: The Making of the Neoliberal Thought Collective*, (Cambridge, MA: Harvard University Press, 2009), 15.

11. Phillip Mirowski, Dieter Plehwe, eds., *The Road to Mt. Pelerin: The Making of the Neoliberal Thought Collective*, (Cambridge, MA: Harvard University Press, 2009), 12-13.

12. Phillip Mirowski, Dieter Plehwe, eds., *The Road to Mt. Pelerin: The Making of the Neoliberal Thought Collective*, (Cambridge, MA: Harvard University Press, 2009), 427.

13. Andrew Rich, *Think Tanks, Public Policy, and the Politics of Expertise*, (New York: Cambridge University Press, 2004), 154-155, 207, 209, 213.

14. Phillip Mirowski, Dieter Plehwe, eds., *The Road to Mt. Pelerin: The Making of the Neoliberal Thought Collective*, (Cambridge, MA: Harvard University Press, 2009), 428.

15. Wilhelm Ropke, *The Social Crisis of Our Time*, (New Brunswick, NJ: Transaction Publishers, fourth printing 2009), 210-211.

16. The Mont Pelerin Society, "Notable Members," www.montpelerin.org/montpelerin/mps-Members.html, accessed 2013.

17. Phillip Mirowski, Dieter Plehwe, eds., *The Road to Mt. Pelerin: The Making of the Neoliberal Thought Collective*, (Cambridge, MA: Harvard University Press, 2009), 435.

18. Phillip Mirowski, Dieter Plehwe, eds., *The Road to Mt. Pelerin: The Making of the Neoliberal Thought Collective*, (Cambridge, MA: Harvard University Press, 2009), 435.

19. Naomi Klein, *The Shock Doctrine: The Rise of Disaster Capitalism*, (New York: Henry Holt and Company, Pan Books Limited, Picador, 2007).

20. Fritz Machlup, *Economic Semantics, Second Edition*, see introduction, by Mark Perlman, (New Brunswick, NJ: Transaction Publishers, 1991), xii.

21. F. A Hayek, *The Road to Serfdom, Fiftieth Anniversary Edition*, (Chicago: University of Chicago Press, 1944), 143, 147.

22. Wilhelm Ropke, *The Social Crisis of Our Time*, (New Brunswick, NJ: Transaction Publishers, fourth printing 2009), 227.

23. David Brunori, "Where Is the Outrage Over Corporate Welfare?" www.forbes.com/sites/taxanalysts/2014/03/14/where is the outrage over corporate welfare, accessed 2013.

24. Richard Wolff, "Is the Massive Shift of the Tax Burden from Corporations to Individuals a Statistical Mirage?" rdwolff.com/content/massive-shift-tax-burden-corporations-individuals-statistical-mirage, accessed 7 Aug 2014.

25. Deepak Lal, *In Praise of Empires: Globalization and Order*, (New York: Palgrave MacMillan, 2004), 63.

26. Karl Brunner, ed., *The First World, and The Third World: Essays On the New International Economic Order,* Karl Brunner, "The New International Economic Order: A Chapter in a Protracted Confrontation," (New York: University of Rochester Center Publications, 1978).

27. Wikipedia, "Efficient-market hypothesis," enwikipedia/wiki/Efficient-market hypothesis, accessed 2014.

28. Phillip Mirowski, Dieter Plehwe, eds., *The Road to Mt. Pelerin: The Making of the Neoliberal Thought Collective*, (Cambridge, MA: Harvard University Press, 2009), 434.

29. Michel Foucault, *The Birth of Biopolitics: Lectures At The College De France, 1978-1979*, Michel Senellart, ed., Graham Burchell, trans., (New York: Palgrave MacMillan, Picador, 2004), "beneficial competition" where both sides of an economic transaction perceive their own benefit in an economic win-win, 53-54; "liberalism is motivated by a sense of danger," 66-67; reference to German neoliberal ordoliberalism where the state should prevent monopoly and encourage small businesses and medium sized enterprises 239-243; "the principle of dissociative association is also a principle of historical transformation," 306-307.

30. Phillip Mirowski, Dieter Plehwe, eds., *The Road to Mt. Pelerin: The Making of the Neoliberal Thought Collective*, (Cambridge, MA: Harvard University Press, 2009), 442-443.

31. Wikipedia, "Ludwig von Mises," enwikipedia.org/wiki/Ludwig von Mises, accessed 2012.

32. Ludwig von Mises, *Interventionism: An Economic Analysis*, Thomas McManus and Heinrich Bund, trans., (USA: Liberty Fund, Inc., 2011, from 1998 Foundation of Economic Education edition), 7.

33. Ludwig von Mises, *Interventionism: An Economic Analysis*, Thomas McManus and Heinrich Bund, trans., (USA: Liberty Fund, Inc., 2011, from 1998 Foundation of Economic Education edition), 78.

34. Ludwig von Mises, *Interventionism: An Economic Analysis*, Thomas McManus and Heinrich Bund, trans., (USA: Liberty Fund, Inc., 2011, from 1998 Foundation of Economic Education edition), 94.

35. Ludwig von Mises, *Selected Writings of Ludwig von Mises: Monetary and Economic Policy Problems Before, During, and After the Great War*, Hillsdale College, trans., (USA: Liberty Fund Inc., 2012), 314.

36. Ludwig von Mises, *Interventionism: An Economic Analysis*, Thomas McManus and Heinrich Bund, trans., (USA: Liberty Fund, Inc., 2011, from 1998 Foundation of Economic Education edition), 93-95.

37. Ludwig von Mises, *Interventionism: An Economic Analysis*, Thomas McManus and Heinrich Bund, trans., (USA: Liberty Fund, Inc., 2011, from 1998 Foundation of Economic Education edition), 2.

38. Ludwig von Mises, *Interventionism: An Economic Analysis*, Thomas McManus and Heinrich Bund, trans., (USA: Liberty Fund, Inc., 2011, from 1998 Foundation of Economic Education edition), 47.

39. Ludwig von Mises, *Interventionism: An Economic Analysis*, Thomas McManus and Heinrich Bund, trans., (USA: Liberty Fund, Inc., 2011, from 1998 Foundation of Economic Education edition), 43.

40. Ludwig von Mises, *Interventionism: An Economic Analysis*, Thomas McManus and Heinrich Bund, trans., (USA: Liberty Fund, Inc., 2011, from 1998 Foundation of Economic Education edition), 82.

41. Ludwig von Mises, *Interventionism: An Economic Analysis*, Thomas McManus and Heinrich Bund, trans., (USA: Liberty Fund, Inc., 2011, from 1998 Foundation of Economic Education edition), p84.

42. Ludwig von Mises, *Interventionism: An Economic Analysis*, Thomas McManus and Heinrich Bund, trans., (USA: Liberty Fund, Inc., 2011, from 1998 Foundation of Economic Education edition), 9.

43. Ludwig von Mises, *Selected Writings of Ludwig von Mises: Monetary and Economic Policy Problems Before, During, and After the Great War*, Hillsdale College, trans., (USA: Liberty Fund Inc., 2012), 310-311.

44. Ludwig von Mises, *Interventionism: An Economic Analysis*, Thomas McManus and Heinrich Bund, trans., (USA: Liberty Fund, Inc., 2011, from 1998 Foundation of Economic Education edition), 47, 43.

45. Wikipedia, "Friedrich Hayek," enwikipedia.org/wiki/Friedrich Hayek, accessed 2012.

46. Fredrich Hayek, *The Road to Serfdom, Fiftieth Anniversary Edition*, (Chicago: The University of Chicago Press, 1994.

47. Fredrich Hayek, Ronald Hamowy, ed., *The Constitution of Liberty: The Definitive Edition*, (Chicago: The University of Chicago Press, 2011).

48. Wikipedia, "Friedrich Hayek," enwikipedia.org/wiki/Friedrich Hayek, accessed 2012.

49. Norman Roth, *Telos and Technos: The Teleology of Economic Activity and the Origins of Markets*, (Lanham, MD: University Press of America, Inc., 2008), 119-120.

50. Fredrich Hayek, *The Road to Serfdom, Fiftieth Anniversary Edition*, (Chicago: The University of Chicago Press, 1994), 80, 81, 87, 88.

51. Fredrich Hayek, *The Road to Serfdom, Fiftieth Anniversary Edition*, (Chicago: The University of Chicago Press, 1994.

52. Fredrich Hayek, *The Road to Serfdom, Fiftieth Anniversary Edition*, (Chicago: The University of Chicago Press, 1994), 227.

53. Fredrich Hayek, *The Road to Serfdom, Fiftieth Anniversary Edition*, (Chicago: The University of Chicago Press, 1994), 227.

54. Fredrich Hayek, Ronald Hamowy, ed., *The Constitution of Liberty: The Definitive Edition*, (Chicago: The University of Chicago Press, 2011), 454-455.

55. Fredrich Hayek, Ronald Hamowy, ed., *The Constitution of Liberty: The Definitive Edition*, (Chicago: The University of Chicago Press, 2011), 456.

56. Fredrich Hayek, Ronald Hamowy, ed., *The Constitution of Liberty: The Definitive Edition*, (Chicago: The University of Chicago Press, 2011), 456-457.

57. Fredrich Hayek, *The Road to Serfdom, Fiftieth Anniversary Edition*, (Chicago: The University of Chicago Press, 1994), 241.

58. Fredrich Hayek, *The Road to Serfdom, Fiftieth Anniversary Edition*, (Chicago: The University of Chicago Press, 1994), 250.

59. Fredrich Hayek, *The Road to Serfdom, Fiftieth Anniversary Edition*, (Chicago: The University of Chicago Press, 1994), 254.

60. Fredrich Hayek, *The Road to Serfdom, Fiftieth Anniversary Edition*, (Chicago: The University of Chicago Press, 1994), 159-160.

61. Fredrich Hayek, *The Road to Serfdom, Fiftieth Anniversary Edition*, (Chicago: The University of Chicago Press, 1994), 143.

62. Fredrich Hayek, *The Road to Serfdom, Fiftieth Anniversary Edition*, (Chicago: The University of Chicago Press, 1994), 216-217.

63. Fredrich Hayek, Ronald Hamowy, ed., *The Constitution of Liberty: The Definitive Edition*, (Chicago: The University of Chicago Press, 2011), 454-455.

64. Fredrich Hayek, Ronald Hamowy, ed., *The Constitution of Liberty: The Definitive Edition*, (Chicago: The University of Chicago Press, 2011), 460-461.

65. Fredrich Hayek, Ronald Hamowy, ed., *The Constitution of Liberty: The Definitive Edition*, (Chicago: The University of Chicago Press, 2011), 465.

66. William Briet, Roger Ransom, *The Academic Scribblers: Third Edition*, (Princeton, NJ: Princeton University Press, 1998), chapter 14.

67. Phillip Mirowski, Dieter Plehwe, eds., *The Road to Mt. Pelerin: The Making of the Neoliberal Thought Collective*, (Cambridge, MA: Harvard University Press, 2009).

68. Milton Friedman, *Capitalism and Freedom: Fortieth Anniversary Edition*, (Chicago: University of Chicago Press, 2002), 15.

69. Milton Friedman, *Capitalism and Freedom: Fortieth Anniversary Edition*, (Chicago: University of Chicago Press, 2002), 8-9.

70. Milton Friedman, *Capitalism and Freedom: Fortieth Anniversary Edition*, (Chicago: University of Chicago Press, 2002), 77.

71. Milton Friedman, *Capitalism and Freedom: Fortieth Anniversary Edition*, (Chicago: University of Chicago Press, 2002), 54.

72. Milton Friedman, *Capitalism and Freedom: Fortieth Anniversary Edition*, (Chicago: University of Chicago Press, 2002), 124.

73. Milton Friedman, *Capitalism and Freedom: Fortieth Anniversary Edition*, (Chicago: University of Chicago Press, 2002), 120-121.

74. Milton Friedman, *Capitalism and Freedom: Fortieth Anniversary Edition*, (Chicago: University of Chicago Press, 2002), 198.

75. Milton Friedman, *Capitalism and Freedom: Fortieth Anniversary Edition*, (Chicago: University of Chicago Press, 2002), 111, 113.

76. Milton Friedman, *Capitalism and Freedom: Fortieth Anniversary Edition*, (Chicago: University of Chicago Press, 2002), 202.

77. Wikipedia, "Milton Friedman," enwikipedia.org/wiki/ Milton Friedman, accessed 2014.

78. William Breit, Roger L. Ransom, *The Academic Scribblers, 3rd Edition*, (Princeton, NJ: Princeton University Press, 1998), chapter 14.

79. Wikipedia, "Milton Friedman," enwikipedia.org/wiki/Milton Friedman, accessed 2014.

80. Milton Friedman, *Capitalism and Freedom: Fortieth Anniversary Edition*, (Chicago: University of Chicago Press, 2002), 8, 9.

81. Milton Friedman, *Capitalism and Freedom: Fortieth Anniversary Edition*, (Chicago: University of Chicago Press, 2002), 84.

82. Phillip Mirowski, Dieter Plehwe, eds., *The Road to Mt. Pelerin: The Making of the Neoliberal Thought Collective*, (Cambridge, MA: Harvard University Press, 2009).

83. Gottfried Haberler, "How Important Is Control Over International Reserve, originally published in 1977, in *Selected Essays of Gottfried Haberler*, Anthony Koo, ed., (Hong Kong: MIT Press, 1985), 221.

84. Gottfried Haberler, "The International Monetary System in the World Recession," originally published in 1984, in *Selected Essays of Gottfried Haberler*, Anthony Koo, ed., (Hong Kong: MIT Press, 1985), 231-232.

85. Gottfried Haberler, "The World Economy Macroeconomic Theory and Policy—Sixty Years of Profound Change," originally published in 1982, in *Selected Essays of Gottfried Haberler*, Anthony Yoo, ed., (Hong Kong: MIT Press, 1985), 439-440.

86. Careerbuilder.com, "Report: Science and Engineering Workforce Stagnant," http:wwwcareerbuilder.com/article/CB-3063-Engineering-Report-science- and-engineering-workforce-stagnant, last updated May 2012, accessed 2012.

87. Eugene Veklerov, American Thinker, "Hollowing Out Science and Engineering Careers," http://www.americanthinker.com/2011/02/hollowing-out-science-and-engihtml., accessed 2012.

88. Michael Teitelbaum, *The Atlantic*, www.theatlantic.com/education/archives/2014/03/the-myth- of -the-science-and-engineering-shortage/284359, accessed 2014.

89. Gottfried Haberler, "How Important Is Control Over International Reserve," originally published in 1977, in *Selected Essays of Gottfried Haberler*, Anthony Koo, ed., (Hong Kong: MIT Press, 1985).

90. Gottfried Haberler, "A Survey of International Trade Theory," originally published in 1961, in *Selected Essays of Gottfried Haberler*, Anthony Koo, ed., (Hong Kong: MIT Press, 1985), 67-68.

91. Gottfried Haberler, "A Survey of International Trade Theory," originally published in 1961, in *Selected Essays of Gottfried Haberler*, Anthony Koo, ed., (Hong Kong: MIT Press, 1985), 93-94.

92. Gottfried Haberler, "A Survey of International Trade Theory," originally published 1961, in *Selected Essays of Gottfried Haberler*, Anthony Koo, ed., (Hong Kong: MIT Press, 1985), 94-95.

93. Gottfried Haberler, "The International Monetary System and the Great Depression," originally published 1983-1984, in *Selected Essays of Gottfried Haberler*, Anthony Koo, ed., (Hong Kong: MIT Press, 1985), 255.

94. Gottfried Haberler, "A Survey of International Trade Theory," originally published in 1961, in *Selected Essays of Gottfried Haberler*, Anthony Koo, ed., (Hong Kong: MIT Press, 1985), 67-68.

95. Gottfried Haberler, "A Survey of International Trade Theory," originally published in 1961, in *Selected Essays of Gottfried Haberler*, Anthony Koo, ed., (Hong Kong: MIT Press, 1985), 93-94.

96. Gottfried Haberler, "A Survey of International Trade Theory," originally published in 1961, in *Selected Essays of Gottfried Haberler*, Anthony Koo, ed., (Hong Kong: MIT Press, 1985), 95.

97. Gottfried Haberler, "How Important Is Control Over International Reserve," originally published in 1977, in *Selected Essays of Gottfried Haberler*, Anthony Koo, ed., (Hong Kong: MIT Press, 1985), 221.

98. Thomas Fitch; Irwin Kellner, Donald Simonson, Ben Weberman, eds., *Dictionary of Banking Terms*, (Hauppauge, NY: Barrons Educational Series, 1990), 389.

99. Eric Pace, *New York Times*, "Professor Karl Brunner Is Dead at 73: Economist and Early Monetarist," www.nytimes.com/1989/05/10/obituaries/Prof karl brunner is dead at 73; economist and early monetarist, updated May 10, 1989, accessed 2013.

100. David Lake, "International Political Economy: A Maturing Interdiscipline," in Barry Weingast, Donald Wittman, eds., *The Oxford Handbook of Political Economy*, (New York: Oxford University Press, 2006), 759-760.

101. Fritz Machlup, *A History of Thought On Economic Integration*, (New York: Columbia University Press, 1977), 219.

102. Deepak Lal, *In Praise of Empires: Globalization and Order*, (New York: Palgrave MacMillan, 2004), 145-148.

103. Karl Brunner, *The First World and the Third World: Essays on the New International Economic Order*, (Rochester, NY: University of Rochester Policy Center Publications, 1978), 2-3.

104. Karl Brunner, *The First World and the Third World: Essays on the New International Economic Order*, (Rochester, NY: University of Rochester Policy Center Publications, 1978), 11, 13.

105. Karl Brunner, *The First World and the Third World: Essays on the New International Economic Order*, (Rochester, NY: University of Rochester Policy Center Publications, 1978), 29.

106. Karl Brunner, *The First World and the Third World: Essays on the New International Economic Order*, (Rochester, NY: University of Rochester Policy Center Publications, 1978), 37.

107. Karl Brunner, *The First World and the Third World: Essays on the New International Economic Order*, (Rochester, NY: University of Rochester Policy Center Publications, 1978), 28.

108. Jennifer Zerk, *Multinationals and Corporate Social Responsibility: Limitations and Opportunities in International Law*, (New York: Cambridge University Press, 2006).

109. Jennifer Zerk, *Multinationals and Corporate Social Responsibility: Limitations and Opportunities in International Law*, (New York: Cambridge University Press, 2006), 12.

110. Jennifer Zerk, *Multinationals and Corporate Social Responsibility: Limitations and Opportunities in International Law*, (New York: Cambridge University Press, 2006), 10-11.

111. Wikipedia, "Allan H. Meltzer," enwikipedia. org/wiki/Allan H. Meltzer, accessed 2013.

112. Karl Brunner, Allan Meltzer, *Money and the Economy: Issues in Monetary Analysis*, (New York: Cambridge University Press, 1993), 51.

113. Karl Brunner, Allan Meltzer, *Money and the Economy: Issues in Monetary Analysis*, (New York: Cambridge University Press, 1993), 171-173.

114. Karl Brunner, Allan Meltzer, *Money and the Economy: Issues in Monetary Analysis*, (New York: Cambridge University Press, 1993), 195.

115. Karl Brunner, Allan Meltzer, *Money and the Economy: Issues in Monetary Analysis*, (New York: Cambridge University Press, 1993), 184.

116. Brunner and Meltzer, *Money and the Economy: Issues in Monetary Analysis*, (New York: Cambridge University Press, 1993), 190-191.

117. Wikipedia, "Peter Thomas Bauer," enwikipedia.org/wiki/ Peter Thomas Bauer, accessed 2013.

118. The Cato Institute, "Peter Bauer: Winner of the 2002 Milton Friedman Prize," www.cato. org/friedman prize/peter bauer, accessed 2013.

119. Peter Bauer, "The Third World Debt Crisis: Can't Pay or Won't Pay," in *The Development Frontier: Essays in Applied Economics*, (Cambridge, MA: Harvard University Press, 1991), 59.

120. Peter Bauer, "The Third World Debt Crisis: Can't Pay or Won't Pay," in *The Development Frontier: Essays in Applied Economics*, (Cambridge, MA: Harvard University Press, 1991), 61-62.

121. Peter Bauer, "Industrialization and Development: Nigeria," in *The Development Frontier: Essays in Applied Economics*, (Cambridge, MA: Harvard University Press, 1991), 130-131.

122. Peter Bauer, "Development Economics: A Retrospective View," in *The Development Frontier: Essays in Applied Economics*, (Cambridge, MA: Harvard University Press, 1991), 190.

123. Peter Bauer, "Development Economics: A Retrospective View," in *The Development Frontier: Essays in Applied Economics*, (Cambridge, MA: Harvard University Press, 1991), 198-199.

124. Peter Bauer, "Development Economics: A Retrospective View," in *The Development Frontier: Essays in Applied Economics*, (Cambridge, MA: Harvard University Press, 1991, reprinted by permission from *Pioneers in Development*), 203-204.

125. William Campbell, introduction to Wilhelm Roepke, *The Social Crisis of Our Time*, (New Brunswick, NJ: Transaction Publishers, 2009, translated from *Gesellschaftskrisis der Gengenwart*, Eugen Reutsch Verlag, 1942).

126. Wilhelm Roepke, *The Social Crisis of Our Time*, (New Brunswick, NJ: Transaction Publishers, 2009, translated from *Gesellschaftskrisis der Gengenwart*, Eugen Reutsch Verlag, 1942), 52-53.

127. Wilhelm Roepke, *The Social Crisis of Our Time*, (New Brunswick, NJ: Transaction Publishers, 2009, translated from *Gesellschaftskrisis der Gengenwart*, Eugen Reutsch Verlag, 1942), 66-67.

128. Wilhelm Roepke, *The Social Crisis of Our Time*, (New Brunswick, NJ: Transaction Publishers, 2009, translated from *Gesellschaftskrisis der Gengenwart*, Eugen Reutsch Verlag, 1942), 87.

129. Wilhelm Roepke, *The Social Crisis of Our Time*, (New Brunswick, NJ: Transaction Publishers, 2009, translated from *Gesellschaftskrisis der Gengenwart*, Eugen Reutsch Verlag, 1942), 95-96.

130. Wilhelm Roepke, *The Social Crisis of Our Time*, (New Brunswick, NJ: Transaction Publishers, 2009, translated from *Gesellschaftskrisis der Gengenwart*, Eugen Reutsch Verlag, 1942), 121-122.

131. Wilhelm Roepke, *The Social Crisis of Our Time*, (New Brunswick, NJ: Transaction Publishers, 2009, translated from *Gesellschaftskrisis der Gengenwart*, Eugen Reutsch Verlag, 1942), 172-173, 131-132.

132. Wilhelm Roepke, *The Social Crisis of Our Time*, (New Brunswick, NJ: Transaction Publishers, 2009, translated from *Gesellschaftskrisis der Gengenwart*, Eugen Reutsch Verlag, 1942), 190.

133. Wilhelm Roepke, *The Social Crisis of Our Time*, (New Brunswick, NJ: Transaction Publishers, 2009, translated from *Gesellschaftskrisis der Gengenwart*, Eugen Reutsch Verlag, 1942), 53.

134. Wilhelm Roepke, *The Social Crisis of Our Time*, (New Brunswick, NJ: Transaction Publishers, 2009, translated from *Gesellschaftskrisis der Gengenwart*, Eugen Reutsch Verlag, 1942), 66-67.

135. Wilhelm Roepke, *The Social Crisis of Our Time*, (New Brunswick, NJ: Transaction Publishers, 2009, translated from *Gesellschaftskrisis der Gengenwart*, Eugen Reutsch Verlag, 1942), 131-132.

136. Wikipedia, "Fritz Machlup," wikipedia.org/wiki/Fritz Machlup, accessed 2014.

137. Fritz Machlup, *Economic Semantics, Second Edition*, (New York: Columbia University Press, 1977), 279.

138. Fritz Machlup, *Economic Semantics, Second Edition*, (New York: Columbia University Press, 1977), 43-44.

139. Fritz Machlup, *Economic Semantics, Second Edition*, (New York: Columbia University Press, 1977), 65.

140. Fritz Machlup, *Economic Semantics, Second Edition*, (New York: Columbia University Press, 1977), 67.

141. Fritz Machlup, *Economic Semantics, Second Edition*, (New York: Columbia University Press, 1977), 68-69.

142. Fritz Machlup, *Economic Semantics, Second Edition*, (New York: Columbia University Press, 1977), 92.

143. Fritz Machlup, *Economic Semantics, Second Edition*, (New York: Columbia University Press, 1977), 95.

144. Wikipedia, "Partition of India," enwikipedia.org/wiki/Partition of India, accessed 2014.

145. Phillip Mirowski, Dieter Plehwe, *The Road from Mont Pelerin: The Making of the Neoliberal Thought Collective*, (Cambridge, MA: Harvard University Press, 2009).

146. "Deepak Lal, Senior Fellow," www.cato.org/people/deepak_lal, accessed 2014

147. Deepak Lal, *In Praise of Empires: Globalization and Order*, (New York: Palgrave MacMillan, 2004), xvii-xxvi.

148. Deepak Lal, *In Praise of Empires: Globalization and Order*, (New York: Palgrave MacMillan, 2004), xvii-xxvi.

149. Deepak Lal, *In Praise of Empires: Globalization and Order*, (New York: Palgrave MacMillan, 2004), 55-56.

150. Deepak Lal, *In Praise of Empires: Globalization and Order*, (New York: Palgrave MacMillan, 2004), 104.

151. Deepak Lal, *In Praise of Empires: Globalization and Order*, (New York: Palgrave MacMillan, 2004), 112-113.

152. Deepak Lal, *In Praise of Empires: Globalization and Order*, (New York: Palgrave MacMillan, 2004), 137.

153. Deepak Lal, *In Praise of Empires: Globalization and Order*, (New York: Palgrave MacMillan, 2004), 154.

154. Phillip Mirowski, Dieter Plehwe, *The Road from Mont Pelerin: The Making of the Neoliberal Thought Collective*, (Cambridge, MA: Harvard University Press, 2009), 438.

155. Deepak Lal, *In Praise of Empires: Globalization and Order*, (New York: Palgrave MacMillan, 2004), xxv.

156. Deepak Lal, *In Praise of Empires: Globalization and Order*, (New York: Palgrave MacMillan, 2004), 63.

157. Thomas Palley, *Financialization: The Economics of Finance Capital Domination*, (New York: Palgrave MacMillan, 2013), 7.

158. Phillip Mirowski, Dieter Plehwe, *The Road from Mont Pelerin: The Making of the Neoliberal Thought Collective*, (Cambridge, MA: Harvard University Press, 2009), 17.

159. Phillip Mirowski, Dieter Plehwe, *The Road from Mont Pelerin: The Making of the Neoliberal Thought Collective*, (Cambridge, MA: Harvard University Press, 2009), 24.

160. Phillip Mirowski, Dieter Plehwe, *The Road from Mont Pelerin: The Making of the Neoliberal Thought Collective*, (Cambridge, MA: Harvard University Press, 2009), 23.

161. Phillip Mirowski, Dieter Plehwe, *The Road from Mont Pelerin: The Making of the Neoliberal Thought Collective*, (Cambridge, MA: Harvard University Press, 2009), 25.

162. Wikipedia, "Credit Mobilier of America Scandal," enwikipedia.org/ wiki/Credit-Mobilier-of-America-Scandal, accessed 2013.

163. Wikipedia, "Teapot Dome Scandal," enwikipedia.org/wiki/Teapot Dome Scandal, accessed 2014.

164. Ropke, *The Social Crisis of Our Time*, (New Brunswick, NJ: Transaction Publishing, 2009, translated from German), 132.

165. Friedrich Hayek, *The Road to Serfdom: Fiftieth Anniversary Edition*, (Chicago: University of Chicago Press, 1994), 227.

166. Fritz Machlup, *Economic Semantics, Second Edition*, (New Brunswick, NJ: Transaction Publishing, 1991), 44-72.

167. Fritz Machlup, *Economic Semantics, Second Edition*, (New Brunswick, NJ: Transaction Publishing, 1991), 9-72.

168. Wikipedia, "Historical school of economics," enwikipedia.org/ wiki/Historical_school_of_ economics, accessed 2014, the later historical school of economics was associated with the ideas of Werner Sombart (promoting the German ideal of the state or the Volkgemeinschaft, which ignored individual happiness and promoted the idea that individuals have duties instead of rights), and Max Weber (the idea that states and not individuals have the only legitimate prerogative to utilize force).

169. Fritz Machlup, *Economic Semantics, Second Edition*, (New Brunswick, NJ: Transaction Publishing, 1991), 29.

170. Fritz Machlup, *Economic Semantics, Second Edition*, (New Brunswick, NJ: Transaction Publishing, 1991), 43-73.

171. Fritz Machlup, *Economic Semantics, Second Edition*, (New Brunswick, NJ: Transaction Publishing, 1991), 9-72.

172. Roger Ransom, *Coping With Capitalism: The Economic Transformation of the United States 1776-1980*, (Englewood Cliffs, NJ: Prentice Hall, Inc., 1981), 3.

173. Fritz Machlup, *Economic Semantics, Second Edition*, (New Brunswick, NJ: Transaction Publishing, 1991), 30.

174. Karl Brunner, Allan Meltzer, *Money and the Economy: Issues in Monetary Analysis*, (New York: Cambridge University Press, 1993), 184, 195.

175. William Briet, Roger Ransom, *The Academic Scribblers, Third Edition*, (Princeton, NJ: Princeton University Press, 1998), 267-273.

176. William Briet, Roger Ransom, *The Academic Scribblers, Third Edition*, (Princeton, NJ: Princeton University Press, 1998), 269-273.

177. Fritz Machlup, *Economic Semantics, Second Edition*, (New Brunswick, NJ: Transaction Publishing, 1991), section two, "Semantic Issues in Economic Methodology", 7-97.

178. Stephen McCarthy, David Kehl, *Deductive Irrationality: A Commonsense Critique of Economic Rationalism*, (Lanham, MD: Rowman and Littlefield Publishers, Inc., 2008), 1-27.

179. Milton Friedman, *Capitalism and Freedom*, (Chicago: University of Chicago Press, 2002), 15.

180. Thomas Sowell, *Basic Economics: A Common Sense Guide to the Economy, Third Edition*, (New York: Basic Books, Perseus Books Group, 2007), 2.

181. Filippo Cesarano, *Monetary Theory and Bretton Woods: The Construction of an International Monetary Order*, (New York: Cambridge University Press, 2006), 4.

182. Anat Amadhi, Martin Hellwig, *The Banker's New Clothes: What's Wrong With Banking and What to Do About It*, (Princeton, NJ: Princeton University Press, 2013), 81.

183. Percy Greaves Jr., and Bettina Greaves, "Letter to the New York Times," in *On the Manipulation of Money and Credit*, Ludwig von Mises, 275.

184. Anat Amadhi, Martin Hellwig, *The Banker's New Clothes: What's Wrong With Banking and What to Do About It*, (Princeton, NJ: Princeton University Press, 2013), 81.

185. Adam Smith, *The Wealth of Nations, Books I-III*, (New York: Penguin Books, 1987), 358-359.

186. Filippo Cesarano, *Monetary Theory and Bretton Woods: The Construction of an International Monetary Order*, (New York: Cambridge University Press, 2006), 33.

187. Filippo Cesarano, *Monetary Theory and Bretton Woods: The Construction of an International Monetary Order*, (New York: Cambridge University Press, 2006), 31.

188. Filippo Cesarano, *Monetary Theory and Bretton Woods: The Construction of an International Monetary Order*, (New York: Cambridge University Press, 2006), 21-67.

189. Filippo Cesarano, *Monetary Theory and Bretton Woods: The Construction of an International Monetary Order*, (New York: Cambridge University Press, 2006), 65.

190. Bill Still, *No More National Debt*, (St Petersberg, FL: Reinhardt and Still Publishers, The Still Foundation, Inc., 2011), 145-146.

191. Filippo Cesarano, *Monetary Theory and Bretton Woods: The Construction of an International Monetary Order*, (New York: Cambridge University Press, 2006), 62.

192. Deepak Lal, *In Praise of Empires: Globalization and Order*, (New York: Palgrave MacMillan, 2004), 49.

193. Filippo Cesarano, *Monetary Theory and Bretton Woods: The Construction of an International Monetary Order*, (New York: Cambridge University Press, 2006), 46, 43.

194. Filippo Cesarano, *Monetary Theory and Bretton Woods: The Construction of an International Monetary Order*, (New York: Cambridge University Press, 2006), 45-47.

195. Filippo Cesarano, *Monetary Theory and Bretton Woods: The Construction of an International Monetary Order*, (New York: Cambridge University Press, 2006), Cesarano, qtd Milton Friedman, 193.

196. Filippo Cesarano, *Monetary Theory and Bretton Woods: The Construction of an International Monetary Order*, (New York: Cambridge University Press, 2006), 2.

197. Filippo Cesarano, *Monetary Theory and Bretton Woods: The Construction of an International Monetary Order*, (New York: Cambridge University Press, 2006), 4.

198. Filippo Cesarano, *Monetary Theory and Bretton Woods: The Construction of an International Monetary Order*, (New York: Cambridge University Press, 2006), 2.

199. Wikipedia, "London Gold Pool," Wikipedia.org/wiki/London Gold Pool, accessed May 2014.

200. Kenneth Morris, Alan Siegel, Virginia Morris, ed., *The Wall Street Journal Guide to Understanding Money and Investing*, (New York: Simon and Schuster, 1993), 10-13.

201. Stephen Johnson, Euro Pacific Capital, Inc., "Experience is the Teacher of Fools," www.europac.net/voices/experience_teacher_fools, last updated June 2012, accessed 2013.

202. Wikipedia, "Fiat money," enwikipedia.org/wiki/Fiat money, accessed May 2014.

203. Kenneth Morris, Alan Siegel, Virginia Morris, ed., *The Wall Street Journal Guide to Understanding Money and Investing*, (New York: Simon and Schuster, 1993), 4-32.

204. Filippo Cesarano, *Monetary Theory and Bretton Woods: The Construction of an International Monetary Order*, (New York: Cambridge University Press, 2006).

205. Richard Peet, *Unholy Trinity: the IMF, World Bank and WTO*, (New York: Zed Books Ltd., 2003).

206. Deepak Lal, *In Praise of Empires: Globalization and Order*, (New York: Palgrave MacMillan, 2004), 112-113.

207. Richard Peet, *Unholy Trinity: the IMF, World Bank and WTO*, (New York: Zed Books Ltd., 2003).

208. 208. Elaine Bernard, "What's the Matter with NAFTA?" www.law.harvard.edu/programs/lwp/nafta.pdf, accessed 2014

209. 208. Elaine Bernard, "What's the Matter with NAFTA?" www.law.harvard.edu/programs/lwp/nafta.pdf, accessed 2014

210. Joseph Stiglitz, "On the Wrong Side of Globalization", *The New York Times,* opinionater.blogs.ny times.com/2014/03/15/on the wrong side of globalization/?_php=true&type =blogs&r=o, and "The Free Trade Charade", Joseph Stiglitz, www.project sindicate.org/commentary/transpacific free trade trouble by Joseph E. Stiglitz, accessed 2014.

211. Steger and Roy, *Neoliberalism: A Very Short Introduction,* (New York: Oxford University Press, 2010).

212. Naomi Klein, *The Shock Doctrine: The Rise of Disaster Capitalism*, (New York: Henry Holt and Company, Picador, 2007), 204.

213. Steger and Roy, *Neoliberalism: A Very Short Introduction*, (New York: Oxford University Press, 2010), 19, 20.

214. Naomi Klein, *The Shock Doctrine: The Rise of Disaster Capitalism*, (New York: Henry Holt and Company, Picador, 2007), "Friedman's triumvirate", 204; Brazil, 81; Chile, 87; Argentina, 121-143.

215. Naomi Klein, *The Shock Doctrine: The Rise of Disaster Capitalism*, (New York: Henry Holt and Company, Picador, 2007), 563, 560-589.

216. Niccolo Machiavelli, *The Prince and the Discourses*, (New York: Random House, Inc., 1950), xxx, xxxii, 64.

217. Office of Management and Budget, "Chapter I. The Role of Economic Analysis in Regulatory Reform, Report to Congress on the Costs and Benefits of Federal Regulations," www.whitehouse.gov/omb/inforeg ch1, accessed 2014.

218. Office of Management and Budget, "Chapter I. The Role of Economic Analysis in Regulatory Reform, Report to Congress on the Costs and Benefits of Federal Regulations," www.whitehouse.gov/omb/inforeg ch1, accessed 2014.

219. The American Presidency Project, Ronald Reagan XL President of the United States: 1981-1989, "Address Before a Joint Session of the Congress on the Program for Economic Recovery," www.presidency.uscsb.edu/ws/ index.php?pid=43425), accessed 2013.

220. Lisa Heinzerling and Frank Ackerman, "The Humbugs of the Anti-Regulation Movement," frankackerman.com/publications/costbenfit/Humbugs Antiregulatory Movement.pdf, "Heizerling and Ackerman, 2002, accessed May 2014.

221. Office of Management and Budget, "Chapter I. The Role of Economic Analysis in Regulatory Reform, Report to Congress on the Costs and Benefits of Federal Regulations," www.whitehouse.gov/omb/inforeg ch1, accessed 2014.

222. Frank Ackerman, Lisa Heinzerling, Rachel Massey, Center for Progressive Regulation White Paper, "Applying cost-Benefit Analysis to Past Decisions: Was Protecting the Environment Ever a Good Idea?" www.progressive reform.org/articles/Wrong 401.pdf, last updated 2004, accessed 2014.

223. Lisa Heinzerling and Frank Ackerman, "The Humbugs of the Anti-Regulation Movement," frankackerman.com/publications/costbenfit/Humbugs Antiregulatory Movement.pdf, "Heizerling and Ackerman, 2002, accessed May 2014.

224. Richard Posner, *Fordham International Law Journal*, Vol. 23, Issue 6, "The Effects of Deregulation on Competition: The Experience of the United States, 1999, http://ir.lawnet.fordham,edu/ilj, accessed 2013.

225. Bethany McLean and Joe Nocera, *All the Devils Are Here: The Hidden History of the Financial Crisis*, (New York: The Penguin Group, 2008), 109, 357.

226. Wilhelm Ropke, *The Social Crisis of Our Time*, (New Brunswick, NJ: Transaction Publishing, 2009), 93.

227. C. H. Sterling, "Deregulation," www.museumtv/eotvsection.php?entry code=deregulation, accessed 2012.

228. Media Reform Information Center, www.corporations.org/media, citing Ben Bagdikian's *The New Media Monopoly.*

229. C. H. Sterling, "Deregulation," www.museumtv/eotvsection.php?entry code=deregulation, accessed 2012.

230. Gene Kimmelman, Consumer's Union, "Deregulation of Media: Dangerous to Democracy, http://www.consumersunion.org/telecom/kimmel-303.htm, accessed 2012.

231. Bethany McLean and Joe Nocera, *All the Devils Are Here: The Hidden History of the Financial Crisis,* (New York: The Penguin Group, 2008), 7, 109.

232. Bethany McLean and Joe Nocera, *All the Devils Are Here: The Hidden History of the Financial Crisis,* (New York: The Penguin Group, 2008), 29.

233. Bethany McLean and Joe Nocera, *All the Devils Are Here: The Hidden History of the Financial Crisis,* (New York: The Penguin Group, 2008), 15-19.

234. Bethany McLean and Joe Nocera, *All the Devils Are Here: The Hidden History of the Financial Crisis,* (New York: The Penguin Group, 2008), 53, 31.

235. Bethany McLean and Joe Nocera, *All the Devils Are Here: The Hidden History of the Financial Crisis,* (New York: The Penguin Group, 2008), chapter two.

236. Bethany McLean and Joe Nocera, *All the Devils Are Here: The Hidden History of the Financial Crisis,* (New York: The Penguin Group, 2008), 169.

237. Sarah Childress, "How Much Did the Financial Crisis Cost?" PBS, www.pbs.org/wgbh/pages/frontline business economy financial crisis/money/power/wall street/how much did the financial crisis cost? May 31, 2012.

238. Charles Ferguson, *Predator Nation: Corporate Criminals, Political Corruption, and the Hijacking of America,* (New York: Crown Business, 2012).

239. Charles Ferguson, *Predator Nation: Corporate Criminals, Political Corruption, and the Hijacking of America,* (New York: Crown Business, 2012), 2.

240. Michael Lewis, ed., *Panic: the Story of Modern Financial Insanity,* (New York: W.W. Norton and Company, 2008).

241. Eric Lipton, *The New York* Times, "House Votes to Repeal Dodd-Frank Provision," Oct 30, 2013, dealbook.nytimes.com/2013/10/30/house passes bill on derivatives/?php=true&type=blogs&_r=0, New York Times, accessed 2014.

242. Bethany McLean and Joe Nocera, *All the Devils Are Here: The Hidden History of the Financial Crisis,* (New York: The Penguin Group, 2008), 109.

243. Charles Ferguson, *Predator Nation: Corporate Criminals, Political Corruption, and the Hijacking of America,* (New York: Crown Business, 2012), 223-224.

244. Wilhelm Ropke, *The Social Crisis of Our Time,* (New Brunswick, NJ: Transaction Publishing, 2009), 211.

245. Timothy Egan, *The Worst Hard Time: The Untold Story of Those Who Survived the Great American Dustbowl*, (New York: Houghton Mifflin Company, A Mariner Book, 2006), 43.

246. Grace Livingstone, "The Real Hunger Games: How Banks Gamble on Food Prices –And the Poor Lose Out, April 2012, *The Independent,* the real hunger games how banks gamble on food prices and the poor lose out-7606263, accessed 2014.

247. Grace Livingstone, "The Real Hunger Games: How Banks Gamble on Food Prices –And the Poor Lose Out, April 2012, *The Independent,* the real hunger games how banks gamble on food prices and the poor lose out-7606263, accessed 2014.

248. Wikipedia, "List of landmark court decisions in the United States," enwikipedia.org/wiki/List_of_landmark_court_decisions_in_the_United States, accessed 2014.

249. U.S. Supreme Court Media, IIT Chicago-Kent College of Law, "*Youngstown Sheet & Tube Co. V. Sawyer (1951),*" www.oyez.org/cases/1950-1959/1951/1951_744, accessed 2014.

250. Wikipedia, "Civil Liberties Act of 1988," enwikipedia.org/wiki/Civil_Liberties_Act_of_1988, accessed Sept 2014.

251. The Skeptical Libertarian, "How Nick Merrill Launched the First Fight Against the Patriot Act," blog.skeptical libertarian.com/2012/04/15/ how-nic-merrill-launched-the-first-fight-against-the-patriot-act, accessed Aug 2014.

252. The ACLU, "National Security Letter Recipient Can Speak Out For First Time Since FBI Demanded Customer Records From Him," www.aclu.org/national-security/national-security-letter-recipient-can-speak-out-first-time-fbi-demanded-customer, accessed Aug 2014.

253. Wikipedia, "List of landmark court decisions in the United States," enwikipedia.org/wiki/List-of-landmark-court-decisions-in-the-United-States, accessed Aug 2014.

254. U.S. Supreme Court Media, IIT Chicago-Kent College of Law, "*Afroyim V. Rusk (1966),* www.oyez.org/cases/1960-1969/1966/1966-456, accessed Aug 2014.

255. "O'Connore v. Donaldson-Significance," law.jrank.org/pages/24781/O-Connor-v-Donaldson-Significance.html, accessed Aug 2013.

256. "ACLU Pros and Cons," ProCon.org, "*Bivens v. Six Unknown Named Agents of Federal Bureau of Narcotics (1971),*" acluprocon.org/view resource.php?/resource ID=3182, accessed Aug 2014.

257. Case Briefs: The Original…Most Comprehensive…digital Legal Content Free, "*Planned Parenthood of Southeastern Pennsylvania v. Casey (1992),*" www.casebriefs.com/blog/law/constitutional law/constititional-law-keyed-to-store/implied-fundamental-rights/planned-parenthood-of-southeastern-pennsylvania-v.casey-4/+2, accessed Aug 2013.

258. History and Government—Supreme Court—Cases, "*Cruzan v. Director, Missouri Dept. of Health (1990),*" www.infoplease.Com/us/Supreme-court/cases/ar08.html, accessed Aug 2014.

259. U.S. Supreme Court Media, IIT Chicago-Kent College of Law, "*Kennedy V. Louisiana (2007),* www.oyez.org/cases/2000-2009/2007/2007_07_343, accessed Aug 2014.

260. Wikipedia, "List of landmark court decisions in the United States," enwikipedia.org/wiki/List of landmark court decisions in the United States, accessed Aug 2014.

261. U.S. Supreme Court Media, IIT Chicago-Kent College of Law, "*Kelo V. City of New London*

(2004)," www.oyez.org/cases/2000-2009/2004/2004-04-08, accessed Aug 2014.

262. *Fox News,* "Seized Property Sits Vacant Nine Years After Landmark Kelo Eminent Domain Case," www.foxnews. com/politics/2014/03/20/seized-property- sits-vacant-nine-years-after-landmark-eminent -domain-case, accessed Aug 2014.

263. U.S. Supreme Court Media, IIT Chicago-Kent College of Law, *"Riley V. California (2013),"* www.org/cases/2010-2019/2013/2013-13-132, accessed Aug 2014.

264. U.S. Supreme Court Media, IIT Chicago-Kent College of Law, *Montejo V. Louisiana (2008),"* www.oyez.org/cases/2000-2008/2008-07-1529, accessed Aug 2014.

265. Hugh, *Montejo v. Louisiana,* a case you probably haven't heard of," myfiredoglake.com/ hugh/2009/06/02/montejo-v.-louisiana-a-case-you-probably-haven't-heard-of/, accessed Aug 2014.

266. U.S. Supreme Court Media, IIT Chicago-Kent College of Law, *"McDonald V. Chicago (2009),"* www.oyez.org/cases/2000-2009/2009_08_1521

267. U.S. Supreme Court Media, IIT Chicago-Kent College of Law, *"Salinas V. Texas (2012),"* www.oyez.org/cases/2010-2019/2012/2012_12_246, accessed Aug 2014.

268. Wikipedia, "Citizens United v. Federal Election Commission," enwikipedia.org/wiki/Citizens_United_v._ Federal_ Election_Commission, accessed Aug 2014.

269. U.S. Supreme Court Media, IIT Chicago-Kent College of Law, *"U.S. Term Limits V. Thornton (1994),"* www.oyez.org/cases/1990-1999/1994/1994-93-1456, accessed Aug 2014.

270. Wikipedia, "List of landmark court decisions in the United States," enwikipedia.org/wiki/ List of landmark court decisions in the United States, accessed 2014.

271. U.S. Supreme Court Media, IIT Chicago-Kent College of Law, *"McDonald V. Chicago (2009),"* www.oyez.org/cases/1970-1979/1975/1975-75-436, accessed Aug 2014.

272. U.S. Supreme Court Media, IIT Chicago-Kent College of Law, *"McConnell V. Federal Election Commission (2003),"* www.oyez.org/ cases/2000-2009/2003/2003_02_1674, Aug 2014, accessed Aug 2014.

273. U.S. Supreme Court Media, IIT Chicago-Kent College of Law, *"Citizen's United V. federal Election Commission (2008),"* www.oyez.org/cases/2000-2009/ 2008/2008_08_205, accessed Aug 2014.

274. Wikipedia, "Citizen's United V. Federal Election Committee," enwikipedia.org/wiki/Citizens_United_ v._Federal_Election_Committee, accessed Aug 2014.

275. U.S. Supreme Court Media, IIT Chicago-Kent College of Law, *"Austin V. Michigan Chamber of Commerce (1989),"* www.oyez.org/cases/2010-2019/2013/2013_12_536, accessed Aug 2014.

276. U.S. Supreme Court Media, IIT Chicago-Kent College of Law, *"New York Times V. United States (1970),"* www.oyez.org/cases/1970-1979/1970/1970_1873, accessed Aug 2014.

277. EPIC, Electronic Privacy Information Center, "Foreign Intelligence Surveillance Court (FISC)," epic.org/privacy/terrorism/fisa/fisc.html, accessed Aug 2014.

278. ACLU, "United States Foreign Intelligence Surveillance Court Washington, D.C., In RE Proceedings Required by 702(i) of the FISA Amendments Act of 2008, Docket Number

MISC 08-01" www.aclu.org/sites/default/files/pdfs/safefree/fisc-decision.pdf, accessed Aug 2013.

279. Shaun Waterman, "Spy Court Says NSA Exceeded Bounds, But Judges Approved All Data Requests Anyway," *The Washington Times,* Nov 19, 2013, www.washingtontimes. com/news/2013/Nov/19/secret-surveillance-court-says-nsa-exceeded-all-bounds/?page=all, accessed Aug 2014.

280. Eric Lichtblau, "In Secret, Court Vastly Broadens Powers of NSA," *The New York Times,* www.nytimes.com/2013/07/ns/in-secret -court-vastly- broadens-the-powers-of -nsa. html? pagewanted =&&r=1& pagewanted=print, accessed Aug 2014.

281. The Skeptical Libertarian, "How Nick Merrill Launched the First Fight Against the PATRIOT Act," blog.skeptical libertarian.com/2012/04/15/how-nick-merrill-launched-the-first-fight-against-the-patriot-act, accessed Aug 2014.

282. ACLU, "National Security Letter Recipient Can Speak Out For First Time Since FBI Demanded Customer Records From Him," www.aclu.org/national-security/national-security-letter-recipient-can-speak-out-first-time-fbi- demanded-customer, accessed Aug 2014.

283. ACLU, "FISA Court Orders Declassification Review of Rulings on NSA Spying Response to ACLU Request," www.aclu.org/national-security/fisa-court-orders-declassification-review-rulings-nsa-spying-response-aclu-request, accessed Aug 2014.

284. Casetext, "United States District court For the District of Columbia, *Klayman v. Obama (2013),*" casetext.com/case/klayman-v-obama#. VAjPootGMSA, accessed Sept 2014.

285. The Skeptical Libertarian, "How Nick Merrill Launched the First Fight Against the PATRIOT Act," blog.skeptical libertarian.com/2012/04/15/how-nick-merrill-launched-the-first-fight-against-the-patriot-act, accessed Aug 2014.

286. Wikipedia, "PRISM-(surveillance-program)," enwikipedia.org/ wiki/PRISM-(surveillance-program, accessed 2014.

287. Shaun Waterman, "Spy Court Says NSA Exceeded Bounds, But Judges Approved All Data Requests Anyway," *The Washington Times,* Nov 19, 2013, www.washingtontimes. com/news/2013/Nov/19/secret-surveillance-court-says-nsa-exceeded-all-bounds/?page=all, accessed Aug 2014.

288. Wikipedia, "PRISM-(surveillance program)," enwikipedia.org/wiki/ PRISM (surveillance program), accessed 2014.

289. U.S. Supreme Court Media, IIT Chicago-Kent College of Law, *"Hamdan V. Rumsfeld, (2005),"* www.oyez.orgcases/20000-2009/2005/2005?05/184, accessed Aug 2014.

290. U.S. Supreme Court Media, IIT Chicago-Kent College of Law, "*Boumediene V. Bush, (2007),*" www.oyez.org/cases/2000-2009/2007_06_1195, accessed Aug 2014.

291. U.S. Supreme Court Media, IIT Chicago-Kent College of Law, "*Massachusetts V. Environmental Protection Agency, (2006),*" www.oyez.org/cases/2000-2009/2006/2006_05_1120, accessed 2014.

292. U.S. Supreme Court Media, IIT Chicago-Kent College of Law, "*Association For Molecular Pathology V. Myriad Genetics, (2012),*" www.oyez.org/cases/2010-2019/2012/2012_12_398, accessed 2014.

293. Jenny S. Lam, "Accountability for Private Military Contractors under the Alien Statute", 97 CAL L REV. 1459, 2009, http://scholarship.law.berkeley.edu/californialaw review/vol97/iss5/4, accessed 2014.

294. Jenny S. Lam, "Accountability for Private Military Contractors under the Alien Statute", 97 CAL L REV. 1459, 2009, http://scholarship.law.berkeley.edu/californialaw review/vol97/iss5/4, accessed 2014.

295. Angela Snell, "The Absence of Justice: Private Military contractors, Sexual Assault, and the U.S. Government's Policy of Indifference, University of Illinois Law Review, 2011, Illinois-lawreview.rog/wp-content/ilrcontent/ articles/ 2011/3/Snell:pdf, accessed 2014.

296. Walter Lippman, *The Good Society*, (New Brunswick, NJ: Transaction Publishing, 2005), 280.

297. Wikipedia, "Aftermath of World War II," enwikipedia.org/wiki/ Aftermath_of_World_War_II, accessed 2014.

298. Lebor, *The Tower of Basel: The Shadowy History of the Secret Bank That Runs the World,* (New York: Public Affairs, 2013), 36-40.

299. Lebor, *The Tower of Basel: The Shadowy History of the Secret Bank That Runs the World,* (New York: Public Affairs, 2013), 36-40.

300. Pierce Nahigyan, Nation of Change, "War," Feb 2014. www.nation of change.org/wars-afghanistan-iraq-cost-us-over-4-trillion.1392732855, accessed 2014.

301. Tim Wiener, *Legacy of Ashes: The History of the CIA,* (New York: Random House, Double-day, 2007), 24.

302. Tim Wiener, *Legacy of Ashes: The History of the CIA,* (New York: Random House, Double-day, 2007), 223.

303. Tim Wiener, *Legacy of Ashes: The History of the CIA,* (New York: Random House, Double-day, 2007), 224.

304. Tim Wiener, *Legacy of Ashes: The History of the CIA,* (New York: Random House, Double-day, 2007), 226.

305. Tim Wiener, *Legacy of Ashes: The History of the CIA,* (New York: Random House, Double-day, 2007), 223-226.

306. Tim Wiener, *Legacy of Ashes: The History of the CIA,* (New York: Random House, Double-day, 2007), 192-193.

307. Tim Wiener, *Legacy of Ashes: The History of the CIA,* (New York: Random House, Double-day, 2007), 13.

308. Tim Wiener, *Legacy of Ashes: The History of the CIA,* (New York: Random House, Double-day, 2007), 239-243.

309. Tim Wiener, *Legacy of Ashes: The History of the CIA,* (New York: Random House, Double-day, 2007), 518.

310. Adam Lebor, *Tower of Basel: The Shadowy History of the Bank that Runs the World,* (New York: Public Affairs, 2013), 84.

311. Adam Lebor, *Tower of Basel: The Shadowy History of the Bank that Runs the World,* (New York: Public Affairs, 2013), 186.

312. Adam Lebor, *Tower of Basel: The Shadowy History of the Bank that Runs the World,* (New York: Public Affairs, 2013), 166.

313. Tim Wiener, *Legacy of Ashes: The History of the CIA,* (New York: Random House, Doubleday, 2007), 514.

314. Tim Wiener, *Legacy of Ashes: The History of the CIA,* (New York: Random House, Doubleday, 2007), 147, 156, 162, 172-173, 189, 190, 192.

315. Tim Wiener, *Legacy of Ashes: The History of the CIA,* (New York: Random House, Doubleday, 2007), 143.

316. Deepak Lal, *In Praise of Empire: Globalization and Order,* (New York: Palgrave MacMillan, 2004), 55.

317. Andrew Bacevich, *The New American Militarism: How Americans Are Seduced By War,* (New York: Oxford University Press, 2005).

318. Tarak Barkawi, *Al Jazeera,* Global Policy Forum, military expansion and intervention/general analysis on us military expansion and intervention/50916-the lost-bases-of-the-us-empire.html?itemid+id#595, accessed 2014.

319. Deepak Lal, *In Praise of Empire: Globalization and Order,* (New York: Palgrave MacMillan, 2004), 55-56.

320. Andrew Bacevich, *The New American Militarism: How Americans Are Seduced By War,* (New York: Oxford University Press, 2005).

321. Andrew Bacevich, *The New American Militarism: How Americans Are Seduced By War,* (New York: Oxford University Press, 2005), 227-232.

322. Naomi Klein, *The Shock Doctrine: The Rise of Disaster Capitalism,* (New York: Henry Holt and Company, Picador, 2007), Iraq, chapters 16, 17 and 18.

323. John Perkins, *Confessions of An Economic Hitman,* (New York: Penguin Group, Plume, 2004), 154-164.

324. William Black, *The Best Way to Rob a Bank is to Own One: How Corporate Executives and Politicians Looted the S&L Industry,* (Austin, TX: University of Austin Press, 2005).

325. Donald Barlett, James Steele, *Vanity Fair,* "US Billions Over Baghdad: The Spoils of War, Oct 2007, www.corpwatch.org/article.php?id+14681, accessed 2014.

326. Greta R. Krippner, "The Financialization of the American Economy, *Socio-Economic Review,* (2005) 3,173-208, cas.umkc.edu/econ/economics/faculty/wray/631Wray/Week%207/Krippner.pdf, accessed 2014.

327. Edward Herman, Noam Chomsky, *Manufacturing Consent: The Political Economy of the Mass Media,* (New York: Random House, Pantheon Books, 2002), xiii.

328. Anat Admati, Martin Hellwig, *The Banker's New Clothes: What's Wrong with Banking and What to Do about It,* (Princeton, NJ: Princeton University Press, 2013), 6.

329. Thomas Fitch, *Dictionary of Banking Terms,* Irwin Kellner, Donald Simonson, Ben

Webermen, eds., (Huappauge, NY: Barrons Educational Series, 1990), 56.

330. Anat Admati, Martin Hellwig, *The Banker's New Clothes: What's Wrong with Banking and What to Do about It*, (Princeton, NJ: Princeton University Press, 2013), 208-228. Daniel Doherty, Townhall Tipsheet, "Grim Milestone: Current Administration Adds $7 Trillion to National Debt," townhall.com/tipsheet/Danieldoherty/ 2014/08/04/grim-milestone-obama-adds-7-trillion-to-national-debt-n1874439, as of July 31ˢᵗ, accessed 2014.

331. Anat Admati, Martin Hellwig, *The Banker's New Clothes: What's Wrong with Banking and What to Do about It*, (Princeton, NJ: Princeton University Press, 2013), 202.

332. Thomas Fitch; Irwin Kellner, Donald Simonson, Ben Weberman, eds., *Dictionary of Banking Terms*, (Huappauge, NY: Barrons Educational Series, 1990), 56, 282.

333. Robert Parenteau, "The Late 1990's US Bubble: Financialization in the Extreme," Gerald Epstein, ed., in *Financialization and the World Economy*, (UK: Edward Elgar Publishing Limited, 2005), 143.

334. Wikipedia, "Financial market," enwikipedia.org/wiki/ financial market, accessed July 2014.

335. Anat Admati, Martin Hellwig, *The Banker's New Clothes: What's Wrong with Banking and What to Do about It*, (Princeton, NJ: Princeton University Press, 2013), 214.

336. James Crotty, "The Neoliberal Paradox: The Impact of Destructive Product Market Competition and 'Modern' Financial Market on Nonfinancial Corporation Performance in the Neoliberal Era," in *Financialization and the World Economy*, Gerald A. Epstein, ed., (UK: Edward Elgar Publishing Limited, 2005), 90.

337. James Crotty, "The Neoliberal Paradox: The Impact of Destructive Product Market Competition and 'Modern' Financial Market on Nonfinancial Corporation Performance in the Neoliberal Era," in *Financialization and the World Economy*, Gerald A. Epstein, ed., (UK: Edward Elgar Publishing Limited, 2005), 90.

338. Wallace Turbeville, "Derivatives: Innovation in the Era of Financial Deregulation," www.demos.org/publication/derivatives-innovation-era-financial -regulation, June 13. 2013, accessed 2013.

339. Wallace C. Turbeville, "Derivatives: Innovation In the Era of Financial Regulation, www.demos.org/publication/derivatives-innovation-er-financial-regulation, June 13.2013, accessed 2013.

340. Wallace C. Turbeville, "Derivatives: Innovation in the Era of Financial Regulation, www.demos.org/publication/derivatives-innovation-er-financial-regulation, June 13.2013, accessed 2013.

341. Wallace C. Turbeville, "Derivatives: Innovation in the Era of Financial Regulation, www.demos.org/publication/derivatives-innovation-er-financial-regulation, June 13.2013, accessed 2013.

342. Michael Lewis, *Flash Boys*, (New York: WW Norton & Company Ltd, 2014).

343. Michael Lewis, *Flash Boys*, (New York: WW Norton & Company Ltd, 2014), 135.

344. Michael Lewis, *Flash Boys*, (New York: WW Norton & Company Ltd, 2014), 215-243.

345. Terrence Casey, Rose-Hulman Institute of Technology, "'Financialization' And The Future of the Neoliberal Growth Model," http://www.psa.ac.uk/journals/pdf./5/2011/6-5.pdf,

April 2011, accessed 2012).

346. William K. Black, *The Best Way to Rob a Bank Is to Own One*, (Austin, TX: University of Texas Press, 2005), 62.

347. John Bellamy Foster, "The Financialization of Capitalism", *Monthly Review*, 2007, Vol. 58, Is.11, April, http://monthly review.org/2007/04/01/the financialization of capitalism, accessed Jan 2013.

348. Paul Kedrosky and Dane Stangler, Ewing Marion Kauffman Foundation, "Financialization and Its Entrepreneurial Consequences, www.Kaufman.org/~/media/Kauffman.org/research %20reports%20 and %20 covers/2011/03/financialization report 32311.pdf, Mar 2011, accessed 2012.

349. Jean Cushen, Paul Thompson, "Doing the Right Thing? HRM and the Angry Knowledge Worker," onlinelibrary.wiley.com/doi/10,1111/j1468-005x.2012.00285.x/full, June 2012, accessed June 2014.

350. Jean Cushen, and Paul Thompson, "Doing the Right Thing? HRM and the Angry Knowledge Worker," New Technology Work and Employment, 27:79-92. onlinelibrary. wiley. com/doi/10,1111/j.1468-005x .2012.00285. x/full, accessed 2014.

351. Ulrich Jurgens, "Ownership Structures, Corporate Governance and Labor, Conference on 'Financialization and Labor,' WZB 27-28 Feb 2014, www.wzb.eu/sites/default/files/u7/05-juergens-ownership-structures.pdf, Feb 2014, accessed 2014.

352. Ulrich Jurgens, "Ownership Structures, Corporate Governance and Labor, Conference on 'Financialization and Labor,' WZB 27-28 Feb 2014, www.wzb.eu/sites/default/files/u7/05-juergens-ownership-structures.pdf, Feb 2014, accessed 2014.

353. Kent Weaver, *The Politics of Industrial Change: Railway Policy in North America*, (Washington, DC: The Brookings Institution, 1985), 1-25.

354. Kent Weaver, *The Politics of Industrial Change: Railway Policy in North America*, (Washington, DC: The Brookings Institution, 1985), 6.

355. Kent Weaver, *The Politics of Industrial Change: Railway Policy in North America*, (Washington, DC: The Brookings Institution, 1985), 5.

356. Kent Weaver, *The Politics of Industrial Change: Railway Policy in North America*, (Washington, DC: The Brookings Institution, 1985), 1-25.

357. Gerald A. Epstein, ed., *Financialization and the World Economy*, (UK: Edward Elgar Publishing Limited, 2005), chap 10-14.

358. Rajiv Sethi, Economist's View, "James Tobin's Hirsch Lecture," economistsview.typepad. com/economistsview/2010/05/james-tobin-hirsch-lecture.html, updated May 2010, accessed 2014.

359. Gerard Dumenil, Dominique Levy, "Costs and Benefits of Neoliberalism: A Class Analysis," in *Financialization and the World Economy*, Gerald Epstien, ed., (UK: Edward Elgar Publishing Limited, 2005), 17-45.

360. Gerard Dumenil, Dominique Levy, "Costs and Benefits of Neoliberalism: A Class Analysis," in *Financialization and the World Economy*, Gerald Epstien, ed., (UK: Edward Elgar Publishing Limited, 2005), 17.

361. Gerard Dumenil, Dominique Levy, "Costs and Benefits of Neoliberalism: A Class Analysis," in *Financialization and the World Economy*, Gerald Epstien, ed., (UK: Edward Elgar Publishing Limited, 2005), 40-41.

362. Gerard Dumenil, Dominique Levy, "Costs and Benefits of Neoliberalism: A Class Analysis," in *Financialization and the World Economy*, Gerald Epstien, ed., (UK: Edward Elgar Publishing Limited, 2005), 35.

363. John Bellamy Foster, "The Financialization of Capital," *Monthly Review*, http://monthlyreview.org/2007/04/01/the financialization of capitalism, April 2007, Volume 58, Issue 11, accessed 2013.

364. Adam Smith, *Wealth of Nations: Books I-III*, (New York: Penguin Books, 1987), 432, 433.

365. ZeroHedge, Elliot Management, Paul Singer, "Elliott's Paul Singer On How Money Is Created...And How It Dies," www.zerohedge.com/news/2013-01-30/elliots-paul-singer-how-money-created-and-how-it-dies, printed Jan 30, 2013, accessed Aug 6, 2014.

366. Anat Admati, Martin Hellwig, *The Banker's New Clothes: What's Wrong With Banking and What to Do About It,"* (Princeton, NJ: Princeton University Press, 2013), 208-228.

367. Anat Admati, Martin Hellwig, *The Banker's New Clothes: What's Wrong With Banking and What to Do About It,"* (Princeton, NJ: Princeton University Press, 2013), 99, 218, 221.

368. Anat Admati, Martin Hellwig, *The Banker's New Clothes: What's Wrong With Banking and What to Do About It,"* (Princeton, NJ: Princeton University Press, 2013), xv.

369. Jennifer Taub, "Taking Stock of Four Years of Dodd Frank," *New York Times*, dealbook. nytimes.com/2014/07/25/taking-stock-of–four-years-of-dodd-frank, July 2014, accessed Jul 2014.

370. Wallace C. Turbeville, "Derivatives: Innovation In the Era of Financial Regulation, www. demos.org/publication/derivatives-innovation-er-financial-regulation, June 13.2013, accessed 2013.

371. Ilene Grabel, "Averting Crisis? Assessing Measures to Manage Financial Integration in Emerging Economies, Gerald A. Epstein, ed., *Financialization and the World Economy*, (UK: Edward Elgar Publishing Limited, 2005), 368.

372. Bethany McLean, Joe Nocera, *All the Devils Are Here: The Hidden History of The Financial Crisis*, (New York: Penguin, 2008) 97.

373. Randall Dodd, "Derivative Markets: Sources of Vulnerability in US Financial Markets, in *Financialization and the World Economy*, Gerald Epstein, ed., (UK: Edward Elgar Publishing Limited, 2005), 152.

374. Robert Pollin, "Applying a Securities Transactions Tax to the US: Design Issues, Market Impact and Revenue Estimates, in *Financialization and the World Economy*, Gerald A. Epstein, ed., (UK: Edward Elgar Publishing Limited, 2005).

375. Robert Pollin, "Applying a Securities Transactions Tax to the US: Design Issues, Market Impact and Revenue Estimates, in *Financialization and the World Economy*, Gerald A. Epstein, ed., (UK: Edward Elgar Publishing Limited, 2005).

376. Michael Lewis, *Flash Boys: A Wall Street Revolt*, (New York: W.W. Norton and Company, 2014), 264-266.

377. Ilene Grabel, "Averting Crisis? Assessing Measures to Manage Financial Integration in Emerging Economies," in *Financialization and the World Economy*, Gerald Epstein, ed., 357-360, 368.

378. Ron Rimkus, CFA, Enterprising Investor: Practical Analysis for Investment Professionals, "Derivatives: The Anti-Money," blogs.cfainstitute.org/investor/2012-01-30-derivatives-the-anti-money, updated Jan 2012, accessed 2014.

379. The Collapse Report: Documenting the Economic Collapse, "A New Theory to Explain Our Current Derivatives Crisis," collapsereport.com/ daily-news/cyclic-money- flow-money-creation- and-the-derivatives-crisis, accessed 2014.

380. Walther Burien, CAFR1.com, in www.zerohedge.com/ news/was-collapse-of- mf-global-pre-meditated-conspiracy –theory, dec 13, 2011, article presenting the argument that derivative monies go somewhere, not nowhere, submitted by Tyler Durden, Dec 2011, accessed 2014.

381. Walther Burien, CAFR1.com, in www.zerohedge.com/ news/was-collapse-of- mf-global-pre-meditated-conspiracy –theory, dec 13, 2011, article presenting the argument that derivative monies go somewhere, not nowhere, submitted by Tyler Durden, Dec 2011, accessed 2014.

382. Shah Gilani, Wall Street Insights & Indictments, www.wallstreetinsight andindictments. com/2013/12/how-the-masters-of-the-financial-universe-use-derivatives-for-fun-and-profit, Dec 2013, accessed Aug 2014.

383. Randall Dodd, "Derivative Markets: Sources of Vulnerability in US Financial Markets, *Financialization and the World Economy*, Gerald Epstein, ed., (UK: Edward Elgar Limited Publishers, 2005), 165-169.

384. Anat Admati, Martin Hellwig, *The Banker's New Clothes: What's Wrong With Banking and What to Do About It,*" (Princeton, NJ: Princeton University Press, 2013), 227.

385. ZeroHedge, Elliot Management, Paul Singer, "Elliott's Paul Singer On How Money Is Created…And How It Dies," www.zerohedge.com/news/2013-01-30/elliots-paul-singer-how-money-created-and-how-it-dies, printed Jan 30, 2013, accessed Aug 6, 2014.

386. Mike Krieger, Liberty Blitzkrieg, "Revelations From the Torture Report—CIA Lies, Nazi Methods, and the $81 Million No-Bid Torture Contract," 12/10/2014, www.zerohedge. com/news/2014-12-10/revelations-torture-report—cia-lies-nazi-methods-and-81-milllion-no-bid-torture-con, accessed Dec 2014.

Neoliberalism Appendix Sources

Essential Characteristics of Neoliberalism:

Most sources were discussed and referenced in the body of the manuscript except for the topic of science politicization:

1. Mark Hendrickson, "The Palpable Politicization of Science," *Forbes*, www.forbes.com/sites/markhendrickson/2013/09/20/the-palpable-politicization-of-science -by-global-warming-alarmists, Sept 2013, accessed 2014.

2. Commission on Social Action of Reform Judaism, 68th Union for Reform Judaism General Assembly, passed Nov 2005, urj.org/about/union/governance.reso//?syspage=article&item-id=1943, accessed 2014.

3. Toby Bolsen, James Druckman, Fay Lomax Cook, "The Politicization of Science and Support for Science Innovation," Institute for Policy Research, Northwestern University, *Working Paper Series*, WP-13-11, May 2013, www.ipr.northwestern.edu/publications/docs/workingpapers/2013/IPR-WP-13-11-REV.pdf, accessed 2014.

4. Wikipedia, "The Skeptical Environmentalist," enwikipedia.org/wiki/The_Skeptical_Environmentalist, accessed 2014.

5. Bjorn Lomborg, *The Skeptical Environmentalist: Measuring the Real State of the World*, (Cambridge, UK: Cambridge University Press, 1998).

CIA timeline:

1. Tim Wiener, *Legacy of Ashes: The History of the CIA*, (New York: Doubleday, a division of Random House, 2007), CIA backing for Latin American dictators, 192, 280.

2. Tim Wiener, *Legacy of Ashes: The History of the CIA*, (New York: Doubleday, a division of Random House, 2007), 279.

3. Tim Wiener, *Legacy of Ashes: The History of the CIA*, (New York: Doubleday, a division of Random House, 2007), 279.

4. Michael Kelley, "Leaked 'Black Budget' Shows How the CIA Progressed From Spy Agency to Paramilitary Force," Business Insider, Aug 2013, www. businessinsider.com/black-budget -about-the-cia- 2013-8, accessed 2014.

5. CIA Museum, "Timeline," CentralIntelligenceAgency www.cia.gov/ about-cia/cia-museum/experience-the-collection/text-version/timeline.html, accessed Feb 2013.

6. Steve Kangas, "A Timeline of CIA Atrocities," www.huppi.com/kangaroo/CIAtimeline.html, accessed Feb 2013.

7. Tim Wiener, *Legacy of Ashes: The History of the CIA*, (New York: Doubleday, a division of Random House, 2007).

8. Wikipedia, "Gary Webb," enwikipedia.org/wiki/Gary Webb, accessed 2014.

Differential pricing to enhance selling within a market under conditions of falling demand.

1. Court Listener, "Katzman v. Victoria's Secret Catalogue, 923F.Supp.580(S.D.N.Y. 1996)," www.courtlistener.com/ nysd/aYNj/katzman-v-victorias-secret-catalogue/?, accessed 2014.

2. Arie Shpanya, "What Is Price Discrimination and Is it Ethical?" e-consultancyLLC econsultancy.com/blog/64068-what-is-price-discrimination-and-is-it-ethical #i1jewn8cyphdtg2, accessed 2014.

3. Uwe Reinhardt/ Disclosures Health Affairs, 2006:25(1):57-69, "The Pricing of U.S. Hospital Services: Chaos Behind A Veil of Secrecy," www.medscape.com/viewarticle/521175_3, accessed 2014.

4. Robert Weiss, Ajay Mehrotra, "Online Dynamic Pricing: Efficiency, Equity and the Future of E-commerce, *Virginia Journal of Law and Technology, University of Virginia*, Summer 2001, 6VA.J.L.&Tech II, www.vjolt.net/vol6/issue2/v612-a11-Weiss.html, accessed 2014.

5. Wikipedia, "Price Discrimination," enwilkipedia.org/wiki/Price-discrimination, accessed 2014.

6. William Breit, Roger Ransom, *The Academic Scribblers*, Third Edition, (Princeton, NJ: Princeton University Press, 1998), 44.

7. Wikipedia, "Price discrimination," enwikipedia.org/wiki/price discrimination, accessed 2014.

8. David Hackett Fischer, *Albion's Seed: Four British Folkways in America*, (New York: Oxford University Press, 1989), 157.

9. Arie Shpanya, "What Is Price Discrimination and Is it Ethical?" e-consultancyLLC econsultancy.com/blog/64068-what-is-price-discrimination-and-is-it-ethical #i1jewn8cyphdtg2, accessed 2014.

10. Uwe Reinhardt/ Disclosures Health Affairs, 2006:25(1):57-69, "The Pricing of U.S. Hospital Services: Chaos Behind A Veil of Secrecy," www.medscape.com/viewarticle/521175_3, accessed 2014.

11. Konkurrensverket, Swedish Competition Authority, Claes Norgren, Director-General, "The Pros and Cons of Price Discrimination," www.konsrrensverket.se/upload/Filer/Trycksaker/Reporter/Pros &Cons/rap_pros_and_ cons_pricediscrimination.pdf, accessed 2014.

Neoliberal timeline

1. Wikipedia, "Timeline of modern history," enwikipedia.org/wiki/Timeline_of_modern_history, accessed 2013.

2. "Globalization Timeline: 1940-2005," http://www wnccumw.org/PDF%20%%20%20 word%20files/Globalization%20Timeline.pdf, accessed 2012.

3. Wikipedia, "Big Bang," enwikipedia.org/wiki/Big_Bang_ (financial_markets), accessed 2014.

4. Glenn Greenwald, Glenngreenwald on Security and Liberty, "Obama's Justice Department Grants Final Immunity to Bush's CIA Torturers," http://www.guardian.co.uk/comments-free/2012/Aug/31/obama_justice_department_immunity_Bush_cia_torturer, accessed 2014.

5. Lachlan Markay, "Operation Fast and Furious Guns Found at 11 U.S. Crime Scenes," http://blog.heritage.org/2011/08/17/operation-fast-and-furious-guns-found-at-11-11-5-crime-scenes, accessed 2012.

6. Mike Masnick, Techdirt, "The Senate Is Sitting On a Devastating Report About How the CIA Avoided Oversight of Unnecessary Torture Program," www.techdirt.com/articles/20131019/02001424935/the-senate-is-sitting-on-a-devastating-report-about-how-the-CIA-avoided-oversight-of-unnecessary-torture-program.shtml, accessed 2013.

7. Washington's Blog, "Senate Intelligence Committee and Head CIA Lawyer Admit Torture Was Unnecessary," www.washingtonblog.com/2013/10/a-devastating-and-secret-report-by-the-senate-intelligence-committee-documents-in-detail-how-the-cias-brutalization-of-terrorist-suspects-during-the-Bush-years-was-unnecessary-ineffective-a.html, accessed 2013.

8. Vassar Bush Mills, Unified Patriots, "Fast and Spurious and a Prosecution by Federal Co-Conspirators," http:www.unifiedpatriots.com/2012/07/08/fast-and-spurious-and-a-prosecution-by-federal-co-conspirators/vassar-business, accessed 2013.

9. Investopedia, "Nixon Shock," www.investopedia.com/terms/n/nixon-shock/asp#, accessed 2014.

10. Wikipedia, "List of wars and anthropomorphic disasters by deathtoll," http://enwikipedia.org/wiki/List_of_wars_&_anthropomorphic disasters_by_deathtoll, accessed 2012.

11. Wikipedia, "COINTELPRO," enwikipedia/wiki/ COINTELPRO, accessed 2014.

12. Mary Bellis, "What is a Microchip? How do microchips work? How are microchips made?" inventors.about.com/od/computersandinternet/a/microchip.htm, accessed 2014.

13. Laserfest, Celebrating 50 Years of Laser Innovation," "The First Ruby Laser," www.laserfest.org/lasers/how/ruby.cfm, accessed 2014,

14. History, "Cultural Revolution," www.history.com/topics/cultural-revolution/print, accessed 2014.

15. This Week In History, "Mao Zedong Outlines the New Chinese Government," www.history.com/this-day-in-history/mao-zedong-outlines-the-new-chinese-government, accessed 2014.

16. American Scientist, "The First Discovery of DNA," www.americanscientist.org/issues/feature/2008/4/the-first-discovery-of-dna, accessed 2014.

17. Marilyn Stokstad, *Art History, Second Edition Volume II,* (Upper Saddle River, NJ: Prentice Hall, Inc., and Harry N. Abrams, Inc., 1995), 1058-9, chapter 29.

18. Jed Rakoff, "Why Innocent People Plead Guilty," www.nybooks.com/articles/archives/2014/nov/20/why-innocent-people-plead-guilty/?utm_medium=emailand utm-campaign=NYR+plea+bargains, accessed 2014.

Index

About the Book

Thank you to Russel Davis at Gray Dog Press in Spokane, Washington, for providing format editing. Illustrations and text were by the author. Born in the Old Western Frontier, Mel Scanlan Stahl has lived in Texas, New Mexico and Washington. She earned two bachelor's degrees, one in microbiology and the other in fine arts with an emphasis on drawing and painting. After a long career in cytogenetics, this is her first book.